SPITFIRE PILOT
AIR COMMODORE
GEOFFREY STEPHENSON

John Shields.

SPITFIRE PILOT AIR COMMODORE GEOFFREY STEPHENSON

THE BIOGRAPHY OF THE PILOT OF DUXFORD'S SPITFIRE MK.I N3200

JOHN SHIELDS

AIR WORLD

First published in Great Britain in 2024 by
Pen & Sword Air World
An imprint of
Pen & Sword Books Ltd
Yorkshire - Philadelphia

ISBN 978 1 03610 540 2

Typeset in INDIA by IMPEC eSolutions
Printed and bound in the England by _____

Pen & Sword Books Ltd incorporates the imprints of Pen & Sword
Archaeology, Air World Books, Atlas, Aviation, Battleground, Discovery,
Family History, History, Maritime, Military, Naval, Politics, Social History,
Transport, True Crime, Claymore Press, Frontline Books, Praetorian Press,
Seaforth Publishing and White Owl

For a complete list of Pen & Sword titles please contact:

PEN & SWORD BOOKS LTD
47 Church Street, Barnsley, South Yorkshire, S70 2AS, UK.
E-mail: enquiries@pen-and-sword.co.uk
Website: www.pen-and-sword.co.uk

or

PEN AND SWORD BOOKS,
1950 Lawrence Road, Havertown, PA 19083, USA
E-mail: Uspen-and-sword@casematepublishers.com
Website: www.penandswordbooks.com

For Victoria and Veryan

Contents

List of Illustrations   viii
Foreword   xi
Acknowledgements   xv
Figures and Tables   xx

Chapter 1   The Early Days – 1910 to 1928   1
Chapter 2   Pre-War in the RAF   13
Chapter 3   Spitfire Command: 19 Squadron, RAF Duxford –
              January to May 1940   27
Chapter 4   Dogfight over Dunkirk   41
Chapter 5   I Walk Alone – 26 May to 5 June 1940   59
Chapter 6   *Dulag Luft*, Oberursel – June to September 1940   89
Chapter 7   *Stalag Luft* I, Barth – September 1940 to August 1941   111
Chapter 8   *Oflag* IVC, Colditz – The Allied Years, August 1941 to
              September 1943   132
Chapter 9   *Oflag* IVC, Colditz – The British Years, October 1943
              to April 1945   159
Chapter 10   A Return to Blighty, then Overseas and Back Again –
              April 1945 to July 1953   183
Chapter 11   Central Fighter Establishment, RAF West Raynham –
              July 1953 to November 1954   200
Chapter 12   Letters From America   212
Chapter 13   The Last Flight – 8 November 1954   221
Chapter 14   Stephenson's Legacy   248
Appendix A   RAF Burials at The Commonwealth War Graves
              Commission Cemetery, Oakwood Annex,
              Montgomery, Alabama   269
Notes   272
Bibliography   296
Index   303

List of Illustrations

1. Geoffrey's grandfather (middle row, centre), father (right-hand side of the rear row) and eight uncles. (Image from Stephenson family archive)
2. A pre-Great War photograph of Geoffrey Stephenson and his younger sister, Eileen. (Image from Stephenson family archive)
3. Between 1918 and 1924, Stephenson attended Castle Park School, a boys-only preparatory school on the outskirts of Dublin. (Image courtesy of Castle Park School)
4. Following six years of schooling in Ireland, 14-year-old Geoffrey returned to England in 1924 to attend Shrewsbury School for his last four years of education. (Image from Stephenson Family Archive)
5. A cheery Flight Cadet Stephenson looking resplendent in his RAF Mess Dress at RAF Cranwell. (Image from Stephenson Family Archive)
6. Cranwell Flight Cadets learning about aero engines. (Image from Stephenson family archive)
7. A July 1929 photograph showing the RAF College Cranwell Boxing Team. (Image courtesy of the RAF College Cranwell archive)
8. The senior Cranwell Flight Cadets during their last term at Cranwell. (Image from Stephenson family archive)
9. Flight Cadet Sergeant Stephenson on his BSA motorbike during early 1930 and his last term at Cranwell. (Image from Stephenson family archive)
10. Stephenson in the cockpit of his RAF Cranwell-based Armstrong Whitworth Siskin trainer. (Image from Stephenson family archive)
11. The Cranwell prize-winners in July 1930. (Image courtesy of RAF College Cranwell archives)
12. In July 1930, after two years of training to be RAF officers and pilots, Stephenson, Bader and 19 other Flight Cadets graduated from RAF Cranwell. (RAF College Cranwell Archives)

13. Flight Lieutenant Harry Day (left) and Pilot Officer Douglas Bader (right) of 23 Squadron. (Image from Stephenson Family Archive)

14. Pilot Officer Bader, Flight Lieutenant Harry Day and Pilot Officer Geoffrey Stephenson stand in front of a 23 Squadron Gloster Gamecock as part of the 1931 Hendon display.

15. Flying Officer Geoffrey Stephenson riding shotgun in the Iraqi desert in the early 1930s while serving with Number 1 Armoured Car Company. (Image from Stephenson family archive)

16. Iraq in the early 1930s – Flying Officer Geoffrey Stephenson cleaning his shotgun. (Image from Stephenson family archive)

17. Iraq 1933 – Stephenson, wearing his trademark white flying suit, is sat in the front seat of a Westland Wapiti. (Image from Stephenson family archive)

18. Stephenson was an accomplished horseman and rode throughout his life; he was an avid polo player and regularly won point-to-point races. (Image from Stephenson family archive)

19. The 1937 Central Flying School aerobatics team honing their skills ahead of the final RAF Display at Hendon. (Image copyright of RAF Museum)

20. King George VI (centre, front) visited the Central Flying School in May 1938. (Image courtesy of CFS Association archive)

21. On 26 May 1940, Stephenson was flying Spitfire Mark I N3200 on his first operational mission over Dunkirk. (Image courtesy of George Romain)

22. After belly-landing on the beach at Sangette, Stephenson's Spitfire would become a tourist attraction for the German occupying force.

23. The RAF cohort at Colditz during the winter of 1942/43. (Image from Stephenson family archive)

24. 22 June 1946, Geoffrey and Maureen's wedding day. (Image from Stephenson family archive)

25. Group Captain Stephenson CBE ADC, circa 1949 as the 23rd Commandant of the Central Flying School. (Image courtesy of CFS Association archives)

26. The newly-promoted Air Commodore Geoffrey Stephenson CBE ADC and his wife Maureen prepare to attend the coronation of Queen Elizabeth II in June 1953. (Image from Stephenson family archive)

27. RAF Odiham in July 1953. The newly-crowned Queen Elizabeth II is escorted by Air Commodore Geoffrey Stephenson around the 300 aircraft

comprising the static display of the RAF Coronation Review. (Image from Stephenson family archive)

28. Air Commodore Geoffrey Stephenson CBE ADC in his last post as Commandant of the Central Fighter Establishment. (Image from Stephenson family archive)
29. The early Super Sabres, as flown by Stephenson on his last flight in November 1954. (Image courtesy of NASA)
30. Under ever-blue skies, Stephenson's final resting place is at the Oakwood Cemetery Annex in Montgomery, Alabama. (Image from author's collection)
31. The 2014 'Guy Martin's Spitfire' documentary followed N3200's two-year restoration at Duxford. (Image courtesy of North One Productions)
32. N3200 is now owned by the Imperial War Museum and flies from Duxford, its original home, thus ensuring Stephenson's legacy is preserved for future generations. (Image copyright of Roland Bogush)

Foreword

W hat do Geoffrey Stephenson and N3200 mean to me? It is pretty straightforward, N3200 is a simply stunning and original Spitfire Mark Ia; it is a project that represents the pinnacle of my warbird career – as the owner of a warbird restoration company, an engineer, and a pilot. My career and passion for warbirds started in the early 1970s, first as a volunteer, then as an aircraft engineer, and ultimately as a warbird pilot. In that time, I have been fortunate to fly over a hundred aircraft types. Without a doubt, my favourite aircraft of them all is the Spitfire, having amassed well over a thousand hours on several different variants of R.J. Mitchell's iconic fighter. However, N3200 is special. It's a thoroughbred, a pure Spitfire, the first of the breed and a manifestation of Mitchell's original vision before war, necessity, and bloody experience adapted the airframe, engine, weapons, roles and tactics throughout the first half of the 1940s. To me, Geoffrey embodies that time. He was a career RAF officer and squadron commander thrown into the cauldron of battle with his squadron, where man and machine were put to the ultimate test. When combined, Geoffrey and N3200 tell quite an extraordinary story. Not only do Geoffrey and N3200 hark back to a bygone and halcyon era, but they also take us back to a place that was once their home; an airfield that I have been captivated by since I was a young lad, a location that remains, to this day, very dear to my heart – Duxford.

A few years ago, one of the Duxford management team compared me to a particular piece of British confectionery. He said that if you broke me in half, it would be a bit like Blackpool Rock – I would have Duxford written through me! It's very true; I have been coming to Duxford since I was 12 years old. That love affair started with the 1969 *Battle of Britain* film, much of which was filmed at the former Second World War Fighter Command airfield that had long been home to 19 Squadron, which in early 1940 was equipped with the original mark of Spitfire and commanded by Geoffrey. I was captivated by the various stories of the Second World War air battles, whether in film, television, comic book or novels, and I wanted to see where the iconic movie was filmed. I travelled by bus from Hertfordshire, where I lived and grew up, and walked from the Royston bus station all the way to Duxford. When I finally arrived, the airfield was derelict, there was no security, and you could just walk through the main gate – how times have changed! I wandered amongst the hangars, which were still painted in a camouflage scheme, a remnant of the film set rather than the war. There was also further evidence of the film scattered around the airfield – partly-destroyed fibreglass Spitfire and Hurricanes still littered the corners of the airfield. My early visits to Duxford pre-date the introduction of the M11 motorway. So, Duxford still had its full-length runway, not the truncated strip that exists today. I was in paradise and immediately fell for Duxford, and my love for the airfield and what it represents has never faltered since. However, the journey has been a long and eventful one. My own story, like everyone else's, has its twists and turns as well as highs and lows, but it is not quite up to the same scale and amplitude as Geoffrey's rather remarkable life. He is an individual that I admire immensely; Geoffrey was a resilient soul who understood and embraced risk. He rose to the challenges he faced and reaped the rewards of his endeavours. It is a mantra that I live by today. Consequently, I feel rather privileged to have rebuilt and flown in his, and my favourite, Spitfire – N3200.

Several decades span from my arrival at Duxford to that momentous day in 2014 when I took N3200 back into the air on its first flight in nearly 74 years. My Duxford journey started small and steadily grew. After my first visit, I started coming to Duxford regularly to volunteer at weekends, sweeping hangars and helping on various old bits of aircraft they had kicking around. It was the early Seventies, and warbirds had just started to arrive at Duxford. Ormond Hayden Baillie was the first of many warbird enthusiasts to set up shop at Duxford. In addition to a Hawker Sea Fury and a Bristol Blenheim restoration project, Ormond also operated two Lockheed T-33 Shooting Stars from Duxford. Ormond set up workshops in Building 66, the first on-site workshop; it is still in operation today with the Aircraft Restoration Company. In parallel to working on these warbirds, I had been accepted onto a Hawker Siddeley Dynamics technical apprenticeship. My life as an aircraft engineer was set, or so I thought.

At the end of my apprenticeship, I moved home and job to be closer to Duxford. I was now working with Graeme Warner, who had taken over the Blenheim restoration project following Ormond's fatal P-51 Mustang crash in West Germany in 1977. At a similar time and cajoled by a supportive group of friends from the warbird community, I started flying lessons at Bourn. I began to build up my hours in Cessna 152s, Chipmunks, Harvards, and the Twin Beech before ultimately transitioning to warbirds, including the Spitfire. It was not all plain sailing. The restored Blenheim crashed, destroying Graeme's business model and my livelihood. In the late 1980s, I acquired a reassuringly expensive commercial pilot's licence with the intent of becoming an airline pilot to earn a living. In hindsight, it was perhaps a blessing that the airlines were not recruiting at that time. I stayed at Duxford and tried to recover my costs by doing what I loved. I set up my own business, the Aircraft Restoration Company, to build, restore and fly warbirds, amongst other types. I was immediately involved in restoring a second Blenheim, a former exhibit at the Strathallan aircraft museum in Perthshire. By 1993, the Blenheim took to the air. Life was good, but the next step led directly to my involvement in my favourite project – N3200.

It all started with a broken Spitfire that landed at Duxford. Air traffic control asked me to come to the flight line to look at the poorly Spit. The aircraft was owned by Karel Bos, who at that time was a part-owner of Historic Flying Limited based out of Audley End. The company, which he would eventually own outright, specialized in restoring Spitfires. He returned the following week with an offer to buy my company as he was looking for a company that could maintain warbirds. I politely refused, but it was the start of a great relationship. Eighteen months later, a similar conversation took place, but this time as equals. Historic Flying Limited and the Aircraft Restoration Company became a partnership, co-located in a hangar at Duxford. One end of the hangar restored Spitfires, and the other maintained anything that was coming through the door. During this era, N3200 and P9374 were rebuilt to exacting standards. When Karel retired, the two companies eventually merged into a single entity - the Aircraft Restoration Company. The business has expanded with a workforce of 60 employees and the construction of a second hangar in 2016, named appropriately after Geoffrey – the Stephenson Hangar.

When the decision finally came to sell both Mark I Spitfires, I made the case to keep N3200 at Duxford and donate it to the Imperial War Museum. I felt passionately that it should be kept at its original home and in its original specification, something that we had fastidiously maintained throughout its build process. Alternative options would not guarantee these two basic premises. An elegant solution was created where P9374 was sold, with proceeds going to the RAF Benevolent Fund and other charitable causes. The owner, Tom Kaplan, magnanimously gifted N3200 to the Imperial War Museum, thus ensuring that it would stay at Duxford and in flying condition. With its future secured, N3200 continues to delight its pilots, engineers and adoring public, all of whom love to see it in its element.

Throughout my life, I've tackled adversity, taken risks to change my direction, and felt the enduring joy of flying as well as the rewards it brings to me as an individual, the team that I lead and those who enjoy the warbird story. Many of these traits echo Geoffrey's own approach to life. When coupled with my personal involvement in the N3200 project, it is perhaps no surprise that if I was to be offered one last Spitfire flight, it would have to be in N3200 and flying from its home today and in May 1940 – Duxford.

John Romain MBE
Director, Aircraft Restoration Company
Duxford, Cambridgeshire

Acknowledgements

I have always been told that you must start with the 'why'. For this project, that is an easy question to answer as I can pinpoint exactly the time and place when I became interested in the story of Air Commodore Geoffrey Dalton Stephenson CBE. It was the bright, fresh afternoon of 9 November 2019 as I stood under the beautiful blue skies at a Commonwealth War Graves Commission site. This site is different from a traditional war cemetery, not one of the multitude of sites that scatter the landscape of northern France. The Oakwood Cemetery Annex in Montgomery, Alabama, is thankfully smaller but it lacks the grandeur of many of its more famous European counterparts. However, the cemetery remains a tranquil, solemn, and reflective site in keeping with its position as the largest of the Commonwealth War Graves Commission sites in the United States.

As the newly-arrived senior RAF officer and Air War College student at the nearby Maxwell Air Force Base, it was my responsibility to oversee the annual Anglo-French Remembrance Sunday event. The parade traditionally comprises five RAF officers, our three French counterparts, our families, and a dedicated group of local supporters. We gather each year to pay our respects and commemorate the 78 British and 20 French trainee pilots killed during their Second World War flying training in Alabama. Therefore, as the new boy, I thought it would be prudent to do a quick reconnaissance of the site the day before the actual event – as we say in the RAF, prior preparation prevents poor performance and all that! What I found during that short visit had a profound impact on me then and now.

I was unfamiliar with the location of the cemetery but was simply told by my colleagues to follow the signs on my Sat Nav for the Hank Williams memorial. Strange, I thought, but I will go along with it! Sure enough, immediately adjacent to the Commonwealth War Graves Commission site is the final resting place of the famed country and western singer – a rather surreal sight! Nevertheless, and in keeping with all Commonwealth War Graves Commission sites, the Oakwood Cemetery Annex is very well looked after. As you look out to the north, there is a lovely, wooded vista where you can see for miles and usually with perpetual clear blue Alabamian skies above.

As part of the reconnoitre, I wanted to familiarize myself with not only the layout of the site, but I also wanted to know the names of those who paid the ultimate sacrifice for their country and would never see that homeland again – Who were they? What were their backgrounds? How old were they? As I walked the site and read each of their names, I was surprised to find two further British graves not from the Second World War era, but from the 1950s. I knew nothing about them, so I jotted down the names of the two senior RAF officers and went home to research what I could about the two individuals – Squadron Leader Christopher Walker and Air Commodore Geoffrey Stephenson. After a quick internet search, I was able to put two and two together. In 1958, Walker was part of a small cadre of RAF exchange pilots operating out of Texas flying with the USAF on the, then still classified, Lockheed U-2 spyplane when he crashed following a suspected oxygen failure at high altitude. However, it was Stephenson's back story that I found utterly fascinating. My brief research that evening showed a link to the fantastic 2014 documentary 'Guy Martin's Spitfire'. I recall watching and enjoying the documentary at the time, but I had thought no more about it, and I had certainly not made the Alabama connection as I was still three postings away from Maxwell Air Force Base.

The next day, and by sheer coincidence, on the 65th anniversary of his burial, I spoke at the Remembrance Sunday service about Air Commodore Geoffrey Stephenson and his incredible career. Some of the group had been coming to the service for over 20 years, they knew the story about the 78 Second World War trainees who had been struck down in their prime and who were simply too young to establish their own legacy. However, and regrettably, no one at the event knew of Geoffrey Stephenson's incredible story. I vowed that I would remedy the problem and I promised that during my tenure in Alabama, I would always speak of the exploits of Air Commodore Stephenson. Nevertheless, my concern was that over time his memory would once again fade. Therefore, I wanted to leave a more permanent reminder of an individual who was laid to rest thousands of miles away from home. The purpose of this narrative was primarily to ensure that his remarkable story would be remembered by future generations here in Alabama. More importantly, the story also puts a face and a life to one of the gravestones and tells the amazing story behind one of the 80 RAF airmen who are laid to rest far from home and their loved ones; I just wish that I could do the same for the others.

While the previous paragraphs explain the 'why', the 'how' and the 'who' are equally important. A biography (obviously) spans a lifetime and numerous significant events; Geoffrey's life had more than the norm. Consequently, getting the depth of necessary information for each of these events was critical to the success of the biography, which in turn, required access to several experts. Knowing where to start is always a good starting point. I was fortunate to have the assistance of William Spencer, the former military archivist at The National Archives, to guide me through the plethora of files at Kew to identify the key primary source material. However, the primary source material is insufficient to tell a story and must be put into context. Therefore, I am indebted to Dilip Sarkar, Paul McCue and Paul Cox for their support, expertise and insights into Spitfire operations, the Special Operations Executive and Colditz. Several dedicated archivists have also helped me along the way, including Philip Mangan at Castle Park School in Dublin, Ian Steward of the Cranwellian Historical Society, Hazel Crozier from the RAF College Cranwell and Jim Gardiner from the Central Flying School Association. I am extremely grateful to them for taking the time to answer my many questions about their organisation and its linkages with Stephenson.

At the centre of the Stephenson story is his Spitfire Mark Ia, serial number N3200, which has been rebuilt to flying condition in 2014 at its former home at Duxford. The team responsible for the project was the Aircraft Restoration Company, under the watchful eye of its Director and then Chief Pilot John Romain, Senior Projects Engineer Colin Swann and Hangar Manager Martin 'Mo' Overall. It was a welcome reunion with John; the last time we met was in 1998 when I was strapping him into the back seat of a Tornado F3 at RAF Leeming! John, Colin and Mo not only allowed me to visit the Stephenson Hangar at Duxford, but also permitted me to get up close to N3200 and we spent quite a bit of time talking about their passion for that particular aircraft, its history, its rebuild and its connection with Geoffrey Stephenson. I was also very fortunate and grateful that John, who flew N3200 on its first flight after the rebuild in 2014, agreed to write the foreword to the book.

Many will be familiar with the Stephenson story via the 2014 Channel 4 documentary charting the rebuild of the Spitfire and its first flight. The programme, hosted by Guy Martin, was produced by North One, and commissioned by its Chief Executive Officer, Neil Duncanson. Without Neil's support, I simply would not have been able to contact Geoffrey's daughters. My original intent was to simply tell them that their father was not forgotten out here in Alabama, and that the small RAF community at the nearby Maxwell Air Force Base would continue to remember Stephenson and his fellow airmen who are buried in Montgomery, far from home. From that initial contact, it quickly became apparent that Stephenson's daughters had several questions relating to their father's service and demise. One thing led to another, and the end result was that I agreed to write Stephenson's biography.

This biography would have been meaningless without the support of Victoria and Veryan, Stephenson's daughters. Both have fully supported the project from its outset. They have both placed great faith in me and provided me with unprecedented access to their father's letters, diaries, memoirs and family photograph albums as well as their recollections of their father. As a result, the family archive gives a greater sense of who Geoffrey Stephenson was rather than just what he did. Additionally, Victoria and Veryan have been supported by a wider group of family and friends including Anna Menzies, Luke Lundin, David Strawderman, Philip Stephenson, William Sclater and Peter Orgain: all have been involved to some extent. I am indebted to them all and I hope I have done their father, stepfather, grandfather, father-in-law, uncle, and family friend justice in this biography.

I would also like to thank the team at Pen and Sword for their support throughout the project. From the outset, Martin Mace and John Grehan have both offered their full backing and sage advice during the research phase. Additionally, Stephen Chumbley's outstanding editorial skills and excellent knowledge have kept me on the right track throughout the editing process. Thank you team Pen and Sword for making this project a reality and a better product.

Last and by no means least, I must thank my family for their support throughout the project. As any author will know, writing a book takes time and a fair degree of commitment. As the author, I take the credit for the book, but the family bears the sacrifice. Consequently, it may be my name on the front cover, but Helen, Euan, Ellie and Maddie also deserve recognition too, for it was they who would see me disappear into my office for hours at a time, only appearing for sustenance and to watch endless TV programmes on Spitfires and Colditz. Thank you!

I have found this project fascinating. Even though he died at the relatively young age of 44, Stephenson led an action-packed life; he worked alongside some incredible individuals, visited many beautiful places around the world and flew in a broad range of aircraft at a time when the pace of technological advancement was simply breath-taking. I hope you enjoy this book and that it gives you an insight into an extraordinary individual who was one of many who made up a quite remarkable generation.

John Shields
Montgomery, Alabama

Figures and Tables

Figure 2.1	Stephenson's RAF Career by Location.	26
Figure 4.1	19 Squadron Composition, Casualties and Claims – Morning of 26 May 1940.	43
Figure 5.1	Stephenson's 'I Walk Alone Journey' – 26 May to 2 June 1940.	88
Figure 6.1	Stephenson's POW Camps in Germany.	110
Table 8A	Colditz Prisoner's Weekly Ration for Late 1941.	139
Table 9A	Colditz Prisoner's Weekly Ration for January 1945.	165
Figure 12.1	The 1954 Central Fighter Establishment Tour of the United States.	218
Figure 13.1	Flight Path of Stephenson's F-100A Super Sabre Sortie.	235
Figure 13.2	Plan View of Stephenson's F-100A Super Sabre Crash.	238
Figure 13.3	Side View of Stephenson's F-100A Super Sabre Crash.	239

Chapter 1

The Early Days – 1910 to 1928

'Intus Si Recte Ne Labora'

The motto of Shrewsbury School

The motto of Geoffrey Dalton Stephenson's *alma mater* would stand him in good stead for the rest of his life. 'If all is right within, trouble not' would be a creed that Stephenson used throughout his career. Many people have heard of Geoffrey Stephenson. In part, due to N3200, his Mark Ia Spitfire, recovered from a French beach, rebuilt and restored to flying condition at its former home in Duxford. Some may know Geoffrey from his other escapades, including his five years as a prisoner of war (POW) or his fatal flight in a Super Sabre jet in Florida in 1954. However, most of these stories have reached near mythical status, based upon part truths. A deeper look into Geoffrey's life using official records as well as personal diaries and letters shows a remarkable career as a fighter pilot and commander, but also as a husband and father. Stephenson was just the kind of character the junior Service wanted; he was bright, sporty, naturally competitive, resilient, and with a healthy appetite for risk. Coupled with his family traits of sacrifice, honour, courage, and country, he was an obvious choice for the Cranwell officer cadet cadre. Nevertheless, his distinguished RAF career was by no means assured.

Indeed, many of his Cranwell cohort had not survived the 12 years of hazardous military service that took Stephenson from Lincolnshire in 1928 to Dunkirk and a Spitfire cockpit in May 1940. Moreover, his entry into Cranwell and the decade-old Royal Air Force very nearly did not happen. The 18-year-old Stephenson almost missed out on an adventure that would last over a quarter of a century. His career would see him join the RAF with one of the most renowned fighter pilots the United Kingdom has ever produced – Douglas Bader. The two Cranwell graduates and lifelong friends would spend their first tour together as fighter pilots, guided by two remarkable flight commanders. While Bader recovered from the horrific injuries from his near-fatal, impromptu, and illegal low-level aerobatic display, Stephenson would head out to the Middle East for the first of two tours in the region. He would also fly in a broad array of cutting-edge fighter aircraft from 1920s-era silver-winged, sedate biplanes to the elegant and iconic Spitfire as well as the sleek, supersonic fighters at the dawn of the jet age. He served as an *aide de camp* to the King and during the transition to the new Queen. Stephenson would also spend nearly a fifth of his career as a POW, culminating in the most infamous of POW camps – Colditz. Throughout his career, Stephenson would meet incredible people, fly in some of the most advanced planes and visit beautiful places. The reason for the near-missed opportunity was that Stephenson's father, William Dalton Stephenson, a once-affluent farmer, was now in financial trouble. You needed money to join the RAF as an elite officer cadet in the late 1920s. In its early days, and in keeping with the other Services, Cranwell charged its students to attend the two-year-long course. Nevertheless, William had a plan to set his son up for a remarkable career. The first entry in William Stephenson's file held at The National Archives is a letter that provides an insight into his approach:

Captain William Dalton Stephenson, Educational Corps (Retired)

Sir,

I am directed to inform you that the above-named officer has made an application for payment of reduced educational fees in respect of the entry of his son G. D. Stephenson, to the Royal Air Force Cadet College, as a result of the recent examination and ask that you will furnish this department with a record of service of Captain Stephenson and state whether such service is considered to be of the nature of active service in the field with an expeditionary force.

I am, Sir, Your obedient Servant,[1]

The letter was dated 3 September 1928 and signed off with an undecipherable scribble from an Air Ministry official in Adastral House. The recipients of the letter were the junior Service's army counterparts in the Under Secretary of

State's section at the War Office in Whitehall. Stephenson's career hung in the balance awaiting a bureaucratic decision regarding funding his Cranwell fees via a scholarship. It was by no means a unique position. The RAF handed out several scholarships to a number of prospective RAF cadets in each Cranwell intake for keen young men vying to be pilots and officers in the new and exciting Service. Indeed, the RAF awarded one such scholarship to Bader, which undoubtedly aided the enduring bond between the two Cranwell cadets. Moreover, the letter and the remaining file on William Stephenson would show that he led a remarkable life dedicated to his nation. However, why did an apparently affluent farmer have to resort to asking for a scholarship for his son to attend Cranwell?

In response to the Air Ministry's letter, the War Office informed them that:

> I am to state his services were satisfactory and that nothing of an adverse nature is recorded against him. I am also to state that this officer served in the ranks of the Imperial Yeomanry in South Africa and was awarded the Distinguished Conduct Medal. (Vide London Gazette dated 27 September, 1901), but that details of this service are not readily available. I am to add that the periods spent overseas in South Africa during the South African War and in France during the Great War are considered to be 'Active Service in the Field'.[2]

While the War Office's note is accurate, it is somewhat economical with the details of William Stephenson's time in uniform. Thankfully, the remainder of William's file provides a more profound and fascinating insight into Geoffrey Stephenson's father. The file documents William's service in the Boer War, the Great War and his time in Ireland, including both the war of independence and the subsequent civil war. The file also details his injuries suffered in combat. William's story demonstrates enduring family traits and sets the scene for why his eldest son, Geoffrey, chose the career he did. William's story echoes Geoffrey's own story. Consequently, the comment attributed to Mark Twain that history may not repeat, but it sure does rhyme, seems rather appropriate.

William Dalton Stephenson was born in 1879 into an affluent farming family who lived in the village of Althorpe on the western bank of the River Trent in North Lincolnshire. He was the eldest of nine brothers in a family of

12 siblings. Sadly, William's mother, Clare, died aged 37 in 1892, a mere three weeks after the birth of her son, Eric. William's father soon remarried, and his second wife, Susannah, gave birth to the youngest child in the family, Urban, in 1896. Like his brothers, William attended Bishop's Stortford College and, according to his early Army records, would go on to Nottingham University.[3] However, post-First World War paperwork later suggests that his postgraduate studies were perhaps a little less stellar. The reality was that he spent six months training at Nottingham Dairy College.[4] Nevertheless, the intent was to continue the family line of business. However, war would intervene not once but twice. The first of his two stints in uniform occurred in 1900 when the 21-year-old William served in the ranks of the Sherwood Rangers Yeomanry during the Boer War. He served until mid-1901 before returning home as a Corporal and to farming. A couple of months after his return to England, he was awarded a Distinguished Conduct Medal for his actions at Lichenburgh. After the Boer War, William Stephenson 'was an extensive farmer, having farmed from 500 to 1,000 acres for 12 years, including three years as a farm manager'.[5] The 1911 Census shows that farming provided William with a comfortable life. He lived on a large farm at Edlington, a few miles north of Horncastle in Lincolnshire, with his wife and two young children and employed four staff on the farm.

William married Jessie Scorer on 24 June 1908 in Newport Pagnell. Jessie was the ambitious driving force behind the family and would remain so until her death in 1986 at the remarkable age of 106. Eighteen months after they married, the Stephensons welcomed their first of four children. Their eldest child, Geoffrey Dalton Stephenson, was born in Edlington on 19 January 1910. Geoffrey would be followed by Jessica Eileen Stephenson (known as Eileen) in October 1911 and a brother, John Dalton Stephenson, in January 1915. By the time of John's birth, the world was changing. The Great War had started the year prior and would directly impact Geoffrey's family and those of his uncles. Moreover, the war would showcase William's sense of duty and sacrifice, traits also instilled in his eldest son, Geoffrey.

Just a couple of months before his 37th birthday, William Stephenson was attested into the Army on 10 December 1915. Although he was deemed an essential worker as a farmer, William once again felt obligated to do the right thing and join up. However, the Army did not call him up immediately.

His attestation card informed that 'You will be required to serve for one day with the Colours and the remainder of the period in the Army Reserve . . . until such times as you may be called up by the order of the Army Council.'[6] William did not have long to wait; he was called up on 16 February 1916 and joined the Inns of Court Officer Training Corps based out of Berkhamstead in Hertfordshire. The Army declared the 5ft-7in and 149lb farmer medically fit on 29 March 1916. His experience and maturity were evident as his unit quickly promoted him to Lance Corporal in mid-June, Corporal in early August, and then commissioned as a Second Lieutenant on 27 November 1916. For the moment, he remained in the United Kingdom. In August 1917, he transferred to the 9th Lancers (Special Reserve) in preparation for a move to the Continent and the battlefields of northern France. He left his young family and 'handed over his farm for a friend to manage' in his stead.[7] After a 17-year absence from the front line, William Stephenson headed to the Somme. The 9th Lancers' War Diary informs that on 23 February 1918, Second Lieutenant W.D. Stephenson joined as a reinforcement.[8] At the time, the 9th Lancers headquarters were at Doingt, a small village a few miles east of Arras. It would not be long before he was in action.

William Stephenson arrived on the front line only a few weeks before the German Spring Offensive of 1918. Known as Operation Michael, the German plan was radical and aimed to break the static trench warfare stalemate across the Western Front. The German gambit was to break through the Allied lines before pivoting north-west towards the Channel ports. With Russian forces surrendering on the Eastern Front, Germany could focus its remaining military forces westwards and, critically, before the imminent influx of US troops into France. The German opportunity was fleeting. Consequently, they planned to employ new stormtrooper tactics to enable quick advances by avoiding heavily defended areas and exploiting gaps. In the early hours of 21 March 1918, Operation Michael began with a ferocious German artillery barrage to soften up the front lines. Next, the Germans unleashed their stormtroopers, who attacked across a broad 40-mile front between Arras, Saint-Quentin and La Fere. Amongst the defending forces facing the German onslaught were the 9th (Queen's Royal) Lancers and Second Lieutenant William Dalton Stephenson. The unit War Diary for 23 March 1918 notes:

The regiment moved in the evening to Athies, where it remained about one hour, subsequently moving to defend Le Mensil and over the Brie bridge.[9] At this place, the remnants of the Pioneer Regiment were found under Lieutenant Jenkinson. Lieutenant O.F. Stapleton-Bretherton killed. Captain C.J. Chisholm and 2nd Lt W.D. Stephenson DCM wounded, three Other Ranks killed, 20 Other Ranks wounded and 56 Other Ranks unaccounted for.[10]

While details provided in the unit's War Diary were sparse, William Stephenson's medical records provide more detail about the injuries he sustained that day.

That when in action on 23 March 1918, he received a [gunshot wound] of the left hand. X-ray showed [foreign body] in palm of hand. This was removed on 25 April 1918. The wound is healing. At the same time he was wounded, he strained his back muscles through being buried by a shell. This is also compromising. The first time his back muscles was strained was ten years ago, before he joined the Army. Since then, from time to time, it has given him trouble with severe exertion.[11]

Tragically, William's injuries occurred on the same day that one of his brothers was killed. Lieutenant Urban Arnold Stephenson, the youngest of the brothers, was only 21 when he was killed in action on 23 March 1918. After spending a year in the ranks of the Royal Fusiliers, Urban received a commission in the First Battalion of the Lincolnshire Regiment. On 23 March 1918, Urban was only a few miles north-west of William's location when he came under a fatal German barrage. Unlike William, Urban had spent significant time deployed in France, including three long, harsh winters.[12] Sadly, Urban was not the first of the Stephenson brothers to be killed during the First World War.

Of the seven Stephenson brothers who served during the Great War, Urban was the last of three fatalities within the family. The first to be killed was 33-year-old George, serving as a Sapper with the First Field Company of the Canadian Engineers. On 15 June 1915, George was killed by shellfire during the aftermath of the Second Battle of Ypres and was laid to rest at the Post Office Rifles Cemetery in Festubert, a few miles east of Bethune in the

Pas de Calais. Nine months later, tragedy struck the Stephenson family once more. On 18 March 1916, a month after William was called up, 24-year-old Second Lieutenant Eric Stephenson of the Lincolnshire Regiment was killed in action at Mont Saint Eloi, located a few miles north-west of Arras. The former medical student now rests at Ecoivres Military Cemetery, not far from where he fell. The inscription on Eric's gravestone reflects the sacrifice paid by the Stephenson family – 'One of Seven Brothers Who Served, Three of Whom Rest in France'. Unfortunately, the Stephensons were not alone, as many families on both sides of the divide paid a similar blood price.

The other three surviving Stephenson brothers who served during the Great War all had an eventful war. Charles and Harold Stephenson were both Mentioned in Despatches and awarded the Military Cross. Harold would also receive a Bar to his Military Cross. Charles, like William, had already served in the Boer War. However, during the Great War, Charles served in Egypt and Palestine. Meanwhile, Harold was besieged at Kut, in Mesopotamia, before being taken prisoner for the rest of the war. The remaining brother, Reginald, survived a German U-boat torpedo attack that sunk the passenger liner RMS *Arcadian* in the eastern Mediterranean in April 1917. The brothers did not solely dominate the Stephenson Great War narrative. Their sister, Lilian, served as a nurse in Belgium for two and a half years and was awarded the Queen of the Belgians' Medal. As the local press suggested, the Stephensons were a 'Family of Fighters', a trait that the next generation would aspire to and emulate.[13]

William Stephenson's injuries were severe enough that doctors sent him back to England to be rehabilitated, arriving in Southampton via ship from Le Havre. The date of his arrival in England would have seemed somewhat irrelevant to William at the time. However, given his eldest son's future career path, it is rather apposite that his arrival coincided with the formation of the RAF – 1 April 1918. In London, doctors assessed William's wounds as severe but not permanent. Consequently, Stephenson was removed from military duty for three months to aid his recovery. William recuperated at the family's new home in Binbrook in the Lincolnshire Wolds and not too far from Geoffrey's school, Surfleets Preparatory School in Louth. However, this was a temporary home as Stephenson's military journey was far from over. The Army ordered William to report to the Curragh in Ireland on 30 September 1918 to take on the role of Chief Instructor at the Agricultural Training Farm at Ballyfair. The training farms gave practical instruction for those still serving but expecting demobilisation and early return to civilian life. The 150-acre farm catered for up to 130 students and exposed them to various tasks associated with running and managing a farm. Stephenson's previous farming experience meant he was an obvious choice for the Chief Instructor role. The family packed their Lincolnshire home and moved to Ireland in late autumn 1918.

The end of the First World War in November 1918 was a time to reflect and celebrate. For the Stephenson family, the loss of three brothers was understandably tragic. Back in their home village of Althorpe in North Lincolnshire, a memorial was erected on Main Street to remember Geoffrey's uncles. However, with the end of the Great War, there was also an element of relief and celebration. William's recovery from his war wounds was clearly progressing rather well, as evidenced nine months after the armistice by the arrival of his fourth child, Urban George Eric Stephenson. Named after the three Stephenson brothers killed in the Great War, Urban was, in many ways, a walking memorial to his lost uncles. Consequently, the family always protected Urban. None more so than his eldest brother, Geoffrey. It would also be a trait reciprocated in times of need.

While there was undoubted elation at the end of the Great War, William's new role in Ireland was far from a straightforward appointment, not because of the position but due to the context. While Stephenson may have missed the last few months of the First World War, his new posting at the largest British Army garrison in Ireland coincided with the tensions and bloodshed over independence. The fight for Irish independence would start in January 1919, only a few months into the start of his tour, and finish in July 1921. With Ireland transitioning into an independent but still divided nation, British military units had left the Irish Free State by late 1922. Stephenson's three-year tour in Ireland would coincide with that period of tension. In October 1921, as British forces began withdrawing from Ireland, William faced a dilemma. Should he leave Geoffrey in Ireland to finish his preparatory education, a pre-requisite for entry into public school, or take him home to the safety of England? Unbeknownst to William, the fight for Irish independence would turn into a year-long Irish Civil War that would last until May 1923.

Despite the turmoil, Geoffrey was benefitting from his time at Castle Park Preparatory School at Dalkey on the outskirts of Dublin and close to the shores of Dublin Bay. The boys-only boarding school catered to the sons of affluent and influential military officers, landed gentry, British administrators, and wealthy Irish industrialists. Due to the educational stability provided by the school, William made the difficult decision to leave his son in Ireland. A similar dilemma would occur later in Geoffrey's own military career, where he would be left behind while the rest of the family escaped from a country in turmoil. Despite 'accounts of occasional skirmishes on the [school] grounds', Geoffrey would remain in the relative safety of Castle Park until 1924.[14] Despite the hardships of isolation from his family and a civil war outside the school grounds, Geoffrey enjoyed his time at Castle Park. The school provided safety, a stable education, friendship and fostered his love of sports. As one of the first members of the school's Old Boys' Society, Geoffrey would update the school each year on his many exploits throughout his career. The Society's annual newsletter also captured Stephenson's sporting prowess, including captaining the rugby team in 1923 and his utility as a wicketkeeper during the cricket tour later that same year.[15]

Back in England, the rest of the Stephenson family moved to Eastgate House, a sizeable 1,500-acre farm in Norfolk. At the same time, William transferred to a regular commission as a Captain in the Army Education Corps but had yet to receive a follow-on appointment. In the meantime, William was reacquainting himself with rural country farming in England. Some six months after returning from Ireland, the Army offered William a posting to Northern Command's vocational farming centre at Catterick in North Yorkshire – a very similar role to the one he had left in Ireland. However, by this stage, William had settled back into his traditional family role of running a large farm. Consequently, he asked to resign his commission from the Army. On 1 May 1921, after five and a half eventful years in service to King and Country, Captain William Dalton Stephenson DCM retired.

In the summer of 1924, 14-year-old Geoffrey finally returned to England. However, after six years in Ireland, he was not heading back to the family but to Shropshire, some 150 miles west of the family's Norfolk farm. Geoffrey attended Shrewsbury School, a private school on the banks of the River Severn, for his final four years of education. Geoffrey immersed himself in his studies and sports, excelling in both. He was a good all-round sportsman and captained the school's swimming, gymnastics, and boxing teams. In his final year at Shrewsbury School, he was a member of the Sports Committee. He also proved to be a fine cross-country runner and was awarded his school colours and the title of 'Gentleman of the Runs'. The short and wiry Stephenson's love of competitive sports would endure throughout his life.

While Geoffrey excelled at school, his father's farming business was in financial trouble. William's father passed away in 1925 and left his inheritance to William and two of his brothers. The sum was not insignificant. The estate's gross value was £55,894 4s and 6d, a princely sum in 1927.[16] The money should have given the Stephensons a very comfortable lifestyle. William elected to invest the money and his efforts into forming a farming partnership that combined three farms at Marham, Narborough, and Wiggenhall St Mary the Virgin into a single company. However, a year before Geoffrey was due to join Cranwell as a Flight Cadet, the farming company, Stubley & Stephenson ultimately failed and folded in October 1927.[17]

Sporty, academic, privately educated and imbued with the family sense of sacrifice and duty, a transition to the military was an obvious pathway for the 18-year-old Geoffrey. The Stephenson family may have had a strong army heritage, but their Great War sacrifices had also scarred them. Consequently, and aided by being a member of the school's Officer Training Corps, Geoffrey was attracted to the decade-old RAF and its relatively new Fenland-based officer cadet college.

While Geoffrey sat comfortably within the 17½ to 19-year-old age bracket for entry into Cranwell as a flight cadet, he also had to pass a written examination, an exacting Interview Board, and a full aircrew medical examination in London.[18] The examination, arranged by the Civil Service Commission, comprised four obligatory papers which included English, English History and Geography, Mathematics (Elementary) as well as one of seven modern languages.[19] Three further papers had to be selected from the following choices: Latin, Greek, one of the seven modern languages not taken as an obligatory subject, Mathematics (Intermediate), Mathematics (Higher), Science (Physics and Chemistry) or Elementary Engineering.[20] While the academic tests may have been a taxing but straightforward challenge for Geoffrey, one significant obstacle required external assistance. Not only was there a £5 fee to sit the written examination, but parents needed to pay a fee for their sons to attend the two-year course at Cranwell. In addition to the £75 per annum fees, parents were liable to pay £35 before entry, and a further £30 payment was due at the beginning of a cadet's second year. The additional fees were to cover the costs of uniforms and books.[21] While these fees may seem somewhat paltry today, these were considerable for 1928, particularly if you had just lost your farming business. However, when setting up their new officer training college, Trenchard and his fellow senior RAF leaders wanted to ensure they were attracting high-calibre individuals. As a result, each intake of two dozen or so students could apply for several scholarships to ease the financial difficulties. Each course had up to five King's Cadets whose scholarship funds covered the costs of fees, uniforms, and books. Other scholarships were also available to those with South African heritage or the 'sons of parents whose reduced circumstances were due to the late war'.[22] The latter scholarship, provided by the industrialist and philanthropist Sir Charles Wakefield, 'provided funds for a period of three years for the annual award of two scholarships each to the value of £75'.[23]

The financial difficulties faced by the family and William's military service meant that Geoffrey could apply for the Sir Charles Wakefield Scholarship. The RAF saw the potential in Geoffrey, and he was duly awarded one of the two Sir Charles Wakefield Scholarships for his intake of 24 cadets. To show the quality of the individuals competing for the various scholarships, and as we will see in the next chapter, Geoffrey would prove his worth by being one of the prize-winners upon his graduation from Cranwell. Also, the other Charles Wakefield scholar would go on to win the Sword of Honour for the best student overall, narrowly beating one of the King's Cadets – a certain Douglas Bader.

The net result was that on 6 September 1928, Geoffrey Dalton Stephenson arrived at the RAF Cadet College at Cranwell in Lincolnshire, only a few miles west of his birthplace, to begin his RAF adventure. He would spend the next two years at Cranwell, learning to become an officer and a pilot. The expectations were high. The Service expected its Cranwell graduates to shape its future and to lead it, both in the air and, more importantly, on the ground as a prospective senior officer. This generation would lead squadrons in the early stages of the Second World War and command fighter wings as well as stations during its latter stages. In the post-war peace, they would lead the reshaping of the organisation and prepare it for the emerging challenges of the Cold War. However, to do so, they had to endure their training, the early stages of their fledgling flying careers, and enemy action. Success and survival were not guaranteed. Many would fall by the wayside along the way. The next quarter of a century would be an eventful adventure for Stephenson and his cohort. However, Flight Cadet Geoffrey Dalton Stephenson had two years of officer and pilot training to look forward to.

Chapter 2

Pre-War in the RAF

'Superna Petimus' – We Seek Higher Things

RAF College Cranwell Motto

RAF Cadet College Cranwell – September 1928 to July 1930

Stephenson arrived at RAF Cranwell in early September 1928. He was one of 24 new Flight Cadets to join course S28. The 'S' stood for September, while '28' reflected the year the course started. The two-year course was split into four terms, with four courses running simultaneously, each six months apart with the cadets of each course divided between two Squadrons – A and B. The 24 new Flight Cadets were a select group of individuals. The vast majority, like Stephenson, were privately educated and from affluent families. However, the RAF also catered for those from a more humble background who had already demonstrated the aptitude and ability to lead the junior Service. Consequently, several Halton apprentices were also added to each Cranwell intake. For S28, three Halton apprentices, including Paddy Coote, joined those from more privileged backgrounds.

Although the airfield at Cranwell was set up during the First World War, the officer training element formed in 1920. Marshal of the RAF Sir Hugh Trenchard was the power behind what would become the RAF College. His intent was that 'first, that the doors of the Air Force should be thrown open to boys of sufficient physical, mental and moral capacity; secondly, that they should be trained for the Air Force rather than general culture by instruction in special technicalities'.[1] From their first day at Cranwell, the Flight Cadets were a small, select cadre of privileged, capable and driven individuals; the camaraderie and bonds formed at Cranwell would last a lifetime and the 'old boy network' certainly aided many throughout their careers. However, their progression and graduation were not assured, and several would fall by the wayside, either through poor academic performance or an inappropriate attitude. The intent for a Cranwell graduate was to 'have a general although somewhat elementary knowledge of the Navy, Army and Air Force – will be a first-class pilot of the Avro – will have an elementary knowledge of the work carried out from flying machines and will have a solid grounding in the duties of the mechanics of an aeroplane squadron'.[2] To meet that goal, the cadets had a focused academic programme. During their first year, the curriculum included the traditional subjects of English, Mathematics and Physics. However, the remainder of the syllabus was more bespoke and incorporated: Aerodynamics, Aeronautical Science, Engines, Rigging, History and Organisation of the RAF, Armament, Wireless Telegraphy, Morse, Air Pilotage, and Army Organisation as well as Drill and General Efficiency. In the second year, Naval Organisation, Law and Administration, Sanitation and Hygiene, Meteorology, Signals as well as Practical Flying were added to the programme.

Academically, Stephenson sat in the middle of the pack, finishing 13th at the end of the first year but rising to tenth by graduation. After barely meeting the minimum academic grade for the first year, Bader became more focused and rose from 19th to 17th. Some were less fortunate. Three of the 24 students from S28 were back-coursed due to failing to meet the academic requirement. Two of the three would eventually graduate six months later than Stephenson. The remaining student withdrew from officer training in July 1930 to return home and 'fly for a firm of fur trappers in northern Canada'.[3] Beyond academics, the Cranwell curriculum had several practical elements to it. The most prominent feature was the flying instruction conducted from Cranwell's grass airstrip, with sport a close second.

The one area where Stephenson stood head and shoulders above his compatriots was flying. He was a natural pilot, a point reflected in his assessments. Stephenson scored 1115 out of a possible 1200 in the Practical Flying examinations and tests. His closest rival was a distant Bader. The students started flying in September 1928 in the two-seat Avro 504N trainer. By the end of the course, Stephenson had accrued 256 flying hours and added the Bristol Fighter, the De Havilland DH9A and the Armstrong Whitworth Siskin to his logbook. Of note, one of his flying instructors at Cranwell was the New Zealander, Squadron Leader Arthur 'Mary' Coningham. The Kiwi would rise through the ranks and become one of the most successful

RAF commanders of the Second World War. Stephenson and Coningham would reunite in the post-war era. However, this was some way off. More immediately, Stephenson's stellar performance in the air ensured that he was awarded the R.M. Groves Memorial Prize for the best pilot of the course. Beyond the classroom and the cockpit, Cranwell invested significant effort in sports, particularly those that built team cohesion and leadership amongst the Flight Cadets.

Stephenson was highly competitive; it would be an enduring trait. At Cranwell, his spirited nature was given an outlet in the sports arena, specifically athletics, cross-country, boxing, horse-riding, and swimming. Given his slight build, Stephenson was a natural long-distance runner, and it is no surprise that he won the 2-mile race against the Old Cranwellians in April 1930.[4] However, he was only placed fifth of 85 cadets in the inter-Squadron cross-country race earlier in the same week. There was some mitigation for the poor form. 'Stephenson's run was especially creditable . . . taking into account his previous very "late night."'[5] It is clear that Stephenson was following the old RAF adage of working hard and playing hard!

In the boxing ring, Stephenson fought in the Lightweight class. He would always put up a good fight, but while at Cranwell, he appears to have been vanquished by most of his opponents.[6] In the annual encounter with their Sandhurst counterparts, Stephenson faced the same opponent in 1929 and 1930 – Gentleman Cadet Arkwright. After being beaten in the 1929 competition, Stephenson sought revenge the following year.[7] The 1930 re-match produced 'the best boxing of the evening . . . They wasted no time in preliminaries, and there was hard, fast and clean punching for three rounds. Stephenson lost by very little, his opponent having an advantage in reach, which probably won for him.'[8] Despite his defeat, Stephenson would continue to box throughout his career.

While Stephenson may have had the edge on Bader in academics and flying, Bader had the advantage regarding sporting prowess and leadership qualities. During the fourth and final term, the senior course would undertake leadership roles. The senior student within the Squadron would be assigned the position of 'Under Officer' supported by two Flight Cadet Sergeants and two Flight Cadet Corporals. In January 1930, Bader was selected as one of the two Under Officers, the lead cadet within A Squadron. However, Stephenson's leadership potential was also recognized; he would be promoted to one of the

Flight Cadet Sergeant positions for A Squadron, subordinate to Bader. The B Squadron Under Officer was Paddy Coote, the former Halton apprentice and the other Sir Charles Wakefield Scholar, who would go on to win the Sword of Honour for the best cadet.

In what little downtime they had, Stephenson and his friends made the most of it. Although Flight Cadets were barred from having cars, they were allowed to own motorbikes. Most of their off-base escapades involved their motorbikes, usually overloaded, travelling too quickly and ending up in hedges or gardens![9] The RAF created a group of young, fearless individuals trained to push boundaries and take risks. Evidently, these traits manifested themselves both at work and at play. Despite their various misdemeanours, 21 of the original 24 Flight Cadets graduated on 25 July 1930. In Stephenson's end-of-course report from Cranwell, the RAF College Commandant, Air Vice-Marshal A.M. Longmore wrote, 'smart efficient Cadet Sergeant who set a fine example to others by his energy and enterprise in work and sports. Will make a valuable officer and good mess mate.' 20-year-old Pilot Officer Geoffrey Stephenson was now a commissioned officer in the RAF with a new set of pilots' wings and heading to a front-line unit as a fighter pilot. He was also heading there with his best friend.

23 Squadron – August 1930 to January 1932

'Semper Aggressus' – Always on the Attack

23 Squadron motto

On 23 August 1930, the 23 Squadron Operations Record Book highlights that 'Pilot Officers D.R.S. Bader and G.D. Stephenson posted to unit from Cranwell'.[10] The two Cranwell friends had made it to a front-line fighter squadron. The Squadron was based at RAF Kenley on the southern edge of Greater London and commanded by Squadron Leader Henry Woollett DSO MC and Bar. The 45-year-old Woollett had arrived on the squadron in January 1930 following the death of the previous squadron commander in North Africa after a failed attempt to break the world's long-distance flying record.[11] While Woollett may have been older than his peers, he had a distinguished flying career. During the Great War, Woollett had initially served with the Lincolnshire Regiment in Gallipoli before transferring to the Royal Flying

Corps in 1916. Already an ace by the time of the German Spring Offensive of 1918, he added ten kills in March 1918 alone. While the Stephenson brothers suffered on the ground during Operation Michael, Woollett was honing his fighter skills in the air. By the war's end, he had amassed 35 air-to-air kills.

Under Woollett's command was a squadron of 10 officers and 88 airmen (including four airmen pilots) looking after 12 aircraft.[12] Stephenson initially flew in the basic Gloster Gamecock before converting to the more advanced Bristol Bulldog towards the latter stages of his tour. Woollett was aided in running the squadron by his flight commanders, Flight Lieutenants Richard Atcherley and Harry Day. Both would shape, inform and influence Stephenson not only on the squadron but throughout his career.

The 26-year-old Atcherley was also a Cranwell graduate but had graduated six years earlier than Stephenson. Like Stephenson, he was a Flight Cadet Sergeant and was awarded the R.M. Groves Memorial Prize for his piloting skills. After a brief front-line tour, Atcherley became a flying instructor and would arrive at Kenley following a stint with the RAF High-Speed Flight and their participation in the 1929 Schneider Trophy competition, a prestigious and highly competitive seaplane race between the major global air power nations. Although Atcherley would only briefly overlap with Stephenson and Bader on 23 Squadron, the other flight commander would be there for Stephenson's entire tenure at Kenley. At 32, Harry Day was older than his fellow flight commander and had a less flamboyant approach. However, he was a capable, credible and experienced pilot who had served in the latter stages of the First World War, not as an airman but as a Royal Marine. He moved to the Fleet Air Arm in 1924 before transferring to the RAF permanently in 1930 and joining 23 Squadron.

The squadron flew affiliation sorties with bomber squadrons and conducted cooperation exercises with Royal Artillery anti-aircraft units as well as searchlight units. The squadron also honed their own fighting skills. For example, in May 1931, the squadron spent three weeks practising air-to-air gunnery at Sutton Bridge during their annual air-firing camp.[13] A week after this, 'four aircraft of squadron participated in Andover air display', that included Day, Bader and Stephenson.[14] On 27 June 1931, the 23 Squadron pilots headed to the highest-profile airshow of the year – the Hendon Air Pageant. Although the Squadron took three pilots to Hendon, only Day and

Bader flew in the display, with Stephenson relegated to the reserve pilot role. Although Stephenson may have been disappointed to not fly in the display, his time would soon come. 'Two months later, on 22 August . . . at Cramlington in Northumberland, Bader and Stephenson, flying the pair together for the first time in public, fashioned a sequence over the top of the airfield which set the great northern crowd alight.'[15] According to Laddie Lucas, Bader's biographer, a fellow fighter pilot and Bader's brother-in-law, the duo 'had lifted their dual and individual skills to a level which was out of reach of all save a small handful of Service pilots. Squadron pride and quest for perfection – to be, in a word, the best – was their spur.'[16] Moreover, Stephenson's tactical flying skills were also recognized. After the successful squadron air-firing camp earlier in the year, Stephenson and Pilot Officer A.E. Dobell were selected to compete in the Brooke-Popham Cup and 'proceeded to Sutton Bridge for best firer's competition'.[17] Stephenson impressed his seniors. In his 1931 confidential report, his squadron commander assessed Stephenson as an 'exceptional' flyer. Woollett also highlighted that 'his energy and enterprise are a fine example, smart and efficient and a great asset. "Full Out" at everything.' The RAF Kenley Station Commander, Wing Commander Robinson, suggested that Stephenson was 'a keen and energetic officer of the right type'.

Despite the accolades and their natural ability, Stephenson and Bader were still inexperienced with relatively few flying hours, less than 500 hours total. To be a truly experienced pilot you needed maturity, ability, and luck. So far, Stephenson's luck had held despite a few close calls. During an aerobatics practice, he 'fell out of a slow roll but luckily was just beyond the end of the Kenley escarpment and had enough space to recover'.[18] On another occasion his engine failed, resulting in a 'forced landing in the grounds of a country estate'.[19] Stephenson had been fortunate; others would be less so. A change in aircraft type would prove to be the undoing of his squadron colleagues. In mid-1931, the squadron retired its Gloster Gamecocks and replaced them with the larger, heavier, but faster Bristol Bulldog. The bulkier Bulldog was more of a handful than the more docile Gamecock. On 30 September 1931, 23 Squadron lost Pilot Officer Ireland, who was killed when his Bristol Bulldog failed to recover from a spin.[20] Ireland had been on the squadron a mere three days. Sadly, the Bulldog would bite closer to home. As the end of 1931 approached, Woollett handed over command of 23 Squadron on 9 December 1931.[21] Five days later, tragedy struck.

While much of Bader's near-fatal crash is well documented, there is still some debate on who was involved. All agree that on Monday 14 December 1931, Flying Officer G.W. Phillips led the formation of three Bulldogs, including Bader, and left Kenley for a lunch stop at the Reading Aero Club at Woodley. The area of contention is the identity of the third pilot. In Bader's memoir, he suggests that Richardson was the third pilot, while Laddie Lucas informs that it was Stephenson.[22] While the group's construction does not influence the tragic outcome, it does question the timing and type of posting that Stephenson moved on to subsequently.

After lunch at Woodley and some interactions with aero club members, the 23 Squadron trio performed a 'Prince of Wales' Feathers manoeuvre after take-off. Phillips was in the lead aircraft and pulled up vertically while the wingmen on each side of Phillip's aircraft peeled away in their respective directions. However, this was not enough for an incredibly capable but equally overconfident aerobatics pilot like Bader. Upon completing the initial manoeuvre on Phillips' left-hand side, Bader returned to the airfield at a low altitude. However, and showing his relative inexperience on the heavier and less manoeuvrable Bulldog, Bader's aircraft lost what little height it had during the subsequent slow roll, which resulted in the left wingtip striking the ground. Bader's aircraft now collapsed around him as it careered across the grass airfield. Overhead, Phillips and the third pilot could only watch on in horror as their squadron colleague fought for his life in the remnants of his fighter.

While Bader started to come to terms with his life's defining moment, the RAF Court of Inquiry convened to determine the cause of the accident. As the most senior of the three pilots, Phillips was ultimately court-martialled for not restraining Bader and flying into a civilian aerodrome contrary to service regulations.[23] Pending the result of the court martial, Phillips left the squadron on 21 January 1932 to 12 (Bombing) Squadron at Andover.[24]

Two days later, Stephenson also left the squadron. On 23 January 1932, just over a month after Bader's crash, the 23 Squadron operations record book informs that 'Pilot Officer GD Stephenson posted from unit to No1 Armoured Car Company, Iraq'.[25] The proximity of the posting to an overseas ground unit so soon after Bader's crash has raised questions by some. Bader suggests that in the summer of 1931, the RAF released the 'A List' roster detailing the young permanent commission officers due for an overseas posting.[26] As recent Cranwell graduates, Bader and Stephenson fell firmly into that category. Consequently, 'it was routine that after a year on a squadron, a young permanent officer would go overseas'.[27] Also, the timing of Stephenson's posting is in keeping with other Cranwell graduates from 23 Squadron of that period. Moreover, there is nothing untoward written in Stephenson's Record of Service, and his confidential report shows no dip in performance or criticism. Additionally, his next post came with a promotion to Flying Officer. However, if indeed Stephenson was the third pilot and was deemed culpable, the punishment doled out may have been limited to moving him into a ground-focused appointment with limited flying opportunities. By comparison, most of Stephenson's Cranwell peers were sent to flying-related second tours, such as flying-instruction duties. Irrespective of the rationale for his move to Iraq, the decision to post Stephenson in early 1932 may have prolonged his life. He would return to the United Kingdom two and a half years later, a more mature, experienced and wiser pilot. Ahead of him was a more sedate flying career in older, more docile aircraft on simple transits with senior officers as his passenger. There was always an inherent risk in flying military aircraft in an unforgiving environment, but it involved less risk than flying in a testosterone-laden front-line fighter squadron.

While Bader and Stephenson barely survived their first tour, many of their Cranwell cohort would not be so lucky. By the end of 1932, less than 18 months after their Cranwell graduation, five, nearly a quarter, of Stephenson's graduating class would be dead, four due to flying accidents.[28] Peacetime flying in the military during the 1930s was a brutal affair. In 1931 alone, the RAF suffered 40 fatal accidents and 97 serious incidents.[29] Immature technology, flying indiscipline and sheer bad luck took their toll. Sadly, more would follow as another world war would claim even more of Stephenson's Cranwell intake. In the meantime, Stephenson was heading to the Middle East while Bader retired from the RAF . . . for now.

Iraq – January 1932 to October 1934

Stephenson set sail for Iraq from Southampton on 23 January 1932 on board His Majesty's Troopship *Somersetshire*. Three days later, as Stephenson was on his way to the Middle East, he was promoted to the rank of Flying Officer.

The RAF had been in the region since the early 1920s conducting 'Air Control' supporting the League of Nations' Mandates in Palestine and Iraq. 'Air Control' used aircraft, armoured cars and locally recruited levies as a cost-effective but efficient means to police the territories. By 1932, Number 1 Armoured Car Company was part of the RAF team responsible for patrolling Iraq. Led by the decorated First World War pilot Wing Commander Vivian Gaskell-Blackburn DSC AFC, the unit was broken down into four Sections dispersed across three locations. The headquarters and workshops as well as Numbers 2 and 3 Sections were located at RAF Hinaidi, on the outskirts of Baghdad. Number 1 Section was based at Mosul in the north of the country, while Number 4 Section was stationed in the south at Basra.[30] In his 1932 letter to his old school in Dublin, Stephenson confirms that he was based in Basra.

Each section had seven armoured cars, and their role was to 'keep tracks open, making ourselves familiar with the countryside, show a bit of strength in the villages and do a lot of training'.[31] Stephenson's photograph album shows him on patrol in the Iraqi desert with the Rolls-Royce armoured cars. While he may have been living an adventurous life, Stephenson remarked, 'I miss the complete lack of greenery here. Just miles and miles of sand with not a living thing on it.'[32]

With the British mandate in Iraq ending in October 1932, the active role of the Armoured Car Companies began to diminish. Although the Mosul and Hinaidi units were involved in countering a potential crisis amongst the Assyrian levies, life was quieter for Stephenson in Basra. Nevertheless, Stephenson's performance received praise from his commanding officer. In his 1932 appraisal, Gaskell-Blackburn stated that Stephenson was 'keen and conscientious, marked ability. Worked hard with marked success. Has shown ability in signals and gunnery.' The following year, Gaskell-Blackburn's successor was also impressed. Wing Commander William Strugnell MC commented that Stephenson was 'recommended for flying duties, very keen and useful. Reliable in all ways.' More importantly, Stephenson's talent was attracting the attention of senior commanders.

On 14 July 1933, 18 months into his overseas tour, Stephenson took on the role of personal assistant to Air Officer Commanding Iraq Command, Air Vice-Marshal Charles Burnett. Stephenson regularly flew his principal around the region in a Westland Wapiti, a large and cumbersome two-seat general-purpose biplane, including a flight to Tehran in late August 1934. Burnett was impressed with his mentee. As Stephenson departed Iraq in October 1934, Burnett commented on Stephenson's confidential report that he was 'very good. Should do well. Keen sportsman.' The two individuals would be reunited later in the decade, but for now, Stephenson was heading back to England and the cockpit.

Flying Instructor – December 1934 to October 1938

Imprimis Praecepta – Our teaching is everlasting,

Central Flying School Motto

After two months of reacquainting himself with home, Stephenson reported to RAF Wittering, near Stamford, on 3 December 1934, to start the Central Flying School's (CFS's) 44th Flying Instructors Course. For Stephenson, this would be the start of a long association with CFS as a student, instructor and, later, its commandant. In late 1934, Stephenson joined 19 other RAF officers and nine airmen pilots as a student on the four-month course aimed at teaching experienced pilots how to instruct student aviators.[33] Although poor weather curtailed the start of the course, the improving weather allowed the student instructors to graduate on time on 9 March 1935. However, not all of the students finished the course. Despite the average student starting the course with 935 flying hours, 'which was rather higher than normal', three pilots were withdrawn from the course and two were deemed unsuitable to be instructors.[34] Eighteen of the remaining 24 graduates were categorised as 'B' instructors, and five were given the lower 'C' grading.[35] Only one pilot on the course was graded as 'A2' – above average in the air and on the ground. Although the CFS Operations Record Book does not promulgate specific student's grades, Stephenson's Record of Service confirms that he was awarded an 'A2' instructional grade on 9 March 1935 – the sole above-average grading on the course and, as a result, the course's top student. Despite spending nearly three years on predominantly ground-based appointments, Stephenson had ably demonstrated that he had not lost any of his natural flying aptitude. Moreover, he showed that he could teach better than his peers in the air and on the ground. His next step was to return to RAF Cranwell and ply his new trade as an 'A2' Qualified Flying Instructor.

Over the next 17 months, Stephenson deepened his knowledge of his new craft, teaching Cranwell flight cadets. He also supported Oxford University Air Squadron's two-month summer camp to RAF Eastchurch in the summer of 1935. However, given his natural piloting skills, it was not long before CFS poached Stephenson to become one of the select few who would teach new flying instructors and examine the existing instructor cadre. In August 1936, the newly promoted Flight Lieutenant Stephenson was posted to CFS' new home at RAF Upavon in Wiltshire. While the School had only moved to Upavon the previous summer from RAF Wittering, CFS was, in reality, returning to the airfield where it was initially established in 1912.

In addition to teaching the *ab-initio* instructors, the CFS instructors would regularly visit the various flying schools at home and abroad to ensure that teaching techniques and standards were being followed. CFS would also examine the instructors and potentially upgrade their instructional categorisation. Few achieved the coveted but rare 'A1' categorisation for exceptional instructional abilities in both air and ground roles. It was not only the instructors at the flying schools who were examined. CFS also applied the same standards and scrutiny to their own instructors. Stephenson was put under the microscope on 4 May 1937 and was assessed as exceptional by CFS examiners. Consequently, after only two years as a Qualified Flying Instructor, Stephenson was upgraded from 'A2' to the exulted 'A1' category. Stephenson was now amongst a small group of elite flying instructors within the RAF.

It was not all work and no play. Stephenson would again be heading back to Hendon as part of a three-man aerobatic team. However, this time he would be part of the flying display team rather than a ground spare, as had been the case with Day and Bader back in 1931. In addition to front-line squadrons providing aerobatic displays, CFS also provided a formation display team. The 1937 CFS display team was led by Flight Lieutenant Herbert 'Tubby' Mermagen, with Sergeant Colin Scragg as the other wingman.[36]

The CFS team flew the rugged two-seat Avro Tutor primary trainer, 'an attractive biplane which had considerable aerobatic potentialities'.[37] However, the aircraft allocated to the aerobatics team were modified to a single-seat configuration with an inverted fuel system where the front seat should have been.[38] Additionally, the upper surfaces of the wings and tail were given an attractive red and white sunburst design. The highlight of the season was the

RAF Display at Hendon. June 27th 1937 saw the eighteenth but last of the annual Hendon displays. Following the end of the display season, Stephenson returned to his core CFS role, teaching new instructors at Upavon and visiting the various Flying Training Schools to examine instructors and students. Before completing his flying instructional tour, Stephenson would meet another individual who would be a central part of his later career.

On 9 May 1938, Stephenson briefly met the Monarch. This would be the first of many interactions with the King and his successor, Queen Elizabeth the Second. The CFS Operations Record Book notes that 'His Majesty the King paid a visit to the Central Flying School on 9 May, arriving by air at 1230 hours accompanied by the Chief of the Air Staff. His Majesty was met by the Air Officer Commanding Training Command, the Air Officer Commanding 23 (Training) Group and the Commandant Central Flying School. After inspecting the station, His Majesty had lunch in the Officers' Mess, leaving the station by air at 1445 hours.'[39] In October 1938, with war looming, Stephenson was moving on and up. Although predominantly ground-based, his new post was high profile, career-enhancing and would see him reunited with two of his former mentors. Despite leaving a flying role that he excelled in, Stephenson would return to CFS a decade later. However, the intervening period would prove to be a very eventful one.

Inspector General's Pilot – October 1938 to December 1939

After just over two and a half years as a Flight Lieutenant, Stephenson was promoted to Squadron Leader on 1 October 1938 and moved to his new role working for the Inspector General. Stephenson's career progression was impressive and destined for greater things. His piloting skills were evident, but more importantly, he was being allocated prime staff appointments as well as being sponsored and mentored by some very influential senior officers. The Inspector General was responsible for the inspection of airfields and was an excellent way to 'review [the RAF's] preparedness and final preparations'.[40] In October 1938, time was of the essence. A few days before Stephenson took up the appointment, Prime Minister Neville Chamberlain claimed that there was 'peace in our time'. However, it was becoming abundantly clear that time was limited and preparing the RAF for the inevitable war was paramount.

As Stephenson arrived, the department was run by a former Chief of the Air Staff. Marshal of the RAF Sir Edward Ellington would later prove to be a valuable mentor for Stephenson. However, that was in the future. Ellington would be replaced by Stephenson's former principal in Iraq, the now Air Chief Marshal Sir Charles Burnett. Another former mentor would join the Inspector General team – Squadron Leader Richard Atcherley, Stephenson's former flight commander on 23 Squadron. He was amongst friends, influential ones at that, who would continue to guide Stephenson's career. Stephenson's post proved helpful in understanding the Service's capabilities as it transitioned and expanded to a war footing. The strategic circumstances and his influential principal allowed Stephenson to compete for highly presitigious, high-profile command appointments. His timing was perfect; not only was the RAF developing rapidly, but the fighter community was also seeing a paradigm shift in fighter design and how they were operated. In his last few months in post, Stephenson saw Britain enter another war against Germany. After eight years away from the front line, Stephenson was heading back to an operational squadron as its commander and one at the forefront of British air defences.

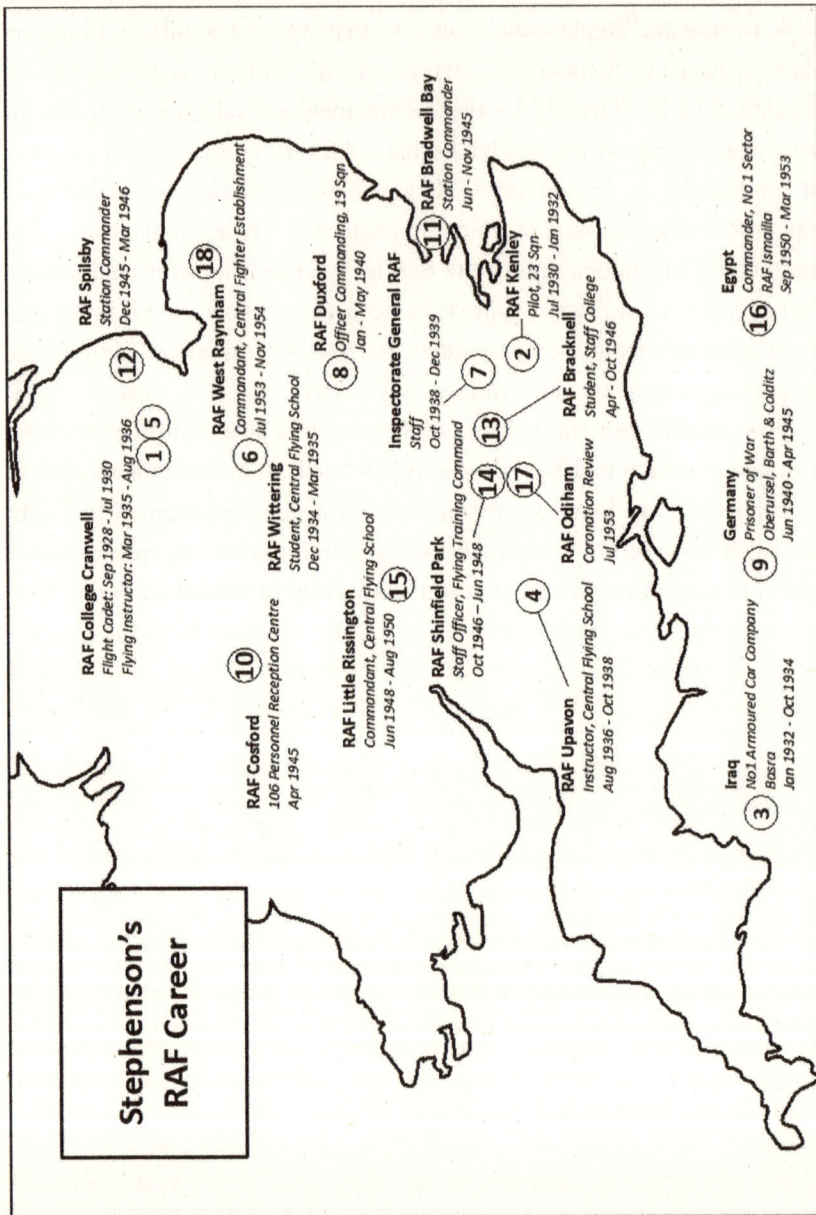

Figure 2.1 Stephenson's RAF Career by Location.

Chapter 3

Spitfire Command: 19 Squadron, RAF Duxford – January to May 1940

'Possunt Quia Posse Videntur' – They Can Because They Think They Can

19 Squadron Motto

1 9 Squadron had transitioned to Spitfires even before Stephenson arrived in Cambridgeshire. The first of the 19 Squadron Spitfires arrived at Duxford in early August 1938 'for intensive flying on re-equipment'.[1] By 19 December 1938, the Squadron was 'completely re-equipped with Spitfires'.[2] During the transition from the Gloster Gauntlet to the Spitfire, Squadron Leader Henry Cozens commanded the Squadron. He had not rested on his laurels; Cozens was active in developing the Spitfire further. Although the Spitfire was a step change in the RAF's fighter capability, its introduction to service was not without issues or areas that required attention. Cozens' early report on the Spitfire, co-authored with his fellow Spitfire squadron commander at Duxford, set the stage for improvements to the propeller, canopy, engine oil seals and starter motor. For his sterling efforts in setting up the first Spitfire squadron, Cozens was subsequently awarded an Air Force Cross on 9 June 1939.[3] Over the next year, 19 Squadron, initially under Cozens' tutelage, was increasingly focused on the German threat. It was a far cry from the earlier inter-war era, where some believed the Squadron was merely a 'happy flying club'.[4] The imminent German menace galvanized the Squadron.

Although the Hawker Hurricane was the first monoplane fighter in the RAF when the first aircraft joined 111 Squadron at RAF Northolt in December 1937, it was an obvious evolution from the Hawker biplanes of the 1920s and early 1930s. In contrast, the Spitfire seemed more revolutionary, cutting-edge and flamboyant. The aircraft shared several common traits. For example, the iconic Rolls-Royce Merlin engine powered both the Hurricane and the

Spitfire. In addition, the fighters looked more tactically focused as they sported the new camouflage scheme rather than the less discreet overall silver finish of previous generations of RAF fighters. Also, the two fighters had a common weapon system as they both initially carried eight wing-mounted Browning .303 machine guns. Despite these mutual bonds, the aircraft were different. The Hurricane was seen as the reliable, functional workhorse, while the Spitfire was the elegant, futuristic thoroughbred. If you were to command a fighter squadron in 1940, a Spitfire squadron was the first choice. Nevertheless, both were complementary and vital; the RAF introduced the Hurricane and Spitfire into service at a critical time.

The 'Phoney War'

Despite the declaration of war in September 1939, the operational tempo on 19 Squadron was relaxed, bordering on monotonous. This period, known as the 'Phoney War', saw little interaction with the enemy for those based in the United Kingdom. However, the deployed elements of the RAF had a quite different experience of the 'Phoney War'. The RAF deployed the Allied Air Striking Force, which comprised light bombers and fighters, to the European continent, and they regularly saw action. Harry Day, one of Stephenson's flight commanders on 23 Squadron at Kenley in the early 1930s, was now a Wing Commander and commanded 57 Squadron, a Blenheim unit. Day's squadron operated in the strategic reconnaissance role and flew from a forward operating base at Metz in eastern France. At 1140 on 13 October 1939, Day took off in a Bristol Blenheim Mark I along with Wireless Operator, Aircraftman Second Class Frederick Moller and Air Observer, Acting Sergeant Eric Hillier. Their task was to conduct a reconnaissance of the 'rail traffic going over the Hannover-Hamm line' to ascertain troop movements.[5] However, 50 miles inside the German border, and with the weather rapidly clearing, three German Me 109 fighters bounced the lone and vulnerable Blenheim. The subsequent fight was swift and one-sided. Moller was killed during the engagement while Day and Hillier bailed out. Sadly, only Day survived the fall to earth, but German troops quickly captured him.[6] While Day was now in German hands, Stephenson was in the process of preparing to leave his staff post in the Inspector General's department. Interestingly, Day and Stephenson would meet again in a few months. But for now, Stephenson was heading back to the cockpit and, after an eight-year sabbatical, a return to the front line. Stephenson had positioned himself well with his influential superiors, and his sponsors had given him a prime squadron command – 19 Squadron at Duxford flying Spitfires.

Back at Duxford, the 'Phoney War' continued. 19 Squadron's operational missions involved sections of three aircraft conducting mundane 'convoy patrols escorting convoy ships up and down the east coast, our parish was East Anglia'.[7] This sedate pace was the norm when, on 20 December 1939, 'Squadron Leader G. D. Stephenson reported from Air Ministry preparatory to taking over command from Squadron Leader H. I. Cozens AFC'.[8] After a short handover over the festive period, Stephenson took command of the unit on 1 January 1940. As he took command of the Spitfire squadron, the Second World War was now in its fifth month. The operational tempo would soon pick up.

After a period in late 1939 with limited operational tasking, primarily due to inclement weather, tasking increased in early 1940. However, Stephenson did not participate in any operational flying during his first month in command; he was becoming familiar with his new aircraft type and bedding into his role as the squadron commander. It was not until the morning of 16 February 1940 that he flew his first operational patrol when he flew on the wing of one of the Squadron's flight commanders, Flight Lieutenant Brian Lane.[9] From then on, Stephenson would invariably lead a section conducting operational patrols. Typically, a section would fly a single patrol per day. However, there were occasions when the Squadron would surge their operational flying to cover the standdown of another unit. With little to no Luftwaffe activity during these patrols, the flying remained predominantly routine, interspersed with brief periods of chaos chasing friendly aircraft. One of the squadron pilots at the time was Flight Sergeant George 'Grumpy' Unwin, who described the unit's activities as 'mainly convoy patrols, chasing phoney plots which usually turned out to be a Blenheim or a Wellington for the first few months of the war'.[10]

The dreary nature of the patrols had a brief respite on the afternoon of 11 May 1940 when a section of 19 Squadron Spitfires intercepted a lone German Junkers Ju 88 bomber over the sea 10 miles east of East Dudgeon on the Norfolk coast. The Squadron record book noted that

Blue Section led by Flight Lieutenant Clouston, went on patrol at 1200. Flight Sergeant Steere and Flying Officer Petre were Blue 2 and Blue 3. After being on patrol for nearly an hour, Blue Section sighted a Ju.88. Blue Leader attacked from the stern and Flight Sergeant Steere did a full deflection attack. Flying Officer Petre then took up the attack and closing to 150 yards or less shot off all his ammunition. The Ju.88 crashed into the sea, and the crew were picked up.[11]

However, this is at odds with the 12 Group assessment that the enemy losses were 'unknown'.[12] Nevertheless, 19 Squadron had engaged the enemy, and many more opportunities for more definitive outcomes would soon follow.

In addition to the operational tasking, the squadron also honed their flying skills and attack profiles. Consequently, the squadron would conduct Fighting Area Attacks which 'consisted of a series of five different types of formation attack'.[13] Throughout the winter period, sections and flights would practice these attack procedures against between three and six Wellingtons and Blenheim bombers.[14] With Stephenson taking command, the emphasis changed; the practice involved the whole squadron, not just sections or flights. For example, on 17 February 1940, 'Squadron Leader Stephenson led the squadron in formation practice. Various manoeuvres in Air Drill successfully completed.'[15] Leading large tactical formations was a skill that Stephenson had to master and quickly. As the squadron commander, he was expected to lead his squadron *en masse* into battle. Consequently, he, and for that matter, the rest of the squadron, had to practice and become comfortable in executing the Fighter Command-mandated but regimented formation attacks against large-scale enemy formations. The Fighting Area Attacks were criticised by many as they tended to compromise the wingman's awareness as they focused on precision formation flying to the detriment of effective stalking of the prey and bringing their weapons to bear in a timely fashion.[16] In just over two months, air combat with the Luftwaffe would test Stephenson's and the squadron's ability to deliver and validate these antiquated tactics.

At this point in the war, the RAF lacked dedicated night fighter squadrons. Therefore, the Spitfires had to conduct 'a lot of night flying' to provide air defence cover both day and night.[17] However, night flying was a high-risk proposition. On 29 February 1940, Stephenson lost one of his young pilots during a Spitfire night sortie. The New Zealand-born Pilot Officer Horace Trenchard, who had only joined the Squadron in October 1939, was 'killed whilst carrying out local night flying practice'.[18] The Court of Inquiry opined that the cause of the accident was that 3–4 minutes after take-off the pilot, with limited experience flying in 'blackout conditions', lost altitude when he changed from instruments to visual flying. The Court offered three recommendations. First, all squadrons conducting night flying should have a dual aircraft to give junior pilots more experience. Second, pilots must experience at least two flights in 'blackout' conditions and carry out dusk landings merging into moonlight for at least 3 hours. Last, units should use all instrument flying aids. Given his extensive instructional background and A1 Qualified Flying Instructor accreditation, Stephenson was a natural choice to give the more junior pilots greater exposure to night flying. Fortunately, the Squadron benefitted from having routine access to the station's Miles Magister, a two-seat monoplane training aircraft, to give the inexperienced pilots a gentler introduction to night flying. The 19 Squadron record book reflects these training flights. For example, the 11 March 1940 entry informs that 'Squadron Leader Stephenson took Pilot Officers Baker and Watson night flying in the Magister'.[19]

Despite this additional training burden, the squadron continued to send sections of three aircraft and flights of six aircraft to the weapons range at Sutton Bridge, located on the southern edge of The Wash on Lincolnshire's east coast. As expected for aircraft operating in the air defence role, the squadron practised 'air firing' at the weapons range. However, what is surprising was that the early marks of Spitfire, often considered a thoroughbred fighter aircraft, also routinely conducted air-to-ground strafing.[20] Despite the regular sorties to the weapons ranges, some criticized the utility of these events. For example, Unwin suggested that when it came to gunnery techniques, particularly the vagaries of air-to-air employment, 'no one was really taught properly'.[21]

Despite their busy schedule, the Squadron also had to contend with visits from senior RAF officers. Air Vice-Marshal Leigh-Mallory, Air Officer Commanding 12 Group, which oversaw the Duxford area, was a regular visitor to Duxford and the Squadron. The Squadron record book often commented on the visits. For example, on 21 February 1940, it was noted that 'the squadron was inspected by the Air Officer Commanding Air Vice-Marshal T. D. Leigh-Mallory'.[22] For some, the visits were unwelcome intrusions, while others saw them as opportunities to influence very senior RAF officers. Stephenson exploited these opportunities even before he took command of the Squadron. The benefactor was his old Cranwell friend – Douglas Bader.

The Arrival and Departure of Bader

The Squadron's official record book notes that on 7 February 1940, 'Flying Officer D. R. S. Bader posted to squadron from Central Flying School, Upavon'.[23] Bader's arrival on 19 Squadron may have been a surprise to many. However, the plan to get Bader back into the cockpit and a front-line squadron had been developing for a few years. Stephenson was a key interlocutor who had orchestrated many of the steps during his previous tour in the Air Ministry. Stephenson leveraged his connections within the corridors of the Air Ministry to get Bader access to the Air Member for Personnel, Air Marshal Sir Charles Portal. There were still several hurdles to cross, but the 'old boy network' allowed Bader to bypass much of the bureaucracy and processes. The German invasion of Poland in September 1939 and the need to expand the RAF was the opportunity Bader needed to remove the remaining barriers. After passing the medical examination, the only thing between him and the front line was a flying test with CFS.

Despite being out of the cockpit for nearly eight years, Bader excelled during his flying test and subsequent refresher course. At the end of the course, on 7 February 1940, Wing Commander George Stainforth, the officer commanding the Refresher Squadron at CFS, assessed Bader's flying ability as 'exceptional'.[24] Although most of his refresher flying was in the Avro Tutor trainer, he took the opportunity to fly in modern operational aircraft, including the Fairey Battle and the Hawker Hurricane. These aircraft were a far cry from anything he had flown in the past. There was a multitude of differences to contend with when compared to his Bristol Bulldog back on 23 Squadron at RAF Kenley in 1931. A few fundamental changes included: radio procedures, retractable undercarriage, wing flaps, constant speed variable-pitch propellers, blind-flying instruments and only one wing!

Bader was keen to get back into the air as a pilot, but it was not just any old cockpit he wanted to clamber into. He was after a return to the coveted fighter cockpit. With his peer group now commanding squadrons across the RAF, Bader used his Old Cranwellian network to leverage the situation. Stephenson's position as the commanding officer of a Spitfire squadron created the perfect opportunity that Bader could exploit; Stephenson was only too happy to oblige. Bader's end-of-course report from his refresher training suggested that 'this officer is an exceptionally good pilot . . . he is very keen and should be ideally suited . . . to single-seater fighters'.[25] However, it was the senior echelons of the Service that Bader needed to influence to ensure he achieved his goal of getting back onto a fighter squadron. So, Stephenson and Bader hatched a plan.

During a visit by Leigh-Mallory to Duxford, Bader just happened to visit the station in a Hurricane during the latter stages of his CFS refresher course. Stephenson undoubtedly orchestrated the visit to allow Bader to influence the 12 Group commander. Over lunch, Bader persuaded Leigh-Mallory to accept him onto the front line. While his dynamic personality, perseverance and drive were without question, his ability to adapt to the demands of modern air combat may still have been questioned by some. However, following lunch, Bader put on an elegant display of aerobatics with Leigh-Mallory watching. Any lingering doubts that senior leaders may have had were now quashed. Bader was heading back to the front line, and as a junior officer on his old friend's squadron – the Cranwell chums would once again be reunited. Bader enjoyed flying the Spitfire and suggested that his new aircraft 'looked good and was good'.[26] Nevertheless, during his early days on the RAF's most iconic fighter, there was a sense of frustration, both at the personal and the tactical level.

Approaching his 30th birthday and 12 years since joining the RAF, Bader was irritated. As a mere Flying Officer, Bader's peer group was now two ranks above him and influential as well as powerful squadron commanders. Bader felt that his flying experience, albeit nearly a decade before on biplanes, somehow trumped the experience and knowledge of his fellow squadron pilots. Bader complained to Stephenson about the quality of the airmanship and tactical leadership within the squadron. There is a debate concerning the validity of Bader's criticisms of his fellow 19 Squadron pilots. However, most suggest that the 19 Squadron flight commanders and the other veteran squadron pilots were more familiar with and comfortable with operating the Spitfire. Bader's concerns reflect his frustrations of being forced into a subordinate role rather than operating in a leadership position, like Stephenson and his other peers from Cranwell days. Compromising Bader's argument was his inexperience on Spitfires, an aircraft that was a far cry from his last front-line aircraft – a significantly slower and demonstrably less agile biplane. Consequently, and despite his natural flying talent, Bader was prone to make mistakes during his rapid transition to a modern front-line fighter. On his first Spitfire flight, he struggled to bring the undercarriage down after discarding instructions from a young but more experienced squadron pilot. On a later sortie, Bader crashed on take-off after failing to select fine pitch on the propeller – a rudimentary mistake. While conducting a low-level practice attack against a bomber, he flew into the upper branches of a tree but managed to recover the aircraft. Despite these embarrassing incidents, all occurring within a very short period, Stephenson constantly protected his friend. Bader's logbook bears testament to Stephenson's benevolent oversight of his friend. Despite a mere two months of experience flying Spitfires with three major incidents, Stephenson wrote his assessment of Bader's ability to fly Spitfires in his friend's logbook – 'Exceptional'.

Despite his misdemeanours and relative inexperience on Spitfires, Bader still had the audacity to challenge his friend and squadron commander on the tactical employment of Spitfires. Bader held forthright views on how the squadron should operate in wartime. However, in early 1940, Stephenson and Bader would have lively debates concerning the regimented tactics employed by Fighter Command.

'There is only one damn way to do it, that is for everyone to pile in together from each side as close to the Hun as they can and let him have the lot. Why only use eight guns at a time when you can use sixteen or twenty-four from different angles.' Stephenson and the others argued: 'but you don't know, do you? No one knows.'[27]

In hindsight and based upon the Spitfire's baptism of fire over France and southern England in the spring and summer of 1940, Bader's views on the squadron level of tactical employment have some merit. However, there was little Stephenson could do to change the rigid tactics enforced by Fighter Command. Indeed, 'so much faith in these tactics did the Air Ministry place that individual squadron commanders were forbidden to experiment with alternative ideas'.[28] Bader's views on Spitfire tactics would develop throughout 1940 and, most controversially, during the Battle of Britain. His opinions on massing 12 Group's firepower to counter the Luftwaffe threat during the Battle of Britain with his proposed 'Big Wing' tactics remain divisive and hotly debated even today.

There is no doubt that Stephenson helped in getting his friend back into a front-line fighter cockpit and protected him during his short tenure on 19 Squadron. However, Bader was irritated with the lack of responsibility and respect doled out to him by his fellow squadron pilots. Bader was ambitious and wanted to be treated as an equal with his cohort of Cranwell graduates rather than an inexperienced Spitfire pilot who had spent eight years in the aviation wilderness. Bader wanted more. Consequently, it came as no surprise that on 16 April 1940, a mere two months after his return to front-line operations, Bader jumped at the opportunity to take on a flight commander position with 19 Squadron's sister unit at Duxford – 222 Squadron. The 222 Squadron commander, Squadron Leader 'Tubby' Mermagen, was also Stephenson's aerobatics formation leader from the 1937 CFS team. The relationship between the two squadron commanders undoubtedly helped the recruitment process for Mermagen's new flight commander. Bader's drive, maturity and charisma were precisely the traits Mermagen needed on his recently-formed Spitfire squadron. Bader's foibles were tolerated by most, if not ignored, and his new role would come with more responsibility as well as a promotion to Flight Lieutenant, a position closer to his Cranwell peer group and a better fit with his ambitions. Stephenson had worked tirelessly to get his old friend back onto the front line. However, it is likely that he was also glad to see him transfer to another squadron. Their friendship would endure, and they would be reunited later in the war. With the temporary departure of one of the main protagonists in Stephenson's life, another central character was about to arrive on the scene – Supermarine Spitfire Mark Ia, serial number N3200.

Arrival of N3200

The 19 Squadron Operations Record Book notes that on 19 April 1940, just a few days after Bader's departure to 222 Squadron, three new Spitfires were collected by members of the Squadron from Little Rissington.[29] The RAF base, located in the beautiful rolling countryside of the Cotswolds, was home to 8 Maintenance Unit, and used as a storage depot for newly-built aircraft before the RAF allocated them to front-line units for operational use.

N3200's story dates back to September 1938 when the aircraft was part of contract B527113/36 for 200 aircraft covering serial numbers N3023 to N3299. With a construction number of 441, N3200 would come off the Supermarine Aviation production line at Woolston in Southampton on 25 November 1939, a few weeks before Stephenson took up command of 19 Squadron at Duxford. Four days later, on 29 November 1940, fitted with the iconic Rolls-Royce Merlin III engine, N3200 took to the air for the first time from the nearby airfield at Eastleigh. With its acceptance checks complete, the aircraft flew north on 2 December 1939 to RAF Little Rissington, awaiting its allocation to a front-line squadron. The aircraft sat in the Cotswolds for over four months before N3200 headed east towards its new home – RAF Duxford and 19 Squadron.

Like other early 1940 Spitfires N3200 had its upper surface painted in the standard Ministry of Aircraft Production Pattern No.1 for Single Engine Monoplanes. The pattern was a dark earth and dark green camouflage, but they came in two schemes, 'A' and 'B'. N3200 wore the 'B' version. The subtle difference between the two patterns was when looking at the left-hand side of the fuselage, the 'B' version camouflage would slant towards the front, whereas the 'A' scheme would slope aft.[30] In May 1940, and to aid identification and reduce the likelihood of friendly-fire incidents, the underside of the wings had a rather distinctive paint scheme. Again, there were two schemes to choose from. Both schemes incorporated contrasting colours between the two wings; the right wing was white, whereas the left wing was painted 'Night' – a near-black hue. While one scheme continued the white/night split across the complete underside of the aircraft, the option carried by N3200 only had the white/night split on the wings while the remainder of the underside was painted aluminium.

While there was some oversight and standardization of the camouflage schemes, there appears to be less control over the size of the roundels and tail flashes. The traditional red, white and blue RAF roundel on the fuselage had an additional band of yellow added to it. The outer yellow ring was applied from 1 May 1940 to further improve recognition of friendly aircraft. The initial Air Ministry guidance was to paint the yellow band the same width as the existing blue band. On N3200, this rule appears to have applied. As a result, N3200's roundels appear oversized. So much so, that if you view the aircraft from above, the yellow bands of the port and starboard fuselage roundels overlap on the spine of the aircraft. Upon reflection, the Air Ministry offered further guidance on 11 May 1940 to reduce the overall size of the roundel to accommodate the yellow band. If that was not confusing enough, there was limited guidance on the fin stripes. The Air Ministry direction 'only stated that the blue section should be adjacent to the rudder on both sides, with this later being amended to include the proviso that the stripes did not have to cover the entire fin area'.[31] Despite the guidance, N3200's fin flash design was taller and broader than the norm. Last, and despite a recent Air Ministry edict on 15 May 1940 to apply roundels to the underside of the wings, N3200 was devoid of these markings.[32] Ultimately, there was a wide array of Spitfire markings in May 1940 and N3200's plumage reflects the guidance in situ in late April and early May 1940.

On arrival at Duxford, the Squadron painter was responsible for applying the finishing touches to identify the aircraft as a 19 Squadron asset. The early 19 Squadron Spitfires carried a large white number '19' on the tail fin to identify the aircraft as belonging to the Squadron. In September 1939, just before Stephenson took command of the Squadron, the squadron code of QV in a light grey colour replaced the '19' on the tail fin. The squadron code was applied ahead of the large RAF roundels located on the fuselage and just aft of the cockpit. Most aircraft would have a third letter added on the other side of the fuselage roundel to differentiate specific squadron aircraft. However, N3200 would not have a third letter added. This apparent omission was perhaps deliberate, as N3200 became Stephenson's personal aircraft.[33] Consequently, the abbreviated Squadron markings allowed squadron pilots to quickly identify their squadron commander visually from a throng of Spitfires in the melee of a dogfight. Stephenson further personalized N3200 by adding a rear-view mirror to the top of his windshield to aid all-round vision. At this stage of the war, this was not yet standard equipment on a Spitfire. As a result, Stephenson had to 'borrow' a rear-view mirror from a car! Within days of the arrival of N3200 at Duxford, the Second World War took on a more sinister guise; the 'Phoney War' was most certainly over as Western Europe faced the so-called *Blitzkrieg* in early May 1940. This change would have profound consequences for 19 Squadron, Stephenson and N3200.

Blitzkrieg

On 10 May 1940, the Germans advanced west into France, Belgium, and Holland with their new warfighting methodology. Having learned the lessons the hard way, the Germans avoided the static, defensive mindset that marred the Great War. The Germans had tested their air arm's tactics during the Spanish Civil War and validated them during the first few months of the Second World War in Poland, Norway, and Denmark. Although the French and British outnumbered the German forces, the Germans' speed, coordination, and offensive mindset would give them a significant advantage. The net result was that the Germans caught the Allies off guard. Just as his father confronted in March 1918, Stephenson would face a rapidly advancing German force.

Facing the German advance was a large French-led Allied force that focused on a fixed defensive posture centred on the 'impregnable' Maginot Line, a continuous chain of underground defences along the Franco-German border. The Allies were further hampered by a turgid command and control relationship. When combined, these issues neutered the Allied numerical advantage. The Germans planned to bypass the Allied strength by making a two-pronged attack through the Low Countries. General von Rundstedt's Army Group A, comprising 45 divisions, would advance west through the rugged Ardennes, outflanking the Maginot Line to its south, and hook right to the north to envelope the Anglo-French forces in the Pas de Calais. To the north of von Rundstedt's force, the 29 divisions of Army Group B, led by General von Bock, would engage Dutch and Belgian troops, draw in British and French forces and secure von Rundstedt's right flank. To the south and opposite the Maginot Line were the 19 divisions belonging to General von Leeb's Army Group C; their role was to prevent French forces from striking von Rundstedt's left flank.

Over the next ten days, the Germans made steady progress. By 20 May 1940, the leading elements of von Rundstedt's force, the now famous German 7th Panzer 'Ghost' Division, commanded by Rommel, had reached Abbeville on the French coast. Calais was under siege. The Belgian Army was pulling back and on the verge of surrender. German troops took Boulogne, and by nightfall on 25 May 1940, they were within 20 miles of Dunkirk. The British Expeditionary Force was now in a perilous situation, trapped within an ever-decreasing perimeter of northern France. The British quickly established an emergency plan to withdraw the beleaguered British forces to Dunkirk for evacuation by sea. Operation Dynamo was born.

Throughout the *Blitzkrieg*, and in sharp contrast to the 'Royal Absent Force' critique, the RAF had contributed to the Allied defence. Six squadrons of Hurricanes were already in France; a further six would follow, with an additional four operating from 11 Group bases in southern England.[34] However, the contribution had come at a cost. By 15 May 1940, only five days into the battle, the RAF had already lost several aircraft. Squadrons were being decimated and losing experienced pilots. Nevertheless, the French-led forces were in retreat and requested more British air assets to stem the German advance. The RAF wanted to preserve their fighter force to defend the UK from the inevitable subsequent German attacks. However, Churchill acquiesced to his French colleagues' request for more fighters to keep the French fighting.[35] In a compromise, 'Sir Cyril Newall, Chief of the Air Staff, subsequently ruled that no further squadrons would be sent to France; instead, they would move to airfields in the south of England, from there they would make sorties over France'.[36] The news was devastating for the French; it was now clear to them that the end was nigh. For Leigh-Mallory, Stephenson and 19 Squadron, the news meant they would soon be in battle.

At Duxford, the dire strategic situation was clear for all to see. To the south of the 12 Group station, the 11 Group units were committed to the Battle of France and paying the price. The situation required more fighters, but there was an understandable reluctance by senior RAF leaders to send them. In contrast to most senior RAF leaders, Leigh-Mallory was a strong advocate for committing his 12 Group fighters to the battle. First in line was Stephenson's 19 Squadron. In the week leading up to their eventual deployment, the Squadron wisely focused on training. As it prepared for battle, Leigh-Mallory visited the unit twice.[37] The German tactics were also changing; they were now patrolling in ever larger numbers. The RAF reacted by requesting fighter patrols in squadron strength of 12 aircraft rather than the smaller section-sized patrols of three fighters. 19 Squadron would be the first unit to patrol as an entire squadron of 12 aircraft, with Stephenson in the lead. Consequently, 'it was five o'clock in the evening of May 25th that the squadron took off and headed south into the gathering dusk'.[38] 19 Squadron were heading *en masse* from Duxford to Hornchurch, located north of the Thames Estuary to the north-east of London and within the 11 Group area of responsibility. The flight was only a short hop, but it was enough to get the Spitfires closer to Dunkirk and, critically, give the fighters more time to patrol the beaches. As Stephenson and his squadron were putting their aircraft to bed, the skies around London appeared peaceful but sombre grey and laden with barrage balloons, perhaps an indicator of the ominous change that would unfold over the next 24 hours. The officers and sergeants retired to their respective messes for the evening. Hornchurch was the home of RAF fighter squadrons who had already operated over the beaches of Dunkirk. In the Officers' Mess, the pilots of the resident squadrons were only too willing to share their stories of success, failure and close escapes with Stephenson and his pilots. Initially, the stories were told in the bar over a few drinks. After dinner, Stephenson gathered his officers in the Writing Room to listen to one of Hornchurch's squadron commanders provide his insights on fighter operations over Dunkirk.[39] After hearing the realities they would face the following morning, the 19 Squadron pilots turned in early. Sunday, 26 May 1940 would be an eventful day for the squadron and, in particular, their squadron commander.

Chapter 4

Dogfight over Dunkirk

It was an early start for 19 Squadron at RAF Hornchurch on Sunday, 26 May 1940. However, the weather over London and the south coast was looking good. 'Save for a layer of hazy cloud high up in the sky, through which the sun shone mistily, the . . . morning dawned bright and clear.'[1] Beyond the upbeat weather forecast, things were looking ominous for the United Kingdom. In recognition of the dire situation unfolding on the Continent, the British Government had also stipulated the 26th as a National Day of Prayer. Despite the gloomy strategic situation, Stephenson's focus was on the upcoming mission. He had only time for a very light fried egg breakfast at 0700. It was a decision he would come to regret over the next few days.

Stephenson's attire for the flight was a far cry from the traditional image of an RAF fighter pilot of that era. Stephenson donned his distinctive white coveralls and a pair of black shoes from Austin Reed. Next, Stephenson put on the more customary yellow life jacket, leather flying helmet and clambered into his parachute. While Stephenson's attire was old-fashioned, it was distinctive – a trait that would be incredibly useful in the aftermath of the upcoming dogfight. Stephenson climbed into his allocated Spitfire, N3200. The aircraft had only been on the squadron for just over a month. With no operational flying the week prior, as well as the inevitable arrival checks, painting and modifications required when the aircraft arrived at Duxford, this would be the first operational sortie for N3200. It would also be its last.

All 12 Spitfires started up, taxied, and took off from Hornchurch without incident at 0740. As the aircraft headed south-east and climbed to 17,000ft towards their assigned task, patrol Calais-Dunkirk, the squadron established its pre-assigned formation positions.[2] The 12 Spitfires comprised four sections of three aircraft each. For ease of identification, each section was named after a different colour. Stephenson led the squadron from the front with Red Section. To his right was Yellow Section led by one of his flight commanders,

Flight Lieutenant Brian Lane. To Stephenson's left was Blue Section led by the other flight commander, Flight Lieutenant Wilf Clouston. The last section flew behind the other three sections to provide top cover for the Squadron; Flying Officer Eric Ball led Green Section.

During Operation Dynamo, the weather generally aided the British plans; late May 1940 benefitted from a spell of settled weather with calm seas and light winds. The light easterly winds helped the British troops awaiting evacuation by blowing smoke over the beaches. Above the beaches, the medium-level cloud cover was causing issues for German bombers endeavouring to strike the beaches. However, the cloud cover also meant that the British fighters had to precariously balance protecting the troops on the ground, finding their opposition, and keeping their large and unwieldy formation of Spitfires together. The Spitfires also faced several other operational challenges.

In sharp contrast to the situation during the Battle of Britain, where the radars of the Dowding System allowed fighter controllers to scramble squadrons and vector them promptly towards incoming raids, this was not the case in May 1940. The radars and radios did not have the range for fighter controllers to support the RAF's fighters over France. Consequently, the Spitfires were operating in splendid isolation over hostile territory. However, the RAF fighters did have radios to communicate between themselves to identify threats, coordinate attacks and deal with administrative issues.

Despite the build-up of medium-level cloud over the French coast, any concerns regarding navigation were quickly quashed as 'the columns of black smoke from the Dunkirk oil storage tanks' were easily visible.[3] At the same time, the Messerschmitt Me 109Es, known as 'Emils', from two *Jagdeschwaders* were launching from their deployed bases to escort Ju 87 Stukas from 3 *Staffel* of *Sturzkampfgeschwader* 76 (3./StG76) as they attacked the Dunkirk area. The German two-seat dive bomber, with its distinctive inverted gull wings and bulky, fixed undercarriage, was slow, lacked manoeuvrability, and had a limited range. As a result, the Stuka was vulnerable to enemy fighters and needed its own dedicated fighter sweep to protect them. However, while vulnerable in the air, the Stuka was feared by Allied ground forces.

One of the escorting Me 109 units was 2 *Staffel* of *Jagdeschwader* 2. The fighter wing was named after the most famous German First World War fighter pilot, Manfred von Richthofen. The 'Emil' unit was originally based at

Red 2
Pilot Officer
Michael Lyne
(Ju.87 Destroyed)

Yellow 2
Flying Officer
Frank Brindsen
(Ju.87 Destroyed)

Red Leader
Squadron Leader
Geoffrey Stephenson
(Ju.87 Destroyed)

Yellow Leader
Flight Lieutenant
Brian Lane
(Ju.87 Possible
& Me.109 Possible)

Red 3
Pilot Officer
Peter Watson
(Killed in Action)

Blue 2
Flying Officer
George Petre

Yellow 3
Sergeant
Jack Potter
(Me.109 Destroyed)

Green 2
Sergeant
Charles Irwin

Blue Leader
Flight Lieutenant
Wilf Clouston
(2 Ju.87 Destroyed)

Green Leader
Flying Officer
Eric Ball
(Me.109 Destroyed)

Green 3
Flying Officer
Gordon Sinclair
(Me. 109 Destroyed)

Blue 3
Flight Sergeant
Harry Steere
(1 Ju.87 Destroyed)

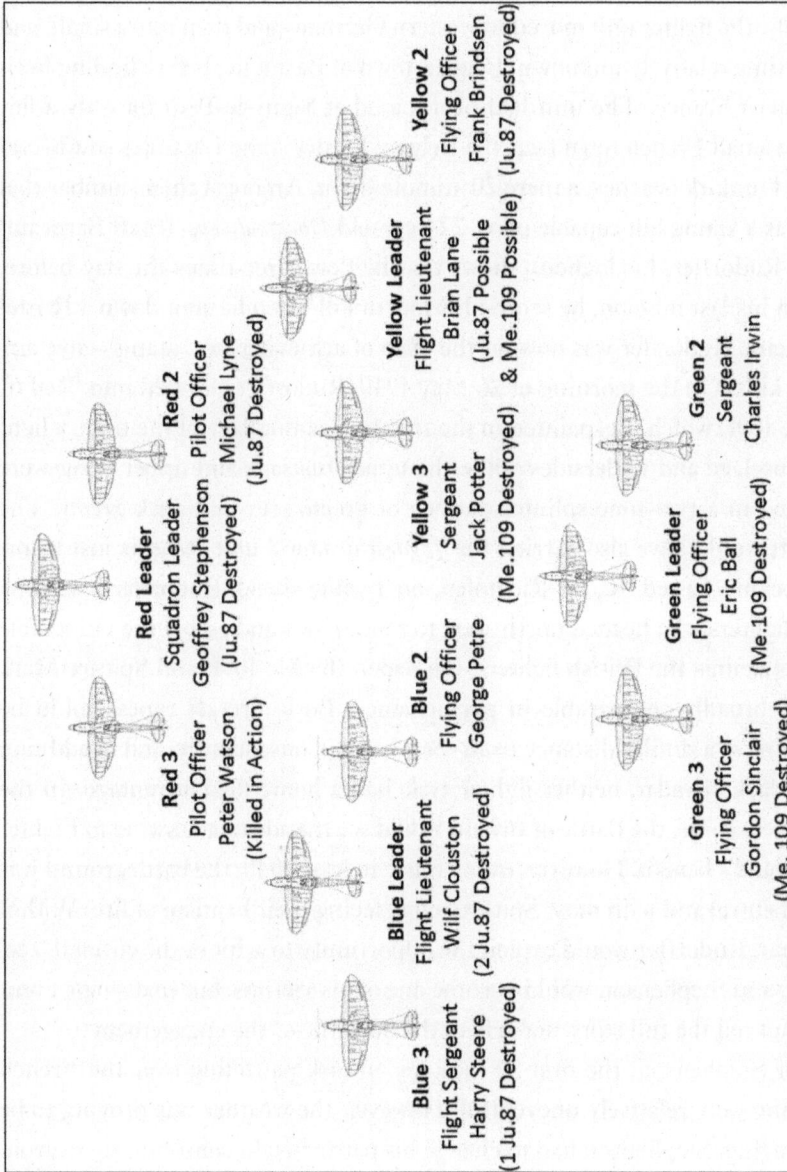

Figure 4.1 – 19 Squadron Composition, Casualties and Claims – Morning of 26 May 1940.

Döberitz, on the western outskirts of Berlin. However, as the *blitzkrieg* moved westwards into the Low Countries and France, 2 *Staffel*, and its parent unit, I *Gruppe*, forward-deployed to support the rapidly advancing ground force. Initially, the fighter unit moved to western Germany and then into a small, and at the time relatively unknown, Belgian town of Bastogne, before finding itself in eastern France. The unit had been based at Signy-le-Petit for only a few days, a small French town near the Belgian border some 120 miles south-east of the Dunkirk beaches, a mere 20-minute flight. Amongst their number that day was a young but capable pilot, 22-year-old *Oberfeldwebel* (Staff Sergeant) Erich Rudorffer; his logbook shows that he flew three times the day before, and on his last mission, he scored his fourth kill when he shot down a Bristol Blenheim. Rudorffer was now on the cusp of achieving 'ace' status – five air-to-air kills. On the morning of 26 May 1940, Rudorffer climbed into 'Red 6', an Me 109E which was painted in the standard camouflage of the time, a light blue fuselage and undersides while the upper fuselage and upper wing were adorned in a two-tone splinter pattern of green/grey and dark green. The aircraft would have also carried the *Jagdeschwader* 2 unit insignia just below the cockpit – a red 'R', for Richtofen, on a white shield. Rudorffer's was one of 30 fighters who headed north-west to rendezvous and escort the vulnerable Stukas against the British fighters. On paper, the Me 109E and Spitfire Mark I were broadly comparable in performance. Both aircraft types would be operating at a similar distance from their bases. Consequently, and in addition to the lack of radar, neither fighter type had a home-field advantage. In the months to come, the Battle of Britain would see the advantage swing to Fighter Command's benefit. However, over France in May 1940, the battleground was more neutral and with most Spitfire pilots facing their baptism of fire. Within the hour, Rudorffer would exploit the opportunity to achieve the coveted 'ace' status, and Stephenson would become one of his victims, but that single event does not tell the full story nor reflect the outcome of the engagement.

For Stephenson, the first 30 minutes on task patrolling over the French coastline were relatively uneventful. However, the weather was proving to be challenging. Stephenson had to change his patrol height continuously to avoid the various cloud layers between 14,000 and 19,000ft. Eventually, Stephenson elected to descend his unwieldy formation of 12 aircraft through the cloud to 7,000ft and the clearer skies below. As Stephenson wheeled his formation west from Dunkirk to head down the coast towards Calais, the RAF pilots spotted a large formation of aircraft west of their position, at a similar altitude and heading out to sea. At this point, the narrative becomes confusing as there are conflicting reports of the subsequent battle. Alas, Stephenson did not write his own account of the dogfight and its outcome. However, multiple combat reports were written by the surviving 19 Squadron pilots who made it back to Hornchurch. The conflicting reports reflect individuals' perspectives of a dynamic, large, and fleeting skirmish over the Dunkirk beaches.

In his combat report, Pilot Officer Michael Lyne, flying as Red 2 on Stephenson's wing, sets the initial scene.

> Red Section, followed by Yellow and Blue Sections and with Green Section patrolling above, spent about half an hour patrolling amongst cloud layers at varying heights from 19 000 to 14 000 feet. Squadron Leader then came through the clouds and started patrolling Dunkirk-Calais area at about 7000 feet. Green section, which had become detached appeared to starboard, the remaining three sections turned at Dunkirk to go down the coast to Calais. After making this turn about 20-30 Me 109s were seen leading about 20 Ju87s out to sea, over Calais, and slightly above them.[4]

Lyne's report suggests that there were two different formations – Me 109 fighters ahead of the Stuka dive bombers. However, other formation members indicated that it was only Stukas in the lead group. For example, Brian Lane, leading Yellow Section, provides a different view in his combat report. 'We were at approximately 10 000 feet over Calais when we sighted 21 Ju 87s proceeding out to sea.'[5] Backing up Lane's perspective is his wingman, Flying Officer Frank Brinsden, who confirms that 'I was Number 2 in Yellow Section led by Brian Lane when at about 7–8000 feet off the coast at Dunkirk we encountered two separate formations of Ju.87s – 21 in all, and further off about 30 Me 109s.'[6] Flying above the rest of the Squadron, Ball's Green Section had a clearer view of the impending fight. In his combat report, Green Two, flown by Sergeant Charles Irwin, informs that 'while flying at 15 000 feet, I saw the other three sections attack 2 formations of Ju 87s flying at about 10 000 feet. We remained in position as previously arranged, and almost immediately I saw about 30 Me 109s approaching from inland and slightly above.'[7]

Consequently, the 19 Squadron Spitfires were engaging a large formation of approximately 21 Stukas that had wheeled through 180 degrees and now heading south over the English Channel towards the French coast. An even larger formation of escort fighters was heading north and diving down to join the fray from the south and the French coast. The Spitfires' advantage of surprise would be fleeting and quickly neutralized by the arrival of the Me 109 fighters. A dogfight of over 60 aircraft was about to form one mile above the French beach, with Stephenson and his squadron outnumbered by four to one. Several aircraft would not survive the fight – Stephenson's N3200 would be one of the first to fall, but he would strike his prey first.

Stephenson's Red Section was the first to attack. While there is no record of Stephenson's account of the dogfight, the Second World War historian Dilip Sarkar interviewed Stephenson's wingman, Pilot Officer Michael Lyne. The following narrative is taken from Sarkar's book, *Spitfire!*:

Stephenson aligned us for an attack in sections of three on the formations of Ju.87s. As a former CFS A1 flying instructor, he was a precise flier and obedient to the book, which stipulated an overtaking speed of 20 miles per hour. What the book never foresaw was that we would attack Ju.87s at just 130 miles per hour. The CO led his section . . . straight up behind the Stukas which looked very relaxed. They thought we were their fighter escort, but the leader had been very clever and had pulled his formation away towards England, so that when they turned in towards Calais he would protect their rear. Alas for him we were coming, by sheer chance, from Dunkirk rather than Ramsgate. Meanwhile, Stephenson realised that we were closing far too fast. I remember his call 'Number 19 Squadron! Prepare to attack!' then to us 'Red Section, throttling back, throttling back.' We were virtually formating on the last section of Ju.87s – at an incredibly dangerous speed in the presence of enemy fighters – and behind us the rest of the 19 Squadron staggered along at a similar speed.[8]

Lyne's combat report from the morning of 26 May 1940 adds further detail.

Red Section and Blue Section went into the 87's first and up to the moment of firing at about 150 to 200 yards the 87's appeared not to be alarmed at us. Squadron Leader Stephenson, leading Red Section, got one Ju.87, which turned over and went down. I had the Ju.87 on the extreme right of the tail of the formation, and Yellow Leader [Flight Lieutenant Brian Lane] said he saw this go down. Red Section then broke up.[9]

The second section into the fight was Brian Lane's Yellow Section. Lane describes his initial battle:

I was astern Red Section, who attacked the starboard rear section of enemy aircraft, Blue Section attacking a section of the port side of the formation. I attacked as soon as I could, selecting an enemy aircraft to the starboard of the formation, as it turned left. I fired one burst at approximately 400 yards from below and astern. Tracers appeared to enter enemy aircraft which climbed and stalled. I fired again from about 200 yards and enemy aircraft went into a dive. The escorting Me 109s were by this time attacking and I was forced to break away, but sighted Ju.87 diving towards sea. No fire was experienced from rear gun, and enemy aircraft appeared to be out of control.[10]

Lane's number two was Flying Officer Frank Brinsden, who was equally successful during the initial phase of the dogfight. Brinsden describes his attack.

While leading up to the attack I saw a Ju.87 crash into the sea as a result of a burst fired by Flight Lieutenant Clouston [leading Blue Section]. I then selected my target and closing to about 200–150 yards fired a short burst. The enemy aircraft immediately went down out of control, and I broke off the engagement. This action was witnessed by Flight Lieutenant Clouston who had turned and was approaching for his second attack. Rounds fired 1000.[11]

Not to be outdone, Yellow 3, Sergeant Jack Potter, also destroyed one enemy aircraft. However, this would come later as the fight developed into a series of chaotic individual battles rather than the pre-planned formation attacks.

The third Spitfire section to attack was Clouston's Blue Section. Clouston's combat report states,

I ordered my section into echelon starboard, and carried out a stern attack on the left-hand rear section of enemy aircraft. The enemy aircraft I attacked, after closing to approximately 50 yards, turned slowly on its back, and dived vertically into the sea. This was confirmed by Red 2 [as noted above it was Yellow 2, not Red 2, that witnessed the kill]. I broke away and repeated the attack on another enemy aircraft and after experiencing severe crossfire from enemy aircraft I saw several pieces break off, and then it burst into flames. I last saw it diving in a spiral turn towards the sea. The second enemy aircraft was taking turning evasive tactics. Range first attack – 100 yards closing to 50 yards. Range second attack – 250 yards closing to 100 yards. Enemy casualties 2 Ju.87.[12]

Blue 2, Flying Officer George Petre, makes no comments in his combat report about the success or otherwise of his initial attack. Blue 3, Flight Sergeant Harry Steere, had a similar initial experience but made amends on his second attack as the dogfight and enemy formation integrity, discipline and mutual support started to break down.

We carried out one attack echelon starboard before the escort fighters arrived – the Ju.87s maintained formation and crossfire was experienced. We broke away to port and climbed up again for a second attack. By this time the formation was broken up and I saw 1 Ju.87 climb slowly and steeply upwards out of the general fight, I closed and gave a long burst of about 8 seconds while he was in a practically stalled position, he dropped his port wing and spiralled down in flames. My ammunition expired and I returned to base. Rounds fired 270 per gun.[13]

Sitting above the initial fight was Green Section led by Flying Officer Eric Ball. His combat report notes,

I was patrolling Calais-Dunkirk with 19 Squadron, myself being leader of Green Section which had been detailed as look-out section for enemy escort fighters, when I saw the rear of the squadron attack a formation of Ju.87s. As pre-arranged, I stationed myself in the best position searching all the while until I eventually spotted a large formation of Me 109s positioning themselves for attack. I accordingly warned the Squadron Leader that he was being attacked. From that moment a terrific dogfight ensued into which I joined.[14]

Green 2, Flying Officer Gordon Sinclair, reinforces the point that his Section was providing high cover for the remainder of the Squadron to make their initial attacks. However, Green section was quickly intertwined into the melee.

We remained in position as previously arranged, and almost immediately I saw about 30 Me 109s approaching from inland and slightly above. I gave warning of these over the R/T and engaged at once. Looking in my mirror I saw an Me 109 on my tail, slightly to port and diving. I throttled back and turned hard to port, to meet the Me 109, which passed by me and climbed. As he climbed, he appeared in my sights about 100 yards range, and I was able to fire a long burst. I saw enemy aircraft burst into flames.[15]

19 Squadron had gained initial success, scoring six kills for no loss. However, the second phase of the dogfight would not be as one-sided as the first. Having throttled back to cater for the slow-flying Ju 87s, the 19 Squadron Spitfires now found themselves low on the one thing that is absolutely critical in a dogfight – energy. On paper, the Spitfire and Me 109 were fairly evenly matched. However, that view was predicated on aircraft flying at similar speeds and heights. This was not the case for Stephenson and his fellow Spitfire pilots on the morning of 26 May 1940. Not only were they outnumbered four to one, but they were also on the wrong side of the Channel and far from home. More importantly, the Spitfires were now flying at slow speed and a lower altitude than the Me 109s swooping down from on high. Stephenson and his squadron pilots were now vulnerable and with limited options to counter the faster and more manoeuvrable Me 109s. The initial advantage gained by the Spitfires had now swung in favour of the Germans. It was now vital that the Spitfires rebuild their energy, defend themselves against the German foe, egress the fight as quickly as possible and escape back across the English Channel towards home and safety. Compounding the error was that the squadron had executed their

massed British fighter attack tactic. The four sections had now dispersed into twelve singletons fighting against coordinated German attacks; it was now a case of every man for himself. The battle had now become a series of fleeting one-versus-one engagements with momentary glimpses of other fights.

After the initial attack, Stephenson's Red Section had split into three separate entities rather than three fighters working together as a single force. During his interview with Dilip Sarkar, Stephenson's wingman Michael Lyne tells his view of the developing dogfight.

> As I was looking round for friends after the break I came under fire from the rear for the first time – and did not at first know it. The first signs were mysterious little corkscrews of smoke passing my starboard wing. Then I heard a slow 'thump, thump,' and realised that I was being attacked by a 109 firing machine guns with tracer and its cannon banging away. I broke away sharpish – and lost him.[16]

Lyne was fortunate to survive the first German fighter attack: his leader and fellow wingman were less fortunate. Nevertheless, Lyne recovered from the situation and subsequently re-entered the fight. His combat report tells the story of the rest of his dogfight.

> I made another brief attack on the 87s and went to look for fighters. By now the enemy fighters had broken up. There were also about 10 Ju.87s, which must have broken off at the beginning of the engagement, coming in from the sea to attack Calais. I made for these, and came up with them over Calais, which they were bombing. Three of them appeared in my sights, apparently preparing to dive, and on one of these I made a head-on attack, closing to about 50 yards. As he rose and turned in this attack one bullet entered my leading edge and punctured my right tyre. I went away to try and get a clear picture of the melee. Two Me 109s shot away from under my tail about 100 yards away but did not seem to shoot. An Me 109 then appeared climbing slowly, and this I gave a full deflection burst of two seconds at 100 yards. I then went home. Enemy casualties: 1 Ju.87 certain. Number of rounds fired 350 per gun.[17]

Of note, Lyne was so consumed by his own personal battle that he makes no specific comment regarding the other members of Red Section – Stephenson and Pilot Officer Peter Watson.

The leader of Yellow Section, Brian Lane, recalls the developing fight in his combat report.

> I looked around and observed an Me 109 attacking a Spitfire which was almost immediately hit forward of the cockpit by a shell from enemy aircraft. The Spitfire went into a steep dive, and I subsequently observed a parachute in the sea about half a mile off Calais. A dogfight now ensued, and I fired a burst at several enemy aircraft, most deflection shots. Three enemy aircraft attached themselves to my tail, two doing astern attacks while the third attacked from the beam. I managed to turn towards this enemy aircraft and fired a good burst in a front quarter deflection attack. The enemy aircraft then disappeared and was probably shot down. But this time I was down to sea level, and made for the English coast, taking violent evasive action. I gradually drew away from enemy aircraft using 12-pound boost which gave an airspeed of 300 miles per hour.[18]

Lane extracted every last ounce of power from his Merlin III engine, successfully exited the fight and returned home to 'one possible Ju.87 and one possible Me 109' claimed.[19]

Although notionally Brian Lane's wingman, Sergeant Jack Potter was now operating alone.

> I was on my own and discovered that the Me 109s seem to fight in pairs or threes. It was impossible to get one without being fired upon by one or more of his friends. However, I did actually find one on the outskirts of the fight and fired a short burst from about 400 yards. He immediately climbed and I followed him up. At the top of his climb, he did a stalled turn to the left which exposed the whole of the top of his aeroplane, whilst he was not moving at more than 100 miles per hour. I immediately lined up my sights on him and fired a long burst starting

at 400 yards and closing to about 150 yards. I saw bullets enter the cockpit of the enemy aircraft, who fell out of his turn, out of control, and since there were very few other enemy aircraft in the vicinity, I followed him down and saw him crash into the sea. Enemy casualties 1 Me 109 claim. Rounds fired 305.[20]

Blue Section were now also operating as singletons. Blue 3, Flight Sergeant Harry Steere, described how he successfully stalked his victim.

By this time the formation was broken up and I saw 1 Ju.87 climb slowly and steeply upwards out of the general fight, I closed and gave a long burst of about 8 seconds while he was in a practically stalled position, he dropped his port wing and spiralled down in flames. My ammunition expired and I returned to base. Rounds fired 270 per gun.[21]

Flying Officer George Petre, flying as Blue 2, was also heavily involved in the maturing fight but, despite opportunities, was not as successful as Steere.

After becoming separated from Blue Section, I became involved with 5 Me 109s and with 4 other Spitfires at 6000 feet off Calais. After firing at odd enemy aircraft, I positioned myself to the rear of a Me 109 opened fire at approximately 250 yards and closed to approximately 100 yards, during which time I observed pieces of the enemy aircraft become detached. After opening fire enemy aircraft carried out no evasive tactics, except to pull up in a gradual climb. Enemy aircraft was not seen again after the break away. Number of rounds fired 2445.[22]

Steere would claim one kill, but despite apparently damaging a Me 109, Petre would make no claim.

With the Me 109s entering the fray, Green Section dived down from their lofty perch to become involved in the dogfight. Leading Green Section, Flying Officer Eric Ball joins the fight; his combat report informs us that,

At no period of this fight were there less than 3 Me 109s whirling round, I eventually managed to get on the tail of one and fired at a range of

100 yards until I saw him go into a spiral dive with smoke pouring out from the engine. I myself had been shot at and sustained injuries in head and arm. Rounds fired 2800.[23]

Green 3 Flying Officer Gordon Sinclair's combat report provides his perspective on the rapidly evolving battle and German tactics. 'I noticed particularly that the Me 109s worked in pairs, apparently covering each other's attacks. The method of attack being a steep dive from above, and then apparently a short gun burst followed by a steep climb again.'[24]

The 10 surviving Spitfires pilots started arriving back at Hornchurch from 0900. Reinforcing the chaotic nature of the dogfight, the first five aircraft arrived as singletons five minutes apart. The first to come back to Hornchurch was Blue 1, Flight Lieutenant Wilf Clouston, followed by Yellow 2, Flying Officer Frank Brinsden, five minutes later. At 0910, Blue 3, Flight Sergeant Harry Steere, arrived at Hornchurch, with Green 1, the wounded Flying Officer Eric Ball arriving at 0915. Stephenson's wingman and the sole survivor of Red Section, Pilot Officer Michael Lyne, arrived at 0920. After a nervous ten minutes, the remaining five aircraft landed back at their forward operating base at 0930. With 10 of the 12 aircraft now safely back at Hornchurch, the groundcrew went to work to repair, refuel and rearm the aircraft for the next mission back across the Channel. Amongst the 19 Squadron pilots, there must have been a strange mix of elation and sadness. Some would have been celebrating their successes while others were having their wounds tended to, trying to comprehend their baptism of fire and the squadron losses, including their squadron commander.

As the pilots were logging their combat reports, it quickly became apparent that several of the 19 Squadron pilots had seen both Spitfires that were in trouble. Moreover, based on what the pilots were wearing, it could be determined which pilot was in which aircraft. Sergeant Jack Potter, flying as Yellow 3, noted in his combat report,

that during the course of the fight, I happened to look to my starboard side and saw a Spitfire about 500 yards away and just as I saw it there was a big burst of flame from its starboard side at about the position of the roundels. I thought he was on fire, but the flames died out and the aircraft dropped its nose and dived vertically towards the sea. The cause was obvious to me as a high explosive cannon shell. The aircraft continued its dive until it was about 3000 feet from the sea, when to my surprise I saw a parachute open and the pilot appeared to be safe.[25]

Potter also noted that the pilot bailing out of the Spitfire was 'Pilot Officer Watson as he was wearing black overhauls, and Squadron Leader Stephenson whom I saw in an apparently controlled glide over the land, was wearing white. The Squadron Leader's aircraft when I saw it was in a straight glide over the land going westwards, with a thin stream of blue smoke trailing behind it.'[26] Others believed Stephenson's descent towards the beach was not as controlled as Potter suggests. Flying Officer Gordon Sinclair's combat report informs, 'While inland I noticed a Spitfire spiralling down apparently with a glycol leak.'[27] Nevertheless, Sinclair's view is at odds with Pilot Officer Michael Lyne's combat report, which confirms Stephenson's aircraft was descending towards the beach in a controlled manner. 'I saw one Spitfire hit by a cannon shell, near the cockpit, on the port side and another going gently down with glycol vapour pouring from the starboard side of the engine.'[28]

Despite their two losses, 19 Squadron's first large-scale dogfight was successful. In addition to their six claims during their initial attack, the Spitfires would claim a further five kills for a total of eleven kills for the entire engagement. However, the subsequent analysis would suggest that the RAF pilots' 5.5:1 kill ratio was optimistic. The exaggeration of air-to-air kills is a common phenomenon and was prevalent on both sides throughout the Second World War. It was only in the post-war period and with access to German records that it became possible to establish a more accurate picture of what happened. The three Luftwaffe units involved in the dogfight with the 19 Squadron Spitfires would confirm that they lost two Me 109s and four Ju 87s. Not the 5.5:1 kill ratio that 19 Squadron believed that they had achieved, but still a creditable kill ratio of 3:1 in their first massed attack. However, more interesting was that access to German records allowed individuals to analyse who had shot down Geoffrey Stephenson.

There is a debate regarding who shot down the two 19 Squadron Spitfires of Stephenson and his wingman Pilot Officer Peter Watson. Bader suggests that the rear gunner of one of the Ju 87 Stukas shot down Stephenson – a rather ignominious end for any fighter pilot.[29] Rather than decrying his friend,

Bader's perspective may have reflected Stephenson's own view of his demise. They certainly had plenty of time to discuss the matter at Colditz. Nevertheless, at this point, Stephenson would not have had access to the various combat reports from his fellow squadron pilots to build a more comprehensive picture of the engagement. However, Rudorffer's logbook provides contrary evidence. His logbook is annotated with two kills on the morning of 26 May 1940. The kills would be his fifth and sixth and got him the coveted status of fighter 'ace'. Other sources infer that the two Spitfire kills are split between two Me 109 pilots. In Peter Cornwell's book, *The Battle of France: Then and Now*, it is suggested that Stephenson's was possibly one of the two aircraft shot down by Rudorffer at 0845, while *Oberfeldwebel* Clade from I./JG1 is perhaps responsible for downing Watson at a similar time.[30] Either way, it is probable that the young 22-year-old Rudorffer delivered the mortal wound to N3200 and sent Stephenson to an emergency belly landing on the beach at Sangatte and his eventual incarceration.[31] While Stephenson was coming to terms with his predicament, back at Hornchurch 19 Squadron were getting set for further missions over Dunkirk. The war may have been as good as over for their now former squadron commander, but the squadron would continue to operate throughout Operation Dynamo.

At 1145, and using pilots not employed on the morning mission, two 19 Squadron Spitfires launched from Hornchurch to support a 74 Squadron mission over Dunkirk. The mission was uneventful and in sharp contrast to 19 Squadron's previous and subsequent mission. At 1445, and flying in the same aircraft that he had flown that morning, Brian Lane led the Squadron on their second large-scale patrol over Dunkirk. The Squadron operations record book stipulates that 'a second patrol was carried out about lunchtime; 10 machines went on patrol. A large formation of Me 109s was met. Flying Officer Petre, Flight Lieutenant Lane, and Flying Officer Sinclair each shot one down. Sergeant Irwin failed to return, and Pilot Officer Lyne landed on the beach at Deal [in Kent] with engine failure and a bullet in his leg.'[32] Irwin was killed in action while Stephenson's wingman from the morning mission, Pilot Officer Michael Lyne, would be out of action recovering from his wounds until February 1941. By the end of the day, 19 Squadron had claimed 12 kills but had lost four of its 14 pilots, with two killed in action, one wounded and their squadron commander unaccounted for.

May 26th 1940 was an eventful day for 19 Squadron. Consequently, the Squadron had to take stock of the events and learn the lessons quickly. 'Grumpy' Unwin was one of the pilots left on the ground for the first mission but participated in a later mission that day. His analysis of 26 May 1940 is succinct and apposite.

> The very first trip over Dunkirk, we followed the book. In other words, there were three fighter command attacks, but they were all in formation, more suited for a Hendon air display. You went in [as] formation of threes in line astern and you picked off your target which was supposed to be only a bomber . . . which flew straight and level and didn't try to evade you. Of course, the first lot we saw were a load of '87s dive-bombers. A very, very slow aircraft. We went in Fighter Command Attack Number One in threes and of course we were only going twice as fast as they were and rapidly overhauling them . . . trying to get a sight on them and forgetting all about the fact that there might be escorts and the escorts came down and clobbered us and the front three, the CO and his two wingmen were shot down.[33]

Unwin's criticism is valid but must be put in context. May 26th 1940 was the first Fighter Command squadron-sized sweep over enemy territory. Consequently, it would have been somewhat irregular if the Squadron had strayed from the standard Fighter Command tactics it had practised in the preceding months. The tactics had to be tested and validated in operational settings. Sadly, the RAF had to learn the lessons, often the hard way, via the loss of blood and treasure. 19 Squadron was the first unit to attempt to validate the tactics as a squadron. Given his Cranwell ethos and precision as an exceptional qualified flying instructor, Stephenson was unlikely to deviate from the stipulated procedures. However, the tactics proved flawed in a dynamic and aggressive air battle. The Germans had learned from their experiences during the Spanish Civil War, and several 19 Squadron pilots noted the German emphasis on mutual fighter support during the dogfights of 26 May 1940. The irony was that despite the perceived superior German formation skills, the outnumbered RAF squadron achieved a higher kill ratio in this particular dogfight. Nevertheless, to survive, the RAF had to learn from their mistakes, adapt their tactics, and do so quickly. The flawed RAF tactics would cost Peter Watson his life, while Stephenson had to rely on his extensive flying experience and skills to safely bring his wounded bird back to earth.

In his first letter home to his parents on 12 June 1940, Stephenson tells his own side of the story. 'I was shot down over Calais by being hit in the radiator. The cockpit became full of steam so that I couldn't see and had to break off the scrap. I was very worried about leaving my boys. I dived down and was drenched with hot water, so that I had to crash quickly onto the sands at Calais. I was not scorched or bruised.' Stephenson's story undersells his piloting skills. Analysis of pictures of N3200 sitting on the beach at Sangatte show remarkably little damage to the Spitfire. Moreover, Stephenson walked away uninjured from the landing. Many others, like Al Deere, bore the scars of getting up close and personal with their gunsight during their own crash-landing on the beaches near Dunkirk.

Beached Spitfires

Stephenson was neither the first nor the last Spitfire pilot to crash land on the beaches at or around Dunkirk in May 1940. In total, nine Spitfires festooned the continental beaches overlooking the English Channel. The first Spitfire to crash land was P9374, flown by 92 Squadron's Flying Officer Peter Cazenove on 24 May 1940. 92 Squadron had been mauled the day before, losing four aircraft, including their commanding officer, Squadron Leader Roger Bushell, who had belly-landed in a field. Like Cazenove, Bushell was captured and taken prisoner. While Cazenove would be released at the end of the war, Bushell's POW experience was more tumultuous. Stephenson and Bushell's paths would cross at both *Dulag Luft* and *Stalag Luft* I, but while Stephenson headed off to Colditz, Bushell would move to *Stalag Luft* III with Harry Day, where they would both be central actors in the infamous 'Great Escape.' N3200 and P9374 would also be reunited, but more on that later . . .

The day before Stephenson crashed, a 54 Squadron aircraft came down at Dunkirk. On the same day that Stephenson belly-landed at Sangatte, a 65 Squadron Spitfire crashed landed at Dunkirk. On the 27th, two 74 Squadron Spitfires came down, including Stephenson's near-namesake, Pilot Officer

P.C.F. Stevenson, who belly-landed at Dunkirk. In contrast, his squadron mate came down towards Calais a few miles further down the coast. May 28th 1940 saw two more Spitfires crash land on the beaches. 65 Squadron's Pilot Officer Smart crash-landed at Dunkirk while Pilot Officer Al Deere from 54 Squadron belly-landed on a Belgian beach at De Panne, a few miles up the coast from Dunkirk.[34] The last incident occurred on 31 May 1940 when 222 Squadron's Pilot Officer G.G.A. Davies brought down his stricken Spitfire near Fort Mardyck to the west of Dunkirk.

In addition to the nine Spitfires that crash-landed on the beaches, the RAF would lose an additional 33 Spitfires during the Dunkirk evacuation. The attrition was a concern for senior RAF leaders and politicians as they prepared for what would become the RAF's defining moment – the Battle of Britain. Stephenson's problems were more immediate and parochial. He was alone. He was far from home. He was without his mighty Merlin-powered steed. He was conspicuous in his white flying overalls. He needed to do something.

The period between Stephenson's crash-landing on a French beach on 26 May 1940 and his letter from the POW camp outside Frankfurt on 12 June 1940 tells a remarkable story. Stephenson's account of his time on the run through occupied France and Belgium gives an incredible insight into the chaotic period. Stephenson displays endurance, resilience, and frustration in a foreign country that is simultaneously both friendly and hostile.

Chapter 5

I Walk Alone – 26 May to 5 June 1940

On 6 June 1940, Stephenson put pen to paper and wrote a memoir detailing his evasion through war-torn France and Belgium. The memoir is titled 'I Walk Alone' and in one of his diaries, he noted that it 'was written in a notebook which I knew would be taken and read from time to time by the Germans. I had to disguise some of my opinions and leave out some events.' Despite Stephenson's own caveat, the document is enlightening and is fully reproduced with only minor edits to correct the odd misspelling of a town's name or a grammatical error.

My engine wrecked. I had forced landed on the beach south of Calais, opposite the town of [Sangatte]. No German soldiers immediately rushed out, so I began to think of rejoining English or French troops besieged in Calais or Boulogne.

Some French men, who came out to me, led me amongst some bushes on the edge of the shore and we discussed the situation. My French was halting, but we got on pretty well. They were splendid chaps and full of enthusiasm.

They told me how there were scattered German motorised units in the town. If none of these discovered me in my uniform, I thought I could pass for a Frenchman in civilian clothes. Some kind lad brought some along and I changed. It was a very disturbing thing to do. My uniform which had belonged to a great friend of mine, I would never see again. My wings, the first ones I had ever won and therefore much cherished, were claimed by one young man as a souvenir. I decided it was not the time for sentiment. I did not want a cursory search to arouse suspicions, so I kept only my watch, some English money, and my identity disc. My fountain pen – Anne's Christmas present – I gave away in exchange for the clothes.[1] My little wallet – H.W.'s present of long ago – I gave to another helper.[2] It was not a time for emotion, but rather cool planning.

So, wearing a beret, a heavily patched pair of slacks of one shade of grey, and a coat and waistcoat of another shade of grey and with a blue silk scarf round my neck, I set off southwards along the beach. Various derelict British Tommies took me for a Frenchman, as also did their officer, Lieut[enant] Rollo, a Sapper, recently of the Stock Exchange, until I drew him aside to hear his news. He had about thirty to forty men with him who had been cut off from the French Army in the south around St. Pol. He had wandered north, blowing up a bridge or two enroute, intending to join forces with the troops in Boulogne, but he could not penetrate the German cordon round the town. He had been shelled out of a chateau in which he had rested and had escaped northwards hoping to get into Calais. This was now impossible, so he and his men had been wandering up and down the beach for four days, hoping that a boat might come to take them off. I wonder what happened to them.[3]

Rollo thought that disguised as I was, I could go anywhere, and I decided to strike south-east, thinking that the French would advance, driving the Germans northwards into Belgium. It was hopelessly difficult to know what to do as I had a very imperfect picture of the situation. I expected that the British would move southwards out of Belgium in the neighbourhood of Lille to cut the communications of the Germans around Calais and Boulogne, and then westwards to relieve these two places. The Germans would then, I thought scramble back northwards. Nothing of the sort occurred.

I was walking for eight days, but no one could give me any news. There were no papers, no letters, and as the electric current stopped, no radio, for no one seemed to have a battery set.

I went south-east for two days. Everything indicated a hasty French retreat – overturned lorries, French helmets and gas masks, bullet-scarred walls, and evacuated trenches – so I tried eastwards for two days. Still, everything looked firmly in German hands. A talk with an educated Belgian made me decide that my best plan would be to go to Brussels with the other refugees and hope to get assistance there.

My hopes of crossing the lines to rejoin the allies seemed to be impossible to achieve. The British whom I had hoped would move across the German lines of communication were being driven westwards towards the sea and it was too late to try to contact them. The French were reported to be holding the Somme, both sides of which would be closely guarded, I thought. I had no money and no bicycle and spoke French very haltingly, and so did not feel attempting this long and uncertain journey southwards.

I had informed no one of my fate and I felt that by longer delay, apart from the worry caused to those at home, the probability of my being shot out of hand or captured was increased and I did not want to disappear ignominiously. My plan was to go to the American Embassy in Brussels and ask them to send off my particulars, and after having the situation from them, decide on the best course of action. This is the outline of my trek which I will now describe in more detail.

I left Rollo at about 1030 on Sunday morning. I had no French money, very little ability to speak French, no compass, and only a torn bit of my flying map, the scale of which was eight miles to an inch, and which showed only the railways, the high ground, the main woods, rivers, and roads, and very few place names.

I could not feel too depressed at my fate. Naturally I felt exasperated that the fruits of all my labours during the difficult months of 1940 to make my squadron ready for battle should not be enjoyed by me. One had longed so much for the stimulus of real action which would cause everyone to work willingly, instead of having to be continually pushed.

I had been very tired up till now, as it had been a hard struggle to combat the boredom and lethargy resulting from months of apparently pointless readiness for immediate action, but I knew that I would quickly recover when the squadron actually saw active service. I felt completely useless to my country, but was full of hope and confidence that I should be back again in England. Also, I was alive and young and walking in France on a warm summer's morning after rain.

For a while I walked along the sands southwards beside the cliffs until some steps led up through a gap. I was then faced with half a mile of open country before reaching a road, and Germans were on neighbouring hilltops. I thought that they would be suspicious, and I should give them a wide berth, so I kept to the fields.

I saw several burnt-out wrecked aeroplanes and felt glad that they had not been my fate. Crossing the rolling country, I met no one, but after several hours I thought I would go into a village to beg a drink of milk. It looked peaceful and quiet and was away from the main road, so that I expected it to be empty of Germans. Imagine my feelings when I found four very large ones in the first farmyard I passed. The village fields were full of motor transports, all very closely concealed under trees and hedges. I had to pass numerous Germans, but none of them took any notice of me.

Perhaps it was as well I was made to realise so early that I was not a suspicious object in the Germans' eyes. I later passed hundreds of them as close as one foot. I suppose they thought I was a Belgian refugee. I slouched along looking rather dejected and never felt unduly worried.

With the French and Belgians, however, it was a different story. The Belgians, particularly, are a hopelessly curious people. They want to know all about you and having been told, they pass the information on to others. Their curiosity and chatter caused me most of my worries. They are embarrassingly kind, and never intended, I am sure, to be anything but helpful.

After this experience, I kept to the roads. Round about lunchtime I was feeling very hungry as I had not had anything since a fried egg at 7 a.m. How little did I know then about hunger.

I entered a little cottage on the roadside. The father and mother and about six children were having lunch. They were obviously very poor people, but they gave me some hot coffee and two large slices of bread and butter. I told them that I was an English pilot and then regretted it, for it was obviously better that they should not know that they were helping an Englishman. For the rest of the day, I said that I was from the north of Belgium and spoke only Flemish.

Whilst I was in the house, a German car drew up outside which caused us to be rather apprehensive, but it only stopped momentarily. I left immediately afterwards and found a field further on in which to rest and eat.

Another air combat was taking place over Calais – the thrilling thunderous clamour of the Spitfires' guns and the purposeful pom-pom-pom of the Germans' cannons. A Spitfire seems to spew out noise when it fires. It is a wonderful sound. I felt very lonely and unhappy. It would have been such a thrill to be amongst one's Squadron, whirling around fighting and being fought! I knew that they were being successful, too, and would be in very high spirits. They would worry about my disappearance, but would not be demoralized, I hoped. Anyhow, all that life was not for me, so I made an effort to live in the present and plan for the future.

How I longed to find a suitable bicycle to pinch! I would have had no scruples about taking one which did not obviously belong to a refugee, but I never found one during my travels. One's motto under these circumstances is 'Sauve qui peut,' and I should never do without a bicycle again.[4] Walking is much too slow and tiring and one's feet never stand up to it, as one is usually incorrectly shod.

My next adventure was when a storm caused me to shelter in a cottage. Of course, they wanted to know where I came from and my destination. When I said that I spoke Flemish and French only badly, one of them spoke to me in Flemish. This was distinctly embarrassing, but I sat there appearing to be very stupid and tired. All the men chattered away suspiciously and occasionally questioned me, but the woman kindly gave me a cup of hot coffee. The village was full of Germans, and I was worried lest someone should jump to conclusions and give me away. When the rain slackened, I made my escape as unconcernedly as I could after thanking madame, but my troubles were not ended. As I was sheltering under a tree further on, two of the men from the house drew up on bicycles and questioned me further. They then went on to a German camp about half a mile ahead. I decided to give them a wide berth and took to the fields for a mile or two.

On these occasions one is naturally very suspicious and probably takes too serious a view of such events. It is all too easy to panic when one is alone and tired.

I got very wet crossing the fields which added little more to the growing discomfort of my feet. I was wearing a light pair of black shoes which I had bought from Austin Reed. They gave most marvellous service but cramped my toes and blistered them badly.

The whole countryside was packed with soldiers and transport, all carefully hidden. It seemed to be a day for rest and repairs, and I expect that these were the troops which moved northwards to harass the B.E.F.[5] The men looked a fine, healthy, upstanding crowd and their behaviour was admirable. All the movements I saw seemed to be at top speed with no regard to conserving petrol. All motor cycles, cars, lorries, gun and tank carriers with their guns and tanks, seemed in excellent condition and I hardly ever saw a breakdown. I noticed that they set up repair and maintenance parks in every locality. Shortage of petrol seemed a complete myth.

That night I found a small out-of-the-way farm at about 8 p.m. Luckily the men folk were out and madame, an old ill-looking woman, was very kind. She said I could sleep on some hay and gave me two plates of soup. My food for the day was – a hasty egg in England, two slices of bread, two cups of coffee, and those two plates of soup, so I enjoyed them very much.

As I was dropping off to sleep in the hay, covered with a blanket I had found, the two men of the house came in to question me. One was slightly tipsy and would keep saying, 'I think you are afraid of the Germans. I am not afraid of them. They are good friends and never try to interfere with me. They give me drinks. Why shouldn't all nations be friends together? I don't want to fight; I want to work so that I can have enough to eat. All friends, plenty of work and plenty to eat.' So much for German propaganda! No one in the invaded parts of France or Belgium seemed to resent the Germans. They were certainly 'tres raisonable' and well behaved. They gave food to the refugees and helped them home in their lorries. Oh, they are clever devils! One felt that they would have been equally cruel and ruthless if ordered to do so.

I was rather glad to say goodnight at last to the two men and snuggled down in the hay. It was lovely to take off my wet shoes and socks and stretch my toes, although they were badly blistered. I tried to dry my socks by lying on them and kept my shoes under the blanket in case someone tried to remove them during the night.

The unfriendliness of the men made me wonder whether they suspected anything, and might report me to the Germans, their friends. Anyhow, despite a continual [squeal] of pigs, I slept pretty well.

Monday, the 27th

I was off again at 5 a.m. aiming for Desores. Again, it was a very lovely warm summer's morning. During my tour there was only one wet afternoon, when I was under cover anyway and glad of the excuse to have a good rest, and at the end of this day I got very wet, but otherwise the weather was perfect. I and all the thousands of refugees could never have carried on if it had been cold and wet. One got very tired and very hungry, and would have quickly contracted pneumonia.

As far as Desores the country was more enclosed than is usual in France and it reminded me poignantly of England. Again, I passed huge convoys of motorised troops. They seemed to camp for the night in orchards and fields around farms which were well off the main road, always hiding themselves carefully with branches under trees. They always take the shortest route to the objective and owing to the caterpillar tracks on the driving wheels, they do not worry about muddy conditions.

That morning I was going through a wood along a little lane which I thought would be shorter than around by the main road, when I met about thirty vehicles preceded by motor cycle outriders. There were large buses for the men; huge lorries for the equipment and stores, sometimes with trailers; several long guns on trailers and some light tanks, also on trailers. The officers brought up the rear in touring cars. Although the lane was narrow and muddy, they were keeping up twenty to twenty-five m.p.h. Dash and initiative have been encouraged. It appears that risks are permitted. Mobility and surprise seem to the two most important principles in their tactics. Later in the day I had a further example of this.

I had passed a cross-roads by about a quarter of a mile when a German motor cyclist came from behind and stopped ahead of me to ask two women the way to somewhere. They told him to return to the cross-roads and go up one of the side roads. He, however, just drove his machine off into a cornfield and cut straight across at good speed to the other road. He did this as a matter of course.

I travelled a long way that day to a large farm about three miles from Fruges. Nothing very eventful happened till I got there. I begged a glass of milk at 7 a.m. and a crust of very old bread later. I had gone into a barn about lunchtime to rest for twenty minutes and before leaving, noticed a sitting hen nearby. The old dear had laid an egg which proved to be very fresh. How I blessed her! I found I had no reluctance about eating it raw!

Later, in another barn where I had rested, there were more hens, but they embarrassed me considerably by the noise they kicked up when I approached. It was very awkward, as people were standing outside the back door through which I had entered, and I had to beat a hurried retreat out through the front yard past the house. Nobody luckily saw me. Cackling, whether human or animal, was my chief bugbear on this journey.

I arrived at the farm at about 3 p.m. feeling very worn out, foot-sore and hungry. It was a huge place with two-storied brick buildings enclosing a rectangle of about seventy-five yards by fifty. A gateway in the middle of one long side led into the yard. The building opposite was divided into the house, which occupied about a third of its length, and stables with granaries above. The other sides were stables, cowsheds, barns, and stores. The used straw and manure are just thrown out and spread in the yard. Pigs walk about as they please, as do the horses, cows, calves, and sheep when they are brought in from the fields before being put into their proper quarters.

Everything seemed warm, simple, and happy. It was very touching. The fruitfulness of nature was apparent on all sides. The children (there were two families of nine), the animals and birds, the well-stocked granaries, the orchards, and the fields of growing corn – everywhere Nature striving to reproduce and being very successful. I could not help thinking what a happy existence these people were leading. It might have been thought dull, insanitary, and uncultured, but it was at least genuine, honest, and kind, with a real co-operative community, friendliness.

I felt rather lonely and tired and tried to absorb as much of the humble kindness of it as I could. I had a wash and then was brought some fried potatoes and a morsel of meat and later some soup, so I did well. This unasked for generosity brought quite a lump into my throat. It was all a very happy interval which was too soon ended by the arrival of eight youths and the next few hours were the worst I have ever spent.

I saw them arrive through a crack in my barn. They looked much too military with carefully rolled blankets and camping accoutrements. What really made me suspicious were the long boots some of them had and the fact that some time before their arrival I thought I had heard Morse being tapped out. Some of the women at the farm had asked me some very searching questions about my nationality and I thought these were perhaps German youths which one of the young farm hands (in German pay), when he heard the discussions about my nationality, had called up to deal with me.

I always consider myself rather a well-controlled, phlegmatic type, but I got rather harassed on this occasion. My summing up of the situation and my subsequent actions sound rather stupid, perhaps. I thought these young men, seeing that I was in civilian clothes, had been sent to put me out of the way so that no one would ever know of my fate. It would be so convenient for the Germans. I knew of a young Englishman touring in Germany who was savagely killed in this way because it became known that he intended to return to England with some military secrets which he had found out quite unintentionally.

Whilst I was thinking what to do, the senior youth was led into my barn by the farm hand to look at me. I pretended to be asleep, and he departed after rather obviously closing both the doors to the place. That decided me. I was off, late though it was and despite my weariness.

I debated whether I should take a bicycle belonging to a Belgian refugee girl which was there but decided that it would be too unkind. Feeling very thankful there was a back door to the barn, I escaped into the fields and back on to the main road. How I hated that long straight stretch with no cover and how glad I was to reach a wood with a track along which I sped.

After walking for some miles, I reached the outskirts of [Fruges] and was feeling more composed and inclined to think how stupid I had been to leave such a good roast with the promise of more food. I had no respite, however, for a young man passed me on a bicycle and turned to stare at me. I had never been stared at before in my travels. He stopped at a house about two hundred yards ahead and spoke to a man before returning. He ignored me rather obviously this time. The man's parting word to him was, 'Silencieux.'

There was a small aerial on top of the house, and I imagined him flashing the news to other such parts on the outskirts of the town. I walked on, wondering what the devil I should do. Suddenly, just ahead, there was a burst of firing and people came running down the street and dashed for cover. I walked on like the village idiot to see what was afoot and found a very excited troop of Germans standing in front of a house shouting threats at some upstairs' windows and brandishing revolvers. They had a machine-gun mounted on a motor bicycle sidecar and had been firing into the upper windows. It was a beat-up and all rather unnerving. I turned down a side street and then continued in my original direction through the town. I passed hundreds of soldiers but was not stopped.

I wanted to get outside the town to think. I did not expect to be attacked openly in daylight, but thought that my movements were being watched, so that I could be pounced upon after darkness. I passed further sentries and walked out about a mile into the country before sitting down to ponder.

It was difficult to think sensibly and weigh the pros and cons of each line of action dispassionately. I was a badly scared man, sitting alone in enemy territory, footsore and weary. It is damned difficult being alone on these adventures. I did not want to be bumped off ignominiously by young thugs. And was very sorely tempted to return and surrender to the German soldiers. Being shot as a spy by them did not seem so bad. I meant to keep going south-eastwards in hope of finding the French, although all the signs I had seen were most discouraging.

Eventually I bullied myself into a more reasonable frame of mind and decided to try to skirt round the north of the town again and then hit off southwards. I meant to keep to the fields and out of sight of the town, so I set off.

It was very difficult to avoid the skyline and the exertion of crawling and bending in my weary condition was great. However, I was getting on all right until I saw two soldiers to the west disappear as I caught sight of them. It was getting dark, and I could not be sure whether they had seen me. I could not help laughing at the game of Red Indians in earnest. I crawled back, getting very wet and hid under a bush to wait till it was darker. I was soon shivering with cold and decided to move to a little hutch I had passed further back which might offer more shelter.

It was quite dark and so I walked upright, but not for long. An aeroplane came flying round with a headlight on, firing star shells to illuminate the ground; also, I realised that a tank proceeded by a motor cycle was moving about all round my position. Of course, it may have been only a night exercise, but I thought they were after me. At last, I got to the hutch and crawled inside. There was only a narrow plank on which to sit, and the inside measurements were very cramped. I lay down balanced on the plank and after listening apprehensively for some time, I slept. I woke up feeling very stiff and cold. There was a cold breeze blowing in underneath and I realised that I must move to better quarters or catch a serious chill.

All was now quiet outside, so I ventured out. To my alarm, I found that the tank had passed within three feet of my hutch while I slept, but I could not help laughing about it. I intended to go to a similar hutch about a mile away which I knew had straw in it. Returning in the darkness across open country in the right direction was not easy. I wanted to avoid growing lucerne, as it made my legs so wet.

At last, I hit a road which I recognized, and walked along it trying to locate the hut. It was now raining slightly and much darker, so that I could see nothing and decided to try to get into a stable at some farm about a quarter of a mile back. Then it poured in torrents. The only place I could find was a pigsty, knee deep in filth and an already overcrowded stable full of grumbling refugees. Even a lorry which

I tried was full of sleepers. I beat it to another farm, getting soaked still further, and eventually, after poking round in the dark, crawled into a draughty barn feeling rather miserable. I lay on the floor, scraping up what straw I could find and shivered till dawn. It was a relief then to get going again to restore the circulation.

Tuesday, 28th

It was a fine morning, and I was surprised and pleased to find in what good spirits and health I was. I intended to continue south-eastwards, but unfortunately the road I took lead me eastwards towards [Aire.] I did not worry about this, as I thought that the British and French would, by this time, have forced a front between Lille and Arras and be pushing back the Germans towards me. How wrong I was! The French were, by this time, trying to hold the Somme and the British were retreating under great difficulties towards Dunkirk.

I decided to keep off the main roads along which the Germans were moving in case they were still suspicious of me, so I had a peaceful walk. A kind woman at a farm gave me a hunk of black bread with paste on it for which I was very grateful. My feet were very painful, and I was worried lest they became poisoned. For a mile or so I got a lift with a girl in a farm cart. Conversation was difficult, but we got on quite well in silence. German squadrons were flying along to the east over what I imagined to be the front and I became quite hopeful. From my map I could not decide exactly where I was, but the general direction seemed right.

I slept in a barn for an hour and then went in search of hot water for my feet. I found a woman who kindly gave me some in which she had been washing some clothes. She scooped it out of the washtub in a tin jerry. It was soapy and rather dirty. I wondered how many germs it contained, but apparently it was all right for my sores got better from then onwards in a very heartening way. She gave me a bit of cloth which I tore into strips as bandages and walked off feeling happier. The feet continued to hurt whilst I wore the shoes, but the sores lost their flushed angry look.

There were many Belgian refugees staying in this district and I wondered how I should get on about food, but fortune was still with me.

It was beginning to rain as I reached a village. I had seen large farm buildings to the right and so made in that direction. I walked in and met madame drawing drinking water. I asked for shelter and some water and told her I had no money and was hungry. How very kind she was. I was taken into the scullery and given some hot milk. The warmth going down into my empty tummy was most heartening. Thank goodness she was not too inquisitive. I was told to come in again at about eight, when I could have something else and until then I could lie down in the barn. It was spacious and had plenty of straw, so that I found a corner to myself. Unfortunately, I could not get very warm. At eight I was given boiled potatoes covered with hot butter and some more cold milk. How good it all was. There were about four young children, all jolly and healthy looking. I was given a blanket for the night, a crust of bread and two eggs, one of which I ate at the time, saving the other for the morning. It really was amazing kindness and I only hope that I conveyed my thankful feelings to madame.

Wednesday, 29th

After a very comfortable night, I was on the road again at 5.30 a.m. The main events of the day were going into the church at Aire, finding some boots, passing an evacuated R.D.F. depot at Ferfay and the talk I had with the Belgians at the place where I stayed the night.[6]

I thought that if I went into the church, I might find a priest who could tell me what the situation was and give me some advice, but I was disappointed. The town was battle-scarred and full of Germans. The church was large and luckily undamaged. Inside was a welcome contrast from the untidy, noisy, unhappy world outside. It was a comfort to be able to think in that quiet atmosphere of reverence and beauty. Various priests were performing certain rites at the brilliantly lit altar in the distance. All were clad in elaborate and costly garments. There was certainly a feeling of permanence and certainty pervading the place. Those clergy were seemingly so detached from the storm outside.

I departed feeling more certain of myself as a result of those few minutes' dispassionate thought. I am afraid I said no prayers, nor did I worship.

Later I saw several pairs of discarded boots on the roadside and went over to find a pair which would fit me. In England I have often watched a tramp stirring over odds and ends in a rubbish heap and thought how, unless he had lost all self-respect, he must have hated been seen doing such a thing. Now that I know when one is up against it, one has plenty of self-respect but no false pride. It is a case of 'sauve qui peut.' I had no scruples about stealing if I could satisfy myself that it hurt no one. But if people are kind and helpful, there is no necessity to steal. These boots were a tremendous relief to my toes, which quickly recovered, but unfortunately the left one rubbed my ankle badly.

At Ferfay there is a large chateau which had been an R.A.F. depot. It was tragic to see a German lorry dragging away an R.A.F. travelling crane.

That night I slept on the floor of a schoolroom. I reached a town after making various fruitless enquiries about accommodation. There were crowds of refugees and the numerous bread queues made me worried as to the chances of getting some food. I saw a youth and a pretty girl entering a yard with an older man. All looked well-dressed and might help me, I thought, so I followed. I found out later that several middle-class Belgian families were there having evacuated themselves by car. The madame of the establishment gave me permission to sleep in the school. I decided to confide in the mother of one of these families and get her to write to Constantia in Switzerland in such a way that she would understand that she should inform my mother that I was alive and well. This had been worrying me since I crashed.

This Belgian woman had two daughters with her who, when they heard my news, were excessively kind. They gave me food and money and a blanket. This was a godsend, as without it I did not look like a refugee and at night I shivered. It was always a tricky business confiding in people because it compromised them and one knew that however much they realised the necessity for secrecy, they could not help telling others.

On this occasion I was sitting in the schoolroom shortly afterwards, when a man entered and questioned me rather pertinently. I told him

I was a Polish miner from Charleroi who spoke only a little French and German. He seemed very suspicious, and when I saw him going out of the gate shortly after leaving me, I imagined him going to inform the Germans about me. I debated doing a bunk on the spot but decided to wait and see. My decision was right, for he returned and was so genuinely friendly, that I told him my story.

He had been in the Belgian Army during the last war and knew England and spoke English quite well. He could tell me about the military situation and confirmed my fears about the hopelessness of trying to regain the Allies by trying to get through the lines. Stories I have since heard from others who tried it, all prove this to be true. He advised me to go to Brussels and see if the American Embassy could help me. I eventually decided to do this, although it seemed to me to be the beginning of the end.

My plan was to get the Embassy to inform the Air Ministry about me and then try to find a safe refuge until I had learnt French better and could make further plans for escape. At the time I could not continue my present existence for more than about four days. I had very little food; I was walking about twenty to twenty-five miles a day and my feet were bad. It was impossible to remain in one place for more than a night as I would not be able to get food and people would become suspicious.

Those Belgians were very kind to me. Apart from food, money, and a blanket, they talked to me so that I felt less lonely and could laugh. I was really in very fine spirits, and it was a relief to be able to give them vent. I slept well on the schoolroom floor and the next morning I was off at 5.30 with the stream of refugees returning to Brussels and other places on the way.

Thursday, the 30th

I was now making for Lens and Douai. All along the road there was a continuous stream of thousands of refugees. Some in cars full of people and loaded up all round and on top with household goods. Some in waggons pulled by horses or oxen; some on bicycles; some pushing carts or prams; the majority just walked. Always the whole family, young and old, had evacuated, taking with them as much as they could carry. Those walking carried blankets and bags of clothes and food. Prams and push-carts were piled high with babies, grandparents, and countless packages. They certainly had to be strong. Children and even dogs were harnessed to help pull them along. Chickens were carried under the carts in many cases and sometimes cows were tied on the back. I saw one foal following a cart until it got tired when it was lifted into a small crate on top. I saw one rather ingenious vehicle – two bicycles had been lashed on either side of a big box two bars supporting it. The steering of this contraption was controlled from one of the bicycles, the steering column of the other being connected by a bar to it, so that the front wheels were always parallel. A man rode each machine and grandfather sat in the box with the luggage.

The fortitude displayed by these people was amazing. They seemed fairly happy, laughing and chattering. They seemed neither sad nor angry. Whilst I admired greatly their spirit and courage, at this time I could not understand their sentiments. They had run away at the first hint of trouble and apparently were not particularly concerned that their country was overrun by an enemy so long as they could get back to their farming. They seemed to lack pride and patriotism. It baffled and disgusted me, so that I did not know what to think. I have met many Belgian and French officers and soldiers and have noticed the same thing. I do not know what they were like before defeat, but they lose all fighting spirit after defeat and accept it apparently unconcernedly. I suspect that they were not very good fighters at any time. There is no doubt also that German propaganda and political disunity have largely contributed to their lack of enthusiasm. It seemed to me tragic and frightening.

Individuals help those in their group, but one group does not help another. There were tragedies. Horses falling down, harness breaking, wheels coming off carts and prams, very old people unable to struggle further with heavy bags. Co-operation between all the people would have helped, but it did not exist. If horses were difficult, passers-by did not run to their heads. No one carried old people in waggons for a mile or two. They were not relieved of their heavy bags by younger men. I was in a hurry, but without inconveniencing myself much, I helped to control frightened horses, disentangled one that had fallen down, stopped a pram which was going too fast downhill, and carried bags for old ladies, but no one else was doing this sort of thing nor seemed to expect it.

British prisoners have complained that when they were very weary and hungry, French officers who invariably had plenty of food and clothes never offered to help in any way whatsoever. French officers came to prison camps with trunks neatly packed with plenty of clothes and food, as though they had been ready to be captured long before they were actually taken. They receive food from the Red Cross long before we do, but they never offer to share it with us. Their mental outlook is entirely different from ours, and this is distressing to us, and we wonder what will happen to the British Isles and Western Europe.

We plodded on through dismal manufacturing districts, but I now had a definite plan, and my hopes were high. I had some biscuits and two bars of chocolate which I was saving for supper. I ate a [Mangel] and got some hot milk for lunch. For breakfast I had a slice of bread.

In the town most of the big houses had been evacuated and subsequently broken into. It was pitiful to see the wreckage in rooms which had been the pride of cultured people. Refugees had camped out in them, leaving their mess. Books were scattered, glasses broken, and empty bottles were strewn about. In two houses I entered, there were beautiful pictures on the walls, and I sat down to look through the books. I admit that I had no compunction about taking anything which would be useful to me but could not find anything. I wish now that I had taken a sheet and towels and some underclothes. I do not think that people should evacuate their houses in these circumstances. I suppose they thought they would be killed if they remained. Those that stayed fared best.

I slept well in a wonderful barn but felt rather empty and my left foot was hurting. Some cavalry passed during the evening singing stirring songs very beautifully.

Friday, the 31st

I passed many signs of the British occupation. It was tragic to see signs such as 'No Entry', 'Speed Limit M.P.H. 20.' I got some milk from a house which had been a British Headquarters and read some orders pinned to a door.

That night I stayed at a farm where I was very well looked after by four old men who reminded me of four of the dwarfs that Snow White met. The oldest and grumpiest was eventually the kindest. They were fairly inquisitive but did not embarrass me unduly. The owner, an ugly middle-aged man (he was ugly, of course) had evacuated and recently returned and was busy putting everything in order again. Two of his cows had been killed and there were some small shell holes to be filled in. I think that three of the dwarfs were brothers and the fourth, a refugee staying with them for a day or two. They were not particularly small, but they had faces and manners like the dwarfs of the film.

I was given some lovely fried potatoes and a slice of sausage meat and coffee to wash it down with. I slept in a stable with three horses who were rather restless.

Saturday, the 1st June

After coffee with the household, I bought an egg and set off for Tournai. The stream of refugees had thinned out, but there were still a great many. The first major event of the day was the finding of a left-footed shoe. It fitted me well and was a very great blessing, as my left boot was rubbing holes in my ankles. By making a nick in the side to give me more room, this shoe was very comfortable.

I found I was getting daily more weary and at about 4.30 p.m. I could go no further, so found a farm and was allowed by madame to occupy a shed with some straw on the floor. Later the patrone and another man and woman returned from the fields. They came in and gave me the most searching cross-questioning. My story was that I was from Holland and had escaped to Calais, where I had lost all my belongings in the siege, so I was now walking to Brussels. They suspected that I was a soldier and went outside where they had a long consultation about it. I felt sure they would give me away to the Germans, so after the others had left, I called in the patrone and told him the truth and asked whether he wanted me to leave. Displaying no emotion, he said

I might do as I pleased. I was quite safe with him. I could not decide whether he meant it or just wanted me to stay till the Germans came. I accused him of sending the others to inform them, but he denied this, so I stayed. Madame came in later to reassure me that I was quite safe.

Shortly afterwards the others returned, and a terrific row started between them and the patrone, so I guessed that they had told the Germans, much to his indignation. The row went on and on, so at last I went out and walked into the kitchen. They all looked rather sheepish and the two younger ones, the man, and his wife, left. When I asked the patrone whether they had told the Germans he nodded and said that the Germans were not interested in Dutchmen. This was a relief.

I was fed on bread and milk and had hard boiled eggs. These two, the man and his wife, were very kind to me in a silent, unostentatious way. They were the first staunch Belgians I had met. They were patriotic and had not evacuated when the country was invaded. We discussed Germany's alarming successes and the probable trend of the war. I think they believed me that England would be a very tough nut to crack, probably too hard for the Germans. I was given two eggs for the morning and was only allowed to pay very little. They bade me a solemn good-night and I slept well.

Sunday, the 2nd

I expected to have another long walk and reach Brussels on Monday. It was, however, a day of surprises, elation, and despair, ending in my surrender to the Germans. I will tell the story of the events as they happened.

I had important decisions to make under difficult circumstances. Since making them, I have often wondered if I could have done otherwise.

After walking a mile or so, I saw a German lorry ahead in which were two Belgians. It was about to start, so I ran up and shouted, 'A Bruxelles?' and was told to climb aboard and we set off for Nivelle. Other refugees, amongst them several Belgian soldiers in civilian clothes, were later picked up and after about 50 kms, we reached Nivelle.

Again, I thought I would have to walk the remaining 18 kms to Brussels but found there was a train which I took.

To arrive in Brussels so unexpectedly, easily, and quickly was rather a shock, as I really had very little idea what I was going to do. By this time, I was looking almost too scruffy for a refugee, so went to a barber's and was shaved. I told the barber I was a Swede who had escaped from Holland when the Germans invaded it. I got him to look up the addresses of the Swedish and American Embassies.

My plan was to go and talk to the Americans, give them my home address so that they could inform the Air Ministry and then decide what to do when I had discussed the chance of escape.

There [were] no outward signs whatsoever of war in Brussels except round a few bridges that had been blown up. I was amazed, as I had expected to find smoking ruins. All the shops were open, and the traffic was running as usual. I went into the very beautiful old square in front of the City Hall and found the flower sellers there as they had been when I visited Brussels two years previously.

It certainly is a very delightful city. I climbed up onto the hill and eventually found the United States Embassy. I knocked and told the butler that I wanted to see someone about a sick American I had seen in Douai. This did the trick, and I was admitted.

I met a very charming middle-aged man called Mr M. P. Groves. He heard my story and then told me the news which was, of course, pretty bad. Immediate escape to the Allies was out of the question. I wanted to know whether there was anyone in Brussels who could put me up till I was rested. I had thought that I might get employment as a chauffeur or valet, but he assured me that this was out of the question. He knew of no one who could give me refuge and getting a job was impossible when everyone was being discharged from the Army and employers were cutting down staff. None of his staff could help me as this would compromise their chances of aiding the British interests for which they had been made responsible.

He had no communications with the outside world, but he would certainly get word to the Air Ministry about me as quickly as possible.

If I gave myself up to the Germans, I wondered whether they would get me out of the way, and we debated the possibility of being handed over through the intermediary of the Americans. Groves did not know if this were possible, and we arranged that he would let me know in an hour or two. Meanwhile, I would sit in some public gardens to try to weigh up the situation and make a decision.

There I sat in the sun on a seat in a peaceful garden during a Sunday lunch hour. Fussy women walked round, exercising their dogs. Babies were taking the air in prams. War seemed far away. I was not unduly miserable but found it difficult to face up to facts and think objectively.

I had about forty Belgian Francs. I was not hungry, but knew that I was rather weak, although I was well. My nerves were good, but a feeling of continuous insecurity is demoralising unless there is the possibility of eventual success to counter-balance this. Every time I spoke, people were curious. I argued that unless I could find a safe berth for some weeks, the alternative was continued wandering in the country. There, as a refugee, I could possibly get the same treatment as I had had during the last week, but I could not see that this way would lead to escape. I felt that every day longer spent at large would lessen my chances of being reasonably treated if captured. I think I possibly magnified the ruthlessness of the Germans as events proved.

I narrowed down the questions to two points of view. Firstly, how could I best help myself. Dead, I was no good to anybody. I would certainly stay at large and willingly incur the increasing risks of being shot if caught and the strain of travelling and existing with difficulty if I could be shown a glimmer of hope of eventually making back to England. Perhaps Groves might be able to make some suggestions. I could not decide till I saw him again. If he had no plan, then the alternative was to walk out to Evere and report to the [German] Air Force there.

It was a miserable thought to have to accept temporary defeat and walk into captivity for an unknown period. How I wished that I had not been alone.

Eventually, Groves came out. The Ambassador was willing to make an official entry to the effect that I had reported to him and that he had arranged for the Germans to collect me, or he would note my name and particulars and I could do as I pleased. I decided on the latter in case anything further turned up. Groves, although extremely considerate and friendly, could offer no helpful suggestions. He said that it would be absolute folly to try to hide in Brussels. The people were so inquisitive and such hopeless chatterers that my whereabouts would be quickly discovered. I took his word for this and had to accept defeat. I felt at the end of my tether. I wonder what would have happened if I had had a companion.

We shook hands and I set out on my one and a half hours' walk to Evere. I had an egg and decided to eat it. Whilst cracking it, it slipped through my fingers and was shattered on the pavement. This seemed in keeping with my situation. My past life, spread out for review, so much desired but impossible to continue. But as yet I was not hungry enough to worry about the broken egg nor unhappy enough with my present prospects to long passionately to get back at any cost.

I walked on with mixed feelings. I was not a bit apprehensive about my reception, just resigned and curious. Eventually I reached the aerodrome gates and reported to the two N.C.O.s who were coming out that I was an English Air Force officer. They looked at my disreputable appearance in amazement and questioned me further before telling me to follow them inside. No attempt was made to search me, and they were absolutely natural and friendly. A car came along which took me to the field headquarters of a Fighter Squadron, which consisted of a converted bus.[7] I was introduced and shook hands all round amid much friendly laughter. A snack and a fresh lemon drink were immediately produced, which I consumed whilst I told of my walk from Calais. I felt almost sinful to feel so at ease and merry. They were a very charming crowd of young men, both in their appearance and manner, most considerate and charming. I felt that if they had been my squadron, I should have thought myself very lucky and well served.

I sat in the bus and talked sometimes in German and sometimes in English for two hours. They really had a very good opinion of the qualities of an Englishman in their hearts, but German propaganda had successfully shaken this. It had told them that we were the pawns of self-seeking financiers and politicians, that our Army had deserted the French and Belgians. 'An Englishman's home is his castle, so you are running there as quickly as possible,' they said. Of course, they felt immensely elated with their successes, but never objectionably aggressive.

They had not contacted our fighters and longed to do so, as they felt so confident of the successful outcome of any engagement. They flew Me 109s for which they had nothing but praise.

The relations between all ranks seemed to be excellent. Except when actually giving instructions, being quite informal and natural. The outward formality is interesting. All juniors salute seniors most punctiliously, even N.C.O.s are saluted. When instructions or orders are given, both parties stand to attention; no emotion is allowed, the information is passed clearly and impassively. There is no 'Would you mind, old boy?' or 'I am sorry to inconvenience you, but . . .'. It is 'The situation is so-and-so.' The recipient is certainly allowed to make suggestions and the senior may alter his mind, but his final orders must be carried out to the letter. This punctilious formality would certainly seem to make it easier for an able but diffident officer to give his commands. The orders having been given, the two may be chatting and smoking together the next moment.

I got many impressions during my very pleasant stay with this Squadron. There was really nothing I could take exception to and many things which I unstintingly admired. Their clothes, their equipment, the personnel themselves and their manner and discipline. I would have liked to see them when really scratched and up against it. The British Squadrons are really at their best under such conditions.

After a very chatty and jolly meal in a house which they used for a mess (separate room, exchange of money, handkerchiefs), I motored off with Lieutenant Seyfert, one of the flight commanders, to prison. We really got quite tearful on the way. He said how sad he was to have to take me under such circumstances. He hoped I would write to his home if I wanted anything and that we would meet again after the war. It really was astonishing that we should be on such terms in such a short time and at such a time. He could not have been kinder to me.[8]

When we reached the prison, there was no officer there and he would not have me go in. I was left outside in the car quite unguarded whilst he made enquiries. We then set off for headquarters which were in the best hotel, and I eventually found myself sleeping in a large double-bedded room with bathroom attached. Still, I had not been searched and no one doubted my word. I had my old blanket with half a loaf and one boot wrapped inside; I might easily have had a gun. Perhaps the Germans were so supremely confident that they could not imagine any further resistance. I was brought chocolate and treated in all ways as if I had been the honoured guest. I must have looked so funny, too, in a muddy suit of clothes, which I had not had off, sleeping and waking for a week, and wearing one Army boot and one shoe with a slit in it to allow more my toes more room, and carrying under my arm my grubby blanket! I was the British Squadron Leader and was treated as such. Their courtesy seemed genuine, too, and not merely a matter of duty.

How I enjoyed that bath and that bed!

Monday, the 3rd

The next morning a razor and all etceteras were brought [to] me, and later, a blue suit, shoes, socks, shirt, and tie, so I sallied forth feeling more civilized, although the suit was too big. The hotel housekeeper had found the suit and chopped about four inches off the trousers and sleeves, and I suppose the Reich paid for it.

A young, rather strutting young German was looking after me till I could be put into an aeroplane for transit to Frankfurt-on-Maine. The aeroplane was not available until after tea, so I had plenty of opportunity to get to know him and his ideas. He was really very charming; he spoke English a little and understood it quite well; his age was probably twenty-three and he was distinctly intelligent. We discussed all the aspects at the time and in the future from both our points of view. Of course, our opinions differed, but we were both sufficiently tolerant to keep on friendly terms. Like all the intelligent young Germans I met, he had thought a great deal about achieving personal happiness and bringing happiness to the world. He was quite clear about his beliefs, and he kept them before him and discussed them constantly, which cannot be said of many Englishmen. I tried to realise what they were and got as far as this:

1. The Fuhrer is a very clever man with great vision and vigour; essentially, he is kind and wants to improve the lot of his own people and at the same time that of the rest of the world.
2. The improvement can not be delayed; old customs and beliefs which are harmful to his idea of a properly run community must be ruthlessly swept away; there is no time like the present.
3. If your intention is to bring about a change which you believe will be for the betterment of mankind, it is policy to be harsh and ruthless now, so that you may achieve your end sooner and start being kinder earlier.
4. If you are clever enough with your methods of spreading your ideas all sensible people will quickly realise their worth, only selfish narrow-minded individuals and communities who have possessions but refuse to share them, will resist the new order and they must be exterminated or forced to co-operate.
5. The Germans are a people of very high culture, having unity and a common purpose. The leaders are the best in the community, and they are toiling untiringly and selflessly for the common good.

My impression was that they were all very proud of their culture and their creed, and very elated at their country's successes. They were sure that their intentions and actions had been hopelessly misrepresented outside Germany. They realised that they were not told the whole truth about their own country and its successes or failures. They accepted the necessity of propaganda in these changing, dangerous, and unsettled times. They said that one should be told only as much as was good for one. The higher one's position and understanding and balance, the more one could know without any fear of being tempted to be uncertain in one's actions.

They realise that they are pawns of their leaders; but willing pawns because of the benefits it has brought them and their belief that Germany has a great part to play in world affairs. You English, they say, are the pawns of self-seeking politicians and unscrupulous financiers. No one in England is wise enough and at the same time strong enough to bring his good ideas forward to the pawns because this selfish ring of vested interests prevents him. They thrive on 'laissez faire' and disunity. 'You people in England are not Spartan enough; you cannot sacrifice your individual comforts to the common good.'

Of course, there is a tremendous lot of sense in their beliefs. Individually they appeared fine men, in the best sense, but I am terrified that they will be exploited by the boundless ambitions of their rulers. I cannot hope that Hitler will be a great and wise enough man with sufficient conscience to make lasting good use of his conquests. It seems that he will probably try to exploit, to bully and dishonour those nations he conquers, and that this treatment will be so hateful to them that they will combine to determine the true principles of peace and eventually exterminate the brutal side of the German movement. Thus, will better living be realised. I do not think that German rule can be really benevolent, despite the fact that in my personal experiences of it, I have everywhere been received courteously and tolerantly and have admired what I have seen.

My flight from Brussels to Cologne was very surprising, it was made in a Ju 52 – an old three-engined troop carrier. The occupants were the N.C.O. pilot with his wireless operator and myself. My request that I be allowed to sit in the second pilot's seat was allowed with enthusiasm. We set off flying low. My pilot was very full out; he swooped down onto a crashed aeroplane and whizzed round it in a vertical bank; he flew low waving to the people he passed and when I wanted to look at Cologne Cathedral, we circled it at 150 feet. I flew the aeroplane myself for about 15 minutes, which made me laugh when I thought of the circumstances and at the same time, I was sad to think that it would probably be a long time before I flew again. There was a pistol behind the pilot; I weighed up the chances of being able to hold up the [crew] and fly to England and decided that it was not worthwhile, but it was a temptation.

At Cologne I spent the night in the guard room, where I was most kindly looked after by the N.C.O. Guard [Commander]. He was very considerate and attentive. The Air Force camp there was splendid: huge barrack blocks of pleasant design and brick, clean and well-equipped kitchens, where I was taken to have a meal. What a memorable day it had been!

Tuesday, the 4th

I travelled by car to Cologne station and thence by train along the Rhine to Frankfurt-on-Maine. It was a very picturesque journey; at first beautifully tilled orchards and fields; then hills coming down on either side of the swift-flowing Rhine. On these hillsides stretched many miles of vineyards and the hilltops were occasionally crowned with old picturesque castles. There were tugs and many barges travelling up and down the river.

All the people I saw looked happy and well-dressed. There were many soldiers travelling, some wounded, some on or returning from leave. It was touching to see the joyful greetings and the good-byes.

Eventually Frankfurt was reached, and I got into the car to motor out to this prisoners' camp at [Oberursel]. The town was very spacious and picturesque and the countryside lovely. The officer in charge of me who is the Adjutant here, is a cheerful, helpful man who has been to America and speaks English quite well.

Wednesday, the 5th, and onwards

We live here on a farm in beautiful country with wooded hills on three sides. There are three long wooden huts, surrounded by a high barbed-wire palisade, which is guarded by sentries, some of whom march round the inside at night only, whilst others are always on duty in two raised penthouses on the corners. There is a small field also fenced with barbed wire in which we walk and play football.

One hut contains the kitchen, dining-rooms, canteen, library, and recreation rooms. The other two, the sleeping quarters and washing rooms. We live in small rooms, each containing three beds and wardrobes. They were crowded, but quite comfortable. The washing facilities are good; there being six showers and ten basins. The water is usually very hot.

A typical day is as follows:

0815	Get up, shave and possibly a shower.
0845	Breakfast – two thin slices of brown bread, lightly spread with butter and jam. Tea.
0900	Roll call.
1215	Lunch – potatoes, gravy, and a very small bit of meat; one slice of bread; sometimes beetroot or lettuce bought by ourselves; sometimes Ersatz coffee made from baked wheat.

Between breakfast and lunch, I do a variety of things, such as (1) wash my clothes if it is a sunny day; (2) write something; (3) read; (4) make something: at present sandals; (5) talk about the latest news; (6) do some digging if it is not too hot.

Between lunch and tea, I sometimes have a nap or learn German or read history.

1600	Tea – two slices of bread with butter and jam.
1900	Supper – soup, potatoes with something from the Red Cross parcels. We have had scrambled eggs or tinned stew or fish or bully beef.

Lastly, we sometimes buy a sweet, such as stewed rhubarb, strawberries etc.

Between tea and supper, I usually take exercise, such as gardening or walking, and then have a shower. After supper I read and later perhaps have a game of chess or backgammon. I played football one night, but unfortunately sprained my ankle.

The days pass very quickly and smoothly, as one is always occupied, in fact, one has to avoid frittering away the time in stupid conversations or one finds that one has left undone important things which one planned to do.

We discuss the news and debate the possible courses of the war. Some people romance and think how wonderful it would be if most unlikely things happened, which is sheer waste of time and makes one depressed, I think.

We have an Army Padre here, a young man from London, who gives very good short addresses during a simple service each Sunday.

We are paid about thirty-five Marks every ten days and can buy drinks, cigarettes, and sundries to a limited extent. Some people have saved up to buy cameras, gramophones etc.

Squadron Leader Stephenson

Stephenson's capture coincided with the end of Operation Dynamo and marked the death knell of the Battle of France. The British may have miraculously rescued over 338 000 British and French troops from the Continent, but they had lost almost all of their equipment. Over the nine days of Dunkirk operations, the RAF carried out 171 reconnaissance, 651 bombing and 2,739 fighter sorties, losing 177 aircraft, including 106 fighters, in the process. The losses over Dunkirk reduced the first-line strength of Fighter Command to a mere 331 Hurricanes and Spitfires, with only 36 fighters in reserve. Despite the heavy losses, the RAF had to recuperate and prepare for its defining fight – the Battle of Britain. Stephenson's war would now take a very different turn. June 1940 would be the start of his near five-year tenure as POW number 253, a *Kriegdgefangener*, more simply known as a 'Kriegie'. Stephenson's war diaries would soon show that the novelty experienced at the first of his three POW camps would soon wear off.

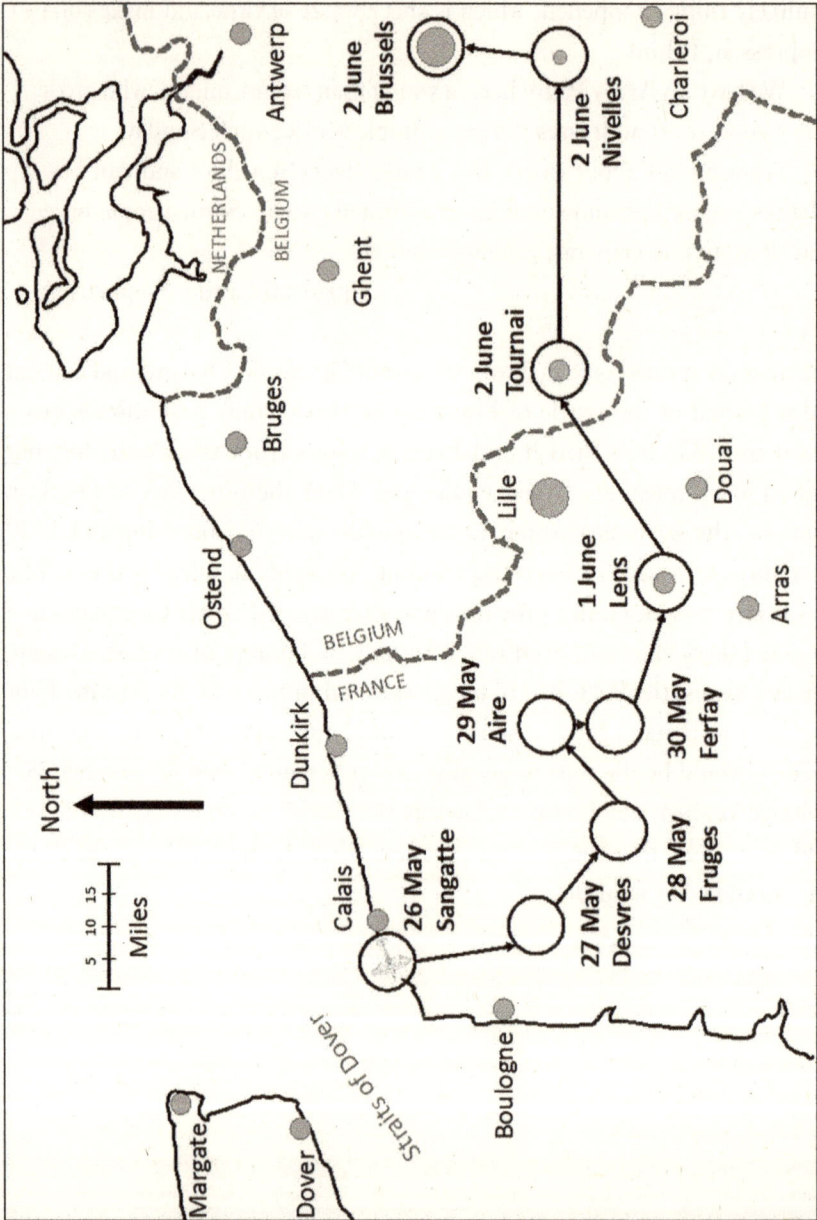

Figure 5.1 – Stephenson's 'I Walk Alone Journey' – 26 May to 2 June 1940.

Chapter 6

Dulag Luft, Oberursel – June to September 1940

S tephenson's memoir 'I Walk Alone' spins a positive picture of his first few days incarcerated as a POW. Moreover, it paints a very different picture from the one portrayed in popular culture. Post-war movies depicted a typical POW camp with searchlights perched on guard towers sweeping across single-storey wooden barrack blocks. Housed within the austere blocks was the stoic Senior British Officer who looked after his men while they endeavoured to get under, through, and over the wire that held them captive. While the basis of the Hollywood stereotype has an element of reality, it is a condensed and exaggerated version of the truth. In reality, the camps came in various guises, and only a small percentage of prisoners participated in escape preparations, while even fewer were active escapers. Nevertheless, Stephenson's initial experiences of life as a POW were bordering on upbeat, but significantly tougher times lay ahead.

The *Dulag Luft* Camp

Stephenson would spend his initial four months in the first of what would ultimately be three POW camps – *Dulag Luft* (*Durchgangslager der Luftwaffe* which translates as 'Transit Camp for the Air Force'). Located on the outskirts of the small town of Oberursel, a few miles north-west of Frankfurt, *Dulag Luft* aimed to act as a reception camp for captured airmen and as the setting for initial POW interrogation.

In addition to Stephenson's memoir about his time on the run, he kept a small red leather 1940 pocket diary covering his time at *Dulag Luft*. The diary does not provide a detailed blow-by-blow account of his travails as a POW but provides insights into his thoughts and activities. Stephenson was a prolific letter writer and fastidiously kept records of his mail in and out of the camp.

Sadly, very few of these letters survive today. Consequently, the complete picture of what went on in the various camps is still debatable.

For security reasons, Stephenson avoided mentioning his fellow prisoners in his letters, one of whom is an obvious omission – Wing Commander Harry Day. Both men knew each other well from their days together on 23 Squadron in the early 1930s. However, as the Germans were monitoring his memoirs, Stephenson's failure to mention Day in his memoir may not have been a deliberate oversight but an effort to protect Day from unnecessary German scrutiny. Corroborating that position further is that in one of his early letters home, Stephenson informs his parents that he is amongst friends and refers to Day positively and via an alternative nickname. Most called Day by his more familiar nickname 'Wings'. However, and perhaps harking back to their days at Kenley, Stephenson refers to him as 'Prickie' Day!

Day also adds to the *Dulag Luft* narrative in a couple of ways. First, his own memoir *Wings Day* was written in 1968 by fellow POW Sydney Smith and told the remarkable POW journey from Day's perspective. Moreover, the United Kingdom produced several Top Secret reports covering each POW camp in the immediate post-war period. Now declassified and available from The National Archives, the *Dulag Luft* document provides the story of the camp from its inception up until mid-1941. The document is detailed, but it only covers Day's tenure at the camp, not the remaining four years of the camp's usage. Consequently, the document appears to be based on Day's testimony and took little consideration of the other airmen who passed through the camp. While Day's memoir and the official document have broadly similar narratives, they do contain subtle differences, primarily based on over two decades of reflection, a broader commercial market, and no longer being constrained by military service and classification issues. The memoirs of other captives both corroborate and reject Day's views. Consequently, the picture at *Dulag Luft* is, at times, contested, and establishing a definitive picture can be challenging. However, the fluid nature of the prisoners transiting through the camp will always lead to many perspectives and understanding. Nevertheless, Day was a central actor at *Dulag Luft* during Stephenson's tenure, and he would play a key role in the British POW story throughout the Second World War.

Day's active, front-line participation in the Second World War was brief. Indeed, he was one of the very first British POWs during the Second World

War, a point reflected in his POW number – 37. After being shot down in mid-October 1939 and treated for his burns, the Germans took Day to the Oberursel POW camp before he was transferred on 3 November 1939 to the *Oflag* IX-A camp located within the austere and apparently impregnable Spangenberg *Schloss*. However, on 15 December 1939, two months into his captivity, Day was nominated as the Senior British Officer amongst a group of six British and six French airmen sent 90 miles south-west from Spangenberg to rejoin the camp at Oberursel again.[1] Initially, the intent was that the remaining French and British prisoners at Spangenberg would join their advance party. However, the influx of prisoners following the Norway campaign, as well as the German advance into Belgium and France, meant that the prison was operating at capacity. Consequently, Day's group was to act as a permanent staff to help newly-captured airmen to become accustomed to camp life. By mid-April 1940, and just over a month before Stephenson's arrival, the permanent staff numbered approximately 25 personnel supported by a further 10 airmen.[2]

Initially, the permanent party lived in a two-storey building known as the Stonehouse, which had lodged farm pupils in the days before the Germans converted the government poultry farm into a POW camp.[3] The ground floor contained their bathroom facilities as well as accommodation. Senior officers had single rooms, while the more junior personnel slept in two-man rooms. The prisoners' dining room was upstairs.[4] The Stonehouse was originally the only building in the camp. However, in early spring 1940, the camp expanded with the completion of three wooden barrack blocks. The latter buildings were available just before Stephenson's arrival, and Day, as well as the rest of the British Permanent Party, moved into the new barrack blocks. The East Block, nearest the road leading back up to the Stonehouse, contained a small recreation room, bathhouse and fourteen rooms, and housed the Permanent Party. Day was one of two officers to have an individual room. The other rooms held two or three prisoners.

> The furniture consisted of one simple white pine wardrobe, a table and two chairs to a room. The next barrack block, known as Middle Block, with four men to a room, could hold 65 prisoners. This was reserved exclusively for the newly captured, after their interrogation and before they were sent to permanent camps in other parts of Germany. The last of the three blocks, West Block, contained a French senior officers'

mess, a general British mess, a general French mess, a general kitchen, and a food store.[5]

Ultimately, the camp layout when Stephenson arrived was:

the farm administration buildings and living quarters were on the west side of a secondary road. The POW barracks lay on the east side of the secondary road. To the north and west of the camp there were woods, and to the east a market garden. To the south was the sports field. Running from east to west, lying south of the barracks and north of the Sports Field was a stream in a ditch, forded by a wooden bridge.[6]

From mid–April 1940, and with the infrastructure now in place, the camp was now ready to accept its new incumbents. As a result, the camp's population steadily grew, but according to the Camp History, prisoner numbers rarely exceeded 100.[7]

On moving into their new accommodation, the British prisoners found more than just basic furniture in the new blocks. An 'electrical cable, apparently originating from the Stonehouse, supported on poles, entered the barrack roof, apparently serving no purpose since it was not an electric light cable' aroused the suspicions of the block's new occupants.[8] Upon further investigation, the British prisoners found microphones secreted away within the dividing walls between each pair of rooms in the East Block that contained the British permanent staff. Additionally, the main distributor box in the roof linked the microphones to the *Kommandantur* (military headquarters).[9] A thorough search of the other two buildings concluded that the Germans only bugged the East Block. Consequently, and in consultation with the French contingent, the prisoners agreed that the microphones would be left in situ 'while ensuring that nothing indiscreet should be said within range of the microphones'.[10] An alternative option was to rip out the microphones. However, Day and his French counterpart felt that a more subtle approach ensured that they could control their captor's intelligence-gathering activities and stop a more brusque measure which would have been more difficult to control. Moreover, as one of the Senior British Officers at *Stalag Luft* I was to find out to their detriment, the Germans would find and punish the culprit.[11] Day's astute solution to the microphone problem paid off. The lack of tangible intelligence captured from the microphones meant that the Germans quickly stopped listening to the activities within the East Block. This change would create an opportunity for the Permanent Party. However, now ensconced within their new accommodation, they were ready for the arrival of the first prisoners.

Unlike Stephenson's personal and luxurious arrival into Oberursel, most prisoners had a more mundane entrance. According to the Camp History of *Dulag Luft*, most POWs tended to arrive in Frankfurt-on-Maine via train and then move the short distance out to Oberursel by public transport, either on a local train or bus. The last part of the journey was on foot, which consisted of a 30-minute walk from the Oberursel train station or a more leisurely 15-minute walk from the tram stop.[12]

On arrival at the camp, the POWs 'were stripped and given coveralls to wear. Their clothes were thoroughly searched for anything concealed in them.'[13] Next, the guards sent the prisoners to the cells for a period of solitary confinement. Within 24 hours, one of three *Sonderfuhrer* interrogators would visit the new prisoner.[14] This initial questioning reflected *Dulag Luft*'s aim of collecting and interrogating newly-captured aircrew before moving them on to the more permanent POW camps. The timing of the transfer depended on the individual's intelligence worth. The interrogator's gambit was to disarm with charm and endeavour to get the prisoner to complete a form asking several questions. In his biography, Day informs that the forms looked like they were from the Red Cross – The Protecting Power.[15] Consequently, the Germans' attempts to glean more information about the individual, their unit and its role often failed at the first attempt. However, the Germans were often aided by POWs' 'private and service background provided by the German Document and Records Section. Each interrogator was issued with twenty cigarettes daily with which to persuade the POW to provide the required information.'[16]

Within a few days of the initial interview, the prisoner would undergo a more detailed and thorough interview while still in solitary confinement. The interrogation was based on the findings of the initial interview and driven by information gleaned from other aircrew from the same squadron or aircraft type.

The initial tranche of interviews did allow the Germans to filter out those POWs whom the Germans did not consider valuable as potential sources of information, who were usually sent away from the camp within a few days. As a result, the Germans now had the opportunity to focus on the more valuable POWs they suspected of knowing and withholding useful information. The POW might then be subjected to 30 days solitary confinement without tobacco or books or undergo physical ill-treatment such as heat-treatment.[17] Nevertheless, the Germans resorted to several surveillance techniques to constantly monitor the prisoners. For example, in addition to the microphones installed in one of the accommodation blocks, the Germans introduced a few agents, or stool pigeons, into the camps in the guise of British or Allied air force personnel.[18] The POWs easily countered the German endeavours to garner information from them. However, with the prisoners' suspicions raised, the second-order effects of the German intelligence-gathering activities manifested distrust within the prisoner community.

The Luftwaffe took over responsibility for *Dulag Luft* from their army counterparts in December 1939, just as Day and his small cohort arrived at Oberursel. Despite the circumstances, the relationship between the German leadership and the British airmen was good. The Camp History of *Dulag Luft* suggests that 'in charge of Camp administration was a *Kommandant*, of the rank of *Oberstleutnant* (Lieutenant Colonel/Wing Commander), a second-in-command, of the rank of Major, and about nine other officers of the rank of *Hauptmann* (Captain/Flight Lieutenant) or *Leutnant* (Lieutenant/ Flying Officer), of which one was the Adjutant, one the Equipment Officer, two the officers in charge of the Company which provided the guards, and the remainder intelligence officers.' In contrast, Day suggests that 43-year-old Major Theo Rumpel was the *Kommandant* during his time at *Dulag Luft*.[19] Rumpel certainly made an impression with Day, and the two developed a strong working relationship. Day found Rumpel to be 'courteous, intelligent, spoke excellent English and was evidently a gentleman'.[20] Over time, Day discovered more about Rumpel's background. He had been a cavalry officer at the outbreak of the First World War but quickly transferred to the air force and became a fighter pilot. During the latter stages of the war, his squadron commander was none other than Hermann Göring. Between the wars, he was a merchant in the Dutch East Indies. However, in the mid-1930s and with Hitler coming to power in Germany, Rumpel was ordered back into the Luftwaffe. In 1938 and after a brief period of flying, Rumpel was promoted to Major and took on a position in the British section of the Luftwaffe intelligence service. The intelligence-related job was an excellent lead-in to his role as *Kommandant* at Oberursel. However, Rumpel reluctantly accepted the job as he believed, based on his British connections during his time in the Far East, that the British would not voluntarily divulge sensitive information. Nevertheless, despite his reservations, 'the best intelligence officer in the Luftwaffe' took on the *Kommandant* role.[21] However, Rumpel and his supporting staff divided opinion among the ranks of the British prisoners.

Despite their common ground, Day was wary of Rumpel. Nevertheless, Day also saw the relationship's value and helped foster the link between the opponents. The rapport was nurtured before the arrival of Stephenson and his fellow non-Permanent Party prisoners and would continue to build as the camp became functional. Rumpel would regularly dine with Day and his team in his private quarters or the Stonehouse.[22] Additionally, Rumpel would take walks with Day in the woods surrounding *Dulag Luft*. The topics covered during these events were broad and included subtle intelligence-gathering techniques.[23]

The strong relationship between the guards and the British Permanent Party created a more collegiate and ordered arrival for the new influx of prisoners. Once the new British prisoners arrived, Day was responsible for their administration, tasking officers from the British Permanent Party 'to be in charge of Canteen, Clothing, Entertainments, Orderlies and Sports, and one officer in charge of catering and parcels combined. He also appointed an NCO (Non-Commissioned Officer) in charge of the Orderlies, and an NCO in charge of the Canteen.'[24] In addition to taking responsibility for the administrative duties, the strong working relationship with Rumpel gave Day leverage for a more lenient approach from the guards and gaining access to privileges. Some were basic needs, such as extra warm clothing. However, some were simply contrary to German orders and even the Red Cross and Geneva Convention protocols, including access to alcohol.

The International Red Cross Society

The International Red Cross Society's role was important for the POW community. The organisation aimed to secure humane treatment and conditions for all detainees. In practical terms, the Red Cross team would visit camps regularly to ensure that the prisoners were looked after appropriately, improve conditions, and enable communications between prisoners and their loved ones. 'Day also dealt with correspondence with the International Red Cross Society and all matters concerning the well-being of POWs and was careful to see that new arrivals were made to feel as happy as possible.'[25] The net result of the Red Cross visits was improved prisoners' welfare through additional clothing, a supply of reading material and sporting goods. Most importantly for the prisoners, the supply of the infamous Red Cross parcels.

The prisoners received clothing parcels regularly. However, the 'Germans were always most reluctant to issue clothing and would do so only in urgent cases where POWs had lost their uniforms or had them badly damaged when they were shot down'. The Germans were wise to be cautious and closely supervised the clothing issue as they were concerned that it would be used or adapted for escape purposes. Nevertheless, 'after an urgent request by Day to the International Red Cross Society, a large consignment of airmen's service issue clothing was received, which included two hundred greatcoats, battledresses and sets of underwear. Day's aim was that every new POW arriving in the camp should be issued with a greatcoat, battledress or uniform, a set of underclothing, a pair of boots and gloves.'[26]

In addition to clothing, the International Red Cross Society, along with the New Bodleian Library, Oxford, and the Young Mens' Christian Association, supplied educational books.[27] The books allowed the prisoners to fill the endless hours of captivity and stave off the tedium of their incarceration. Stephenson was a voracious and eclectic reader. His 1940 diary meticulously lists the many books he read during his relatively short stay at *Dulag Luft*.[28] In addition to the fiction works, Stephenson was also starting to look at more academic-related works, a theme that would continue throughout his time as a prisoner. At *Dulag Luft*, he began researching law, science, and astronomy.

However, the most famous and arguably the most important item gleaned from the International Red Cross Society was their 'Red Cross parcel'. These packages originated from nations but were transported to and distributed via the Red Cross' headquarters in Geneva, Switzerland. The parcels augmented the often meagre and deficient diets in the various camps. Consequently, the parcels contributed greatly to not only a prisoner's morale but very often to their very survival. At *Dulag Luft*, the 'Red Cross parcels arrived regularly from December 1939 onwards, and in sufficient quantity to allow two each week for each POW'.[29] The prisoners at *Dulag Luft* were fortunate; the local catering was considered good and sufficient. Many would find out that the conditions at other camps were not as luxurious. This situation was particularly relevant, since as the war progressed German-supplied food would reduce in quantity and quality. Additionally, Red Cross parcels were arriving at a reduced frequency. Even so, Stephenson's diary shows that despite the relatively comfortable existence at Oberursel, his weight was slowly but steadily dropping. While not life-threatening, the resultant reduction in strength, stamina and increased fatigue would have consequences on an individual's ability to orchestrate an escape. Although the individual's ability to escape may have diminished, it certainly did not vanquish their desire to escape. Consequently, the importance of the Red Cross parcels to supplement and vary the prisoners' basic meals cannot be underestimated. As a result, the management of the parcels came under very close scrutiny from the prisoners. However, different camps operated under different procedures. This situation is perhaps not surprising given that each Senior British Officer was operating in isolation, had no guidance from the United Kingdom and was making decisions based on what they thought was the most appropriate course of action for their specific location and circumstances. As we will see, the inevitable scrutiny regarding the distribution of the parcels and perception of favouritism would lead to angst among prisoners, both at *Dulag Luft* and beyond.

At *Dulag Luft*, Day's plan to distribute the Red Cross parcels was that

> from the beginning, all food parcels were pooled, together with any food which could be purchased from the German canteen. It was for this reason that the duty of Parcels and Catering was a combined duty. It was considered by Day that this system promoted and maintained a feeling of friendliness between veteran POWs and a new arrival who was prevented, in this and many other ways, from feeling that veteran POWs received special consideration while he received none at all.[30]

However, linked to the new prisoners' perception that the British Permanent Party were too close to their German captors, the management of the Red Cross parcels would be questioned. In the view of the new cadre, the strength of the relationship between the British Permanent Party and the Germans did not directly extend to them. There was a palpable perception that there was a two-tier system for prisoners within the camp, and the advantage was with Day and his cohort. This view was the tangible downside of the burgeoning relationship between Day and the other members of the British Permanent Party with their German guards.

Despite the friction, the Camp History reflects that morale within the camp was 'excellent at all times'.[31] High prisoner morale also aided the Germans. A strong relationship between the guards and their prisoners also facilitated conversations which could easily elicit helpful information. However, some criticized the relationship and standards within the camp. For example, one prisoner found the 'holiday camp atmosphere . . . both unreal and disturbing'.[32] Several British prisoners felt that 'we were being softened up and the Germans were getting a lot of useful information, particularly during the evening fraternisation with wine flowing'.[33] The divide between the prisoners would leave a lasting legacy.

Dulag Luft Lifestyle

Stephenson's diaries also provide an insight into camp life and the collective well-being of himself and the wider group. They make little reference to the interrogation phase of his arrival. However, his top-secret debrief with MI9 conducted only a few days after his release in April 1945 suggests that he underwent a 'normal interrogation as for RAF personnel of the period'. Instead, Stephenson's small red pocket diary provides glimpses into his life as a POW. With a few comments here and there but written exceptionally neatly in pencil, the diary adds little details but rarely adds names and provides the odd snippet of routine information. Understandably, there is no mention of escape plans or associated activities and individuals. Stephenson was conscious that the Germans could confiscate the diary at any time. Consequently, there was no need to give the Germans *gratis* intelligence. Nevertheless, his thoughts reveal a period of reflection and decompression after the stresses and strains of command, his first combat and his time on the run. However, the honeymoon period would soon switch to the realities of an extended time in captivity that would last just shy of five years and cover three very different POW camps. Each camp would bring its own challenges, threats, and opportunities.

Nevertheless, Oberursel was a soft landing and certainly not the norm. Indeed, and on reflection, several of its former inmates described '*Dulag Luft* as the best camp in Germany'.[34]

While Stephenson was settling into his new life at Oberursel, frantic activity was going on back home to establish his status. Stephenson was initially reported as 'missing' in an Air Ministry telegram to his father on 28 May 1940, two days after his crash-landing at Sangatte.[35] The telegram was backed up with a letter to Stephenson's father's home in Thetford, Norfolk, confirming Stephenson's 'missing' status. The rather anodyne letter explained that missing did 'not necessarily mean that he is killed or wounded and that if he is a prisoner, he should be able to communicate with you in due course'. The letter said that the Air Ministry would enquire through the International Red Cross Society to establish if Stephenson was a prisoner. After what must have been an agonising wait for the Stephenson family, good news finally arrived. On 12 June 1940, the Red Cross in Geneva telegraphed the Air Ministry to confirm that they had received a card from 26165 Squadron Leader Geoffrey Stephenson confirming he was a POW at *Dulag Luft*.[36] A telegram informed Stephenson's father of the good news the following day. On 20 June 1940, the Air Ministry added further detail in a letter to Mr Stephenson by informing him of the procedures regarding communicating with POWs and how to process any requests from his son for items such as clothing to be despatched to Germany. The letter also informed the family that 'the treatment and general conditions in the German POW camp is good, and there is no immediate cause for anxiety'.[37] It was not until the end of July that the letters from the United Kingdom started to arrive at Oberursel.

By the time his family knew of his predicament, Stephenson was now settled into his routine. Second only to food, mail was important for prisoner morale. Letter-writing was not only a means to stave off the ever-present boredom associated with imprisonment, it also allowed Stephenson and his fellow prisoners to remain connected with their friends and family back in the real world and retain some sense of normality. However, the number of postcards and letters a prisoner could write each month was limited. In his very first letter from the camp, dated 12 June 1940, Stephenson informed his parents that he was limited to four postcards and three letters monthly. However, prisoners had to be careful to ensure that the letters contained no harmful information that either side could use. Consequently, the Germans vetted all outbound and inbound mail to gather intelligence and censor any information that could be useful to the Allies. Consequently, one of the sections within the *Dulag Luft* intelligence department looked after the censorship of mail with specific staff who 'had the care of certain prisoners' mail, thereby gaining a personal interest and knowledge of a prisoner's affairs'.[38]

Due to the limited opportunity to communicate with family and friends, prisoners sent their letters to a specific family member for onward distribution to the wider relative and colleague group. Stephenson fastidiously took note of who and when he wrote to individuals but also of the mail he received. Fortuitously, a few of his early letters survived and they provide an insight into the individual, the camp, and his surroundings. From those letters, Stephenson clearly kept himself busy and focused from his very first days at *Dulag Luft*.

The emphasis of Stephenson's first letter home to his parents on 12 June 1940 was to reassure them that all was well. Stephenson informed his parents about the basic circumstances of his crash and his time on the run. More importantly, he soothed any concerns they may have had about his well-being by informing them that he was unhurt and the Germans were treating him well. He also provides a broad overview of *Dulag Luft* including its surroundings. An astute move was to paint a picture that a farming family could comprehend. He described the camp as 'a farm in the country surrounded by wooded hills, a pleasant spot'. Stephenson also mentions the facilities that were available at the camp. 'There are huts consisting of sleeping quarters, very comfortable, with showers and hot water, dining rooms, play room, kitchens' as well as a 'library and a canteen, a camp barber and tailor.' Next, Stephenson describes the food available to the prisoners, a topic that would dominate many of the prisoners' subsequent conversations and letters home. Although the quantity and quality of the food made available to the prisoners throughout the war would vary, Stephenson's initial views were that 'the food is plain and well-cooked, and we all look very well: rations are supplemented by Red Cross parcels. These are very welcome.' However, the camp food may not have been totally agreeable with Stephenson as he did ask his parents to send him a 'gentle laxative'. Nevertheless, Stephenson paints a positive picture of *Dulag Luft* and suggests, 'I would like to stay here but will probably move on. We are all happy here and the other prisoners are a splendid crowd.'

Stephenson's second letter, again to his parents, on 20 June 1940, was a much more focused affair. The letter was, first and foremost, about getting his family, finances, and future arrangements in order. There is a sense that Stephenson knew that the war would not be short. He set out a list of tasks for his parents. First, he wanted them to contact the 19 Squadron adjutant and send some of his clothes to him. Second, he wanted to get his finances managed appropriately as well as offering advice to his younger sister, Eileen, to also make investments. Stephenson was keen that his finances were working during his time in captivity as there was 'no use in it lying idle'. He also gave his parents' permission to access his accounts and 'not to hesitate about taking any which is urgently required by you'. His third task was to have several non-fiction books sent out to him. He noted that although the camp had a broad collection of fiction, he wanted to learn more and for a specific reason. Stephenson was astute enough to recognize that the war would create a shift in the European, if not world, order. Consequently, he wanted to use his time as a prisoner to read up on economics, history, social organisation and psychology. He also suggested that his 21-year-old brother, Urban, should use his time convalescing to also read up on the subjects to prepare him for the future adequately. Last on his list of requests was a monthly review of current events. However, Stephenson knew his last request might not get past the German censors. He also asked his parents to distribute his letters to several people. The first on the list was his girlfriend, Anne Farrer.

Anne was actually the Honourable Anne Lucy Farrer, the youngest daughter of the late Thomas Cecil Farrer, the 2nd Baron Farrer, and the Dowager Lady Farrer of Abinger Hall, Dorking in Surrey. It is unclear when and where the couple met. However, there may have been an RAF connection via her brother, Oliver Farrar, who served as a Wing Commander during the Second World War. The relationship appears to have been serious and, according to Stephenson's daughters, one that Stephenson's mother very much endorsed. Indeed, a note in Stephenson's diary suggests that he 'write to Anne that I do hope we decide to marry'. Stephenson's incarceration allowed him to consider his future plans with Anne, and there are frequent comments in his diary regarding his intentions.

Beyond the domestic arrangements and distribution, the remainder of the letter gives a sense of his frustrations regarding the state of the war. Stephenson notes that it is 'exasperating writing when one does not know what the situation in England is'. Despite his concerns, Stephenson sends a reassuring message of support to his parents: 'We all feel that England will be very stout-hearted, and we try not to think too much of how we long to be there to help you.' He further comforts his parents by giving them a feel for the conditions and his fellow prisoners. He lets his farmer father know that hay-making is in full swing. He also gives his parents an insight into the camaraderie and morale amongst the prisoners by suggesting that 'there are a grand crowd of fellows here'. Moreover, he lets his parents know that he is remaining physically active by telling them about his swimming activities twice a week.

However, the 20 June 1940 letter ends with a downbeat assessment. Despite his own vision for the future, Stephenson is less sure of his starting point. 'It is so difficult to think in these days objectively and dispassionately, and for a man with wisdom and sound ideas to get [a] hearing. I hope the self-seeking unscrupulous money-grabbers are forced to play the game, and that everything will be so organised that each person who wants to can do his best willingly, not for personal, but for common good.'

On 26 June 1940, in the last of his three letters for that month, Stephenson reflected on his first few weeks in captivity. Naturally, and as with all prisoners, he reinforced his focus on food and the criticality of the Red Cross parcel at the very start of the letter. Next, he complained bitterly about how his 'pocket money' of 108 Marks a month (approximately £8 at 1940 exchange rates) was not only subtracted from his pay back home but halved due to a squabble between the United Kingdom and Germany regarding exchange rates! The first two comments reflect the transition to the routine gripes of a prisoner. However, his third point was the most telling. His comment highlighted the brutal conditions some faced during the first few days in captivity at *Dulag Luft*. It is perhaps more surprising that Stephenson's insight survived the censor's black mark:

I hope that the British will – no matter what happens, treat prisoners chivalrously, a captured man has his self-respect and is very sensitive. Treatment he receives will be remembered all his life. It engenders real understanding or bitter hatred. So long as your enemy is in a position to fight you, you must have at him tooth and nail, but when he is captured, you should be as courteous and considerate as possible. Whatever sort of person he is, his human attitude will have a good effect on him, which will be lasting. An Englishman is proud of his country, as I would wish to be. Some Officers who come here, amongst many hundreds of prisoners, have had a hard time, and some have experienced inexcusable bullying, but for the most part, have been reasonably treated.

Two months into his stint at *Dulag Luft*, Stephenson paints a more positive note in his 8 August 1940 letter to his parents. In the previous week, he spent a surprisingly large amount of time outside the confines of the camp. He had two swims at the local swimming pool and two walks, one of which was an extended trip to the local Roman camp and museum. The trip was with a large group of 41 prisoners and took all day. The group passed through a landscape which reminded Stephenson of home and 'the countryside on the London-Portsmouth road near Liphook'. The group stopped for a sandwich lunch washed down with suitable refreshments from a nearby beer garden. Remarkably, Stephenson could purchase 'two glasses of wine and a piece of cake and could not have enjoyed a meal at The Ritz more'. On the way back, Stephenson could not help but notice that the harvest was in full swing, and it looked like it was going to be a good one – it reminded him of his younger days on the family farm, and he reflected that 'the simple things in life are the best'.

Although his weight was now down to '9 [stone] naked', Stephenson commented that he now had access to 'plenty of fruit' to supplement his diet. He also noted that the secondary benefit of the plentiful supply of fruit was that he no longer had any constipation concerns! Although Stephenson was in fine form, others were not faring as well.

Stephenson commented that the Germans took Day to an 'old country house converted into an efficient modern hospital. Day had been hospitalised due to a poisoned hand.' In contrast, Day's memoir tells a subtly different story. Smith suggests that Day went to the hospital in late September as he was suffering from a poisoned knee, an infection caused by a cut during one of his regular tunnel inspections. He would spend a month in the hospital recuperating.[39] Stephenson's diary adds further detail by informing that the '[Wing Commander] went to hospital' on 2 August 1940. According to Stephenson's diary, he was able to visit him in the Hohemark hospital the following day – an insight into the strength of the relationship between the two. Stephenson clearly respected Day; the former noted in his letter that 'we miss him'. Stephenson also commented that 'the change will do him good as the rations there are better than here – being on a higher scale, and the change of surroundings will be beneficial'. Stephenson's diary also reports that Day left the hospital and returned to camp on 14 September 1940, some six weeks later, not the four weeks suggested by Smith in Day's memoir. A year in captivity was taking its toll on Day. Those who were merely transiting through *Dulag Luft* often misconstrued Day's absence as a sign of weakness.[40] This lack of understanding of cause and effect created a legacy and a narrative that would damage the prisoner community.

Stephenson continued to look forward and planned accordingly. Even though it was the height of the summer and Stephenson was 'very brown all over', he was looking ahead to the approaching winter. As a result, he asked his parents to send out winter clothing, including dyed RAF breeches, skiing suit and skiing socks, jerseys, gloves, mittens, mufflers, stockings, and scarves.

The first tranche of letters gives an insight into Stephenson's ways of dealing with adversity and the values he held dear. Stephenson did not wallow in the misery of his situation; he looked to the future and set himself a plan. He had a logical, safe, considerate, and astute approach. He was not only capable of looking after himself, but he also cared deeply about his family and friends. Stephenson's focus on his own finances and those of his family perhaps reflect the harsh lessons from his family's financial mismanagement in the 1920s. He had the capacity and drive to improve his situation and saw his incarceration as an opportunity to better prepare himself for the post-war world. In contrast, many of his fellow prisoners were focused on the daily routine and lacked Stephenson's vision. His comments to his parents highlighted the traditional values he held dear as well as the deep sense of honour and respect instilled into him and reinforced at Cranwell.

While Stephenson may well have had a long-term plan, he had to get through the near-term drudgery of the mundane life within the camp. Most narratives associated with Second World War POWs focus on tales of the various escape attempts. Pearson suggests that the prisoners belonged to one of several sub-groups: 'The leading spirits, the experts, the escapers, the self-effacing but thoroughly cooperative men and the "not-interested" class.'[41]

Although Pearson does not quantify the distribution between the various groups, the reality shows that only a tiny percentage of prisoners embraced the challenges of supporting or actively participating in escapes. Moreover, as Stephenson would demonstrate throughout the war, it was possible to shift from one group to another. Unsurprisingly, Stephenson's early letters and diary entries do not refer to outwardly supporting any escape endeavours. However, he would become increasingly involved in escape activities as the war continued, predominantly from a supporting perspective rather than as an active escapee. The difference between those supporting escape attempts and a man on the run was a lack of opportunity rather than intent. Only a very small proportion of prisoners had the intent, knowledge, ability, and opportunity to get outside the wire. Stephenson was game, but his opportunities were few.

The daily routine at *Dulag Luft* was somewhat varied, much of it deliberately designed to stave off a monotonous routine. In Stephenson's letters home, he mentioned sharing a room with Squadron Leader Charles Lockett. Lockett was a fellow squadron commander and had been leading 226 Squadron flying Fairey Battles when he was shot down on 14 May 1940 over France. It would appear that Stephenson and Lockett were accommodated in a three-man rather than a two-man room, that the pair lived in the Middle Block for the transitory prisoners rather than in the East Block used by Day and his Permanent Party.

Once the guards completed the 0900 roll call, the prisoners continued their business. The Camp History highlights that there was no formal education programme in place. However, several prisoners, Stephenson included, adopted a self-help approach to education. During his time in captivity, Stephenson started to learn several subjects, including foreign languages and dabbled in French, Spanish, Arabic and German.

Keeping physically and mentally fit was an important aspect of prisoner life. However, physical activity had to balance against their physical capabilities in light of their dwindling calorific intake. The sports field adjacent to the camp was used for running, football, and rugby. Stephenson was an active and enthusiastic participant in these sports. As a natural and gifted sportsman, it was an obvious avenue for him to let off steam, keep fit and compete against his fellow airmen, most of whom were significantly younger than him. His competitiveness led him to suffer several, albeit minor, sports-related injuries. His diary also mentioned that he played various sports, including deck tennis, ping pong, skipping and running. Stephenson's competitive nature was not limited to the sports field; it also migrated into the board games he played. His diary not only noted each time he played chess or backgammon but also named the competitor and whether Stephenson won or lost!

A surprising aspect of life at *Dulag Luft* was the ready supply of alcohol. Not only was it available during the prisoners' walks, but it was also available inside the camp. Stephenson's diary regularly talks about the prisoners drinking wine, beer and whisky in the evenings. While some would argue that it was 'in contravention of one of the articles of the Geneva convention forbidding alcohol in POW camps',[42] others, such as Rumpel, saw the opportunity to loosen a few lips and glean additional intelligence. Stephenson comments, perhaps naively, that on 8 September 1940 that 'Major [Rumpel] sent over cigarettes for everybody and six bottles of whisky – very kind indeed. Drank whisky in evening – very jolly.' However, at times the situation could get out of hand. Stephenson mentions an 'awkward situation with drunk Sergeant' in one of his diary entries.

Despite the relatively comfortable lifestyle at *Dulag Luft*, there was still a desire, if not a sense of duty, for the prisoners to escape. Post the Dunkirk withdrawal, the number of prisoners flowing into Oberursel had eased to a trickle, and the Germans were now attacking the British mainland, including the homes, families, and livelihoods of those incarcerated at *Dulag Luft*. There was now a dawning realisation that the prisoners' predicament would be an enduring one. Someone had to address the subsequent frustration and anxiety. Something had to be done. In May 1940, Day formed an escape committee led by Squadron Leader Roger Bushell, who, like Stephenson, had been shot down over Dunkirk while commanding a Spitfire squadron. Lieutenant Commander Jimmy Buckley assisted Bushell and Day. The triumvirate held their escape committee meetings 'in the barrack, which was known not to have any wall-microphones'.

From July 1940, work began on three escape tunnels. Two of the tunnels were incomplete, but the third showed potential.[43] Twenty prisoners were known to have worked on the tunnel, including all three members of the escape committee, but progress was slow.[44] In the autumn and with the project half complete, the tunnel began to suffer from flooding issues.[45] Reluctantly, the escape committee elected to close the tunnel for the winter period. Work would not recommence until the following spring, by which time Stephenson was well and truly ensconced within his next camp.

Moving On

There is conflicting evidence regarding the date of Stephenson's move to *Stalag Luft* I. On Stephenson's POW debrief form, he infers that he arrived at Barth in February 1941 as the Senior British Officer.[46] The Camp History of *Stalag Luft* I confirms Stephenson in the Senior British Officer role from February 1941. However, Stephenson's small red leather-bound diary shows that he was informed on 15 September that he would be departing for the Baltic. Two days later, he departed for Barth on 17 September 1940. The date's significance will become relevant later as it clarifies the actors involved in an internal dispute between Senior British Officers at *Dulag Luft* and *Stalag Luft* I.

While the timing of Stephenson's arrival at Barth is known, the rationale for the move is less clear. Given the length of his tenure at Oberursel, it was evident that the Luftwaffe were interested in Stephenson. As a senior RAF officer and a Spitfire squadron commander, he could be a valuable resource to his captors. Most airmen would only spend a couple of weeks at *Dulag Luft* before moving on to their permanent POW camp. However, Stephenson would spend nearly four months at the camp. Nevertheless, his utility to the Germans was also a finite resource. Working in Stephenson's favour was that during his stint at Oberursel, the camp received approximately 50 new prisoners per week, and there were capacity issues.[47] Stephenson's knowledge of the Spitfire and its tactics would wane as the new Spitfire variant, the Mark II, entered service, and the outdated tactics seen over Dunkirk were updated to reflect the rapidly-changing character of war. The *Stalag Luft* I Camp history highlights that there may be a more practical reason for Stephenson's extended tenure at *Dulag Luft*. *Stalag Luft* I was a purpose-built facility and was still under construction during the summer of 1940. Although the camp received its first tranche of 21 prisoners from *Dulag Luft* in July 1940, the camp infrastructure remained limited and it simply did not have the capacity to receive the next wave of prisoners until September 1940, when the Germans built an additional barrack.[48] Day also comments on an event in September that may have triggered Stephenson's departure. 'The German Camp Authorities had what we used to call a "Purge." That is to say, the Germans used to select all the chaps who they thought were keen escapees or made a nuisance of themselves and send them away.⁴⁹

Life Beyond *Dulag Luft*

Stephenson's time at Oberursel coincided with the battle that became synonymous with the RAF and its fighter pilots – the Battle of Britain. Despite his fighter pilot background, Stephenson's diary makes only passing comments on the battle. The 10 September 1940 entry reads, 'Fighter boy came in and gave us news of battles over London'. Although the battle had still to reach its peak, the discussion must have pricked Stephenson's interest and forced him to reflect on how his old squadron was getting on.

19 Squadron was heavily involved in the fighting during the summer of 1940. After temporarily taking command of the Squadron following Stephenson's crash-landing, Brian Lane handed over command to Squadron Leader Philip 'Tommy' Pinkham only a few days later. However, that position changed again when Pinkham was shot down and killed on 5 September 1940. The 23-year-old Lane led the squadron for the remainder of the battle and into mid-1941. Under Lane's command, the squadron had performed well. However, half of the 12 Spitfire pilots that flew with Stephenson over Dunkirk on 26 May 1940 were no longer operational. Three pilots were killed in action (two on 26 May 1940 and one during the Battle of Britain); Stephenson and Potter were both POWs, while Lyne was still recovering from the wounds sustained on 26 May 1940. However, that number would dwindle even further as the war progressed.

Bader also saw action over Dunkirk with 19 Squadron's sister Spitfire unit at Duxford, 222 Squadron, and claimed two kills during Operation Dynamo. In late June 1940, Bader was promoted to Squadron Leader and took over command of 242 Squadron flying Hurricanes. Bader was joined by a new flight commander and former 19 Squadron pilot, Eric Ball who had recovered from his wounds of 26 May 1940. During the Battle of Britain, Ball would make ace and be awarded the Distinguished Flying Cross. Although Bader's squadron was based at RAF Coltishall in Norfolk, it remained under the command of Leigh-Mallory's 12 Group. Bader had a successful as well as controversial Battle of Britain. He proved to be an effective combat leader, quickly gaining 'ace' status and, by the end of the battle, had accrued the vast majority of his 22 wartime kills. Consequently, and at the height of the battle, Bader received the Distinguished Service Order. However, Bader wanted even more action for himself, his squadron, the Coltishall wing and 12 Group. He advocated that the 12 Group assets, located north of London, were not being introduced into the engagements early enough and in sufficient weight. As a result, he demanded that 11 Group scramble their northern neighbours earlier to gather the various units before entering the fight *en masse*. The counterargument was that it simply took too long to bring the 12 Group assets to bear. The 'Big Wing' debate was predominantly at the very senior levels at Fighter Command and was, in essence, a mechanism to debate the future ownership of Fighter Command. To aid Leigh-Mallory's argument, he brought along Bader, a lowly squadron leader, to add the tactical detail. The architects of the Battle of Britain victory, Dowding and Park, would ultimately lose out to Leigh-Mallory in the battle for Fighter Command's future direction. After the Battle of Britain and the 'Big Wing' furore, Leigh-Mallory took over at 11 Group in December 1940; Bader now had a powerful ally and mentor.

As Bader's profile increased, it contrasted sharply with the fortunes of Stephenson. The former Spitfire commander had missed the battle – he was not there for their finest hour and would never be one of 'The Few' with the associated gallantry medals and array of impressive post-nominals. However, he was alive unlike many of his cohort. Nevertheless, he was leaving behind the relative luxuries of *Dulag Luft* for a much more austere and chaotic life at *Stalag Luft* I. In hindsight, Stephenson would undoubtedly miss the simple *Dulag Luft* lifestyle.

Meanwhile, at Sangatte, Stephenson's Spitfire continued to lie where it fell. Over the summer months, N3200 had become a minor tourist attraction for the now local German troops. Several photos exist of the aircraft as a backdrop for group photographs for inquisitive Germans. Slowly over time, items from the aircraft began to disappear. The rudder, engine cowling, canopy, cockpit side entry hatch, tailwheel and radio compartment access hatch were soon missing, no doubt taken as trophies by either locals or the occupying forces. The soft, shifting sands were also taking their toll on N3200. Stephenson's two-ton steed soon began to sink gradually and become enveloped by the sands of the French beach. It would be over 45 years before Stephenson's Spitfire would see the light of day again.

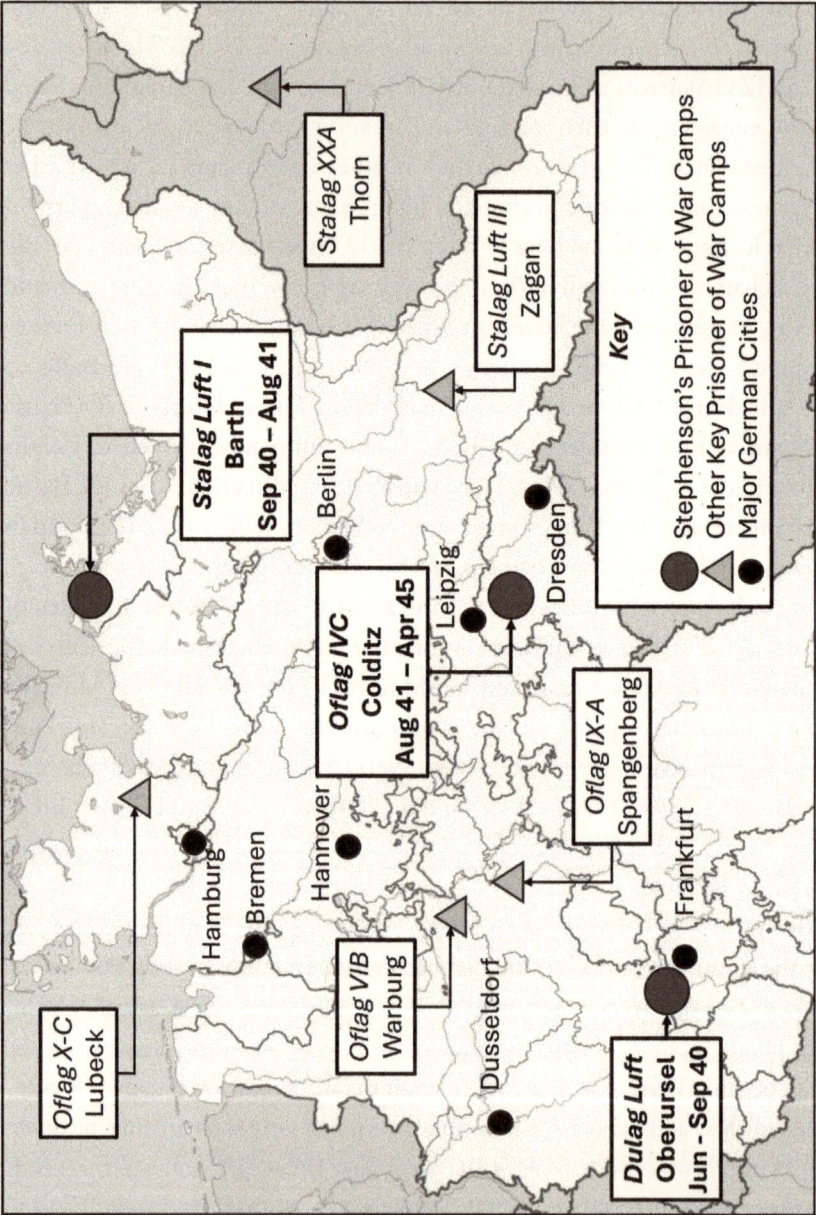

Figure 6.1 Stephenson's POW Camps in Germany.

Chapter 7

Stalag Luft I, Barth – September 1940 to August 1941

S tephenson departed Oberursel on 17 September 1940 for the 400-mile overnight journey to the north-east, the Baltic coast and *Stalag Luft* I. However, this was not before a send-off from his comrades. Stephenson notes that he had a 'delightful evening with friends' consuming 'wine, cake, and cocoa.' As he reflected on his time at Oberursel and his experiences with what he considered to be 'real friends', Stephenson felt 'rather sorrowful'. As he departed for the next chapter in his POW experience, Stephenson noted that 'everyone embarrassingly kind. Paddy gave wine and shirt.' Stephenson also had a 'pleasant chat with Major [Rumpel]' as well as a walk and a chat with his roommate, Charles Lockett. Unbeknownst to either of them at the time, Lockett and Stephenson would be reacquainted soon enough and, once again, sharing POW accommodation in the not-too-distant future. Nevertheless, Stephenson 'felt very sad at departure'. It was almost as if he knew that life would get tougher and there was no end in sight.

Although he does not confirm the mode of transport for his transit to Barth, there is a simple note in Stephenson's diary which says 'third class', inferring the transfer was by train. In Stephenson's diary, he also comments that the journey took them via the German capital. 'Berlin flats neat and practical.' As he approached his new home, he was struck by the similarity between his home for the next 12 months and where he grew up as a child by suggesting that the countryside was 'like Norfolk then like [the] Fens'.

The *Stalag Luft* I Camp

The camp was situated 'one and a quarter miles north-west of the town of Barth . . . on the western side of a small, flat peninsula projecting northward into the large inlet between the Der Darss peninsula and the mainland. The

Camp, which was constructed specially for the accommodation of air force personnel, was built on sand. The water level was about five feet below the surface.'[1] Located just to the north of a Flak training school, *Stalag Luft* I comprised two prisoner compounds, one for the officers and an adjacent but separate compound for the other ranks. The officers' camp initially consisted of two wooden, single-storey barracks. However, a third accommodation block was added in September 1940. Each of the barracks was divided into 28 small rooms. Three of these were used as a kitchen, lavatory, and washroom. One barrack block had an extension built on it which was used as a dining hall. The barracks were enveloped by simple anti-escape measures, including a

> double barbed-wire fence about eight feet in height with a space of six feet between the fences. This space was filled with a concertina wire to a height of about three feet. There were three sentry towers fitted with searchlights and machine guns. These were situated at the compound's north-east, south-east and south-west corners. Sentries patrolled outside the fence throughout the 24 hours. Arc lights were situated about twenty yards apart along the compound fence. A warning wire was situated about three feet inside the main fence, and it was a German order that any POW touching it would be fired upon. This threat was not put into effect.[2]

The camp opened in July 1940 when a party of 21 officers arrived from *Dulag Luft*. Further prisoners were added from other camps, including a French contingent of 40 prisoners. However, by the time Stephenson arrived in mid-September 1940, the French prisoners had been moved to another camp leaving approximately 230 RAF, Fleet Air Arm and Dominion airmen. As with the camp at Oberursel, the new camp was administered by the Luftwaffe, numbering about 200 officers and men. However, as Stephenson was to find out, the atmosphere was very different to the comfortable lifestyle he had experienced at *Dulag Luft*.

On arrival at *Stalag Luft* I, Stephenson and his fellow POWs 'were subjected to a thorough search in a building in the *Vorlager* [administration area] before they were permitted to enter the compound'.[3] All POWs 'were photographed and finger-printed on arrival at the Camp, and these, together with a full description of the individual, were kept by the *Abwehr* department'.[4] However, the new prisoners were initially cooped up in an 'unfinished and primitive' barrack block for two days. Stephenson suggests in his diary that this extended period confined to the barrack block during in-processing was as much to do with the French moving out of the camp as it was with the arrival of the new prisoners. Stephenson was frustrated that during the obligatory initial search, and as his particulars were being taken, his Red Cross-supplied suit was confiscated by the Germans. Clothing was at a premium. Many prisoners only had the clothes that they were wearing when they were captured. Consequently, it was not uncommon for several items of clothing to show the wear and tear of their owner's travails over the last few weeks. However, 'the Germans issued a limited amount of captured uniform, underwear etc in necessitous cases. All officers were dependent upon the arrival of their next-of-kin clothing parcels, which began to arrive about six months after capture, though in some cases, the period was much longer.'[5] Nevertheless, as was the case with Stephenson, the Germans tended to confiscate civilian attire in case the prisoners used it during their escape attempts. The net result was that prisoners' wardrobes were bare, and winter was approaching. Removing civilian clothes from the new prisoners did not aid their mood. Stephenson's group was 'restive, impatient and hungry' but were finally released at 1730 on the second day. Despite the frustrations, Stephenson commented that he was 'very pleased to meet old faces'. The vast majority, if not all, of the prisoners, would have passed through *Dulag Luft* during Stephenson's stint there.

September 21st 1940 would be Stephenson's third full day as a *Stalag Luft* I POW. His diary entry highlights the routine daily events that would become the norm over the next year. 'Got up at 7:30. Roll Call 9:00. Lunch 13:00. Appel 18:00. Cooking – Supper – Ovaltine. Bed.' It was also on this day that he had his arrival interview with the Senior British Officer – Squadron Leader Brian 'Auntie' Paddon.[6]

Like Stephenson, Paddon had also been shot down during the Battle of France. He was commanding 40 Squadron at the time, a Bristol Blenheim Mark IV unit. On 6 June 1940, two days after the end of Operation Dynamo, Paddon was flying one of 12 Blenheims tasked to attack troop concentrations in northern France when he was shot down by an Me 109. The Germans quickly captured Paddon, and he was eventually transferred to *Dulag Luft* on

15 June 1940. Within just over a month, Paddon had been whisked through three different POW camps to ultimately take over the duties of the Senior British Officer at Barth as of 12 July 1940 and the responsibility for over 200 fellow aircrew officers. Unlike Day back at Oberursel, Paddon had little time to consider his role, develop key relationships or have an in-depth knowledge of how the system worked.

From his diary entries, Stephenson confirms that he was settling into the new lifestyle and that the days were passing quickly. He continued to keep his mind and body fit. In addition to German classes, he remained competitive at chess and backgammon and would run, skip as well as participate in team sports such as football, handball and 'rugger'.[7]

Stephenson remained an avid reader and had a constant supply of books on various topics from the ever-growing camp library. As the Camp History informs, 'the nucleus of a library was formed in the autumn of 1940. The books contributed by POWs who had retrieved them in parcels from the UK. In early 1941 large quantities of these parcels arrived, as well as books sent to the Camp by the International Red Cross Society.'[8] By June 1941, the officers' compound had access to 1,800 books.[9] The library was in a room in one of the barrack blocks. However, beyond individual study, the opportunities for collective education were initially more limited.

The camp's official history file suggests that 'there were no educational facilities for the first 6 months' in the camp.[10] However, 'during the winter of 1940-1941, one or two classes were started'.[11] Moreover, there is evidence from Stephenson's diary that he was involved in some early education classes. For example, in late October, Stephenson delivered lectures, which included lessons on the theory of flight. While Stephenson's talks were on a one-to-one basis, there were also group activities, including a debating society.

Stephenson's diary also paints a picture of a cohesive social network within the RAF prisoner community in his first few months at Barth. Many of his diary entries at that time talk of having various individuals over for 'Tea' and dining with them. 'Dining' may be an extravagant term as resources remained limited. The prisoners often used their own stoves within their barrack room to cook for themselves. Stephenson's first solo cooking experience was on 29 September 1940 when he cooked 'Potato cake – delightful and savoury'. He would get more ambitious with time. Over the next few weeks, his culinary skills showed ambition and covered marmalade-making as well as baking an orange and lemon tart. The latter was registered as a 'great success' in Stephenson's diary. However, basic ingredients were not always available to make mouth-watering items such as tarts. At times, he was limited to cooking the less-than-appealing cabbage au gratin! Even access to the occasional bottle of wine or beer did not make the smell or taste of some of these meals more appealing.

The bond had extended to the adjacent airmen's POW camp. On 30 September 1940, Stephenson attended and enjoyed a concert organized and led by the airmen. The officers' compound had its own amateur theatrics organization. 'The first entertainment which was attempted was a pantomime at Christmas. This took place in the Dining Hall. Scenery and costumes were made from coloured paper, obtained through the Camp Canteen, and cardboard. A stage was made by placing all the tables together.'[12] According to his diary, Stephenson was involved in the planning and rehearsals for the event. However, due to German concerns that these events created escape opportunities, the prisoners had to offer their parole for these events – a promise not to escape. This system did not appear to work. During a June 1941 interview with the Red Cross, the camp commandant, *Hauptmann* Simmeleit, stipulated that communal band concerts were no longer allowed as 'these celebrations permitted so many attempted escapes that they had to be abandoned'.[13] Nevertheless, the show must go on! The Red Cross noted that during their June 1941 visit, the officers were preparing a dramatic production of 'Treasure Island'.[14]

Stephenson's *Stalag Luft* I honeymoon period was short-lived. His diary reflects that Stephenson had a growing sense of frustration; unsurprisingly, he would have good and bad days. On 20 September 1940, he noted that he was 'inclined to be awkward'. In contrast, on 30 September 1940, after receiving photographs of his girlfriend Anna, he felt very pleased. However, a few days later, on 5 October 1940, his diary simply says 'ungracious'. The pages covering the period 10–16 November 1940 give an insight into how his incarceration started affecting how Stephenson viewed the future. His reflections include the following:

1. I think I shall seek beauty more in the future. I shall find more in dancing, painting, nature and all the arts.

2. I feel it is my duty to be pleasant and timid to the Germans most of the time, but I have moments of rebellion.

3. Can we safely treat other people as if they were children, with a child's reactions, thoughts, and impulses? Without being condescending, of course; but then one is not with children.

Stephenson's growing frustration is evident, and a sense of revolt emerges. Although Stephenson does not come across as the naturally rebellious type, there is a hint that he had a recalcitrant side to his character. In mid–October, contrary to King's Regulations, he began to grow a beard. Although the camp took a more lenient view of the implementation of the rules than back home, it gives a sense that Stephenson was willing and able to push back against the system. His diary continues, 'This life is so cut and dried that I find myself resenting any intrusions on my thoughts and time. This is bad [underlined in original].' One of his last comments in his 1940 diary, dated 20 November, highlights that Stephenson was being punished for some undisclosed reason. 'Cigarettes issued to everyone except Carr and myself.' There are few comments in his diary for the remainder of that year. Perhaps, Stephenson's punishment did not end with the cigarettes. One of the few things Stephenson notes in his diary at the latter stages of 1940 is the excitement and frustration regarding escape attempts. In contrast to *Dulag Luft*, *Stalag Luft* I would see several escape attempts during Stephenson's time there.

The Camp History documents 'in addition to the 38 unsuccessful tunnelling projects involving a large number of men, 38 personnel who were resident in this Compound attempted to escape in 25 separate escape attempts' covering the period July 1940 to April 1942 – some eight months after Stephenson's departure.[15] Sadly, the Camp History only covers the significant escape attempts, and many less successful ones have not been captured for posterity. However, several minor escape attempts are recorded in Stephenson's diary. For example, he mentions a 'short-lived' escape attempt on 1 October 1940 and a 'fatuous attempt to escape' eight days later on 9 October. Additionally, he notes 'much excitement over tunnel' on 19 November. Unfortunately, neither the official Camp History nor his diary expands on the source and outcome of the excitement.

The British escape enterprise at *Stalag Luft* I was clearly an energetic affair but had yet to mature. The Camp History file notes that the endeavour lacked organisation and the escapees were poorly prepared. All intending escapers were required to inform the Senior British Officer, or his deputy, of their plans and to obtain his authority for the attempt. During the first year, this control was largely nominal, and there were instances where individuals making attempts did not obtain the authority to do so.[16] As the Senior British Officer, Padden nominated Squadron Leader Doran as head of escape activities. However, this construct was changed in January 1941, just before Stephenson took over as Senior British Officer, to a committee comprising one member from each of the three barrack blocks.

Although there is no diary for 1941 or letters to give insights into Stephenson's thoughts, the Stephenson family hold some interesting artefacts that provide an insight into their father's activities at the camp. However, the picture is incomplete and as a result, two areas remain contested in various secondary sources and prisoners' accounts of their time at *Stalag Luft* I. One discusses the challenges faced by Stephenson during his tenure as the Senior British Officer, and the other is a dispute over the distribution of Red Cross parcels between the Senior British Officers at *Dulag Luft* and *Stalag Luft* I.

Red Cross Parcel Controversy

The issue of the Red Cross parcels is first raised in Day's memoir. In the book, Smith notes that during the winter of 1940/41, Day received a letter from the Senior British Officer at *Stalag Luft* I. Unfortunately, German censors had opened the letter and, recognizing the sensitive nature of the letter, it was hand-delivered to Day by the *Dulag Luft* leadership. The letter openly criticized Day for his distribution of Red Cross parcels. According to Day's memoir, the accusation was that he 'was responsible for diverting – to put it bluntly, stealing – personal and Red Cross parcels for the use of himself and the *Dulag* [*Luft*] Permanent Party'.[17] Day was enraged by the suggestion but wisely elected to not reply to the letter as 'it would only start an inter-camp feud, and on no account must there appear any disunity among RAF prisoners'.[18] Nevertheless, he struggled to comprehend why such an accusation would be made against him, his team and the *Dulag Luft* camp. 'Every one of the 250 prisoners there had passed through *Dulag* [*Luft*] . . . among the senior officers at Barth, there were some of his old pre-war friends, Service regulars. The others included many whom he had served with him or were ex-pupils of his. Yet this letter which so shocked him was, in fact, symptomatic of a regrettable and unpleasant mood building up at Barth.'[19]

In his memoir, Day does not name his accuser. However, he does leave a few clues about the individual's identity. First, he highlights that the individual was the Senior British Officer at Barth and held the rank of squadron leader. The *Stalag Luft* I Camp History file highlights only four Senior British Officers at Barth during its tenure. The first Senior British Officer at *Stalag Luft* I was a relatively junior Royal Navy officer, Lieutenant Wood, who held the post only for a few weeks in the summer of 1940. The last Senior British Officer at *Stalag Luft* I was Day himself, a Wing Commander who took up the post in the summer of 1941. By dint of rank and time, the first and last Senior British officers can both be ruled out. The spotlight falls on the second and third Senior British Officers, both squadron leaders and both in charge at Barth during the winter 1940/41 period – Squadron Leader Brian Paddon and one Squadron Leader Geoffrey Stephenson.

Like Day, Paddon was a Blenheim pilot and a squadron commander. Consequently, it is likely they both knew each other before the war. Paddon arrived at *Dulag Luft* on 15 June 1940, nine days after being shot down, only a handful of days after Stephenson and with Day already in situ as the *Dulag Luft* Senior British Officer. However, unlike Stephenson and Day, Paddon's tenure at *Dulag Luft* was brief. Although his departure date is not articulated, he was sent initially to *Oflag* IX-A at Spangenberg before moving swiftly on to *Stalag Luft* I and taking on the Senior British Officer role as of 12 July 1940, his third POW camp in less than a month. Nevertheless, Paddon would remain as the Senior British Officer at Barth until February 1941. Moreover, with a large portion of his already short tenure at *Dulag Luft* spent in solitary confinement, Paddon would have spent very little time in the main *Dulag Luft* camp to gain first-hand knowledge of the camp's ways of working, its culture, and its personalities. Moreover, Day's memoir suggests that the originator of the letter had already departed *Stalag Luft* I by the time he arrived in June 1941.[20] However, Day also informs that unlike the more subtle approach used at *Dulag Luft*, the Germans expelled the letter's author from the camp for having blatantly 'fused and burned out the whole microphone system' that the Germans were using as listening devices embedded within the prisoners' barrack blocks.[21] The timing of Paddon's move to *Stalag* XXA appears to be a consequence of his escape attempt in February 1941 rather than an act of deliberate vandalism. However, in his memoir, Peter Tunstall recalls that it was Paddon who had destroyed the listening devices.[22] Consequently, Paddon's rank, position, timing, actions and limited understanding of Day and *Dulag Luft* make him the most likely contender to be the letter's author. Although Day does not point the finger directly at Paddon, others, like Tunstall, do. In Roger Bushell's memoir, *The Great Escaper*, written by journalist Simon Pearson, the author suggests that Paddon is the most likely author of the letter.[23] While strong evidence supports the case, Pearson does not discuss the possibility that it could have been the other candidate – Geoffrey Stephenson.

Although Stephenson arrived at Barth in September 1940, he would not take the Senior British Officer role from Paddon until February 1941 – at the latter stages of the 1940/41 winter period. Although Stephenson was the correct rank and in the Senior British Officer post at the tail-end of the timeframe stipulated by Day, there are some factors that rule him out of contention. First, Stephenson was a long-term acquaintance, if not friend, of Day, as evidenced by referencing his alternative nickname and his regular hospital visits at Oberursel to see his former flight commander. Second, after spending four months at *Dulag Luft*, Stephenson understood how the camp worked, its culture and how the key personalities operated. Stephenson understood the camp's *modus operandi* far better than someone who had only spent, at best, a few days within the camp. That said, Stephenson's diary entries during his latter days at *Dulag Luft* and his first days at *Stalag Luft* I highlight issues with parcels and their distribution.

On 20 July 1940, a simple note in Stephenson's diary says without further explanation or context, 'Mess Officer with major discovery of crooked dealing of quartermaster parcels'. Another comment was made in his diary on 9 September 1940, during his last week at *Dulag Luft*, 'conference on distribution of ration parcels in the evening'. Of note, on 9 September 1940, Day was not present at the conference as he was still in hospital convalescing. Perhaps most telling is that Stephenson fastidiously noted who he was sending his limited number of letters to and from whom he was receiving them. His diary for 1940 has a comprehensive list of letters sent and received that runs through until early 1941 – there is no mention of a letter to Day or his various pseudonyms. Rather than being viewed as nefarious, Stephenson's diary comments may be innocuous and show the prisoners' continued and enduring fixation on Red Cross parcels. Nevertheless, it is difficult to make a definitive assessment without further context and supporting evidence. On balance, it is more likely that Paddon was the author of the letter to Day rather than Stephenson. However, a broader question of why the letter was written is worthy of further examination.

At *Dulag Luft*, and as mentioned previously, Day's approach to distributing Red Cross parcels was to pool all of them together to promote and maintain a feeling of shared hardships and benefits amongst the prisoners rather than a 'them and us' mentality. The Red Cross parcel distribution system at *Dulag Luft* had become a well-oiled machine: it was mature, well-stocked and shared. The early system at *Stalag Luft* I was none of these.

The *Stalag Luft* I Camp History highlights the issue of Red Cross parcels and its consequences on the prisoners.

> During the first few months, a small number of individually addressed Red Cross parcels arrived in the Camp. About October 1940, consignments of Red Cross parcels began to arrive, addressed to the Senior British Officer. These were issued to officers in rotation, starting with those who had been POWs for the longest period. This system was adopted because not enough parcels were received at a time to issue one to each officer. There was a gradual increase in the number of parcels arriving in the camp and, from June 1941 onwards, there was a weekly issue of one parcel per POW. During the period when insufficient Red Cross food parcels were arriving, the German rations were inadequate, and most of the POWs were hungry. It is estimated that the ration was about 1500 calories daily. After the arrival of the parcels, the German rations were reduced. Limited quantities of fresh vegetables could be purchased through the canteen.[24]

One prisoner provided a more severe assessment of the situation in mid-1941, the same time as the Red Cross report. 'For the first six months in the camp on the Baltic, we were hungry – really hungry – and food became an obsession. Hunger is bad. Real hunger is very bad; starvation is catastrophic . . . we were nowhere near starvation, but we were always hungry.'[25]

There was a stark difference in the situations at *Dulag Luft* and *Stalag Luft* I. The prisoners held at Barth in the summer and autumn of 1940 saw a very different side of German hospitality than their compatriots at Oberursel. *Dulag Luft*'s reputation had filtered its way back to the United Kingdom, and later tranches of captured aircrew were told to be wary of the comfortable lifestyle at the camp. This wariness manifested into distrust and accusations from those who quickly transitioned through the camp and onto much more austere conditions at the more permanent camps. Squadron Leader Donald MacDonnell was one of those new incumbents who criticized the *Dulag Luft* lifestyle. He arrived there in March 1941 after being shot down in his Spitfire and bailing out into the English Channel. MacDonnell's comments on Day are, to say the least, forthright. MacDonnell critiques Day as he 'was too often in the company of the commandant'.[26] MacDonnell's criticism is harsh, but it was a sentiment that reflected the feelings of those who were fleeting visitors at *Dulag Luft*. Few, including MacDonnell, had any insight into what Day was up to in those spring days of 1941. Under Day's stewardship, the prisoners were in the final planning stages of the first British mass escape from a POW camp. MacDonnell and Day would be reunited later at *Stalag Luft* III, where MacDonnell would finally recognize that Day 'distinguished himself as a magnificent leader in a number of camps and was awarded a Distinguished Service Order'.[27]

Complicating matters further was that mail was slow at the best of times. This situation would be compounded further by the transitory nature of the prisoners' addresses and made even more difficult because *Stalag Luft* I was a new facility and had been called by another name. Consequently, it is unsurprising that the delivery of Red Cross parcels took some time to sort itself out. The situation at *Stalag Luft* I began to improve in September 1940, with each prisoner receiving one Red Cross parcel per week. However, the underfed individuals with too much time on their hands needed a target to vent their anger and frustration. As Day would find out first-hand, that sense of injustice would last well into the summer of 1941. Nevertheless, Day wisely elected to not add fuel to the fire by replying to the letter. Time and his actions would resolve the issue.

Day had the opportunity to name the letter's author but elected not to – why? One consideration is that it is part of his character; it was simply an act of old-fashioned chivalry to protect a prolific and decorated escaper in the case of Paddon or the honour and reputation of a friend, colleague and, by the time of the book's release in 1968, a deceased senior officer. Although Paddon and Day would not meet again as POWs, Day and Stephenson would be reunited at *Stalag Luft* I, while Stephenson and Paddon's time at *Oflag* IVC overlapped. Stephenson and Day would have a rough ride during the last few months of the former's tenure at *Stalag Luft* I. The trigger for the angst was the attempted escape of the Senior British Officers at *Dulag Luft* and *Stalag Luft* I. Paddon's failed escape attempt in February 1941 elevated Stephenson to the Senior British Officer role at Barth, whereas Day's escape attempt at *Dulag Luft* 1, the first mass RAF escape of the war, forced his transfer to *Stalag Luft* I and relinquished Stephenson of his Senior British Officer role in June 1941.

Stephenson – The Senior British Officer

The failed escape attempts of both Senior British Officers bookended Stephenson's time as the Senior British Officer at Barth. From February to June 1941, Stephenson had to fill in the leadership void at *Stalag Luft* I left by Paddon until relinquished by Day's eventual release from solitary confinement. Stephenson's task was a challenging one. He had inherited a much larger and less well-organised camp than the one he had known at the well-resourced, well-managed and well-fed *Dulag Luft*. Consequently, despite the high morale, the level of turmoil within the prisoner compound was significantly higher. Nevertheless, the Red Cross were able to provide a constant and independent view of the camp.

Although Stephenson mentions in his diary that the Red Cross visited the camp as early as 21 October 1940, just over a month after his arrival, the *Stalag Luft* I file held at The National Archives only contains Red Cross visit reports from 7 June 1941. The first report shows that Stephenson still held the Senior British Officer appointment. However, unknown at the time, Stephenson was in his final few days of the post as Day would soon arrive at *Stalag Luft* I after his failed bid for freedom at *Dulag Luft*. Moreover, the report paints the camp in a positive light, although it recognizes several challenges. The Red Cross team suggests that

> *Stalag Luft* seems to be an unusually good camp although at present considerable tension exists between the prisoners and the German authorities due to the large number of attempted escapes, not all of which have been unsuccessful. This development has arisen with the advent of warm weather, which enables fugitives to travel through Germany with less chance of detection. Relations, nevertheless, remain correct, almost cordial, between captor and captive, and the former have refrained from taking any measures of reprisal but have limited themselves to increasing their vigilance and to refusing to accept prisoners' paroles. It must be expected, however, that these attempts to flee, which take place at least weekly will result eventually in the shooting of one or more of the escaping captives.[28]

In the Red Cross report, Stephenson is interviewed and says, 'there was a good deal of tension due to the many attempted escapes and to measures taken by the Germans. Specifically, prisoner officers no longer can take walks when given their paroles; they will be unable to swim in the nearby Baltic Sea beach; civilian shorts have been taken away from them, and also suitcases.'[29]

The tension mentioned by the Red Cross team and Stephenson reflects the aftermath of the first successful escape from the camp, which occurred only a few days before the visit.[30] The German backlash was immediate. The only mass reprisal taken by the Germans during the camp history occurred after the escape and consisted of 28 successive days of searches within the officers' compound. Of note, the Red Cross visit coincided with the early stages of this period and captured the mood of the prisoners during this upheaval. Additionally, during this period, a 'system of carbon microphones was installed along the north and west boundary fences of the compound'.[31] These were connected to a control room in the German compound. It was several months later before the POWs learned that some electrical system of indicating the vibrations caused by tunnelling had been installed. It was also at this time that punishment for prisoner offences was increased. 'At first, the usual punishment for escape activities was five days in the cells for the first offence, ten days for the second offence etc. Normal German rations and Red Cross parcels were permitted.'[32] However, in June 1941, sentences were increased to '14 days in the cells for all offences, and Red Cross food was disallowed'.[33]

As a consequence of the reprisals, there was a noticeable increase in the level of 'Goon Baiting' – the colloquialism for the deliberate act of the prisoners antagonizing the guards. The *Kommandant* understood the situation but also highlighted his frustrations and possible consequences.

> It is my duty and desire to make life for the prisoners as pleasant as possible. It is also my duty to prevent them from escaping, which they are continually attempting to do. To date, these conflicting duties have been compromised in a more or less satisfactory manner, and at least I feel sure I have the respect and understanding of the prisoners. We get along well, although frankly, I feel I need the patience of an angel. It is a sport between us and the British, a sport in which no one yet has lost his temper, although with, these many attempted escapes, life is extremely trying for me. It is just my bad luck to be a professor of philosophy in civil life and to speak English which caused my appointment at this post.[34]

In response to the Red Cross delegates' questions, Stephenson suggests that the 'camp commander was satisfactory and that there was a good spirit between the German guards and the British'.[35] In response, Simmeleit requested that the 'British forebear from making jokes, because as he stated, the guards were not so clever as the prisoners, did not always understand, and he feared some unpleasant incident might develop'.[36]

One of his fellow prisoners, Squadron Leader Donald MacDonnell, believed that Stephenson was 'doing a reasonable job under difficult circumstances'.[37] However, MacDonnell suggests that 'the camp was disorganised . . . There was no escape committee as such, no organised activities, nothing intellectual.'[38] The criticism is harsh as the Camp History shows clear evidence of an escape committee in existence as well as broader individual and group activities. Consequently, it is fairer to say these activities were developing and continued to mature rather than non-existent. MacDonnell also informs that Stephenson 'represented the "old guard" of the RAF. Most of the other POWs were in their twenties and far less class and rank-conscious.'[39] Again, MacDonnell's comments appear to be on the severe side. Stephenson was 31 years old and just over three years older than MacDonnell, a fellow public school boy and Cranwell graduate. MacDonnell and Stephenson may have had similar values and experiences, but these were not necessarily the same values as their younger subordinates. Nevertheless, Stephenson's tenure as the Senior British Officer was a turbulent one; it was a mixture of what he had inherited, his approach and the events during his tenure. Even with the arrival of Day and the handover of Senior British Officer responsibilities, Stephenson would continue to have an unsettled time at Barth. The pressure and challenges came from both inside and outside the camp.

From inside the camp, the pressure came from an event in May 1941 that would have consequences for Stephenson's remaining time at Barth and set the course for his remaining time as a POW. One of the few artefacts from 1941 that still exist in the Stephenson family archives is a one-page letter written by the German authorities and translated into English. The document reads:

> I punish the British POW Squadron Leader Geoffrey Dalton Stephenson in *Stalag Luft* I with three weeks of solitary confinement for offending against the camp regulations by spreading an order of insubordination in May 1941. Legal proceeding entered for the same reason against him have been stopped by the *Aussenstelle* [branch office] of the Court Martial of Rostock under the command of the General in Command and Commander in Chief of the *Luftgau* XI on June 23rd, 1941.

The typed letter was signed on 25 July 1941 by General Ludwig Wolff, the commander of *Luftgau* XI, a Luftwaffe unit based in Hannover responsible for all administrative activities within a region to include training, maintenance, recruitment, and the like. POWs also came under its purview. The note was countersigned by Stephenson on 4 August 1941 to confirm that he read and understood the order. Stephenson would spend the majority of August in solitary confinement.

The Camp History does not refer to the specifics of Stephenson's case, but it does note that 'with a few exceptions, all POWs were returned to the compound upon completion of their sentences'.[40] The exceptions were sent elsewhere; Stephenson would be one of those exceptions. Upon his release, he would be transferred to the *Sonderlager, Oflag* IVC, more commonly known by the town in which the medieval *Schloss* is situated – Colditz. He would remain there for the rest of the war. While Stephenson's timeline for his transfer can be established, the reason for his punishment lies in comments by a fellow prisoner and those contained within the Red Cross files.

In one of the Red Cross reports following a visit to the camp, the team provide an insight into an issue. In response to a complaint from the British prisoners that the lights of their barrack rooms were being switched off at 9 p.m., two hours earlier than the norm, the Red Cross team provided the following answer:

> Concerning the turning off of the light at 9 o'clock pm, this is in line of cutting all extra privileges for the officers. The reason for this is a scandalous poem about Adolf Hitler found on a search of the quarters after some attempts to escape. The Commander stated, and the Senior British Officer has included the same story in a letter to the Embassy, that when the poem was found, it was brought to the attention of all the British officers upon which the Senior British Officer apologised on behalf of all the British officers. The Commander then gave him the ultimatum that if the guilty one gave himself up before a certain time, the whole matter would be treated as a disciplinary one, but that he otherwise would have to bring it to the attention of higher authorities. As nothing happened, the whole matter was forwarded to higher German authorities, upon which the commander received an order to cut off all extra privileges. Nothing more had happened concerning the matter so far.[41]

The report does not add significant detail regarding timings or naming specific individuals. However, in his memoir, MacDonnell was demonstrably more forthcoming with his forthright views on individuals and their actions. In this case, MacDonnell provides the glue between General Wolff's decision and the Red Cross report. MacDonnell suggests that it was Stephenson who was caught 'possessing an infamous piece of doggerel written by a fellow POW which heaped filth on the Fuehrer . . . Stephenson kept it among his papers which were found during a routine search'.[42]

In the aftermath of Burton's escape and the backlash of recriminations from the German guards, Stephenson was caught with the incriminating evidence. Although it was in his possession, he was not the originator of the poem. The Germans were after the originator, not Stephenson. However, as the originator's name was not disclosed, Stephenson bore the brunt of the penalty. The case was serious enough to be elevated beyond the camp and reached the *Luftgau* level. Although the charges were quashed by higher German authorities, an example was to be made of Stephenson, the Senior British Officer at the time of the incident. Although the process took a couple of months to resolve, Stephenson was sent to solitary confinement before onward movement.

In isolation, the event appears relatively innocuous and does not merit the transfer to the most infamous of POW camps. However, in Pat Reid's history of Colditz, he provides several examples where prisoners found themselves there for what, at face value, appears to be a fairly minor infraction. For example, one British prisoner was accused of having "'a housebreaking instrument – a jemmy – for escape purposes." Actually, it was a piece of wire he used for propping up the lid for his battered suitcase. This was enough to send him to Colditz!'[43] Therefore, Stephenson's transfer to Colditz with the associated annotation of a red seal to his prisoner record identifying him as a '*Deutschfiendlich*' or an 'Enemy of Germany' appears to be in keeping with the standard at that time.[44]

Beyond the camp and adding further angst to Stephenson's predicament was the sad news that Stephenson's father died on 1 July 1941 at the relatively young age of 62. Although Stephenson's reaction to his father's death is not recorded, he must have felt frustrated due to his isolation and inability to support his family, particularly his mother. The timing was also unfortunate as his father's death overshadowed happier news. On 12 July 1941, British newspapers announced that Stephenson and Anne Farrer were now engaged to be married.[45]

Life Beyond *Stalag Luft* I

Stephenson was not the only one who had found love during this turbulent period; Jean François Georges Mennesson was in a similar situation. Although

Stephenson and Mennesson never met, they would have a yet-to-be discovered connection. One thing they both had in common was that they were both sons of affluent farmers. However, as his name suggests, Mennesson was French, born in 1916 and six years younger than Stephenson. He was brought up in the Aisne region of war-torn northern France. After the cessation of hostilities, his family returned to their farming roots. Mennesson was educated at a prestigious French boarding school and, after a brief period in London to improve his English, returned to France in the mid-1930s to join the French Army. When his three-year Army term expired in August 1938, he returned to London to work as an Assistant Master at the *Institut Français*. At the outbreak of the Second World War, Mennesson immediately returned to France and military service. Due to his English-language skills, Mennesson worked as a liaison officer with the BEF. However, shortly before the fall of France, he returned to Britain with his assigned British Army unit. Now devoid of a country to call his own or an army to serve, Mennesson elected to join the British Army in August 1940. In doing so, he was permitted to adopt the assumed name of James Francis George Menzies. He served six months as a Sergeant before volunteering for the French Section of the Special Operations Executive. Mennesson's file in The National Archives informs that he was accepted into the organisation in February 1941 and commissioned into the British Army the following month.

According to his Special Operations Executive training reports, Mennesson was intelligent, keen and popular, as well as a natural leader and organiser.[46] However, despite 'his boyish sense of humour', he was initially critiqued for being too impetuous, clumsy, and acting like a bull in a china shop.[47] Nevertheless, over time, Mennesson developed into a capable asset with potential. He was latterly described as 'the best man for very dangerous and very hard work' and 'although he deliberately plays the fool, he is one of the most brilliant members of the party'.[48] It was not all work and no play for Mennesson.

During the latter stages of his training, Mennesson met and began dating 21-year-old Anne Jean Maureen Booth, known as Maureen, a First Aid Nursing Yeomanry telephonist. Maureen had only recently tragically lost her first love and fiancé, Donald Smith, who was serving in the Royal Navy at the time, to a burst appendix. Maureen was the daughter of Sir Paul and Lady

Agnes Booth who had recently moved from London to Burnham-on-Crouch on the Essex coast to take over the family business and home. Sir Paul was a former Army major and had previously helped his father run the Booth and Brookes foundry, which specialized in piano frames and gaming machines. After finishing his training in the late stages of 1941, Menzies returned to London and asked Maureen to marry him. She accepted. The couple quickly planned their wedding, only too aware that his first operation back in his native France was only a few short months away.

The aerial engagements over the United Kingdom had also dwindled since the successful completion of the Battle of Britain. With Leigh–Mallory now in charge, 11 Group's focus changed from defensive to offensive operations. Consequently, the fighter squadrons began to conduct patrols across the English Channel and into France. The intent was to attrit the Luftwaffe. However, and in a similar manner to the Luftwaffe's challenges faced during the summer of 1940, the advantage lay with the defender. As a result, RAF fighter losses mounted, and several experienced fighter pilots were lost during this period. On 19 Squadron, Brian Lane had turned over command of the squadron in June 1941 and took on a staff appointment at the 12 Group headquarters. After a year of operations covering Dunkirk, the Battle of Britain, and fighter sweeps over France, the respite was long overdue. Of the original twelve 19 Squadron pilots who flew on Stephenson's Dunkirk mission on the morning of 26 May 1940, the number of pilots who were still operational remained constant at six. Michael Lyne returned to action in February 1941 following his convalescence from the wounds received on that fateful day in late May 1940. However, the return of Lyne was offset by the downing of Flying Officer Eric Ball. After a successful Battle of Britain flying as one of Bader's flight commanders on 242 Squadron, he was now serving in North Africa and flying Hurricanes when he was shot down in April 1941. He survived the incident but was captured by the Germans and taken prisoner. Four months after Ball's incarceration, Douglas Bader would meet a similar fate. Bader's aggression in the air and forthright views on the ground ensured that he quickly became a prominent figure within Fighter Command. He was promoted to Wing Commander in March 1941 to take over the wing at RAF Tangmere. His bravery and leadership continued to be recognized; he was awarded the Distinguished Flying Cross in January 1941 and a bar to his Distinguished Service Order in July 1941. However, Bader's luck was about to change.

On 9 August 1941, Bader led a large formation of British fighters in his personalized Spitfire Mark Va, W3185. Bader's force were on a 'Circus', a fighter sweep, over the Pas de Calais when they were engaged by Luftwaffe fighters. After shooting down one Me 109F, the remainder of the engagement becomes disputed. Bader thought he had a mid-air collision with another Me 109. Indeed, in his logbook, he claims, 'a good fight near Bethune. Shot down one Me 109F and collided with another. POW.'[49] As a result of the action, Bader claimed two Me 109Fs destroyed in his logbook, bringing up his total to 30 enemy aircraft destroyed.[50] However, others suggest he was shot down by a Messerschmitt Me 109 pilot from *Jagdgeschwader* 26.[51] Two pilots from the unit each claimed a kill that day, but neither a non-commissioned officer, *Oberfeldwebel* Walter Meyer, nor *Leutnant* Kosse could determine who shot down Bader. While the shootdown of an experienced ace and senior officer by a lowly non-commissioned officer pilot may have been an 'intolerable idea' as suggested by the German ace Adolf Galland, it was not as bad as the alternative.[52] Contemporary analysis of events suggests that Bader may have been shot down by friendly fire from one of his own Spitfires.[53]

Irrespective of the cause of his demise, Bader had a more immediate concern; he could not bale out of his fatally damaged Spitfire. Eventually, he freed himself from his stricken aircraft but lost one of his artificial legs in the process. The one-legged landing was, as expected, a hard one, and with little apparent ability to evade, Bader was quickly captured. Although Bader had now completed his last operational flying mission, he still had plenty of fight. Consequently, he would spend the rest of the war as a prisoner, but his desire and intent were to make life as difficult as possible for his captors. As a result of his drive, determination, and single-mindedness, Bader would eventually be reunited with Stephenson. However, that event would not occur for another year. In the meantime, Bader made the Germans suffer for his captivity.

After the stagnation of their Western European operation, the Germans turned their attention towards a bigger and potentially more lucrative target in the east – Russia. Operation Barbarossa, the campaign to conquer Russia, commenced in late June 1941. It would be a long and bloody campaign for both sides but ultimately fatal for the Germans. However, in the next few months, the war would explode beyond Europe and North Africa and become a truly global affair. The Japanese attack on Pearl Harbor in early December 1941 would draw the United States of America into the war. The consequences were palpable for Stephenson. In early 1941, it would have been incomprehensible that a British fighter pilot shot down over France and captured in Belgium by the Germans could envisage which nation would eventually release him in 1945. The scene was set for a rampant Russia heading west and a US-led force marching east. Both sides were marching towards victory, and the most infamous of German POW camps – Colditz.

Chapter 8

Oflag IVC, Colditz – The Allied Years, August 1941 to September 1943

I f you were to ask a member of the British public to name a German Second World War POW camp, it is most likely that the answer would be Colditz. The castle is renowned within British culture as a haven for hardened and persistent British escapers. Colditz's reputation was brought into the public domain by Pat Reid's memoir of his successful escape from Colditz. Reid's book *The Colditz Story* was turned into a 1955 film of the same name, with John Mills playing the role of Reid. The book was then adapted for the small screen in the early 1970s with a TV series starring Robert Wagner and David McCallum. For those not old enough to remember the film or the television series, the board game 'Escape from Colditz' kept the next generation enthralled for hours in the days before social media. The book, film, TV series and board game reinforce the notion that Colditz contained only the most daring of British prisoners who were focused on only one thing – escape. The reality is more nuanced, and Stephenson is a case in point. The British Official History of the camp informs that there were several different categories of prisoner held at Colditz.

> *Oflag* IVC (Colditz) was a special camp set up by the Germans for POWs who had proved themselves to be a nuisance at other camps; either because of their attempts to escape, or their general attitude towards the Germans. In addition, there were certain personnel who had been dropped as 'agents' in occupied territories and the 'prominent persons' who were held at the camp because of their connection with the British Royal Family, or with members of the British or Allied governments. It is believed that the Germans intended to hold these men as hostages to be used as a bargaining weapon should the need arise, though at the

end of hostilities, owing to the chaotic conditions prevailing, the plan was never put into effect.[1]

Many Colditz prisoners fell into the first of the four POW categories. Hence Colditz had the reputation of being a 'bad boys' camp for persistent escapees. By way of example, a Red Cross report from 16 August 1941, just before Stephenson's arrival at Colditz, informs that 'of the 59 British officers, it was stated that 41 have tried at least once to escape from this or other camps'.[2] However, Stephenson fell into the second category – one of a general malevolent attitude towards the Germans rather than a serial escaper.

Stephenson arrived at Colditz on 31 August 1941 and would spend the rest of the war there, a few months shy of four years. It was a very different camp to *Dulag Luft* and *Stalag Luft* I. His previous camps were predominantly for British airmen and for all ranks, albeit usually separated into various compounds. However, Colditz was an *Oflag* (*Offizier-Lager*), an officers' camp. Consequently, it was not only tri-service with a mix of British Army, Royal Navy and RAF officers but also multinational. Upon their arrival in November 1940, the first British officers were in the minority. The castle already contained a large contingent of Polish officers; French and Dutch officers would join them in early to mid-1941. However, the prisoner apportionment would vary widely throughout Stephenson's tenure at *Oflag* IVC. For most of the latter half of his captivity in the castle, the British were the majority, bordering at times on exclusive stakeholders.

The Colditz file in The National Archives opens by painting a picture of the small town in Lower Saxony and its infamous *schloss*.

The surrounding country was hilly, and the river valley of the Zwickavee Mulde was very steep-sided in the vicinity of the town, especially on the east bank, to the north of the camp where the ground rose to a height of 720 feet. This river joins the Freiberger Mulde about 2 miles north-west of the camp, and they, together with two large wooded areas of the forest Colditz, were the chief landmarks of the area. The camp was built on the ruins of a castle situated in the Saalhaus/Colditz district, about 12 miles south of Dresden and 24 miles south-east of Leipzig, on the north side of a small town called Colditz. Owing to the nature of its construction, the Germans believed the camp to be escape-proof because there was a dry moat with a high outer wall surrounding the castle. On the outer side of this wall, there was a drop of nearly 30 feet to the terraced gardens below, which were built above a fairly high perpendicular wall.[3]

In sharp contrast to other POW camps and based on the previous activities of their charges, Colditz had a large security force. 'The garrison manning the camp outnumbered the prisoners at all times. The Castle was floodlit at night from every angle, in spite of the blackout. Notwithstanding the clear drops of a hundred feet or so on the outside from barred windows, there were sentries all around the camp within a palisade of barbed wire. Beyond the palisade were precipices of varying depth.'[4] Despite its conversion into a POW camp, even the Red Cross, acting as the Protecting Power for British POWs, saw the splendour behind Colditz's new façade. 'The castle itself is quite a beautiful building without the gloomy aspect of decay, and anciently these chateaux present very often.'[5] Nevertheless, highlighting the stark reality of Colditz for any potential escaper, the castle is 'in the heart of the German Reich and 400 miles from any frontier not directly under the German heel'.[6]

Reid was one of the first British POWs at Colditz, arriving at the camp in early November 1940. He noted that Colditz 'was supposed to be impregnable and certainly looked like it for a long time. It was the German fortress from which there was no escape. It had been escape-proof in the 1914-18 War and was to be so again in this war, according to the Germans.'[7]

Once inside Colditz's walls, the building was no less imposing. 'The Castle was divided into two main sections built around two small courtyards. The German officers and guards occupied the southern section in which there were two main gates, one leading to the town, the other leading into the park. Both these gates were manned by sentries.'[8] The southern section or *Kommandantur* was 'administered and guarded by German army personnel who numbered, to begin with, about 300 men, 200 of which were guards. With the exception of the *Kommandant*, who changed three times during the war, the majority of the administrative staff remained at the camp throughout the period. The number of guards, however, was increased from 200 men to 350 men and finally to 500 men.'[9]

The northern section of the castle contained the prisoners. The three main blocks holding the prisoners were the *Saalhaus*, the *Furtstenhaus* and the *Kellerhaus*. After entering the courtyard via the main gate, the *Saalhaus* was located on the right-hand side of the entrance. The first and second floors of the *Saalhaus* housed all the British officers of the equivalent rank of major or higher; Stephenson lived in *Saalhaus* 220.[10] 'Living accommodation was divided into a number of small rooms, the largest holding six.'[11] Above the British senior officers on the third floor was the theatre, while the showers and kitchens were below them on the ground floor. The orderlies lived in a room above part of the kitchen, which jutted out into the courtyard. The Red Cross reports from late 1941 and early 1942 were mostly complimentary regarding the *Saalhaus* accommodation. 'Eleven of the officers live in a set of two rooms on another staircase. These are attractive and satisfactory.'[12] Moreover, 'in those rooms are only comfortable single beds', rather than the bunk beds in the larger communal rooms for the more junior officers.[13] There was a very different view on the other side of the building. 'From the dormitories of the British, there is a very beautiful view over the town at the foot of the castle and over the surrounding country.'[14] The British vista of the town was a mixed blessing. It may have been frustrating for the prisoners to watch the population move around freely below them; other views were greatly appreciated by the prisoners . . .

The accommodation allocated to the junior officers was not as lavish. Located opposite the main gate and the senior officers' accommodation was the *Furtstenhaus*. It 'was divided into two blocks. The Chapel was situated in the first block, occupying the ground and first floors, while the British occupied the second and third floors. The dispensary, dentist's room, and barber's shop were on the ground floor and the Poles the second floor.'[15]

Within a month of Stephenson's arrival, the Red Cross visited Colditz. The October 1941 report describes the prisoners' accommodation.

Most of the officers and all the orderlies live in the same group of rooms . . . on the second floor of one of the castle staircases opening from the inner court. These rooms consist chiefly of a fairly large room for eating and recreational purposes, wash and toilet rooms, a room in which the orderlies eat and sit and sleep, and three rooms in which the officers sleep.[16]

The December 1941 Red Cross report added further detail.

> The men sleep according to the size of the rooms, six to forty per room on double-tiered wooden bunks. Each one has a palliasse and one or two blankets. A certain number of dormitories are overcrowded and produce a depressing effect because they are lit by small windows so feebly that the electric light has to be on almost continuously. All the rooms are well-heated and well-ventilated, but there are not always enough tables and benches. The prisoners have a cupboard between three or four men for their personal effects. This installation is inadequate, and parcels, parts of uniform, underclothing etc, are piled on or under the beds. This is certainly bad for the atmosphere of the rooms.[17]

The last of the three blocks was the *Kellerhaus*, situated to the left of the main gate. This was 'where the cellars store potatoes and mangel wurzels, the ground floor used for the sick bay and parcels office, while the upper stories were occupied by the French'.[18] While the first sight of their new home may have been daunting for the new inhabitants, it quickly became apparent that the castle had a design flaw. Colditz was designed to keep people out rather than keep people in! Complicating the Germans' problem further was that they had gathered the serial escapers in a single location.

Life at Colditz

By the time of Stephenson's arrival at Colditz, British prisoners had been held at the castle for nearly a year. According to the Red Cross report from the following month, the British group at Colditz comprised 63 British officers and 13 orderlies.[19] Although it was an officers' camp, several junior ranks from each nation acted as orderlies to conduct the more menial tasks around the camp. The British group came under the command of the Senior British Officer, Lieutenant Colonel Guy German. German was a 39-year-old reservist from The Leicestershire Regiment who was captured during the 1940 Norway campaign. 'A handsome, young-looking

Colonel, he was broad-shouldered, tall, well-built, with bright blue eyes. His nature was very down-to-earth and good-tempered,' and he held his initial Senior British Officer post from November 1940 to January 1942.[20] According to Reid, German 'brooked no nonsense and was feared by the Germans'.[21] Consequently, German was removed from his Senior British Officer appointment 'owing to his sympathies with escape activities'.[22] His active participation in the failed Canteen tunnel escape attempt on 29 May 1941 probably did not help the situation!

As mentioned previously, the British were a minority amongst the eclectic mix of continental European POWs. The Belgians were the smallest community at Colditz, with 35 officers and 11 orderlies.[23] However, the British group was outnumbered by their Polish, Dutch and French counterparts. Although the numbers ebbed and flowed with constant arrivals and departures, the largest group was French, numbering approximately 250, followed by the Poles with 140. Next, the Dutch outnumbered the British with 68 personnel. Overall, the camp numbered around 500 prisoners. According to the German view, the camp was busy but not operating at capacity. While the Allied prisoners may have questioned the German rationale, the Protecting Powers held the Germans to account during their quarterly visits. Their subsequent reports would describe the conditions and challenges Stephenson and his fellow prisoners faced and any progress on their previous recommendations. It would be fair to say that Colditz and its regime did not emerge well from the Red Cross reports. Comments from the mid-1942 reports were not exactly fulsome in their praise for Colditz. The more positive Red Cross comments included 'this camp is mediocre' and 'the camp is indifferent'. Other comments would be more damning.

While Stephenson may have benefitted from a more private and comfortable room in the *Saalhaus*, there was a general British complaint that Colditz was unsuitable and too crowded.[24] However, in October 1941, the Red Cross team suggested that 'was not found to be the case'.[25] Nevertheless, the camp population continued to grow and added further pressure. During the December 1941 visit, the Red Cross delegation noted that there were now 533 officers and 92 orderlies, 66 of whom were British officers supported by 14 orderlies.[26] The camp was now operating very close to the German's ambitious view of Colditz's theoretical capacity of 520 prisoners and 120 orderlies.[27] The overcrowding, limited resources and inadequate infrastructure would only fuel the fire of the self-proclaimed 'bad boys' camp.

Colditz was starting to show its age, and the odour from the nearby cesspit did not help to engender a convivial ambience. In October 1942, the Red Cross team noted that the camp suffered from a poor water supply, particularly on the top floor where the British officers were quartered.[28] Additionally, the limited water supply also meant that prisoners were limited to one shower or bath per fortnight, although at times even this derisory allowance was reduced.[29] Outside of these times, the 53 British prisoners were forced to share three toilets and six basins in a small, narrow, poorly-lit room; the former was deemed adequate by the Red Cross inspectors, the latter not entirely adequate.[30] The British prisoners' quarters were located

> in the oldest part of a castle, characterised by its thick walls. The walls, which in places are more than a metre thick, keep the interior cool in summer; but in winter, this will be a great drawback, as the rooms cannot be sufficiently warmed because of the small quantity of fuel. The prisoners dread the winter because they have already been told that they will have to reduce the cooking of private provisions and the supply of fuel will be diminished by 30 per cent.[31]

With their heating becoming increasingly limited, the prisoners needed blankets to keep themselves warm during winter. However, even their bedding was restricted. The prisoners slept on a straw-filled palliasse with a German-provided blanket. However, the blankets were not always available, either as German retribution for prisoner misdemeanours or a lack of supply. The British prisoners highlighted the issue to the Red Cross in late 1941. After 100 Red Cross blankets were requested, it was noted that in early 1942 during the subsequent Red Cross visit that 'all beds are provided with one German and two Red Cross blankets'.[32] Nevertheless, fuel for stoves to heat the rooms and cook food from their Red Cross parcels was still in short supply as the war and the prisoners' confinement continued.

Table 8A - Colditz Prisoner's Weekly Ration for Late 1941.

Product	Weight (g)	Product	Weight (g)
Meat	400[33]	Sugar	225
Fat/Margarine	268	Marmalade	175
Cheese (Seret)	62.5	Bread	2,250
Farines	100	Potatoes	3,900
Coffee (Substitute)	100	Fresh Vegetables	600

Food was always a topic of conversation for the prisoners. The official history of Colditz stipulates that the provision of 'German rations throughout the period was inadequate and decreased in quality and quantity towards the end'.[34] Even during the early stages of their captivity, the British POWs complained about the German-supplied rations. In December 1941, the Senior British Officer informed the Red Cross delegation that the German-provided 'food is insufficient . . . The prisoners chiefly nourish themselves with the contents of the parcels which they receive from home.'[35] 'At the time of our visit, at midday, they had received a small plate of soup, very thin and transparent, in which floated some small morsels of beetroot and potato pairings.'[36] The standard weekly allowance for a prisoner is shown in Table 8A and highlights the limited and basic nature of the prisoners' diet. However, not all ingredients were edible. One Red Cross report in August 1942 noted that '90 per cent of potatoes are black and uneatable'.[37] Fresh vegetables were rare, bordering on non-existent for prisoners, guards and the local populace alike, as they were scarce within the local area. Nevertheless, 'Root vegetables could be obtained from the canteen when in season, but no green vegetables were available apart from a small amount of cabbage and a little lettuce. Tomatoes could be purchased sometimes.'[38] During the early Red Cross visits, the inspectors considered that the general health of the prisoners appeared excellent. However, as time progressed and food supplies were reduced or more erratic, malnutrition-related cases rose steadily. Despite German claims that prisoners were receiving the required daily calorie intake, the prisoners were forced to supplement their meagre rations with external food supplies in the form of the Red Cross parcel.

However, it was rare for Stephenson and his fellow prisoners to receive their intended allocation of one parcel per prisoner per week. For example, the January 1942 Red Cross report informs that there was sufficient stock of Red Cross parcels to issue at the intended rate.[39] When looking at the issue more holistically over time, Reid suggests that 'in Colditz, we received normally one, on rare occasions two, parcels per person in three weeks'.[40] In addition to the limited inventory, it was often found that the parcels had been tampered with before they were handed out, with luxury items such as cigarettes and chocolate often being removed from the boxes while in German hands. Ultimately, as their tenure in Colditz extended, the prisoners became increasingly hungry and weaker. From Stephenson's perspective, his already slight frame began to lose even more weight which he took regular note of in his diaries.

The Red Cross' remit was more than just welfare visits and food parcels; they also provided bedding, clothing, games, sports equipment and writing materials. The lack of writing materials at Colditz may explain why Stephenson was forced to reuse his 1940 pocket diary in 1943! Beyond writing materials, clothing was also in short supply. The October 1941 Red Cross report informs that the British POWs 'recently received some supplies from the Red Cross in Geneva, particularly greatcoats and shoes, to supplement those handed out by the Germans. Lieutenant Colonel German reported that about 20 suits of British battle dress would be most welcome, and it was noted that he is still wearing that in which he was captured over a year ago.' During the December 1941 visit, it was noted that the prisoners' uniforms were in good condition, albeit prisoners were forced to mix RAF blue uniform with khaki Army uniform. Indeed, there are several photographs of Stephenson during his time at Colditz wearing battle dress that is not of UK origin. The net result was eclectic dress standards.

As with previous camps, it was important for the prisoners to keep busy. Stephenson was an avid listener to classical music. In his diary, he reflects on the joy of listening to Beethoven and Tchaikovsky on his gramophone. In addition to listening to music, Stephenson continued to be a prolific reader. Colditz had an impressive array of books to choose from. So much so, the prisoners loaned out surplus books to other camps.[41] However, the Germans vetted all the books before being added to the library. The Red Cross noted that

complaints were made about the censoring of books, not so much the time required, which is admittedly long, but the types of books

Geoffrey's grandfather (middle row, centre), father (right-hand side of the rear row) and eight uncles. Seven of the brothers served during the Great War. However, by the end of the war, three had been killed in action and Geoffrey's father wounded, while two other brothers were decorated with the Military Cross and another survived being torpedoed by a German submarine. (Image from Stephenson family archive)

A pre-Great War photograph of Geoffrey Stephenson and his younger sister, Eileen. Two brothers would follow – John born in 1915 and Urban in 1919. (Image from Stephenson family archive)

Between 1918 and 1924, Stephenson attended Castle Park School, a boys-only preparatory school on the outskirts of Dublin. Despite the fight for independence and the subsequent civil war, the boarding school was a safe haven for Stephenson, front row third from left, and his fellow students. (Image courtesy of Castle Park School)

Above: Following six years of schooling in Ireland, 14-year-old Geoffrey returned to England in 1924 to attend Shrewsbury School for his last four years of education. Geoffrey is ninth from left, in the front row, with his hands by his sides. (Image from Stephenson family archive)

Right: A cheery Flight Cadet Stephenson looking resplendent in his RAF Mess Dress at RAF Cranwell. (Image from Stephenson Family Archive)

Cranwell Flight Cadets learning about aero engines. With the ever-attentive SNCO supervising in the background, Bader is on the left leaning forward with Stephenson second right. (Image from Stephenson family archive)

A July 1929 photograph showing the RAF College Cranwell Boxing Team. Stephenson is wearing the dark blazer and would continue to box throughout his RAF career. (Image courtesy of the RAF College Cranwell archive)

The senior Cranwell Flight Cadets during their last term at Cranwell. Flight Cadet Sergeant Stephenson is front row on the right with Under Officer Bader to his right, with pipe in hand. (Image from Stephenson family archive)

Flight Cadet Sergeant Stephenson on his BSA motorbike during early 1930 and his last term at Cranwell. (Image from Stephenson family archive)

Above: Flight Cadet Stephenson in the cockpit of his RAF Cranwell-based Armstrong Whitworth Siskin trainer. (Image from Stephenson family archive)

Left: The Cranwell prize-winners in July 1930. Stephenson (bottom right) with the R.M. Groves Memorial trophy. Sat next to him is the Sword of Honour winner Paddy Coote. Stephenson, Angell (back left) and Coote would all be killed in aircraft accidents. (Image courtesy of RAF College Cranwell archives)

Above: In July 1930, after two years of training to be RAF officers and pilots, Stephenson, Bader and 19 other Flight Cadets graduated from RAF Cranwell. Bader and Stephenson would both depart for RAF Kenley and 23 Squadron. By the end of 1932, five of the graduates would have been killed. (RAF College Cranwell Archives)

Right: Flight Lieutenant Harry Day (left) and Pilot Officer Douglas Bader (right) of 23 Squadron. Along with Stephenson, the pair would participate in the 1931 Hendon Air Display. A decade later all three would be prisoners of war. (Image from Stephenson Family Archive)

From left to right – Pilot Officer Bader, Flight Lieutenant Harry Day and Pilot Officer Geoffrey Stephenson stand in front of a 23 Squadron Gloster Gamecock as part of the 1931 Hendon display.

Above left: Flying Officer Geoffrey Stephenson riding shotgun in the Iraqi desert in the early 1930s while serving with Number 1 Armoured Car Company, a forerunner of today's RAF Regiment. (Image from Stephenson family archive)

Above right: Iraq in the early 1930s – Flying Officer Geoffrey Stephenson cleaning his shotgun. As expected from a fighter pilot, he was a naturally competitive individual and a keen shot, as ably demonstrated by his participation in the Iraq Rifle and Pistol Association's competitions. (Image from Stephenson family archive)

Iraq 1933 – Stephenson, wearing his trademark white flying suit, is sat in the front seat of a Westland Wapiti. Clambering into the rear cockpit is Air Vice-Marshal Charles Burnett, Air Officer Commanding HQ Iraq and Stephenson's principal. (Image from Stephenson family archive)

Stephenson was an accomplished horseman and rode throughout his life; he was an avid polo player and regularly won point-to-point races. (Image from Stephenson family archive)

The 1937 Central Flying School aerobatics team honing their skills ahead of the final RAF Display at Hendon. The Avro Tutors were flown by Flight Lieutenants 'Tubby' Mermagen, Geoffrey Stephenson and Sergeant Colin Scragg. All three would go on to achieve Air rank. (Image copyright of RAF Museum)

King George VI (centre, front) visited the Central Flying School in May 1938. Flight Lieutenant Geoffrey Stephenson is sat front left while his aerobatics partner (and fellow Spitfire squadron commander at Duxford in 1940) 'Tubby' Mermagen is sat front right. Of note, Stephenson would later become the Monarch's *aide-de-camp*. (Image courtesy of CFS Association archive)

On 26 May 1940, Stephenson was flying Spitfire Mark I N3200 on their first operational mission over Dunkirk. After shooting down a Ju 87 Stuka, Stephenson's Spitfire suffered damaged in a dogfight with an Me 109, forcing him to crash-land on the beach at Sangatte. (Image courtesy of George Romain)

After belly-landing on the beach at Sangette, Stephenson's Spitfire would become a tourist attraction for the German occupying forces. Over time, parts of the aircraft would be taken as souvenirs and it slowly sank into the French sands and would not re-emerge until 1986.

The RAF cohort at Colditz during the winter of 1942/43. Bader, as the senior airman, is sat in the centre of the front row while Stephenson is second from the left on the front row. The designers of the 'Colditz Cock' glider are on the flanks of the rear row – Flight Lieutenants Jack Best (right) and Bill Goldfinch (left). (Image from Stephenson family archive)

22 June 1946, Geoffrey and Maureen's wedding day. Front row: Eileen Stephenson (sister), Sir Paul Booth (father-in-law,) Lady Booth (mother-in-law,) Geoffrey, Maureen, Anna (stepdaughter,) Jessica Stephenson (mother). Standing behind Geoffrey is his best man, Douglas Bader, and his wife, Thelma. (Image from Stephenson family archive)

Group Captain Stephenson CBE ADC, circa 1949 as the 23rd Commandant of the Central Flying School. (Image courtesy of CFS Association archives)

The newly-promoted Air Commodore Geoffrey Stephenson CBE ADC and his wife Maureen prepare to attend the coronation of Queen Elizabeth II in June 1953. (Image from Stephenson family archive)

RAF Odiham in July 1953. The newly-crowned Queen Elizabeth II is escorted by Air Commodore Geoffrey Stephenson around the 300 aircraft comprising the static display of the RAF Coronation Review. (Image from Stephenson family archive)

Air Commodore Geoffrey Stephenson CBE ADC in his last post as Commandant of the Central Fighter Establishment based out of RAF West Raynham from July 1953 until his death in November 1954. (Image from Stephenson family archive)

The early Super Sabres (right), as flown by Stephenson on his last flight in November 1954, had a small tail fin. As a result, they were difficult to handle and had a notorious reputation amongst their pilots. Following Stephenson's fatal crash, the USAF grounded the Super Sabre fleet. The aircraft were subsequently modified with a larger tail fin and longer wingspan to improve stability (left). (Image courtesy of NASA)

Under ever-blue skies, Stephenson's final resting place is at the Oakwood Cemetery Annex in Montgomery, Alabama – the largest Commonwealth War Graves Commission site in the United States. (Image from author's collection)

The 2014 'Guy Martin's Spitfire' documentary followed N3200's two-year restoration at Duxford. Guy stands in front of N3200 with its recently installed Merlin III engine and alongside the Aircraft Restoration Company's Hangar Manager, Martin 'Mo' Overall. (Image courtesy of North One Productions)

N3200 is now owned by the Imperial War Museum and flies from Duxford, its original home, thus ensuring Stephenson's legacy is preserved for future generations. The image shows John Romain, the Managing Director of the Aircraft Restoration Company, putting N3200 through its paces at the IWM Duxford Flying Day on 1 August 2022. (Image copyright of Roland Bogush)

censored. For example, it appears all H.G. Wells books are prohibited, as well as all books by Jewish authors. The Commander stated that he has asked the German High Command for permission to give the British a list of books which have been prohibited. (The Embassy will also endeavour to obtain the list.) In addition to the German High Command List, which apparently changes from time to time, the camp authorities also confiscate any books which they censor and find objectionable. For example, they have banned 'Mathematics for the Million' and 'Science for the Citizen,' both by Hogber, because both books contain critical remarks about German people, culture or institution.[42]

Additionally, the Germans removed hardback covers of many books to ensure that escape materials could not be secreted inside the cover and passed on to the prisoners.

Stephenson continued to write letters and postcards to his loved ones back home. He persisted in keeping a meticulous note in his diary of who and when he was sending to and receiving letters from. His mother, siblings and his fiancée, Anne, were all regular correspondents. However, the transfer of mail for RAF officers was significantly slower than that of their army and naval counterparts. The reason for the five to six-week delay was the *Luftwaffe*'s demand for all RAF prisoner mail to be vetted at *Stalag Luft* III.[43] The delay in receiving their mail clearly frustrated the RAF prisoners, and the issue was raised with the Red Cross, but to no avail. In the meantime, the prisoners were given access to another avenue which they fully exploited. 'A very large room on the top-floor (an old theatre) is now at the disposal of the prisoners. There is a ping-pong table, fencing masks and fleurets up there; also a piano.'[44] The theatre housed not only films such as *The Music Maker*, as noted by Stephenson in his diary, but also staged several elaborate theatre productions ranging from 'Ballet Nonsense', 'French Without Tears' and 'The Importance of Being Earnest'. Stephenson criticized the latter as 'too slow but very good'. The Dutch also got involved in putting on a show, including a Caribbean-based escapade. Theatre production was also an excellent cover for escape activities and another location to launch bids for freedom. Overall, the Red Cross team believed that 'indoor recreational facilities at this camp continue to be only satisfactory, in view of the crowded condition of the castle and the large number of different nationalities confined. Sufficient books and games are on hand; some study courses have been organized.[45] Throughout his time in captivity, Stephenson continued to dabble in various languages. At Colditz in mid-1943, he again started learning Spanish, French and Arabic. While there were sufficient opportunities to keep the mind active, there were fewer opportunities for physical activity at Colditz.

The biggest constraint for the prisoners was access to a secure space where guards could watch over them while they exercised. Inside the camp, the courtyard, slightly larger than a tennis court, was all the 500 prisoners had to exercise in; it was simply too cramped for any meaningful exercise. Nevertheless, the prisoners endeavoured to make do, including creating some rather unique sports, including deck tennis, courtyard cricket and stoolball. The latter sport aimed to defend your own stool, gain control of a medicine ball, and place it upon the opponent's stool. There were few rules and numerous injuries; it was most certainly a contact sport.[46]

Theoretically, prisoners were mandated by the Geneva Convention to have two hours of exercise per day. In addition to the courtyard, the prisoners had access to a nearby park located 100m away from the castle. Although the park was of limited utility for ball games due to the numerous tree stumps, 'the British have had permission to go twice a week to the football ground in the town. They go in a party of 25, which makes it possible to have two teams.'[47] Stephenson also highlights that other ball games were available as he 'played Rugger in the town'. However, the Germans could and would 'withdraw privilege at any time, if they do not behave'.[48] The Red Cross reports in October 1942 and April 1943 highlight that this was a regular occurrence. First, 'this privilege was stopped on account of so-called unsoldierly demeanour of some of the officers'.[49] Later, 'the football field has been forbidden as a punishment for the prisoners who whistled at the commander when he appeared in the courtyard to take the daily roll-call'.[50]

The Red Cross team believed that the

general impressions of this camp remain poor. Relations between the prisoners and captors remain bad, with considerable tension and bad feeling on both sides. It is believed that the personality of the Camp Commander has much to do with this situation. Though he can be very charming on occasions, he seems to lack the prisoners' point of view and regards his charges as a group of bad prisoners who have not behaved in other camps, have been sent to him for special watching, and who must therefore be kept under special discipline.[51]

To be fair, the *Kommandant* did have cause for concern.

'The Bad Boys' in Action

For some of Stephenson's compatriots, escape was their sole focus and drove their *modus operandi*. 1941 and 1942 proved to be the zenith for escapes from Colditz. In 1941, there were 25 British escapes; 23 were caught inside the castle and two outside. There were no British home runs in 1941.[52] The international nature of the inmates drove collaboration and friendly competition. Consequently, the British were frustrated with their poor performance compared to their European friends. France led the way with ten 'home runs' from 30 attempts, while the Dutch got four prisoners home and the Poles only one, but critically one more than the Belgians and Brits.[53] Although the geographical advantage lay with those born and brought up on the Continent, it was a disappointing result.

In 1942, the tide began to change, and the British had their first successful escapes and, more importantly, 'home runs'. A more formalised escape committee helped as well as deconfliction and cooperation between the various nations. In early January 1942, the future Member of Parliament, Lieutenant Airey Neave, was the first British officer who made it home. Neave and a Dutch prisoner escaped via the theatre stage and dressed as German guards. A few months later, Stephenson's predecessor as the Senior British Officer at Barth, Squadron Leader Brian 'Auntie' Paddon, made a successful return to the United Kingdom. In September, Flight Lieutenant Bill Fowler escaped via a German guard's office, again working alongside a Dutch officer. The following month Pat Reid made it home with three others.

On reflecting on his time in Colditz in 1942, Stephenson's diary entry in late December 1942 has a register of all the British POWs in the camp. At the end of the list, there is a simple note which says 'To Absent Friends', which lists the names of those who had made it home in 1942. Colditz was not escape-proof, and the British had proved their worth and reputation. However, the last British home run occurred in October 1942, two and a half years before the end of the war. It was not for the lack of trying and invention. The spirit of the British prisoners was personified by one infamous individual who arrived at Colditz in late summer 1942.

The Arrival of Bader

In August 1942, Stephenson was reunited with an old friend.[54] After a year in captivity, Wing Commander Douglas Bader, DSO and Bar, DFC and Bar, arrived at Colditz. There are perhaps two surprising elements to the story. First, Bader had a meteoric rise through the ranks, accelerated by his ability, mentorship and survival. On arrival at Duxford in early 1940, Bader was a lowly Flying Officer, two ranks below Stephenson, when he joined his friend on 19 Squadron. Now a combat veteran and decorated ace, Bader outranked his former squadron commander. The second surprise was that Bader had taken so long to arrive alongside the other 'bad boys' at Colditz. His persistent escape attempts and ability to antagonize his captors were becoming legendary!

After bailing out of his damaged Spitfire over France, Bader was immediately captured and sent to a clinic in nearby St Omer, where he had the audacity to escape via bedsheets tied together and clambered down to the street below. After a brief period on the run, he was re-captured and sent on to *Dulag Luft* outside Frankfurt. He was processed through the *Luftwaffe* interrogation centre and continued his journey to *Oflag* XC at Lübeck – a coastal town north-east of Hamburg. However, Bader's stay on the Baltic coast was brief. 'In October 1941, the whole camp was moved to Warburg, near Cassel', located between Hannover and Frankfurt.[55] Bader moved from *Oflag* VIB in May 1942 to the *Stalag Luft* III camp at Sagan, and would be reunited with his former flight commander from his first tour back in the early 1930s on 23 Squadron, Harry Day. Following his stints as the Senior British Officer at *Dulag Luft* and *Stalag Luft* I, Day reprised the same role at *Stalag Luft* III. However, the reunion was brief, and Bader was transferred to *Stalag* VIIIB at Lamsdorf. Bader was a constant thorn in the Germans' side during his early days as a POW. In his sixth and last POW camp, his attitude did not change!

As Bader entered Colditz Castle for the first time, he was immediately greeted with the following:

> 'Douglas! There you are!' [Bader] swung round. Geoffrey Stephenson, in an old sweater and army trousers, was grinning by the steps. An incredibly warm sight. He looked much the same, though not so dapper, and came bounding up the steps. 'Heard you were shot down. Been expecting you. Knew you wouldn't behave.'[56]

Bader did not take long to continue his antics with the German guards at Colditz. Despite the considerable complexities associated with an escape attempt, Bader was driven and embraced the challenge, irrespective of the risk to himself or his fellow prisoners. 'He had hardly been in Colditz a few weeks when he – a man with no legs from the knee downwards – volunteered for partnership in an escape attempt over the roofs of the Castle!'[57] Bader proposed a three-man escape team comprising himself, Stephenson and Lieutenant Peter Storie-Pugh. However, much to Bader's chagrin, the escape committee turned down his plan. Undeterred by his unsuccessful proposal, Bader continued to harangue those around him. However, these events often had consequences. On 23 December 1942, five people, including Bader, were given five days of solitary confinement for either smoking or shouting during one of the parades. Despite Bader's absence, Stephenson and those remaining in the main camp celebrated Christmas as best they could with a Christmas Eve party. Stephenson's diary entry notes:

> This started at 1845 and finished at 0130. We drank before and during dinner in our own room, and Poles went up to join a party in the English quarters. This was great fun and very gay. We finished off by going to see Wilmet and his table. The French were sitting having a late supper, and there were songs sung and much noise and laughter. We finally came back to the Saalhouse to wish various rooms a merry [original underlined by Stephenson!] Christmas. Got quite lit up.

Christmas Day started with a morning church service and, undoubtedly, a sore head. The rest of the day was more subdued with a group tea and news of the assassination of the Vichy French General Darlan in Algeria. The day culminated with a Christmas dinner at 1930 with the tables adorned with 'very amusing painted place cards. Harry's stories and [Flight Lieutenant Vincent] Bush's [Parker] conjuring were the highlights of the evening.'

Following the Christmas revelry, Stephenson became more contemplative; he reflected on his upbringing and his thoughts on his own post-war plans. His diary entry for 28 December 1942 noted:

thinking about bringing up young people. The aim in life seems to be to direct your efforts towards improving the lot of man for the future, and I got to thinking that the most efficient way to expend effort is tidily and artistically, and children must gradually realise that tidiness and beauty are desirable means to an end. These two standards were instinctive for my mother, but as children, we did not realise why they were worthwhile because they seemed to us ends in themselves. What an amazing force a lesson stamped in during youth has during life if it is workable.

The following day, normal operations resumed. Stephenson's diary for 29 December 1942 recalls that 'Douglas came out of the clink having made friends with all his jailers as usual'. With Bader back in circulation with the rest of the British prisoners, New Year's Eve was never going to be a dull affair. Stephenson's diary entry for 31 December 1942 informs that:

The party in the evening started with an attempt to imbibe the party spirit by drinking the [Squadron Leader Malcolm] McColm brew. Owing to a faulty brew, this was a failure. However, [Flight Lieutenant] 'Bush' Parker's brew over in the other quarters did the trick. Just before Midnight, we went up to the French and there found Douglas, who, having dined with the Poles where he had some 'vodka,' was in very high spirits. Singing national anthems in the [court]yard was the next move. They sounded very fine. Then there was a crocodile around all the yard and through the entire building. It was all a good example of mass excitement. Douglas and I visited the Poles next. They had made their Dining Room like a nightclub – Blankets around the wall, decorated light shades, streamers and flags. The general air was extremely gay. The people were sitting around at small tables. There was a bar in one corner, an orchestra in another. Our companion was a Russian who was very tight but very friendly and amusing except when Russians were mentioned when he became very ferocious and noisy picking up plates and hurling them to the ground and jumping on them. After another visit to the French, where we sang, and then back to the Poles. I got back to my room just after 0200. It certainly was a great evening. The French say 'Bonne Année'.

Stephenson and his multi-national group had every right to celebrate. The British had seven home runs in 1942, the French had five, the Dutch had three and the Belgians had one. Even after a hard night the night before, 1943 started with more celebrations.

Douglas and I went to a French tea party and stayed talking and singing till 2130. The French had turned their beds out of their room and decorated it marvellously – shaded lights, flowers, pictures and flags. The whole character of the room had been changed from a grim barrack to an intimate salon. We sat at small tables eating innumerable spreads and pastries, drinking tea and chocolate and talking. They are all about only one subject, but the tunes are marvellously lively. Douglas was in terrific form and loved by everyone.

The German guards also seemed to have been more tolerant over the Christmas period and made little or no effort to intervene in the prisoners' festive celebrations. There was a distinct sense of optimism from Stephenson and his fellow prisoners over the festive period. Stephenson encapsulated the positivity in his diary. 'And so ended our New Year celebrations, and I hope it is the last time in captivity.' However, the reality was far different. Stephenson would spend another two and a half years, including two further festive seasons, confined to Colditz. With the festive period now complete, the normal routine would return, the antagonistic relationship between the German guards and Allied prisoners continued, and Stephenson would be caught up in the backlash.

Escape Activities and Consequences

In his post-war debrief with MI9, Stephenson notes in the report that he made 'several abortive attempts from *Oflag* IVC'. Alas, the report contains no specific details on the dates, scale and types of escape that Stephenson was involved in. However, the Colditz Official History file does note that Stephenson actively supported escape activities including tunnelling.

Despite the castle's thick walls and bedrock foundation, tunnelling was one form of escape that the prisoners attempted to use to extract themselves from the confines of Colditz. Indeed, the British made 15 escape attempts via tunnels.[58] Sadly, all were unsuccessful. At least 50, or 25 per cent of all, British prisoners were involved in the tunnelling projects in one form or another, including Stephenson.[59] However, the Colditz Official History document from The National Archives file rarely identifies the names of those involved in the specific tunnelling projects. Nevertheless, the document adds detail to nine of the 15 tunnelling projects, eight overlapping with Stephenson's tenure at Colditz.

Following initial issues with deconflicting escape attempts across the various nationalities housed at Colditz, the British escape committee was formed in November 1941. According to the file in the National Archives, the escape committee was initially headed by Lieutenant Colonel George Young rather than Reid. However, Reid was responsible for intelligence.[60] As part of the escape committee, there was a dedicated Tunnelling member. The post was held by Stephenson's roommate, Squadron Leader Malcolm McColm, until May 1943, when the responsibility was handed over to Flight Lieutenant J.C. Wilson.[61]

Tunnelling at Colditz was a complex affair.

Tunnelling in this camp differed from that of any other owing to the fact that it was built on the foundations of a castle. Thus, all tunnelling had to begin with breaking through a floor or wall, which necessitated skilful camouflage of the tunnel entrance. In many cases, rock was encountered during excavations. Whenever an attempt was made to construct a tunnel leading outside the castle, it was necessary to break through the castle wall and the ramparts, both of which were built of stone.[62]

Stephenson makes no direct comment about his support to escape attempts, other than the days he acted as a 'Stooge'. The omission is more likely due to the regular searches of the prisoners' quarters and the possibility that the Germans would seize and analyse his diary. However, in June 1943, there is a cryptic note in his diary which simply says, 'decision to use "tu"'. This could be a reference to the escape committee approving the use of a tunnel?

Stephenson had the ideal diminutive stature to move around and operate within the tunnels. The task was not a simple one. 'The personnel concerned with tunnelling activity displayed remarkable ingenuity and tenacity. The fact that the camp was in a castle, built of stone on a foundation of rock, made their task much more difficult than was experienced in the majority of POW camps.'[63] However, the Germans were equally agile and innovative. As was the case at the other camps, 'Electric sound detectors were used throughout the period and POWs found it impossible to do any tunnelling without the Germans at once being aware of it, the immediate result being increased vigilance on the part of the *Abwehr* and frequent searches of the POW quarters.'[64] Once found, the repair bill was usually quite steep, and the Germans were not averse to penalising the culprits. For example, for the 12,000 Reichmarks worth of damage caused during the tunnel escape in the castle's chapel, each prisoner was deducted 27 Reichmarks from their pay.[65]

While the tunnels may not have led to an escape or a 'home run', they did keep both the prisoners and the guards busy. Consequently, it distracted the prisoners from the reality they faced, kept them physically and mentally sharp and, perhaps most importantly, gave them hope. The tunnelling projects also distracted the Germans; their limited resources were pulled in multiple directions. As a result of the deluge of escape attempts, it was inevitable that some escapes would be successful and ultimately lead to several 'home runs'. It is no coincidence that most of the tunnelling projects occurred in 1942 and 1943, the same timeframe that saw seven British 'home runs'. Stephenson's support of the escape franchise may not have led directly to his or another prisoner's escape. However, by simply being there and being involved in escape activities, he indirectly supported those who made it back to Blighty.

Early 1943 – The End of the Beginning

Bader was not the only one to fall foul of the German authorities at Colditz. Scattered throughout Stephenson's various Colditz diaries are brief notes and mentions about him being sent to solitary confinement – either in the Castle or the jail in town. Although the reason for Stephenson's punishment is rarely mentioned, it would appear that the events were for relatively minor infractions. Some periods lasted for a couple of days while others lasted a week or two, not the month-long sentences associated with escape attempts.

Parades or *appels* were held between two to four times per day based upon the level of nefarious activity by the prisoners. The *appels* took place in the prisoners' courtyard where the prisoners formed a hollow square. 'The British contingent were drawn up in files of five, later reduced to three, in parties representing each floor of their quarters.'[66] The prisoners were then counted to ensure all were present. Each prisoner had their own space to stand during the *appel*. Therefore, 16 months into his tenure at Colditz, it is surprising that Stephenson was penalised for a minor infraction. Stephenson's diary entry for 24 January 1943 states that 'I went to the town "cooler" for seven days for standing in the wrong place on parade'. However, the Colditz History file highlights the rationale for Stephenson's apparent oversight or ambivalence.

> The covering up of POWs who had escaped or were engaged in subversive activities was done by the transfer of one or more men from one party to another so that they could be counted twice. The POWs often upset the counting by changing places with other nationalities on the parade ground which meant that they had to be segregated before another count could be affected. All this took up a great deal of the Germans' time and harassed them considerably.[67]

It would appear that Stephenson's actions indirectly supported escape attempts and applied pressure on the German security apparatus.

Irrespective of the cause, Stephenson headed off to solitary confinement. His diary not only highlights the reason for his jailing, but he also writes about what he did during his solitary confinement. While most of Stephenson's activities will come as no surprise, we already know from his previous time at *Dulag Luft* and *Stalag Luft* I that Stephenson was an avid reader and liked to learn languages. However, perhaps revealing is what he was thinking about during his period of isolation. Consequently, Stephenson was, perhaps understandably, looking to the future again.

Whilst there I read 'The Brothers Karamazov' by Dostoevsky, played patience, read some French, wrote two letters – one home and one to Anne and did a bit of thinking about things. The Brothers Karamazov is a stupendous book, which I was better able to appreciate for having listened to the French Padre [a lecture a few days previously] and for having met Poles and Russians. It is an amazing study of the inner depths of the minds of some of the characters. Then again, the conflicting beliefs according to which these characters try to work out their lives is interesting. The popular opinion and people of the time are wonderfully realistically portrayed. I felt that his Russians had a tremendous upsurge of energy which was going to waste undirected. I thought about what I would tell a child of mine and how I thought about everyday life and what was needed to allow one to make the best of oneself. I think I have got the answers to lots of the uncertainties of life, and I wondered if these will seem very real when I get back into life and how much, in any case, I would hand on. I thought of the need to be aware of more and more of one's surroundings and how an attitude of wonder is a balancing factor in one's opinions. The best sequence of events in learning is the friction of events followed by an analysis of them aided by the wise advice of a good teacher. I certainly hope that Mummy will be able to answer some of my questions about Daddy. He was very inarticulate towards me about his inner feelings and beliefs. Also, I hope that Anne will be sympathetic with my tendency to inspect experiences, analyse them and produce theories to work on. But, I hope she brings me down to practical things and makes me decide on a direction to follow.

As Stephenson returned to the Castle from the town's jail, accommodation was becoming increasingly strained. The January 1943 Red Cross visit noted that the British contingent had grown to 99 officers and 12 orderlies. Moreover, despite the apparent relaxation during the festive period, the atmosphere within the camp remained toxic. 'The impression this camp gives is not pleasant. One feels that there is a very strained atmosphere resulting from the frantic wish on one side to escape and on the other the stern decision to prevent this.'[68] Stephenson's diary entry for 13 April 1943 reinforces the prisoner's collective frustration about their treatment during a visit by the Red Cross delegation. 'Many complaints about underhand, immoral and unjust behaviour done in a spiteful spirit. Polish money, parcels and clothes thefts during searches. Letters to Swiss and OKW [*Oberkommando der Wehrmacht* or German High Command] held up. In this camp, many things are withheld because they are considered as privileges.' The Red Cross report from the visit reflects several of Stephenson's concerns.

> The Theatre has been closed for two months because of sabotage, some panelling having been removed by the POWs. The spirit in this camp is still rather bad; the material conditions are not very satisfactory by the camp commander following the numerous attempts to escape as well as those of sabotage (closing of the theatre, park and football ground, 4 roll-calls a day, lights out at 10 or 10.30 pm) certainly don't contribute to ease the strained atmosphere. The camp authorities on the one side and the POWs on the other are daily stiffening in their attitude and it is difficult to see a way out of this tense atmosphere.[69]

Something had to be done. The Germans would make a significant alteration that changed the dynamic within the Castle.

The Germans enacted the much-needed change during the summer of 1943. It was decided that the British prisoners would remain at Colditz, and further British prisoners would be added while the French, Belgian, Dutch and Polish officers would be moved to other camps. Stephenson's diary notes on 6 June 1943, exactly a year before the Normandy landings, that he attended a Dutch farewell party before they departed on Tuesday 8 June 1943. His diary also informs that the French and Belgians left for Lübeck in two groups on 8 and 12 July 1943. Stephenson missed the international flavour within the castle, particularly the French contribution. Stephenson's diary entry for 8 July 1943 laments the departure of the French contingent as 'a loss as they pick out the amusing things in life to talk about and are wickedly witty'. The void was filled in mid-June with two new batches, the first group arriving from

Spangenberg. Stephenson notes in his diary that 'Second batch from [*Oflag*] VIIB [in Eichstatt in Bavaria] come in, including Canadian VC Colonel.'[70] The last big move was the Poles who departed Colditz for Lübeck on 10 and 23 August 1943. Stephenson attended a tea party to celebrate with the Poles the day before the first group transferred.

The group dynamic was not the only change at Colditz. Stephenson's diary during this period reflects the Allies' slow, steady and indirect approach via the Mediterranean. On 13 May, Stephenson highlights 'Fall of Tunis', followed on 11 June 1943 with the note that 'Pantelleria fell' and two days later 'Lampedusa fell'. In one diary entry, Stephenson identifies his source of information when he suggests 'German rumour re landing in Sicily (this is true)'. Stephenson added the parenthesis in his diary! However, the British were starting to get their intelligence from another source rather than the newspapers or via the German guards. Stephenson's later diaries became increasingly focused on the Allied advances in the Mediterranean and the East. Although the land battles were still some way away from Colditz, other aspects of the war were getting ever closer. In his 11 June 1943 diary entry, Stephenson notes 'air raid warning twice during previous night'. It would become a regular comment in his diaries, and the bombing a more brutal affair, leading to one of the most controversial raids of the war, not far from Colditz and during the last few months of the war. The Allied noose was tightening on Nazi Germany, but, frustratingly, for the British prisoners that sense of hope would take another two years to come to fruition.

Despite the personnel changes, some things inevitably stayed the same. Food remained a problem. A Red Cross report from mid-1943 reinforced the continuing problem. 'The food is bad and insufficient, especially the beetroots, which are almost uneatable.'[71] There were no fresh vegetables, and the prisoners only had spinach twice in five months![72] Stephenson's diary shows the extremes the prisoners were willing to go to enhance their diet. 'Cat dies – autopsy carried out and later dissected.' One can only imagine what the dissection actually meant.

Another certainty during this period was the continued escape attempts. Stephenson's diary highlights several attempts. The diary entry for 11 June 1943 notes that 'attempt via quarters, foiled by wires in the roof'. A later entry records, '[Flight Lieutenant Dominic] Bruce and [Lieutenant Charles] Elwell [Royal Navy] caught in store'. Undoubtedly, Bruce's subsequent punishment would be a small part of his eight months in solitary confinement. Despite the volatile lifestyle, some aspects were so normal that they stand out as borderline bizarre. One example occurred in June 1943 where there is a simple annotation in Stephenson's diary that stated 'watch sent to Rolex for repair'. The watch was duly repaired in Switzerland and returned to Stephenson at Colditz a couple of months later.

August 1943 started well after a much-needed morale-boosting sight for a bunch of red-blooded males couped up in prison without female company. Stephenson's diary entry for 1 August simply states, 'four girls in bathing dresses on a balcony'. Some of the prisoners' dormitories overlooked the town below, and aided by a homemade telescope, the prisoners could take full advantage of the views before them. However, and not linked to the above incident, Stephenson had once fallen foul of his German captors. His diary entry for 18 August 1943 states bluntly 'put into security arrest'. The incident must have been minor, as he was released the next day. However, his diary notes that 'Germans took two great coats'. As it was summer, the loss of the heavy wool coats was unlikely to have been a significant issue.

With the Poles now departed, Colditz contained 228 British and a few Free French officers; the overcrowding issue was literally halved.[73] Consequently, and as highlighted in the Red Cross report, 'the rooms previously occupied by officers of other nationalities are now being cleaned and whitewashed then some of the British officers will be moved into them, and that will give more space in the rooms and improve the sanitary conditions'.[74] It was all change at Colditz. More good news would follow in September.

> The largest consignment of Red Cross parcels ever arrived consisting of 2000 British Red Cross parcels, 45 Tobacco parcels, 40 of invalid comforts, 8 surgical, one of 200 tins of tooth powder, one of 144 rolls of toilet paper, plus sugar from Buenos Aires and coffee from Venezuelan Red Cross. The store of food parcels had now reached 5000, estimated at five months' supply at one per head per week. The impression was anticipating a period of disorganised transport to Germany.[75]

However, angst remained, and escape attempts continued. Stephenson's diary entry for 2 September 1943 comments 'Sinclair as Franz Josef. Sinclair shot in hysterical flap. Given no attention.' Lieutenant Mike Sinclair was shot during a brazen escape attempt when he tried to walk out of the camp dressed as a well-known German guard known as 'Franz Josef'. Despite his injuries, Sinclair made a miraculous recovery and returned to the camp three days later, on 5 September 1943.[76]

The make-up and atmosphere at Colditz had changed through Stephenson's first two years at the Castle. The cosmopolitan, international but chaotic life had settled down into a British-centric institution. However, frustration lingered, not helped by the German attitude. As noted by the Red Cross team, 'life in this camp, under the prevailing conditions, has become almost unbearable. Conclusion – *Oflag* IVC appears to be a bad camp, on account of the present commandant, and particularly in regard to the way which discipline is maintained.'[77] Three years into Stephenson's captivity across three very different POW camps, he was only too aware that the experience was leaving an indelible mark upon him. In June 1943, his diary comments 'how one's views and ideas have changed in 3 years'. Little did he know that although the tide was beginning to turn in favour of the Allies, it would be another two years before he was back home on British soil.

Life Beyond Colditz

During Stephenson's initial period in Colditz, the 12 pilots from 19 Squadron that he had led over Dunkirk in May 1940 continued to diminish further. Squadron Leader Brian 'Sandy' Lane was one of the 19 Squadron flight commanders and had stepped up to take command of the unit after Stephenson's crash-landing on the beach at Calais. After a year of staff duties in the United Kingdom and the Middle East, Lane returned to command a training unit in the United Kingdom from mid-1942. He returned to operations on 7 December 1942 and flew with 167 Squadron flying Spitfire Mark Vs based at Ludham in Norfolk. However, on 13 December 1942 and on his first operational sortie with the new unit, Lane was posted as 'missing in action'. He was last seen chasing after two Focke-Wulf Fw 190 fighters over the North Sea. The RAF had lost a highly regarded as well as experienced fighter pilot, ace and leader.

'Wilf' Clouston was the other flight commander on 19 Squadron during Stephenson's time in command of the unit in early 1940. Clouston, from

New Zealand, served throughout the Battle of Britain with 19 Squadron and achieved ace status, eventually accruing nine confirmed kills. He would command his own fighter squadron, of Hurricanes, in November 1940. However, aware of the growing Japanese threat, Clouston was sent out to the Far East in September 1941. He initially commanded a New Zealand fighter squadron before moving into a staff appointment in Singapore. However, he was captured by the Japanese in Singapore in February 1942 and would spend the rest of the war as a Japanese prisoner. It would be fair to say that his POW experiences were significantly different to those of Stephenson. Despite the hardships, Clouston survived the ordeal.

Flying Officer Frank Brinsden was another Kiwi who served on 19 Squadron during the Battle of France. On 26 May 1940, Brinsden flew as Yellow 2 on Brian Lane's wing. He fought during the Battle of Britain. However, on 31 August 1940, he was forced to bail out of his Spitfire when his aircraft was hit by a Messerschmitt Me 110. After various training and operational appointments, Brinsden flew De Havilland Mosquitoes in the night-fighter role. On 17 August 1943, Brinsden was the captain of a Mosquito FB Mark VI from 25 Squadron, supporting bombers raiding Peenemunde – the German V-rocket research facility. However, as he was attacking a German airfield, he was detected and blinded by searchlights. With his vision almost lost, he headed out to sea but struck the water's surface. Incredibly, Brinsden and his navigator escaped unhurt but were eventually captured. Brinsden would be held at *Stalag Luft* III for the rest of the war.

By the end of summer 1943, of the original 12 pilots from 19 Squadron who took part in Stephenson's 26 May 1940 morning mission, three had been killed in action, and another five were POWs. The war still had another 20 months to run, and the toll would only increase further.

As Stephenson was settling into life at Colditz, a tragic and seemingly unconnected pilot training incident occurred several thousand miles away at Maxwell Field, Montgomery, Alabama. Even before the US entered the Second World War, the RAF was keen to bolster its aircrew cadre to feed the front line as it grew, provide respite for the combat veterans, and mitigate the growing number of combat losses. Due to improved weather conditions and safe training airspace, much of the aircrew training was conducted overseas in Canada, South Africa and the United States. Consequently, as part of the Lend-Lease Act of March 1941, the United States Army Air Corps agreed to offer the Royal Air Force one-third of its pilot training capacity. As a result, the first RAF trainee pilots arrived in Alabama in the summer of 1941. Over 2,000 RAF cadets would pass through training at Gunter and Maxwell Fields from June 1941 to March 1943, when the British training programme culminated. Pilot training is a high-risk proposition for both students and instructors. As a result, there were the inevitable accidents.

November 13th 1941 was a typical autumnal day in Alabama, and the skies were clear and bright. It was a perfect day to go flying, and two RAF trainee pilots were scheduled to undertake another sortie of their advanced flying phase. Leading Aircraftsman (LAC) Frank Marhoff was unusual because he was older than his peers and married. Marhoff was 29, a former civilian clerk and infantryman. His wife, Viona, and two young daughters were back in Hertfordshire, north of London. In contrast, LAC Richard Moss was more typical of the RAF flight cadets. Moss was a mere 20 years old, a former bookkeeper from Preston in north-west England. The two pilots, flying solo in their own two-seat advanced trainer variants of the T-6 Texan/Harvard but flying in two different formations, collided in mid-air two miles south-west of Maxwell Field while returning to the airfield. Both were killed instantly. They were the first RAF fatalities buried at the bare plot allocated to the Commonwealth War Graves Commission site at the Oakwood Cemetery Annex in downtown Montgomery. Over the next 18 months, there would be a further 76 British fatalities. Unfortunately, they would not be the last RAF airmen to be buried at the cemetery, but the next event was over a decade away.

The toll was not only paid by the military personnel; it was also a burden shared by those conducting more nefarious activities. Indeed, the Special Operations Executive agents like Jean François Mennesson did not have the same protections as the uniformed POWs. Nevertheless, Mennesson and his ilk were more than willing and able to accept those risks. Mennesson's training had gone well, and by March 1942, he was ready to be inserted back into his country of birth.[78] However, it cannot have been an easy decision; after a whirlwind romance, he had only just married Maureen a few months earlier, in November 1941. They had also set up their first home together in Maureen's home town of Burnham-on-Crouch, a small village on the Essex coast. By the time of his departure, Maureen would also have been approximately four months pregnant. Mennesson was consciously leaving behind his new bride and their unborn child.

Despite the considerable distractions, Mennesson focused on the task at hand. In Mennesson's file held at The National Archives, Major General Gubbins describes Mennesson's first mission into France.

> Landed by sea on 22 March 1942 with a propaganda and intelligence mission in Southern France, and for five days after his arrival, he was unable to make contact with the organiser who was to have received him. By his ability and diplomacy, he obtained an important position in the '*Secours National*' in the Rhône department which gave him excellent facilities for carrying out his task. He travelled a great deal and spent some time at Vichy where he sent important information to London via W/T [Wireless Telegraphy]. Pursued by the *Gestapo*, he was eventually arrested in June 1943 and stood up to severe interrogation and brutal treatment with outstanding courage and coolness. He escaped from prison in July 1943 and returned to England via Spain.[79]

Gubbins may have exaggerated Mennesson's final few weeks in France. A separate report suggests that German authorities took him from a train in Paris for further questioning when he gave the guards the slip. Nevertheless, Mennesson arrived back in the United Kingdom on 2 September 1943, some 18 months after the start of the mission and just over a year after the birth of his daughter, Anna.[80] Incredibly, and despite becoming a person of interest to the *Gestapo*, he volunteered to return to his country of birth for another mission. On 15 November 1943, a mere two months after the completion of his first mission, Mennesson said goodbye again to his wife and young daughter and headed back to France for his second undercover mission. On this occasion, he was successfully inserted by air from a Lockheed Hudson which flew from RAF Tempsford in Bedfordshire to the landing ground codenamed 'Achille,' located near the town of Soucelles in north-west France.[81] Ominously, nothing was heard from him after his successful insertion into France. When confirmation of Mennesson's status finally reached the United Kingdom, it was not good news.

Chapter 9

Oflag IVC, Colditz – The British Years, October 1943 to April 1945

The Beginning of the End

The Red Cross files from late 1943 paint a rather bleak picture at Colditz. In an interview with the Senior British Officer and an unnamed Royal Navy Lieutenant, the Swiss delegation noted that they were 'stubborn characters, embittered due to long imprisonment and humiliations, however with unbroken spirit and morale. They received the delegate with cordial hospitality, a pleasure to meet such men.'[1] As the winter approached in a cold, dank castle, the prisoners' morale would not have been bolstered by the prospect of their coal ration being cut down to one-third of what it was the previous year.[2] Even the British history of Colditz highlights the waning morale, but it identifies two different causes.

> A slight lowering of morale was noticeable in the camp during the winter of 1943/1944 due largely to the failure of many carefully laid plans for escape on which numbers of POWs had worked for long hours; it was also due to the removal of the foreigners from the camp when the British POWs missed the rivalry of escaping interests and political differences which had arisen among the different nationalities.[3]

The British may have had more physical space in the castle's confines without their European compatriots, but they missed the camaraderie and competition that the eclectic group brought.

Stephenson's first entry to his 1944 pocket diary reinforces the downbeat atmosphere in the castle. In pencil, he scribbles that the 1944 New Year celebrations were 'very tame after previous years'. Although the New Year celebrations were more subdued than the wilder, international affair of earlier years, 1944 had much to offer Stephenson and his fellow prisoners. However, it would appear that being a captive was a zero-sum game. With every win, there seemed to be an inevitable loss. Nevertheless, the risk always seemed worth the reward for many who had been in stasis for an extended period. 1944 started well for the prisoners. However, by autumn, escape attempts would be forbidden by British authorities. Additionally, they were slowly starving; each prisoner's daily ration was down to a mere 1,300 calories per day by the end of the year.[4] Without two of their main ingredients for morale, Stephenson and his fellow prisoners would face a rollercoaster ride during their last 18 months in captivity.

Underpinning the team's upbeat morale throughout the period was the knowledge that the war was tipping in favour of the Allies. In addition to the national trait of constantly talking about the weather, Stephenson's 1944 diary is littered with the Allies' progress. Throughout the diary, Stephenson notes the number and timing of air-raid sirens. Not only does the frequency of the raids increase as the war progresses, but sirens are occurring both night and day. The seemingly continuous nature of aerial bombardment reflects the US Army Air Force's propensity to strike during the day while the RAF's Bomber Command attacked by night. During one daytime raid on 7 July 1944, Stephenson comments on seeing 'many high bombers and [a] group [of] Mosquitoes'. Stephenson's Mosquito comment is interesting as he had never seen the two-seat, multi-role De Havilland Mosquito before. The 'Wooden Wonder's' first flight occurred on 25 November 1940, some six months after Stephenson had been shot down and captured. The technology and character of the war were changing rapidly. Nevertheless, within 18 months, Stephenson would be flying in a Mosquito. However, that was still a long way off.

The progress of the war was also evident on the ground. Stephenson's 1944 diary highlights Russian advances as they pushed west through Ukraine and Belarus and onwards towards Romania and Poland. The Italian campaign is referenced, including the fall of Rome, and the Normandy landings appear by the middle of the year. The diary maps the progress from Caen, St Malo and the Allied push into the Low Countries. Even US advances in the Pacific are mentioned. The information is timely and accurate, although place names are often misspelt. This is a strange oversight, as Stephenson often suggests that the comments are taken from German newspapers. While German newspapers were available, the news appeared to be more Allied-centric rather than based on German propaganda. A more plausible source also accounts for the misspelling of the various foreign place names. As the Colditz official history explains, 'morale rose rapidly during the last 12 months owing to the advance of the Allies which was available to the POWs by the means of a secret radio receiver'.[5]

The Colditz history file suggests that the 'British POWs were not in possession of a wireless receiver until the summer of 1943 when the French left the camp and handed over to them their AC-mains receiver . . . in the autumn of 1943, a small AC-mains wireless receiver reached the camp from [MI9]. This wireless was never used because the first wireless was in operation by this time and considered to be a better receiver.'[6] However, Pat Reid refers to a third radio, including one discovered by the Germans in early 1943. Thankfully, the later radios, known as Arthur II and Arthur III, were never found.[7] The report goes on to inform us that:

the radio receiver was hidden in a cabin in the attic of the *Kellerhaus* in a small cabin hollowed out of the wall. Approach to it was through a small, camouflaged trap door which led into the eaves of the castle. From here, there was a drop down between the outer wall of the castle and the inner wall of the attic, which was a false wall built by the POWs. The radio was hidden in a cabin in the outer wall. Only the radio operators and the POWs, whose task it was to let the operators in and out of the trapdoor, knew where the radio was kept. Although the Germans were aware of its existence and spent a great deal of time searching for it, they were unsuccessful.[8]

Coincidentally, the availability of the former French radio also corresponds to the increased number of comments in Stephenson's diary on the developing strategic situation. He not only devoured the news streaming out from the clandestine radio, but his diary entry for 10 January 1944 suggests more. His note 'working at wireless' infers he was also involved in operating the radio or gathering and potentially disseminating the information.

Throughout 1944, the Colditz theatre was a hive of artistic and nefarious activity. Located in the *Saalhaus,* the theatrical productions were elaborate affairs, and a new show was put on every few weeks.[9] In addition to the amateur dramatics, 'a small orchestra was formed under Lieutenants J.W. Beaumont and J.M. Courtenay, which produced a certain amount of entertainment once or twice a week. Instruments were brought by POWs from other camps and obtained from the International Red Cross Society. A few were brought from the canteen.'[10]

For those involved in the production and rehearsals, the preparation and practice consumed time and energy from the reality that they were living in. Their endeavours brought a smile and the occasional laugh to their audience, a pleasant diversion from the strain of being a POW if even only for a couple of hours every fortnight or so. Stephenson was a regular attendee at the shows, and his diaries often commented on the show's quality. Most of his comments were lavish in their praise, but he was not averse to criticizing a performance that did not quite hit the usual standard.

The shows were a collection of contemporary comic plays, thrillers, traditional festive pantomimes, recitals, and homemade cabarets. However, not all of the events went off without a hitch. For example, Patrick Hamilton's 1929 play 'Rope' had its opening night delayed. Stephenson noted in his diary on 16 January 1944 that the 'Play "Rope" was postponed due to a light failure'. However, the show must go on, and 24 hours later, Stephenson noted that despite its dark storyline, 'the play was excellent'. The March show was another Patrick Hamilton play, 'Duke in Darkness', a psychological drama set during the French wars of religion.[11] Rather appositely, the play dealt with imprisonment, survival, and escape. Over the next few months, the productions had a lighter, more comedic focus. On 21 April 1944, Noel Coward's 1941 comic play was well received by Stephenson. '"Blithe Spirit" – a wonderful show'. More comedy plays followed, including 'The Man who Came to Dinner' and 'George and Margaret'. Nevertheless, another Coward comic production on 6 August 1944 was critiqued by Stephenson, 'went to play "Hay Fever" – not as good as previous'. However, this was not the norm; the remaining plays that year generated rave reviews from Stephenson. The 1935 comedy farce 'Three Men on a Horse' was 'great fun'. Likewise, on 22 October 1944, Stephenson was fulsome in his praise for the production of a 1938 Patrick Hamilton thriller. 'The play "Gas Light" was wonderful, props, room and lighting also dresses.' The year ended with traditional Christmas fayre, a 'very creditable' concert and a pantomime. The Christmas 1944 pantomime was another home-grown affair entitled 'Hey Diddle Snow White'.[12] The plays continued into early 1945.[13]

Another more cerebral group activity that continued during the period was the series of lectures given by the prisoners. Stephenson participated as both a student and teacher. He also showed off his new-found language skills by lecturing on the theory of flight in French. A broad array of lectures was available covering diverse topics such as The Evolution of the British Empire and Commonwealth, The Beveridge Plan, The Geneva Convention, Wireless, Physics and Physiology. In the physical realm, sport was an enduring pastime. However, the demand to play the competitive, rough-and-tumble sport of 'Stoolball' waned with the departure of the international cohort.[14] Stephenson's diary regularly mentions the playing of its replacement – 'Dolly Ball'. Although not as physical as its predecessor, 'Dolly Ball' was a derivation of basketball and played at high speed. The sport was also the subject of one of William Faithfull Anderson's many watercolours from his time at Colditz. Several of his paintings are held in the Imperial War Museum archives, including a portrait of Stephenson. Ultimately, sport kept the prisoners busy, keeping them fit and working as a team as well as out of the infirmary with the inevitable 'Stoolball'-related injuries.

When it all became too much, the prisoners could always turn to alcohol or something vaguely resembling it. In the early days at Colditz, beer was available to purchase, but it soon became a thing of the past in mid-1941.[15] Consequently, the prisoners quickly created their own alcoholic concoction. Known colloquially as 'firewater,' the brew was made from sugar and sultanas, currants or dried figs, all obtained from Red Cross parcels.[16] Later, the brew was refined using the German-supplied jam made from sugar-beet waste and dyed red. The foul-smelling ferment tasted of old rubber tyres.[17] Despite its shortcomings, 'Jam-Alc', as it was known, was popular and potent. According to his diary, Stephenson partook in drinking the concoction. 'Drank some of the wine.' Of note, this was Stephenson's only diary entry for that day . . .

Another reason for the prisoners' increased morale in early 1944 was the plentiful access to Red Cross parcels. Previously, the supply of the parcels was somewhat erratic. However, by 1944 the Red Cross stockpile was in a very healthy state. As highlighted in their July 1944 report, the Red Cross delegates noted that the camp had a reserve of 5,617 parcels, sufficient for the current strength to receive a parcel per week for 19 weeks or, in other words, to the end of the year.[18] The prisoners had no significant complaints regarding food during this period. Nevertheless, there was a point made by the Red Cross team that would prove prescient. 'The ration provided by the Detaining Power would, of course, be quite inadequate were it not augmented by Red Cross Parcels.'[19] While the situation in mid-1944 looked promising, it was fragile.

The November 1944 report highlights a rapidly declining stockpile of 862 parcels that had not been replenished in the interim. The February 1945 report was even more damning. 'Since April 1944, the *Oflag* IVC has not received any consignment of additional Red Cross supplies. Prisoners have been on a half-parcel per week. Since 11 September to 13 December [1944] when they came to an end of Red Cross parcels altogether. From that date, they depend exclusively to the rations supplied by the Detaining Power, which may be considered to be completely inadequate.'[20] The Red Cross understood the reality that the prisoners 'get their nourishment . . . almost exclusively from the foodstuffs in the Red Cross Parcels'.[21] 1945 was going to be a challenging year for the prisoners; without access to Red Cross parcels, they would have to rely upon the notoriously poor-quality German food: the weekly menu for January 1945 is shown in Table 9A. To make matters worse, their already parlous ration was reduced even further. Moreover, the bread ration was cut by 200g per week and potatoes by 150g per day; the loss was offset by introducing the same weight in millet and peas.[22]

Nevertheless, the prisoners were now slowly starving, and even if they had the intent and were authorized, their ability to sustain an escape attempt was questionable. Many prisoners spent their last few months in captivity fighting hunger from their beds as they simply had no energy to do anything else. In 1945, the battle in Colditz was no longer about escaping or eradicating boredom; it was now increasingly becoming a battle against hunger.

The prisoners' morale was fragile; it required constant attention and effort to maintain it. Their morale undoubtedly ebbed and flowed throughout the war based on a variety of factors, both internal and external. In early 1944, the Red Cross noted a significant shift in the dynamic within the Castle. 'The tense atmosphere has greatly relaxed. No incidents, such as threats or ill-treatment, have occurred since last visit on October 13, 1943. There appears to exist a better understanding, at least a spirit of mutual toleration. A happy achievement.'[23] However, that peace was short-lived. The prisoners continued baiting their guardians which would cause reprisals. In their May 1944 report, the Red Cross delegate recounted that 'the young prisoners naturally try and succeed in keeping up their morale by acts which are admittedly childish. I am convinced, however, that this would all cease if the prisoners were provided with the exercises and recreation facilities in other camps.'[24] While the delegate's comment has some merit, it is perhaps naïve to suggest that one simple solution would fix the problem. As an example of the prisoners' intransigence, the Red Cross team noted that 'the prisoners make havoc with the material equipment of the camp. During the delegate's visit, someone came to inform the German commandant that a whole bed (including the wooden frame and all the bedding) had just disappeared.'[25] Something had to be done to curtail the prisoners' enthusiasm. However, the inevitable German backlash would only inflame the situation further. Beyond the individual penalties, the Germans also imposed group reprisals. Electricity and water would be denied. For example, 'baths were stopped for 5 months owing to the stealing of German equipment'.[26] Beyond utilities, the prisoners' ability to conduct physical exercise was also curtailed when the courtyard and sports field were closed. The chapel and theatre were also susceptible to embargo. In isolation, the events were frustrating but not definitive. However, there would be an accumulated toll.

Table 9A – Colditz Prisoner's Weekly Ration for January 1945.[27]

Day	Breakfast	Lunch	Dinner
Mon	4g Coffee Substitute	400g Potatoes 600g Turnip	20g Jam Substitute 300g bread
Tues			
Weds			
Thurs			
Fri			20g Jam Substitute 300g bread 31.25g Cheese
Sat		400g Potato 75g Millet 112.5g Peas 62.5g Oats 68g Cooking Fat 37.5g Barley	20g Jam Substitute 175g Sugar 300g Bread 175g Jam
Sun	3.5g Coffee Substitute	350g Potatoes 250g Fresh Meat 600g Turnips	30g Jam Substitute 425g Bread

As noted by the Swiss visitors, the net result was that 'the strict discipline and the permanent feeling of friction between the German authorities and the officer prisoners does not make the camp a very agreeable one'.[28] Colditz was a dilemma, a point aptly brought out during the Red Cross testimony from October 1944.

> The great majority of the prisoners live in a state of discontent, the chief causes are the long-term captivity under extremely harsh measures and lack of recreational facilities. It must be borne in mind that these prisoners represent an excellent elite of remarkably strong characters, stubborn, proud and uncompromising. On the other hand, they live in a medieval castle, situated on an elevated position, commanding a beautiful view on the surrounding country.[29]

Despite their idyllic surroundings and increasing hardships, the British prisoners continued to provoke their captors. In response, the Red Cross emissary believed that 'it is the deliberate intention of the German authorities to subject the POWs detained in *Oflag* IVC to harsh and arbitrary treatment which in many cases is likely to have a lasting effect on the health of those concerned'.[30] Some British prisoners' physical and mental health deteriorated quicker than others.

As the prisoners' stay became extended with no end in sight and exacerbated by a poor diet, their physical and mental health began to suffer. In one of their later reports, the Protecting Power noted that 'four cases occurred of POWs who were not equal to stand up to the strain of their enforced captivity. These men were removed to Sick Quarters and finally to a Sanatorium.'[31] Although not solely an RAF issue, Tunstall reflects on why several airmen incarcerated at Colditz were susceptible to mental health issues during their captivity: 'they were the "free spirits" rather than the stolid, stoic, severely disciplined soldiers of spit and polish, ceremony, dignity and indifference about trench warfare, or the salty, tar-encrusted, "Hearts of Oak" sailors.'[32] In addition to the mental health issues, the physically-weakened prisoners were also vulnerable to numerous ailments. Stephenson's diaries make several comments about his bed-ridden messmates who frequently suffer from minor disorders. Moreover, the Red Cross noted that there was 'a decided increase in nervousness, insomnia, and dyspepsia. There was an attack of a mild type of influenza which had affected 50 per cent of the strength.'[33] The Colditz prisoners were a weakening cohort who were becoming increasingly vulnerable.

Escape Attempts

Although they may have been physically weakened, most prisoners remained mentally attuned to their environment. Central to the prisoners' morale was their ability and desire to challenge their opponent. The most direct and effective way of competing with them was via continued escape activities. Stephenson's 1944 diary articulates the constant struggle. His entries are becoming bolder when compared with his earlier war diaries. He starts to give greater insights into what is happening within the camp. Stephenson was always aware that the guards could be take his diaries as part of the regular searches of prisoners' quarters. Consequently, he had to be careful about what he wrote to not compromise himself or his fellow prisoners. Nevertheless, Stephenson would regularly start to comment on escape attempts. On 19 January 1944, during the week he was acting as 'stooge', Stephenson highlights the 'brilliant escape by Barnes and Sinclair'. There are a couple of interesting points to come out of this comment. First, this escape attempt is a mere three months since Sinclair's shooting during a previous escape attempt, but Sinclair remains undeterred. Second, there is no record of a British prisoner named 'Barnes' at Colditz at the time. Is Stephenson mistaken? No, it is merely a bit of deliberate misdirection and recognition of a well-executed plan. 'Barnes' was, in fact, Flight Lieutenant Jack Best, who had been at Colditz since September 1942 and was well known to Stephenson. However, in April 1943, Best volunteered to become a 'ghost', an individual secreted away within Colditz by his fellow prisoners and away from prying German eyes. From a German perspective, Best had escaped and was no longer on their books. To mask later escape attempts, Best would be brought out from hiding to make up the correct prisoner numbers during *appels* before being hidden away again. With his morale starting to ebb, Best's 'ghost' role was terminated, and he was selected for the escape attempt with Sinclair. At dusk and with the 'stooges' confirming that all was clear, Sinclair and Best/Barnes escaped from the quarters and scrambled down the outside of the castle via a rope made from bedsheets to the terrace below. After a quick run across the terrace, another makeshift rope was required to clamber down the final descent to the orchard. They were out and now on the run. However, their freedom was short-lived; they were recaptured on the Dutch border a few days later. Upon recapture, Best's true identity was eventually discovered. He was sentenced to extended solitary confinement, 28 days for his escape attempt and a further month for being a 'ghost'.[34] Upon his eventual release, Best was immediately recruited into the most audacious escape plan of the entire war. Sinclair was also undaunted; he would continue in his independent endeavours to escape from Colditz.

Stephenson's diary also contains several apparently innocuous statements. However, when interrogated and cross-referenced with other Colditz documents, it is clear that they relate to other escape attempts. For example, on 27 January 1944, Stephenson comments, 'another birthday party – Bill Millar'. The note just so happened to coincide with Lieutenant Bill Millar's escape from Colditz. However, after escaping through a window and hiding in a lorry to escape, no one at Colditz saw or heard of the Canadian engineer again.[35]

With the increasing effectiveness of German countermeasures, the prisoners' attempts to escape via tunnel began to wane. However, there were four significant tunnel projects in late 1943 and early 1944. All were discovered by the Germans. Moreover, the penultimate tunnel project stirred the most emotion among the British POWs at Colditz. In November 1943, a tunnel known as 'Crown Deep' was begun, and a new technique was adopted. The tunnel had a camouflaged entrance constructed in a way that prevented it from sounding hollow when tapped. The tunnel began on the first floor of the *Kellerhaus* and led down a hollow flying buttress to the ground floor, whence it was intended to emerge outside the boundary wall. Of note, only senior officers, all of whom were above the rank of major or squadron leader, worked on this tunnel.[36] When the tunnel was eventually discovered on 17 March 1944, the German security officer commented that from the tunnel entrance on the first floor, 'it was a very narrow way down to the main working tunnel, and I think only those of very slender build could have been employed on that job'.[37] Consequently, while neither Reid nor Eggers mentions specific names, the rank, stature and activities point to Stephenson's involvement in the project. 'It is believed that the location of the entrance was revealed by a

British informer planted in the camp. Before its discovery had withstood eight severe searches.'[38] The informer was Sub-Lieutenant Walter Purdy, Royal Navy Reserve.

Purdy had been captured in Norway in mid-1940 and turned by the Germans. His tenure at Colditz was short; Stephenson notes that 'a Naval chap' arrived at Colditz on 8 March 1944 and the 'collaborator' departed two days later on 10 March 1944. Prisoners are a wary bunch at the best of times, even more so when unknown new arrivals are inserted into their midst with little prior warning. During his initial questioning by his fellow British prisoners, it became apparent that Purdy's story did not quite add up, and he confessed to his treacherous German-facing role. For Purdy's own safety, the Senior British Officer asked the *Kommandant* to remove him from the prisoners' quarters. However, Purdy was initially held by the Germans at Colditz. Within days of leaving the prisoners' quarters, not only was the 'Crown Deep' tunnel discovered but as noted in Stephenson's diary, 'a large and expensive hide found'. Reid backs up Stephenson's account and adds further detail by saying that 'everything was removed, including a liquor still and typewriter parts'.[39] The discoveries within days of Purdy's removal are, perhaps, a coincidence. However, there is no doubt that although his tenure at Colditz was short, Purdy had a detrimental impact on escape efforts. Conversely, he unified the prisoners even more and spurred them in a new direction.

The toil in the tunnels was not giving the prisoners the reward they sought. With the demise of the tunnel projects, a new and radical change of direction was required. Consequently, as plans began to develop, Stephenson and many of his fellow prisoners turned their attention to an alternative means to support future escape efforts – carpentry. 'The bulk of the carpentry work which was done in connection with forbidden activities fell into two main categories: Hiding places for forbidden articles, etc and the construction of various gadgets, etc.'[40] Unlike the tunnelling projects, which involved over 50 prisoners, the carpentry team was a much more exclusive affair involving only nine personnel, including Stephenson and his messmate, Squadron Leader Charles 'Lucy' Lockett. In addition to a lathe that allowed the prisoners to fashion German rifles to be used in 'walk out' escapes with prisoners dressed as German guards, the carpentry team had a more ambitious project – a glider.

The 'Colditz Cock'

It all started with a snowflake. It was January 1944, and Flight Lieutenant 'Bill' Goldfinch was standing by the window of Keith Milne's room, gazing outside towards the town of Colditz below and watching the wintry vista. However, he noticed something odd. Due to the updrafts around the castle, the snowflakes were drifting up and over the castle; Goldfinch had the genesis of an idea that would keep a small army of British prisoners, including Stephenson, busy for the next nine months. That idea would, arguably, be the most ingenious of escape plans from the Second World War – the 'Colditz Cock' was born.[41]

The plan was to design and build a two-seat glider 'built from wood and bed sheets treated with glue', launch it from the castle's roof, some 160ft above the courtyard and land it on a small, flat stretch of a grassy field on the far bank of the river.[42] The flight would be short, covering approximately 500 yards and lasting only a few precarious seconds. To turn his idea into reality, Goldfinch needed a small team to lead the project. The first person Goldfinch inducted into the project was the former racing driver Lieutenant Tony Rolt, from the Rifle Brigade.[43] Next to be summoned was Jack Best. However, Best's invite was delayed until he could be released from solitary confinement following his recent escape attempt with Mike Sinclair. The Colditz file in The National Archives also identifies two key characters in the project, another infantry officer Captain David Walker from the Black Watch and Lieutenant Wardle from the Royal Navy. Walker and Wardle would join the group as part of the construction team and run 'stooges'.[44] The 12 principle 'stooges' were known as 'The Disciples' and were supported by a wider group of 40 assistants.[45] Sadly, most of the prisoners associated with the project are unnamed.

Stephenson's role in the glider project is somewhat ambiguous. The situation is not helped by the fact that Geoffrey Stephenson was a renowned glider pilot. However, this is a different Geoffrey Stephenson! It was not Squadron Leader Geoffrey Dalton Stephenson but the British engineer Geoffrey Leonard Huson Stephenson. The latter was the first individual to fly a glider across the English Channel in 1939. Moreover, there appears to be no primary source material that directly links Stephenson with the 'Colditz Cock'. However, there is plenty of circumstantial material to show that he was involved. As a bare minimum, Stephenson would have continued his stooge role as he had done throughout his time at Colditz. The National Archives file also highlights that Stephenson was one of the relatively few carpenters amongst the British POWs. The nine-man carpentry team included Jack Best, and their main project was the glider. His messmate, Charles Lockett, was not only a fellow carpenter but was also responsible for producing all of the metal components for the glider.[46] Perhaps most compelling is that Stephenson was an A1 Qualified Flying Instructor. Even today, exceptionally few flying instructors reach that ultimate grade; within the small cohort at Colditz, it was a unique qualification. It is a prestigious qualification rarely awarded and only to the most gifted instructors who excel in the air and on the ground. Additionally, Stephenson was one of the few pre-war RAF officers who had spent considerable time in the flying instructor role. A review of Stephenson's journal shows his meticulous attention to detail in his preparation for the various theory of flight lectures, which included aerodynamics and principles of flight – both were essential components for the construction of the glider. Consequently, it would seem incongruous that such a talented and rare resource would not be involved in the glider project. More so, when the discovery of the 'Crown Deep' tunnel freed up Stephenson and several other experienced and senior aviators.

Although Goldfinch and Best were both pilots, they had no practical experience in designing or building aircraft nor the depth of Stephenson's technical knowledge. However, the Colditz library came to their rescue. Despite the Germans vetting each book that went into the library, the German veto appears to focus on books that were counter to their politics and culture rather than those with a practical purpose. Consequently, and surprisingly, one book that made it onto the shelves of the Colditz library was the 1939 book *Aircraft Design, Volume II: Aero Structures* by British aircraft designer Cecil Hugh Latimer-Needham.[47]

Goldfinch used Latimer-Needham's book to produce a meticulous set of blueprints showing a 20ft long, two-seat glider with a wingspan of 33ft. The airframe was to be constructed out of scavenged wood, covered in the blue and white checked bedsheets and made taut, thus more aerodynamically efficient, with a paste made from ground millet. The all-up weight, including the two-man crew, was a mere 560lbs. While the technical drawings for the glider were impressive, the concept for the launch was a more primitive affair. In principle, the plan was to launch along a runway made of tables along the 60ft apex of the rooftop adjacent to the clock tower of the *Furtstenhaus*. To generate sufficient lift to fly the glider, it needed to be accelerated rapidly to its launch speed. Pat Reid suggested that the launch would be achieved by connecting the glider to a concrete-filled bath via a pulley system. When released, the bath would fall under gravity several storeys to the ground below, thus generating the necessary launch speed for the glider.[48] However, Bill Goldfinch explained that the bath would be too heavy to position, but a similar launch could be achieved by replacing the bath with ten people.[49] Goldfinch readily admitted that the volunteers would travel quickly as they approached ground level and require mattresses to arrest their fall.[50] Goldfinch and Best now had a viable plan to take to Dick Howe, the head of the Escape Committee, for his approval. Howe was incredulous at first, but he knew Goldfinch and Best were thorough, patient and persevering, and he approved the plan.[51] With the approval in place, the team could now switch to the construction phase, which started in May 1944.

Designing the glider and the launch system was one thing, but turning the theory into reality was another. Consequently, a plan was needed to allow the glider to be built and easily transported to its intended launch site. Although many of the smaller components were made by the prisoners in their own rooms, a more substantial space was required to build and store the larger components. The workshop had to be adjacent to the launch site and secure from prying German guards. The prisoners' plan was to exploit the vacant and unused spaces in the two garret storeys in the roof above the *Furtstenhaus*.[52] The ingenious element of the plan was to partition off and camouflage the last 10ft of the 80–100ft room on the upper floor via a false wall. Behind the dividing wall was a small workshop that was big enough for four prisoners to work on the glider simultaneously. 'Access to this secret workroom was through a false wall, up through a trap-door in the ceiling to a small room under the eaves of the building. This secret workroom was never discovered by the Germans.'[53] Consequently, the glider was built without interference from the Germans. By the autumn of 1944, the glider was ready to fly. Yet, it would remain completed but unbuilt in its attic hangar until liberation some six months later. Why?

While the approaching winter was a factor, two further issues would freeze escape attempts at Colditz.[54] First, the extreme German reaction to the 24 March 1944 'Great Escape' from *Stalag Luft* III was starting to be understood. The mass escape of 76 prisoners caused the Germans much embarrassment. As a result, German authorities ordered that 50 of the 73 recaptured prisoners be shot. Harry Day was lucky; he was one of the 23 survivors. Squadron Leader Roger Bushell, the former Spitfire squadron commander who also crash-landed during the May 1940 Dunkirk operation, was not – he was among the 50 prisoners gunned down in cold blood after being recaptured. In the aftermath of the horrific event, 'attempts to escape were not formally forbidden, but they were discouraged'.[55]

The second issue was the slow but positive progress of the war. In the autumn of 1944, three months after the Allied invasion of Northern Europe, the war's outcome was no longer in doubt; the key variable was when. Consequently, on instructions received from the UK, the Senior British Officer issued an order that no POWs were to attempt to escape. 'It was generally understood, however, that in the event of a move from the Camp, POWs would seize any opportunity of escaping, though all plans of this nature were left to individuals.'[56] The order put an end to the glider project. However, it was an order that was too late or irrelevant for some. At Colditz, another tragedy unfolded.

On 25 September 1944, the last escape attempt from the Castle would be fatal. The perpetual escaper, Mike Sinclair, tried to replicate the Frenchman Lebrun's escape from the playing field back in early 1941. Sinclair successfully vaulted the barbed wire fence but was shot by one of the guards while running towards cover and freedom; Sinclair was killed instantly. The glider stayed where it was, gathering dust and totally undetected by the German guards for the remainder of the war. Stephenson and his compatriots' liberty were no longer in their own hands; they now had to wait for the arrival of the allies, but who would liberate them? Would it be the Russians from the East or the Americans in the West? More importantly, how would the Germans treat their prisoners in the last few days of their war?

The End Game

While there was a sense of hope, this had to be offset by the day-to-day hardships of no escapes, limited food and fuel, as well as an approaching winter. As Reid appositely points out, 'The spirit was unconquered, but the flesh was weak'.[57] Their task was not easy, but it was not insurmountable. While the Allied progress was frustratingly slow, there was clear evidence that the Allies were closing in on the Germans. Allied advances also meant that German POW camps further east were evacuating their prisoners to more secure camps, including Colditz. The net result was that *Oflag* IVC was returning to a crowded, multi-national affair.

> The camp continued to remain almost entirely British until February 1945, when five French Generals arrived. A little later, General Bor-Komorvski reached the camp with a contingent of Polish officers who had been captured after the Warsaw rising. March 1945 saw the arrival of 1200 French Officers evacuated from a POW camp East of the Elbe. From this time until the liberation of the camp on 16 April 1945, there was no change in the camp strength, with the exception of the removal of the 'prominent persons' a day before the liberation.[58]

The last few days at Colditz were a fraught affair. News began filtering in via radio that the US First Army was approaching Colditz from the west. Soon enough, the battle for Colditz began when artillery fire started to land in and around the town. The Germans were ordered to move the prisoners. However, Lieutenant Colonel Tod, the Senior British Officer, wisely refused the order. Although the *Prominenter* prisoners were moved, they were not harmed. A larger movement of POWs may have warranted undue attention from both sides. Nevertheless, although relatively safe, the Castle continued to come under bombardment. 'Half a dozen shells landed in the Castle, splintering glass everywhere and leaving ragged holes in the roof. Nobody was seriously hurt. Bader was knocked off his tin legs. The prisoners ordered to the ground floor.'[59] With hastily arranged POW and national flags flying from the windows of the Castle's upper storeys, shelling ceased. Eventually, the town of Colditz was liberated. Late morning on Monday, 16 April 1945, a US soldier, Private First Class Alan Murphy, cautiously entered the prisoners' courtyard. After an awkward silence, he was quickly greeted by a throng of grateful and emotional multi-national prisoners. Stephenson and his fellow prisoners were now free men. The celebrations were instantaneous. 'Food reserves, laid in for a siege, were broken into, and the Americans brought wine and beer from the town. Colonel Tod wisely kept the prisoners inside the Castle until the first exuberance at their deliverance had worn off.'[60] However, two of the former prisoners needed closure on an unfinished project.

Upon liberation, Goldfinch and Best immediately returned to the attic and built the glider. By 5 pm on the day of liberation, they took great pride in showing off their audacious handiwork to their astonished former German guards and American liberators. Only one photograph of the actual glider exists; it was taken by Lee Carsen, one of the three American journalists embedded with the liberating force. Little is known about the glider beyond this point as Colditz quickly became part of the Soviet area of interest in the post-war period. The prisoners did not care. They were literally joining the exodus of tens of thousands of prisoners heading home. Ultimately, Stephenson survived his POW ordeal. Moreover, after 1,778 days in captivity, Stephenson was now free but in limbo, awaiting a plan to return the mass of former POWs.

Operation Exodus – Going Home

The former prisoners spent a couple of days at Colditz while the logistics caught up to not only support the last few weeks of the war in Europe but also enable the return of the former POWs. However, some were more fortunate than others and were singled out for a more bespoke and expeditious return journey. Bader was a case in point. He was quickly whisked away from Colditz on the afternoon of the liberation by the three American news correspondents and headed off towards the First Army Headquarters in Naunberg.[61]

Although Colditz was liberated on Monday, 16 April 1945, the repatriation of Allied prisoners from POW camps in Europe had started nearly a fortnight earlier on 3 April 1945. Allied planners realized that many prisoners were suffering from illness plus malnutrition and needed urgent support. 'Consequently, RAF bombers were tasked to fly the POWs home. At the height of the operation, the repatriation aircraft were arriving in Europe at a rate of 16 per hour bringing more than 1,000 people a day into British receiving camps.'[62] Utilizing transport aircraft and now seemingly redundant bomber aircraft, Operation Exodus lasted until the end of May 1945 and recovered 354,000 former prisoners to the United Kingdom.[63] Albeit over a more extended period, the operation recovered more personnel than from the Dunkirk beaches some five years earlier and the start of Stephenson's European adventure.

After a couple of days of pseudo-freedom at Colditz, the Americans gathered the former Colditz prisoners and began transferring them to a nearby airfield that was now in Allied hands for their return journey. According to Pat Reid, 'On Wednesday, April 18th, the evacuation began'.[64] The prisoners were loaded onto open-topped trucks, and the convoy headed south towards Kaledar, an airfield near Chemnitz.[65] After a hot meal of American Army rations and bedding down for the night, the prisoners boarded a fleet of American Douglas DC-3 Dakota transport aircraft and headed home via a refuelling stop in Rouen in France.[66] Although Reid does not mention where the prisoners finally landed in the United Kingdom, Bill Goldsmith suggests the airfield was Bovingdon, near Luton.[67] Stephenson's MI9 report confirms his arrival in the United Kingdom on Thursday 19 April 1945. However, their arrival was met with neither pomp nor fanfare. The war in Europe was in its last throes, and the war in the Pacific continued as American forces, slowly but surely, made their way towards the heart of the Japanese empire. Nevertheless, the former prisoners' arrival was a hastily-arranged but functional affair.[68] Stephenson and his group were taken to a hangar where they were in-processed, aided by a bun and a mug of tea provided by the Salvation Army.[69]

Before being finally released for their next stage of their repatriation, the prisoners were debriefed by MI9, the military intelligence section within the War Office responsible for overseeing the activities of POWs. The product of that discussion was the completion of a three-page top secret questionnaire covering 20 questions relating to their time and experience as a POW. Part One of the questionnaire covered basic administrative items such as name, rank, unit, date of birth, place of capture and the subsequent location of POW camps, as well as any period of illness and subsequent medical treatment. Stephenson's replies were functional but basic. Part Two looked for more specific details on preparatory lectures before capture, interrogation, escape attempts, sabotage, collaboration, and war crimes. Despite knowing and commenting on the activities of Purdy in his diary, Stephenson made no comment on collaboration. However, Stephenson did remark on interrogation and escape attempts, although, again, his comments were limited. On interrogation, and in response to the question 'were you specially interrogated by the enemy?' Stephenson responded with a rather generic response, 'Yes. Normal interrogation as for RAF personnel of the period.' Regarding escapes, Stephenson added a little more detail with his answer to the question 'Did you make any attempted or partly successful escapes'. In response, Stephenson's reply was far from comprehensive:

> Shot down south of Calais on 26 May 1940. Changed into civilian clothes. Failed to cross Somme, so walked to Brussels. American Ambassador refused to help [original underlined,] and I gave myself up to German air force in Brussels 4 June 1940. Made several abortive attempts from *Oflag* IVC.

Despite the clear desire to get through the MI9 debriefing process as quickly as possible, the parsimonious nature of Stephenson's replies highlights two factors. This was nearly his last act before being released back into British society. Consequently, he was keen to complete the document as quickly as possible and made several omissions. Although he was clearly aware of the detail, Stephenson elected not to comment on his time as the Senior British Officer at *Stalag Luft* I, or to add details of his abortive escape attempts. Stephenson's questionnaire was minimal in comparison to some of his compatriots. While every prisoner wanted their liberty as soon as possible, it was clear that Stephenson wished to look to the future rather than dwell on his extended period in captivity. However, there was one more process to go through before he was given his liberty.

Stephenson's Record of Service provides evidence of the next stage of his repatriation. Stephenson was posted on 19 April 1945 to 106 Personnel Reception Centre, a unit at RAF Cosford, west of Birmingham. The unit had been established in March 1945 to deal with a capacity of 1,000 ex-prisoners of war. The unit's role was

> to receive and register between 9,000 and 10,000 RAF prisoners of war to be evacuated from Germany; to cleanse, clothe and pay them; to give them a quick medical inspection; to furnish them with information on certain relevant matters; to obtain information from them with regard

to the manner in which they were shot down and subsequently treated by the enemy; to accommodate them during these and other processes; and to send them on 28 days leave.[70]

Upon arrival, the prisoners had a bath and a medical examination. Their clothes were discarded and replaced temporarily by hospital blues until they were kitted out. While this was going on a telegram was despatched to inform next of kin that their loved one had arrived in the United Kingdom. Next, they were taken to the dining-hall where they ate 'slowly but heavily'.[71] All were very emaciated, and most suffered from diarrhoea. After resting, they were taken to a hangar to undergo clothing issue, tailor's shop, X-ray, accounts, medical inspection, issue of temporary identity cards and a welfare interview. Due to their physical and mental condition, many were detained for further treatment. Stephenson was more fortunate. He arrived at Cosford as part of a group of 30 officers and 117 airmen at 0500 on 21 April 1945.[72] The group were the 16th intake at Cosford and as such, the compulsory bureaucracy was becoming slick. The principle at Cosford was simple – 'the stay of each man at Cosford before proceeding on leave must be kept to the minimum and the medical officers at the Personnel Recovery Centres are to cooperate very fully towards this end'.[73] Although his posting on paper was for a few weeks, it was predominantly leave. In reality, Stephenson only spent one day at 106 Personnel Reception Centre, before finally getting his long-awaited liberty.

With a 28-day leave pass, a rail warrant and a ration card in his hand as well as a wallet full of his advance of pay, Stephenson was now free to do as he pleased and ready to restart his life and career. After five years in captivity, a grateful nation gave him a few weeks of leave to sort his jumbled life out before he had to report back for work. His next stop was to his mother's home at Dell Cottage in Egham, Surrey. Many of his colleagues and friends would not be so lucky.

Life and Death Beyond Colditz

During the last 18 months of the Second World War, one further 19 Squadron pilot would be killed from the cohort of 12 that flew over Dunkirk on the morning of 26 May 1940. The last casualty was Flight Sergeant Harry Steere.

On 26 May 1940, Steere flew as 'Blue 3' on the wing of his flight commander Wilf Clouston. He remained with the squadron throughout the Battle of Britain, achieving the coveted ace status. After a period as an instructor and gaining his commission, he converted to the De Havilland Mosquito in the pathfinder role. On 9 June 1944, three days after the Normandy invasion, his Mosquito came down in north-west France during an attack against rail targets. Both Steere and his Australian navigator were killed. Four of the 12 pilots from the 26 May 1940 mission led by Stephenson were killed during the war. Five of the eight survivors would become POWs, with Stephenson spending the longest period in captivity.

However, Stephenson's old flight commander from his time on 23 Squadron, Harry Day, would spend an even longer period in captivity than his former charge; Day was captured eight months before Stephenson and, after a convoluted journey, would finally be released a month after him. As Day's interactions with Stephenson began to wane as the war progressed, the influence of his other flight commander at Kenley in the early 1930s started to become more prominent and would remain so for the rest of Stephenson's life.

Richard 'Batchy' Atcherley's wartime experience was less volatile than his former 23 Squadron compatriots. Nevertheless, he played prominent roles in various theatres and operations throughout the War. In October 1939, Atcherley commanded 219 Squadron based at RAF Catterick in North Yorkshire. Atcherley's squadron flew Blenheims that were initially tasked with shipping protection missions before being converted to the night fighter role in February 1940. Atcherley's command tour was cut short as he was appointed to command the Air Element of the British Expeditionary Force in Norway in May 1940.

Following the withdrawal from Norway, Atcherley would spend the next three years commanding several RAF stations in Scotland, Wales and Yorkshire. However, his next tour threw him back into front-line operations. It was a welcome return to RAF Kenley, the airfield in South London where Atcherley, Day, Bader and Stephenson flew from with 23 Squadron in the early 1930s. More recently, it was one of the key 11 Group fighter stations during the Battle of Britain. As the Sector Commander, Atcherley regularly flew on sweep missions into France. However, not all were successful; he was shot down during an engagement with a Focke-Wulf Fw 190. Despite his wounds, he successfully bailed out over the English Channel and was rescued by a minesweeper.

In April 1943, Atcherley became Air Officer Commanding 211 Group at Tripoli in Libya. 'His job was to control the close-support fighter and fighter-bomber wings in the advance from El Alamein to Tunis and later in the Sicilian and Italian campaigns.'[74] His knowledge and experience of broader fighter operations in the Western Desert was ideal preparation for his next appointment later that year when he returned to Headquarters RAF Fighter Command before moving to Headquarters Allied Expeditionary Air Force in 1944 to prepare for Operation Overlord, the invasion of Normandy.

The challenge facing Atcherley in his new post was the divergent thinking on the use of fighter aircraft. 'It was a question of converting pilots from the tradition of air fighting to ground attack tactics. The craft had been learned by trial and error in the Desert Air Force in support of the Eighth Army. Even with the authority of that experience, the job was something of a challenge. Ideas in Britain were still anchored to the famous flying sweeps in the Pas de Calais.'[75] Atcherley formed a small unit to develop tactics centred around allocating the maximum effort towards the offensive, retaining only the minimum for the defensive task. The success of the trial gave Atcherley the idea for a Central Fighter Establishment (CFE). The unit's aim was 'to promote leadership, efficiency and skill in both the interception and ground-attack roles'.[76] CFE became a permanent and centralised tactical laboratory for the RAF. The unit's goal was to establish good practice and disseminate it to the broader RAF fighter community rather than the localised, squadron-centric approach where ideas and concepts were rarely shared. Atcherley would become the unit's first commandant, and he needed talented pilots and leaders to sustain the change. Bader and Stephenson would both become involved with the CFE in the coming decade, Bader almost immediately as the commander of the Fighter Leaders School and Stephenson much later as the Commandant.

The role of the single-seat fighter had evolved since the start of the war. In addition to the traditional counter-air roles, fighters were now operating alongside the Allied bombers operating at scale over Germany on a routine basis. However, the increase in operational tempo was not without risk. As a result, the number of RAF and USAAF airmen shot down increased as the war progressed. One of the USAAF pilots was Captain Lonnie Moore who flew the B-26 Marauder medium bomber with the 596th Bomb Squadron as part of the 397th Bomb Group. In all, Moore flew 54 operational missions during the Second World War. However, his landings did not match his take-offs! He was forced to bail out of his stricken aircraft on two occasions. Thankfully, Moore was more fortunate than Stephenson as his abandonments tended to occur over friendly, rather than hostile, territory. Moore and Stephenson's journeys would connect nearly a decade later. Moore was a lucky pilot: he would have more luck in the future, but it was a finite resource. Others were less fortunate.

By the time of his second covert Special Operations Executive mission into occupied France in November 1943, Jean François Mennesson's name had been formally anglicized to James Francis Menzies. Confusing the situation even further was that for his mission, Menzies operated under the codename 'Birch', the field name 'Henri' and the pseudonym 'Jean François Martinet'. However, the various *noms de guerre*, nicknames and aliases did not help his current predicament. After his insertion into France, nothing had been heard from Menzies until some three months later when in mid-February 1943, Maureen received a message from the Red Cross informing her that 'Captain Menzies is now in a German prison in the suburbs of Paris at Fresnes. His health is good. Somebody brings him packages.'[77]

Menzies' arrival was compromised by a double agent. Although not immediately captured upon their arrival, Menzies and two other group members were quickly detained after reaching Paris on a train. For the next few months, the Germans appear to have held Menzies at the Fresnes prison in the suburbs of Paris. However, in early February 1944, Menzies was one of a group of Special Operations Executive agents that were transferred to Flossenbürg concentration camp, located north-east of Nuremberg on the Czech border and 120 miles south of Colditz. Each prisoner was held in solitary confinement at their new camp until the morning of 29 March 1945. As witnessed by a Danish prisoner, Menzies left Cell 13 sometime between 0900 and 1000; he was naked with his hands tied and escorted by two guards. He was taken towards the end of the yard of the *arrestbau* where executions traditionally took place. There was no sound of gunfire. The scene was repeated every three to four minutes until, eventually, all 13 prisoners hung silently in the cell block courtyard. The bodies were then cut down and immediately cremated at the camp's own facility. However, it would take some time for British authorities to confirm Menzies' status. His wife, Maureen, knew that her husband was missing in action and had been since November 1943, but it would be nearly two years before it could be confirmed that she was indeed a 26-year-old widow with a young child to bring up on her own. There would be little solace in the Special Operations Executive's assessment of her late husband that he was 'a brave and determined officer who undertook his duties very seriously and performed valuable work'.[78]

Chapter 10

A Return to Blighty, then Overseas and Back Again – April 1945 to July 1953

Coming Home

Stephenson's POW file notes that he was reported safe in the United Kingdom on 20 April 1945.[1] The following day, he was in Egham at his mother's cottage, a few miles south-west of what is now Heathrow Airport. From there, Stephenson was slowly starting to get his affairs in order, including gathering up his personal effects that he last saw at Duxford in May 1940. After confirmation of his POW status, his personal items were gathered from Duxford and temporarily held at the Central Depository at Colnbrook in Slough in early October 1940 before being forwarded to his parents later that month. However, upon his release, it became apparent that a few items appeared to be missing. After a phone call to the Central Depository, Stephenson wrote to the unit explaining his predicament.

> I wish to inform you of the loss of the undermentioned items of my personal effects: One RAF Greatcoat, one sporting 12-bore gun in leather case, one silver cigarette case, two cut glass decanters, one electric razor, and hats various . . . On my return last Saturday, the above losses were noted by me, and there may be a few others. Perhaps a case belonging to me is still in the depot. I shall be grateful if you will make enquiries as soon as possible.[2]

In the minutes of Stephenson's POW file, it appears that by 17 May 1945, most of the items had turned up in a package. However, his shotgun was nowhere to be found, a matter that Stephenson would pursue further himself.[3] Nevertheless, he had more pressing matters to attend to. After five years away, and with Victory in Europe being declared during his leave period on 8 May 1945, Stephenson was returning to the cockpit.

A Return to Flying – June 1945

After five weeks of leave, Stephenson reported back for duty on 1 June 1945 at the Empire Central Flying School at RAF Hullavington in Wiltshire. Sadly, his logbook is unavailable to confirm the amount of flying conducted and the types of aircraft he flew in June 1945. However, Bader was going through a similar process at the same time, and his logbook provides an insight into their return to flying. According to Bader's logbook, he flew dual with Group Captain Rupert Leigh in a Harvard two-seat trainer on 2 June 1945.[4] It was another reunion of old friends; Leigh had been at Cranwell with Bader and Stephenson, albeit on one of the more junior courses. Additionally, Leigh was a CFS instructor with Stephenson before the war and was also the CFS instructor who assessed Bader's flying abilities to allow him to rejoin the RAF in late 1939.[5] With their dual checks complete, Spitfires were next. A single sortie was flown in the Mark I followed by the Mark V. While Stephenson and Bader were both familiar with the Mark I from their days on 19 Squadron, only Bader had flown the significantly more powerful Mark V. Bader had been flying a Mark V when he bailed out over France in August 1941. Even more powerful aircraft were to follow in the coming weeks.

On 14 June 1945, Stephenson moved on to the newly-formed CFE at RAF Tangmere, a few miles east of Chichester on the south coast. Bader had arrived a week prior and was no stranger to Tangmere, the base where he led his fighter wing during his last operational sortie back in 1941. Unlike Stephenson, Bader was not there to be simply reacquainted with modern fighters; he was at the CFE to command one of its subordinate units, the Fighter Leader School. Consequently, the flying rate was intense for the rest of the month; Bader flew the Spitfire Mark IX on 23 occasions that month, sometimes twice a day. The Mark IX was a new variant for both Bader and Stephenson. It had entered RAF service in October 1941, two months after Bader was shot down and as Stephenson arrived at Colditz. Although it looked similar to the Mark V, the Mark IX was powered by an upgraded Merlin engine which could produce approximately 1,650 horsepower. The new powerplant was sufficient to swing the fighter advantage back towards the RAF after a period where the Focke-Wulf Fw 190s dominated the Mark Vs.

Bader also managed four trips in the Hawker Hurricane Mark IV, an upgraded version of the fighter he flew at the start of the Battle of Britain.

His last flight at the CFE was also his first flight in a jet aircraft – a Gloster Meteor. Despite the heady mix of nostalgia and cutting-edge modern fighter tactics, Bader did not enjoy the CFE experience. The modern RAF fighter community embraced the multi-role utility of fighter aircraft based upon hard-won lessons from North Africa and the latter stages of the War in Europe. For Bader, the pure, thoroughbred fighter pilot hardened by his experiences in the Battle of Britain and fighter sweeps over France, this new world of fighters diluted what it meant to him to be a fighter leader. Consequently, Bader quickly decided to transfer to lead the North Weald fighter sector. On 24 July 1945, Bader flew from RAF Tangmere to North Weald in an Airspeed AS.10 Oxford twin-engined training aircraft. However, rather than flying direct between the two RAF bases, Bader elected to take a more circuitous route via a small airfield on the Essex coast – RAF Bradwell Bay.

RAF Bradwell Bay – June to November 1945

RAF Bradwell Bay sits on a broad, rural headland on the southern shore at the mouth of the River Blackwater as it enters the North Sea. The nearest major town to the airfield is Burnham-on-Crouch, located 10 miles to the south-west. The airfield was built during the early stages of the Second World War and hosted a variety of units, aircraft types and nationalities throughout the war. However, by mid-1945, RAF Bradwell Bay was one of a plethora of airfields that were now surplus to requirements. Consequently, the RAF had selected the airfield to be shut down. Upon completing his short flying refresher courses, Stephenson was chosen to be RAF Bradwell Bay's last station commander and would be responsible for closing the airfield. His new role may not have been as high-profile as either of Bader's command tours, but this short command tour would have a lasting effect on the rest of Stephenson's life. It also came with the added benefit that, at long last, Stephenson would be promoted to Wing Commander, albeit in acting rank, on his first day in the job – 25 June 1945.[6]

Although the airfield remained open, the station no longer had its own resident aircraft. Despite the imminent closure of the base, the RAF elected to create a new organisation with Stephenson in command. Number 2 Armament Practice Station (or No. 2 APS) was, in effect, a lodger unit at RAF Bradwell Bay which would host a pair of squadrons for a month to conduct air-to-air gunnery practice against banners towed behind Miles Martinet target tugs.[7] Stephenson was perhaps an apposite individual to take command of the unit as he was in the relatively rare position to have been both an exponent and victim of the art of aerial gunnery.

The policy was enacted quickly. In mid-July, the Mosquito NF Mark XXXs of 25 Squadron and Spitfire Mark IXs of 124 Squadron were flying from Bradwell Bay.[8] A month later, Mosquitoes of 85 Squadron and the Spitfires of 287 Squadron took up residence at Bradwell Bay. However, their Armament Camp was disrupted on 15 August 1945 to celebrate Victory in Japan Day and the end of the Second World War. The RAF Bradwell Bay Operations Record Book informs that 'this was treated as a Rest Day by the Station Commander's orders'.[9] Wisely, Stephenson also elected to have the next day as a Rest Day too! The last two squadrons in the Armament Practice Camp roulement at Bradwell Bay were 307 Squadron Mosquitoes and the P-51 Mustangs of 126 Squadron.[10] Both units would arrive on what would become an exalted date for the RAF, Fighter Command and 'The Few' – 15 September, Battle of Britain Day. As the squadrons were arriving at Bradwell Bay, a few miles to the south-west, Douglas Bader was leading the inaugural Battle of Britain flypast over London in a Spitfire Mark IX emblazoned with his initials 'DB' on the aircraft's fuselage – a detail that harks back to when he led the Tangmere Wing on fighter sweeps over France in 1941.

Despite the challenges of leading his own fighter group and the distractions associated with the Battle of Britain flypast, Bader was also a regular visitor to Bradwell Bay, landing there on various occasions to visit his old friend and his squadrons detached to the unit. According to the Bradwell Bay Operations Record Book, Bader visited Bradwell Bay for a second time on 28 July 1945, but Bader arrived by means other than aircraft.[11] However, it would be another two months before he revisited Bradwell Bay. Bader and his Spitfire returned on 21 September 1945, six days after his triumphant Battle of Britain flypast. He revisited Stephenson's base in a Spitfire on 2 and 22 October 1945, as well as an overnight stop on 22/23 November 1945.

The Spitfire was not the only aircraft type Bader flew into Bradwell Bay. In what seems like an unusual activity for a devoted fighter pilot, he also visited on 16 October 1945 and 14 November 1945 in the small and rather cumbersome-looking Percival Proctor communications aircraft. However, the former visit is worth a closer inspection as there may have been an ulterior motive for taking the ugly duckling rather than the goose to visit Stephenson. The benefit of the Proctor is that it could carry two to three passengers. Bader's logbook informs that his passenger for the visit on 16 October 1945 was 'Major Dollar'. Bader's passenger may have been, in fact, Peter Dollar, who had been a fellow Colditz POW with both Stephenson and Bader.[12] Indeed, at Colditz, Dollar regularly escorted Bader on his walks outside the Camp.[13] Bader's trip in the Proctor may have been an opportunity for an impromptu Colditz reunion between three friends with a shared experience.

Beyond his professional life, which was now starting to get back on track following a five-year lull, Stephenson's personal life was in turmoil. His relationship with his fiancée, Anne Farrer, ended. However, it is unclear when this event occurred or the reasons for it. Stephenson's predicament was not unusual for POWs who came back to find a different domestic situation to the one they had left. For both parties, five years apart is a significant period; people change and can simply drift apart. Nevertheless, during his short tenure at Bradwell Bay, Stephenson would meet his future wife.

Maureen Menzies and her three-year-old daughter, Anna, remained in their cottage, Crouch Haven, in the coastal town of Burnham-on-Crouch, the local town to RAF Bradwell Bay. Maureen's domestic situation was equally as complex as Stephenson's. Maureen's husband was the French SOE agent Jean François Georges Mennesson/James Francis George Menzies. Since he was declared missing in November 1943 on his second mission in the country of his birth, Maureen had heard very little about her husband's status. Besides a note in February 1944 confirming that her husband had been captured and held by the Germans, she had heard nothing. Maureen had been in limbo for over 15 months awaiting news about her husband. With the war's end in Europe, information slowly trickled back to Maureen, confirming the worst possible news. On 7 September 1945, Maureen was eventually informed that her husband had been killed in March of the same year.[14] However, within a short period, her husband's sacrifice was recognized and rewarded by both his nation of birth and his adopted country. On 15 November 1945, Captain Menzies' efforts were posthumously recognized by a grateful United Kingdom with the award of Member of the Order of the British Empire. Menzies' country of birth would follow suit. France awarded him the *Croix de Guerre avec Palme* on 16 January 1946. Despite the tragedy, Maureen and Geoffrey became a couple. A Stephenson family photograph shows the pair dancing. Stephenson kept his promise from his early days as a POW; he was dancing more, and his plan, created as a POW, was certainly paying dividends! However, he was on the move again. With the closure of RAF Bradwell Bay on 30 November 1945, Stephenson would take No. 2 APS north to Lincolnshire, the county of his birth, and its next temporary home.

RAF Spilsby – November 1945 to March 1946

The RAF Spilsby Operations Record Book for 1 December 1945 informs that '[Number] 12 Group, Fighter Command took over RAF station Spilsby, Lincolnshire from 5 Group, Bomber Command with Wing Commander G.D. Stephenson as station commander'.[15] Located between the town he was born in, Horncastle, and the coastal town of Skegness, RAF Spilsby was situated in the heart of the wartime Bomber Command. However, as with the rest of the RAF, Bomber Command was re-brigading itself as part of the peace dividend. Consequently, the last of RAF Spilsby's Avro Lancaster bomber units, 207 Squadron, had left the airfield on 30 October 1945. The remainder of December, 'was spent settling down and unpacking equipment from RAF Bradwell Bay. No. 2 APS had aircraft flying on practice trips and ferrying between Bradwell Bay and here, in preparation for the air firing course due to commence on 10 January 1946'.[16] On 23 March 1946, Stephenson handed over command of RAF Spilsby and No. 2 APS to Wing Commander J.R. Cree DFC.[17]

The war may have been over, but peacetime flying was still a high-risk affair, as sadly, Eric Ball, one of the 12 pilots from the 19 Squadron mission over Dunkirk was to find out. On 1 February 1946, less than a year from his release from captivity, four months into his marriage and recently taken command of 222 Squadron, the 27-year-old squadron leader was killed when his Gloster Meteor failed to recover from a spin during a training mission over Devon.

RAF Staff College, Bracknell – April to September 1946

With two short but successful command tours under his belt, Stephenson had made a solid start to his rejuvenated RAF career. However, he needed to attend the RAF Staff College at Bracknell to progress his career further. The six-month course was a critical gateway for anyone serious about reaching the higher echelons of the Service as well as the key to the more prestigious command and staff appointments. Staff College was an essential requirement for a career-minded Cranwell graduate like Stephenson. Stephenson, alongside many former POWs, was selected to attend the RAF Staff College at Bracknell starting on 1 April 1946. 34 Course/17 War Staff Course was 'the most decorated course ever' with approximately 100 RAF students and a dozen or so students from both the Army and the Royal Navy.[18] Stephenson's course was the last of the foreshortened wartime staff courses, which would soon return to their year-long, pre-war format. In amongst his academic studies, Stephenson and Maureen were married on Saturday, 22 June 1946, at Maureen's local parish church, St Mary the Virgin, which was literally a stone's throw from her parent's home in Burnham-on-Crouch. The service was presided over by Reverend Williams. In one of his last acts as a serving RAF officer, Bader was Stephenson's best man and signed the marriage certificate as one of the witnesses.[19] A few days later, on 1 July 1946, Stephenson was promoted to the temporary rank of Group Captain. He would have to wait another year for the temporary annotation to be removed. Although Stephenson 'was still mad keen on flying', the cockpit would have to wait for now as he was heading off to a staff appointment.[20]

Headquarters Flying Training Command – October 1946 to February 1948

Upon graduation from Staff College, Stephenson headed back to the flying training world. However, before Stephenson took command, he had to endure a 17-month staff appointment at Headquarters Flying Training Command based at Shinfield Park in Reading. He arrived on 14 October 1946 as the Senior Personal Staff Officer to the Air Officer Commanding, Flying Training Command. His principal was Air Marshal Arthur 'Mary' Coningham, one of the standout operational air commanders of the Second World War. Moreover, Stephenson would certainly have known Coningham at RAF Cranwell when Stephenson was a Flight Cadet and Coningham, then a squadron leader, commanded B Squadron. At Shinfield Park, the pair worked together again for a year before Coningham's eventual, but sadly short-lived, retirement.[21] For Stephenson's last few months in post, the laid-back Coningham was succeeded by another successful wartime leader. Ralph Cochrane was 'a dynamic and initially unpopular hard-hitting man'.[22] Stephenson left the post with his first daughter, Victoria, and an excellent overview of the challenges facing his subsequent appointment as the CFS commandant. In February 1948, Stephenson left for Hullavington for four months of refresher flying as a supernumerary instructor.

Commandant, Central Flying School – June 1948 to August 1950

On 22 June 1948, 'Group Captain W.L.M. MacDonald CBE DFC relinquished command of RAF Little Rissington. He is succeeded in command by Group Captain G.D. Stephenson.'[23] Stephenson was no stranger to CFS, having graduated as a Qualified Flying Instructor in the mid-1930s. While the unit's role had not changed, its name and location had changed during the Second World War. However, in May 1946, the unit reformed, adopting its original name and task. The school had moved from its former location at RAF Upavon on Salisbury Plain to its new base in the rolling Cotswold countryside at RAF Little Rissington. The unit also had satellite units at South Cerney, Hullavington, Brize Norton and Moreton-on-the-Marsh.

'The object of the course at Little Rissington is to turn out proficient instructors with a basic knowledge of Service-type aircraft and the ability to teach both in the air and on the ground.'[24] While the unit's role remained unchanged, the way the course was delivered had evolved. The first 'all-purpose course' for students, 100 Flying Instructors Course, started on 10 April 1947. The 6-month course involved 110 hours of flying time, 'the majority of which are on the Harvard and Tiger Moth. The Tiger Moths are used to give a sound knowledge of elementary training and its difficulties, whilst the Harvards are used for advanced training. On the Harvards, not only is basic training completed, but also night flying, navigation, bombing, gunnery, beam flying and formation'.[25] 'Each student flies all the service types and so gains the all-important experience he requires for his task as a flying instructor.'[26] The aircraft types in the CFS inventory were diverse. In addition to the Harvard and Tiger Moth, several wartime and modern aircraft were used at Little Rissington, including 'Lancasters, Mosquitoes, Buckmasters, Spitfires and Vampires'.[27] Meteors would join in due course, as well as new training aircraft types that had to be evaluated and integrated.

The intention was to have three courses running simultaneously. Under his command, Stephenson had a staff that comprised 88 RAF, one WAAF, four Royal Navy, one USAF and one Pole, with the student population consisting of 92 RAF, 16 Royal Navy, seven Indian, one Pakistani and an Australian. The unit also comprised 648 Warrant Officers and non-commissioned officers as well as 129 WAAFs and six Jamaicans.[28] During his tenure, the student body became increasingly eclectic and included Irish, French, Belgian, Egyptian, Siamese and Iraqi students. There was plenty of flying to be had, and across an eclectic fleet of aircraft; Stephenson was in his element.

As part of his command role, Stephenson was heavily involved with the local community. The major public event of the year was the 'At Home Day', where the unit opened its doors to the public. Held in September each year to tie in with Battle of Britain commemorations, the September 1948 event hosted 8,000 visitors and raised £240 for the RAF Benevolent Fund.[29] The event was a far cry from today's airshows. For a start, the event had no entry fee. The entertainment started with a pyrotechnics display, followed by the first of three stints by the band. Meanwhile, there were various showings of combat footage in the Ground Instruction Centre. Later, there was the obligatory firefighting display outside the air traffic control tower. Mingled around these events was a static display of aircraft comprising not only the CFS fleet but also the stars of the show, a Hurricane and a Spitfire Mark XVI. Most aircraft types on static display would also participate in the two-and-a-half-hour flying display. Number 4 Hangar not only played host to Afternoon Teas but also showcased the skills of the various RAF technical trades. There was even the ability to view a junior ranks barrack block and their modern dining facility. For those feeling brave enough, and for the princely sum of ten shillings, they could take a pleasure flight in one of Gloucester Aviation Services' aircraft. There were also several amusements and sideshows. However, these were home-grown affairs rather than the commercial entities we see today at modern airshows. There was a traditional treasure hunt and the chance to ride in one of the Link Trainers. Also, for an entry fee of one shilling, the lucky individual who could guess the height and speed of the Spitfire on its pass over the airfield received a free flight in one of Gloucester Aviation Services' aircraft. However, a few events were very much of their time. For some punters, there was the chance of starting up the engine of an operational aircraft! The most bizarre spectacle was the chance to talk to an airborne Harvard trainer and request an aerobatic manoeuvre of your choice! Today's Flying Display Committee would have had a field day. Air shows were very different in the late 1940s!

Stephenson's career was further bolstered when he was appointed as an *aide de camp* to His Majesty King George VI on 28 March 1949. Stephenson was not the sole *aide de camp* to the King. The 1950 Air Force List shows 11 male *aides de camp*. The role allowed Stephenson to add the post-nominal ADC to his signature block. For Stephenson, further post-nominals were to follow shortly afterwards. To add to the celebrations, Stephenson's second daughter, Veryan, was born in April 1949.

To celebrate King George VI's birthday on 9 June 1949, 'the Station paraded in full strength under the command of the Commandant'.[30] The King's Birthday Honours List was also released on the same day. RAF Little Rissington had much to celebrate. In addition to the award of four Air Force Medals and a King's Commendation to station personnel, it was announced that Stephenson had been awarded a Commander of the Order of the British Empire (CBE.) At first glance, the timing of the award may seem a little strange. Ordinarily, state awards, such as the CBE, are bestowed after completing a successful command tour or a significant praiseworthy event. However, Stephenson's CBE award occurred during his tour as the CFS Commandant. The award was likely linked to his appointment to the *aide de camp* role. Indeed, Air Commandant Felicity Hanbury, who was also announced as an *aide de camp* at the same time as Stephenson, was awarded the Dame Commander of the Order of the British Empire (DBE) on the same list as Stephenson. Adding further evidence to the linkage between the *aide de camp* role and a state award was the fact that of the 11 male *aides de camp* mentioned previously, eight had CBEs, two of whom had Companion of the Order of the Bath (CBs) as well, one has a CB alone, and the remaining individual had a mere Officer of the Order of the British Empire (OBE), a lower-level award than the CBE.

At a similar time, Stephenson wrote to his old school in Dublin to give them an update on his career. He noted, 'It's a wonderful job, and we are very busy'.[31] However, Stephenson also added that 'at the moment, for one reason or another, the right type of young man was not coming forward'.[32] Although he did not expand on the type of character he wanted, his own personality showed a rebellious side! Most of the surviving images of Stephenson from his later years show a serious-looking senior officer. His daughters also recall a strict father at home. However, he also had a lighter side. One example is told by Ron Allen, one of the CFS instructors who had flown with Stephenson to Hendon to drop him off for a meeting at the Air Ministry, a short Tube ride away. American C-47 transport aircraft also frequented Hendon. Allen recalls

> having taxied in and parked fairly close to one such Dakota, which had about a dozen, or so rather untidy GIs lounging around aimlessly on the grass eating apples. In their full view, [Stephenson] had quickly shed his flying suit and withdrawn from the back seat of the Prentice in his pinstripe city suit jacket, his rolled umbrella and bowler hat. Thus instantly kitted out, this City Gent apparition strode purposefully off from the antique-looking Prentice, both so strange to the American airmen. The sight became just too much for their jokey mood, and soon not just ribald comments overtook [Stephenson] but several apple cores. Just beyond range and with a remarkable degree of both *savoir faire* and *sang froid*, the Commandant turned in their direction, took off his bowler, bowed graciously and shouted out: 'Good day gentlemen, each and every one of you missed!'[33]

As his time in command was running out, Stephenson exploited several opportunities. First, on 22 May 1950, Stephenson flew in a Fleet Air Arm Fairey Firefly. While flying in another Service's training aircraft was not unusual, perhaps more surprising was where he landed – onboard the aircraft carrier HMS *Illustrious*. He stayed overnight onboard the veteran of the Battle of Taranto and the war in the Pacific.[34] Next, on 22 June 1950, he headed off to West Germany on a six-day liaison visit.[35] During this visit, war broke out, not on the European continent but on the Korean peninsula.

While Fleet Air Arm fighters, operating from aircraft carriers off Korea's west coast, were in regular action on the peninsula, the RAF had a limited role during the war. Nevertheless, the Korean War would directly affect some of the CFS staff and indirectly impact Stephenson later in his career. However, in late June 1950, the war in the Far East was not yet the focus of Stephenson nor his CFS team; their attention was on the upcoming RAF Display at the Farnborough airshow. The CFS were responsible for delivering four separate flying acts for the display. First, the well-honed crazy student/ instructor act comprised two De Havilland Chipmunk trainers flying around in an apparently haphazard and dangerous manner. The display, accompanied by its commentator, was a regular feature of CFS 'At Home Days' and other air displays around the country. Next, two further Chipmunks put on an aerobatic formation display. The last two acts would be far grander and more impressive affairs. The grand finale of the CFS display was a mass formation of aircraft led by Stephenson. On 1 July 1950 and as a prelude to what the public would see at Farnborough, Stephenson led 'a formation of 37 Harvard aircraft from this unit, forming the letters "RAF" flew along a specified route over London as publicity for the RAF Display at Farnborough'.[36] The 37 Harvard aircraft also conducted a second formation flypast at the Farnborough air show, honouring King George VI.[37] The 'GRVI' formation flew past Farnborough and took in the Henley Regatta as part of its route.[38]

July 1950 was a busy and eventful last full month for Stephenson and the CFS team. The Commandant and his team were in the limelight and consequently attracted many visitors, including Air Vice-Marshal Dermot Boyle CB CBE AFC. On 4 July 1950, in his role as Director General of Manning at the Air Ministry, Boyle arrived at Little Rissington by air and was immediately flown to Farnborough to see the rehearsals of the CFS items at the RAF display. Although his current post did not directly connect with the CFS activities at Farnborough, Boyle had a professional interest. Not only was he a flying instructor during Stephenson's last six months as a flight cadet at Cranwell in 1930, but he would later be the unit's Chief Flying Instructor. Moreover, Boyle also flew formation aerobatics with Stephenson's former flight commander at Kenley, Richard Atcherley, when 'Batchy' and Boyle were CFS instructors. On his return to Little Rissington, Boyle stayed overnight with the Stephensons and attended the graduation dinner of 115 Course.[39] While the touch points between Stephenson and Boyle may have been limited to date, they had followed similar paths, albeit Boyle was a few years ahead of Stephenson. Boyle was a Cranwell graduate, a fighter pilot, served in the

Middle East, a flying instructor, formation aerobatics pilot, *aide de camp* to the King and had been awarded a CBE. Boyle was an excellent mentor. There was a clear connection between Boyle and Stephenson, and that bond would extend to the family, which would become evident in the years to follow.

On 21 August 1950, Stephenson handed over command of RAF Little Rissington and the role of Commandant, CFS to Group Captain G.T. Jarman DSO DFC. Jarman had arrived from the Air Ministry while Stephenson was 'shortly leaving for an appointment at Headquarters Middle East Air Force'.[40] Stephenson and his family were heading overseas. Moreover, he was heading back to the Middle East after a 20-year absence. However, this time, Stephenson was destined for Egypt and command of a fighter sector.

Egypt – September 1950 to March 1953

For the next two and a half years, Stephenson was based at RAF Ismailia, located halfway down the western bank of the Suez Canal. Although the 1936 Anglo-Egyptian Treaty was still in force, the stationing of British forces on Egyptian soil was unpopular. However, basing military assets in Egypt remained important to the United Kingdom and its allies as it was seen as a vital mechanism to deter Soviet aggression in the region. The recent Arab-Israeli battles only added further complexity to the turbulent strategic situation. Consequently, the RAF maintained its footprint in the country, but it collapsed around the area of the Suez Canal, known as the Canal Zone.

The RAF units in Egypt came under the purview of Air Marshal Sir John Baker, Commander-in-Chief Middle East Air Force. Subordinate to Baker was 205 Group, commanded in the latter stages of Stephenson's tour by Richard Atcherley's identical twin brother, David. 205 Group was responsible for operating the assigned aircraft. The headquarters was co-located with its reconnaissance and transport aircraft at Fayid, further south of Ismailia, but still on the west bank of the Suez. Between Ismailia and Fayid was Deversoir, the home of three Vampire fighter/ground attack squadrons. One of the key challenges facing the RAF in Egypt was that although they had the various tactical component parts, the associated operational command and control arrangements were antiquated and not fit for the modern battle. Change was required.

RAF air defences in Egypt were to 'be reorganised on a Sector basis and in accordance with the principle of command and control now adopted for the air defence of Great Britain and approved by Air Ministry'.[41] As a result, No.1 Sector formed on 1 October 1950, with the recently arrived Stephenson taking the role of Sector Commander working for the Air Defence Commander, Atcherley, in 205 Group. The set-up resonates with Fighter Command's Group and Sector construct during the Battle of Britain. However, 205 Group had a single subordinate Sector, unlike the multiple Sectors under 11 and 12 Group during 1940. Stephenson's Sector Headquarters and Operations Room were located at El Firdan, a few miles north-east of Ismailia on the west bank of the Suez. The Sector covered the full geographical boundaries of the Canal Zone. Stephenson's new role had three key responsibilities. First, the 'set up of a system of command and control which can by the maximum of time saving, effectively handle the interception problem'.[42] Second, 'knit together the elements which form the nucleus air defence of the Egypt base so as to permit rapid expansion in time of war'.[43] Last, 'to decentralise the operational control of fighter squadrons and the control and reporting system, and the responsibility for the individual and collective training of these elements'.[44] After a period in the training world, Stephenson was back in the front-line air defence game.

His diaries tell of multiple exercises and visits around the country and the wider region, including Malta, Cyprus, Amman, Jerusalem, Beirut, Aqaba and Petra. On many of these trips, Stephenson would fly in an RAF fighter or transport aircraft. On one such trip to Aden, Stephenson mentions that he met Wing Commander Eric Clouston, one of his former flight commanders on 19 Squadron in early 1940 but was now the station commander at RAF Khormaksar. The Stephenson family enjoyed their time in Egypt; they were housed on base on the edge of the Suez Canal and regularly sailed or swam in it. Geoffrey continued to box and showcased his horse-riding skills by playing polo. However, after a thoroughly enjoyable year in the country with his family, the dynamics changed.

In October 1951, 'Egypt abrogated the Treaty without warning and without consultation. The country was immediately convulsed with violence.'[45] At Ismailia, local rioting and disturbances were dealt with by British forces. However, the increased risk to families forced British authorities to evacuate a large proportion of the military families. Although there were 7,500 British military dependants in the Canal Zone, a partial evacuation of 4,000 personnel by the end of the year was planned.[46] The full complement was not evacuated as British authorities were 'utterly opposed to wholesale evacuation of families'.[47] The priority evacuees were those who had recently arrived or those who were coming to the end of their tours. However, this was insufficient to meet the 4,000 target. Consequently, those who lived outside the protective umbrella of British forces were also earmarked for return to the United Kingdom. Although not in any of the initial target groups, Maureen and the girls were part of the 4,000 dependants who returned home by mid-December 1951. There were two modes of transport for the return journey to the United Kingdom. Half of the evacuees returned via passenger ships that were transiting the still-busy Suez Canal. Maureen and the girls took the quicker flying option. To assist in the evacuation the RAF had surged to four daily Handley Page Hastings trooping flights that flew from Egypt to RAF Lyneham in Wiltshire via an overnight stop in Malta. With his family now safe and staying with Maureen's parents at Burnham-on-Crouch, Stephenson would spend the next 15 months alone in a contested country and separated from his family. For Stephenson, it must have felt like history was repeating itself again. The situation in Egypt in 1951 must have brought back memories of Ireland in the early 1920s or Germany in the early 1940s.

1952 was a tough year for Stephenson; not only was he separated from his family, but two deaths would have a profound impact on him. First, in February 1952, King George VI died at the young age of 56 and his eldest daughter, Elizabeth, became the new monarch. Stephenson would continue in his *aide de camp* role for the new monarch and one which would put him in the limelight during the following year. Second and closer to home, Air Vice-Marshal David Atcherley, who commanded 205 Group, was killed on 8 June 1952 when his Gloster Meteor disappeared over the Mediterranean as it flew from Egypt to Cyprus. Better news was on the horizon the following month. By July 1952, a 'colonels' revolt' led to a temporary improvement in Anglo-Egyptian relations, which would last until the end of Stephenson's time in the region. Despite the recovering situation, Stephenson remained in Egypt on his own. His letters home show a more reflective period and one of frustration. In one of his letters, he pondered on his time as a prisoner of war and its enduring impact on him.

My burning desire when I got home from Germany was to cope again as soon as possible as a complete RAF officer. I reckon I only got abreast of where I wanted to be last year – seven years. Of course, there was married life to manage too. I certainly haven't lost the zest, in any way, to want to go head in all endeavours, but I, like you, have more confidence now.

At work, there was the inevitable frustration as he approached the end of his tour. In his letters home, Stephenson noted that he hoped to 'leave on a crest of a wave after a successful exercise season'. However, this had to be tempered with the fact that in his view '205 Group and Canal Group really is bad for morale. Of the two, 205 Group is at least three times the worst.' Despite the Air Officer Commanding 205 Group 'messing around with the Exercise' and 'thwarting planning and training', Geoffrey was heading home to his family, promotion and a much sought-after appointment flying the latest fighters. His next post was as the CFE commandant – the same position set up by Richard Atcherley in the latter stages of the Second World War. In a letter to Maureen, Stephenson was ecstatic about the prospect of leading CFE as 'they provide the fighter gospel'. Also, he commented that 'I continue to get hints that the projected change at CFE is looked forward to'. Before taking up his post and new rank, he would be involved in the ceremonial duties associated with the new Monarch's coronation.

Coronation Activities – April to July 1953

After two and a half years away from home, Stephenson may have expected a slow and gentle reintroduction to family life and the United Kingdom. However, that was not to be the case. He was immediately thrust into the planning for the RAF's contribution to the Queen's Coronation Review at RAF Odiham. Specifically, he was responsible for the vast static display of 321 aircraft. Geoffrey confessed to Maureen that he found the whole thing 'quite exciting'. Before the Review, Stephenson was also involved in two significant events. First, he and three guests attended the Queen's Coronation at Westminster Abbey on 2 June 1953. Stephenson took part in the military parade, Maureen sat inside the Abbey, while his mother and Anna sat outside.

Second, this was one of his last acts as a Group Captain, as on 1 July 1953, he was promoted to Air Commodore and notionally relinquished his *aide de camp* duties.

Two weeks later, on 15 July 1953, the new Monarch's Coronation Review of the RAF opened with a parade of 1,125 personnel. The parade concluded with four Venoms from CFE, Stephenson's next unit, writing the letters 'ER' in white smoke above the airfield. Following lunch, the Queen, escorted by Stephenson, reviewed the impressive static display. The Royal party initially viewed the display from an open-top car before walking part of the display. On completion of the static display, the Royal party returned to the dais to view the culminating event – the flypast. Over the next 27 minutes, a remarkable 641 aircraft comprising 47 formations of 26 different aircraft types from 43 bases flew past the airfield. The flypast finished with the next generation of aircraft, including the three 'V' bombers and the latest fighters – the Supermarine Swift, the Gloster Javelin and the Hawker Hunter. Stephenson would get to know the new fighter types well at CFE. The event was a huge success. Consequently, for his contribution to the Coronation Review, Stephenson received the commendation of the Air Officer Commander-in-Chief of Fighter Command, Dermot Boyle. Five days later, Stephenson moved to his last appointment with the RAF.

As Stephenson was planning and delivering the Coronation Review, the Korean War was in its final stages. One of the pilots involved in the Sabre versus MiG-15 aerial duels over the infamous 'MiG Alley' was Captain Lonnie Moore of the USAF. The Second World War B-26 Marauder bomber pilot had come a long way from his experiences in the European Theatre of Operations. On his return to the United States, Moore transitioned to fighter aircraft and was assigned to Eglin Air Force Base in Florida in 1951, where he served as a project officer.[48] He deployed to the Korean War during this tour, flying and testing upgraded F-86F Sabres with the 335th Fighter-Interceptor Squadron.[49] Moore flew 100 combat missions in Korea and destroyed ten MiG-15s, becoming the USAF's 33rd ace of the war when he scored his fifth aerial victory on 18 June 1953.[50] On completion of his operational deployment, Moore returned to Florida in late 1953 to become the chief project officer for the Air Force's first supersonic jet fighter, the F-100A Super Sabre. Moore and Stephenson's paths would soon cross and end in tragedy.

Chapter 11

Central Fighter Establishment, RAF West Raynham – July 1953 to November 1954

'Parvi arma sine consilo' – Arms are worth little without counsel

CFE Motto

Following the success of the RAF Coronation Review, Stephenson moved on to what would be his final appointment – Commandant of Central Fighter Establishment (CFE). On 20 July 1953, he arrived at his new command at RAF West Raynham, located five miles south-west of Fakenham in Norfolk.[1] After a week's handover, he took command of the unit, which was charged with increasing 'the efficiency of the fighter aircraft and the man who flies it, in all roles in which day and night fighters can be used'.[2] As one of Stephenson's subordinates at CFE suggests, it was 'the place where every keen fighter pilot had dreams of being posted'.[3]

The nucleus of CFE was formed during the latter stages of the Second World War at RAF Tangmere in September 1944. However, the unit officially formed at RAF Wittering on 1 October 1944 before moving to RAF West Raynham on 1 October 1945. The Norfolk base would become the unit's home for the next 17 years before moving to RAF Binbrook in the Lincolnshire Wolds in late 1962. At its inception, the Air Officer Commanding-in-Chief of Fighter Command laid out a vision for CFE at its first conference in December 1944 at RAF Wittering. Air Marshal Roderic Hill said:

> Let me sketch for you, in essence, the aims of the Establishment. First of all, we shall study fighter tactics both theoretically and practically. We shall try to arrive progressively at the most suitable tactical methods for general or specific operational purposes. To this end, qualified and experienced officers of the CFE will pay regular visits to all operational

theatres to obtain first-hand information. These visits, as you know, are already underway.

We believe that the doctrine we evolve, never static but always growing, will be of invaluable use to the appropriate research and development establishments, the aircraft industry, in developing fighter aircraft, equipment and ground control apparatus. So that the striking power of the fighter as a weapon in both defensive and offensive roles may enable this country to hold its own in those respects with any country in the world.

We believe that our links with the Royal Navy and the Army will be continually strengthened both technically and by an increased mutual regard and understanding.

Finally, the importance of handing on the torch to the next generation must never be lost sight of. Our doctrine must be passed on. In CFE, we shall try and evolve the best possible training methods and train new wing leaders, squadron commanders, flight commanders and navigators so that they look on us with tolerance and with, I hope, gratitude,

In short, CFE will serve fighter formations of all RAF commands and the Dominion air forces. Its aim is to increase the efficiency of the fighter aircraft and the man who flies it in all roles which day and night fighters can be used.[4]

Despite being only nine years old, the remit of CFE was continually evolving. By the time Stephenson had taken over as its Commandant, the unit was 'constituted to advise the Air Ministry, all RAF commands at home and overseas, and Commonwealth air forces on all matters relating to the operation of fighter aircraft'.[5] Stephenson's new unit worked for 12 Group and then on to Fighter Command, commanded by the now Air Marshal Dermot Boyle. Stephenson's immediate boss was initially his old flight commander from 23 Squadron days at Kenley in the early 1930s and the very first CFE commandant, Air Vice-Marshal 'Batchy' Atcherley. However, Atcherley was replaced in October 1953 by Air Vice-Marshal 'Paddy' Crisham, Stephenson's predecessor as the CFE Commandant. Consequently, Boyle, Atcherley and Crisham regularly visited West Raynham and often flew with the unit.

CFE's flying wing comprised three main operational units: the Air Fighting Development Squadron, the All-Weather Wing and the Interception Analysis Unit. In addition to the three operational units, CFE also had two training units: the Day Fighter Leaders School and the Instrument Training Squadron. The latter would eventually transfer to its natural home, CFS. However, the former unit can trace its lineage back to the early days of CFE when Bader led the team.

The Day Fighter Leaders School 'continued in its aim of promoting leadership, efficiency and skill in interception and ground attack roles. The six-week course comprised 46 sorties and was attended by RAF officers from all over the world as well as members of the Fleet Air Arm and Commonwealth air forces. All aspects of fighter operations were undertaken.'[6] The Day Fighter Leaders course started with four against four dogfighting scenarios before building up to eight versus eight fights and culminating with a graduating exercise comprising 24 aircraft fighting against an entire wing of aircraft.[7] In 1954, the fighter of choice for the Day Fighter Leaders School was the venerable Gloster Meteor and was about to transition to the Hawker Hunter towards the end of Stephenson's time in command. The course was designed to develop the tactical leadership and technical expertise of specific, selected individuals and return them to the front line to increase their units' tactical and operational effectiveness.

The CFE pilots were not merely limited to the aircraft on the CFE books, or just the RAF for that matter. Throughout 1953 and 1954, CFE's operations record book notes that pilots regularly visited aircraft manufacturers around the United Kingdom to familiarize themselves with and evaluate the latest aircraft types and the upgraded versions of existing fighters. For example, one of the CFE stalwarts throughout the late 1940s and early 1950s was Wing Commander 'Birdy' Bird-Wilson, the commanding officer of the Air Fighting Development Unit for the majority of Stephenson's time at West Raynham, who flew several sorties with the aircraft manufacturers. Bird-Wilson travelled to Dunsfold in September 1953 to fly the Hawker Hunter. In March 1954, he visited Supermarine at Chilbolton in Hampshire to fly their new Swift variant, the F4. A few months later, in September 1954, he would visit Boscombe Down in Wiltshire to fly the diminutive Folland Midge technology demonstrator, a forerunner to the Folland Gnat advanced trainer. For any RAF fighter pilot, whether a lowly (but capable) Flight Lieutenant or the Air Commodore Commandant, CFE was a dream posting.

CFE's remit was broad and, more importantly, at the forefront of tactical air power employment within the RAF. For Stephenson in the Commandant role, this was an important, varied, and high-profile appointment for a senior officer and aviator. Not only were pilots flying the latest fighter aircraft in the RAF's inventory, but they were also at the forefront of technological advances and tactical development. Moreover, they were also witnessing the transition from the first generation of jet fighters to the next generation of faster, more agile, and more complicated fighters. With the Cold War backdrop coupled with the lessons of the Korean War, CFE was a much sought after appointment and an excellent stepping stone for a career-minded individual such as Stephenson. Several previous Commandants had progressed through the ranks; Crisham and Atcherley were prime examples. Stephenson's prospects were good, and there was evidence to support his onward progression within the Service. Early in his tenure at CFE, Stephenson relays to his wife in a letter that a senior Air Ministry official informed him that 'I should probably not be moved much before January 1956 and that I should not necessarily look for my next job as an Air Commodore. He thought that only one job in the rank could be considered quite reasonable.'

Although Stephenson had one eye on the future, he undoubtedly relished command of CFE and the broad, varied, and relevant tactical flying opportunities it presented. Consequently, he flew most days.[8] His subordinates regarded him as an active flyer, not a desk pilot.[9] With several thousand hours of flight time in his logbook dating back to the late 1920s, he was seen as a very highly qualified fighter pilot.[10] However, Stephenson's recent experience made him stand out from his peer group. He was generally considered to be one of the experts in jet fighters in the RAF not only by dint of his appointment but the fact that he had the practical experience to back up the exposure that his appointment gave him. He had access to and flew all the latest types of British jets, including the Hawker Hunter, Gloster Javelin, Gloster Meteor, De Havilland Venom and Supermarine Swift, as well as the US-designed North American F-86 Sabre. After an enforced hiatus during the Second World War, Stephenson was making up for lost time and led the early 1950s RAF's fighter pilot cadre by example.

Life at West Raynham

The CFE operations record book from 1953 and 1954 is a mixed affair. It captures much of the tactical action within the various sub-units that make up CFE, such as trials work, the progress of the various courses, visits to and from the sub-units, as well as the inevitable flying-related incidents and accidents on the unit. Some of the detail delves into the minutia of the unit. Frustratingly, there is little recorded at the higher levels of the station, CFE, or the Commandant's thoughts. For example, there is little or no mention of the Commandant's activities other than the odd fleeting comment regarding Stephenson flying with a specific unit. Nevertheless, the monthly diary builds a picture of a busy unit, effectively managing a plethora of technologically complex problems and constantly delivering high-tariff courses. Stephenson was in his element at work, but it was not without its dramas.

In keeping with the period, West Raynham saw several aircraft accidents during Stephenson's command. Despite a cadre of experienced pilots, the more demanding nature of the sorties flown from West Raynham meant that aircraft incidents were inevitable. The unit's official history notes a number of Meteors, Hunters and Venoms involved in landing or take-off incidents during this timeframe. The aircraft typically landed wheels-up or skidded into the overrun area of the runway. Fortunately, despite the odd fire, there were no fatalities associated with these incidents. However, the events undoubtedly shook up the aircrew and the odd passenger. Others were less fortunate. In two separate incidents in August and September 1954, two Day Fighter Leaders School students were killed in flying accidents, one of which was noted as an 'avoidable incident'.[11] The crashes were not limited to students; even experienced instructors were susceptible to the vagaries of emerging but fragile technology. Sadly, on 19 March 1954, a Hawker Sea Hawk jet crashed off the Lincolnshire coast and claimed the life of the pilot, the commanding officer of the Naval Air Fighting Development Unit, Lieutenant Commander Reginald Taylor.[12]

Beyond work, the Stephenson family enjoyed life at West Raynham. Although Stephenson's ten-year-old stepdaughter, Anna, was attending boarding school in Clacton, the rest of the family lived on base in the Commandant's residence, not far from the end of the runway. The house felt familiar to the family as it had the same layout as their previous home at Little Rissington. Of the two parents, Geoffrey was stricter; Maureen was more liberal and open. Despite his firmer approach, Victoria remembers her father being a cheery, confident, and fun individual, particularly when the chips were down. One incident stands out. On a family walk along the Norfolk coast, the family became stranded on a sand bar with a rapidly changing tide. Not one to panic, Stephenson kept his tribe calm and ensured they were all successfully rescued by a boat. Stephenson also instilled his passion for sport into his children. He taught Victoria to ride her bike and shared his love of golf with his daughter. Victoria tells of her father cutting down a larger golf club for her to use. However, he may have had ulterior motives. He would go to the golf club with his playing partners, Victoria and their poodle, Albert. The golfing four-ball would head off to play a round of golf while Victoria and Albert were left to their own devices on the practice ground!

Work inevitably pervaded into the Stephenson family and their recollections. Anna recalls that the Royal Family regularly flew into West Raynham to visit Sandringham. Consequently, Stephenson used to greet the Royal party upon their arrival. More impressively, Victoria also tells the story of a helicopter landing in the garden of their married quarter and her father disembarking from the aircraft. Victoria was suitably amused by her father's grand entrance. However, not all the Stephenson family were impressed by the patron's dramatic return from work. The noisy arrival was much to the chagrin of the family's cats.

The Stephenson family remained close with the Mennesson family in northern France. Victoria remembers regularly visiting the large family farm near Laon with her father, mother and sisters. The farm was 'a big old place with lots of rooms, but only one toilet and a single shower'. The lack of amenities did not detract from the fun element of the trip. There were always plenty of children to play with and lots of running around the farm. As expected, the French cuisine was plentiful and delicious. Occasionally, Stephenson would fly the family to and from France in a small, borrowed private aircraft. Victoria and Anna both recall one return trip from Le Touquet to Lympne in abysmal weather. While her father battled the low cloud, wind and rain, her mother, who was not a keen flyer, distracted herself from the maelstrom outside by keeping her head down and focusing on her latest knitting pattern!

The life of the CFE's Commandant was busy but very enjoyable, both at home and at work. Additionally, and unsurprisingly given the nature of its work, CFE played host to an array of senior officers throughout the year. The visitors wanted to hear about the unit's work and fly in the Service's latest aircraft. This oversight and scrutiny reached a crescendo during the annual West Raynham-hosted Tactical Convention. The event showcased to all within the Service, its sister Services, Commonwealth air forces and allies the activities, research and conclusions carried out by the unit over the preceding year.

Tactical Conventions

The highlight of the CFE year was their Tactical Convention which was usually held over one week between June and August.[13] Group Captain Frederick Rosier, who held the post of Group Captain Operations at CFE in the early 1950s, describes the purpose of the week-long event:

> CFE presented its most up-to-date ideas on fighter operations. The experts in the audience were allowed to freely comment on the views expressed, and practical conclusions were hammered out. There were also flying and static displays in which the latest fighter aircraft and aircraft were put on view. The conventions grew in size and scope. In my time, we had more than 300 delegates from all corners of the globe – squadron commanders, wing leaders, sector commanders and fighter station commanders. They were joined by representatives of the Royal Navy, the British army, the air forces of the dominions and US Air Force and Navy representatives . . . There was, of course, also a galaxy of distinguished senior officers.[14]

The conference was a veritable who's who of the RAF fighter community. There was a vast array of senior officers ranging from the highest echelons of the Service down to station and squadron commanders, many of whom had distinguished themselves during the Second World War and had the post-nominals to back up their lived experience. The delegates also included RAF personnel deployed overseas, including several attendees from RAF

Germany and the Middle East Air Force. Indeed, before taking up the CFE Commandant role, Stephenson had attended the 1951 and 1952 conventions as a Sector Commander within 205 Group out in Egypt.[15] The notes from the 1952 conference show that Stephenson was heavily involved in discussions. In particular, Stephenson was keen to understand how the limited detection ranges of the Type 15 ground control intercept radar could be improved. Beyond the RAF, UK and Commonwealth fighter community, the various US air arms were well represented at the conventions. The US delegation also included six members from the Air Proving Ground Command, a Florida-based unit that would become inextricably linked with Stephenson.

Despite the executive-level attendance of the conventions, the subject matter discussed during the event was broad. Topics discussed ranged from tactical procedures to operational-level subjects, technological advances, and multi-national integration. Over the week, the briefings covered: day fighter as well as night and all-weather problems, tactics against escorted bomber raids and low-level raids on coastal targets, use of radar poor weather let-down procedures, the operation and control of fighter aircraft between the United Kingdom and Continental air defence systems as well as airborne radar interceptions with collision-course weapons. However, pertinent to CFE and the wider RAF was the first real exposure to their Cold War foe and their equipment. The RAF played little direct part in the Korean War. Nevertheless, several pilots from CFE were seconded to the USAF and flew operational missions with North American F-86 Sabre units. Small groups of five pilots would spend six months embedded within different USAF F-86 units to give them jet combat experience. The first group flew the F-86A Sabre, while later groups flew the upgraded F-86E variant. Consequently, a large proportion of the Fighter Conventions was devoted to CFE pilots, many with MiG kills, providing insights into their Korean War experiences.

Many felt that their Korean experiences were unique, with limited read-across to the Cold War challenges at home. This perspective is reflected by Squadron Leader J.R.H. Merifield, who led the RAF contingent in late 1952. Merifield believed that 'the air war in Korea is highly artificial and it should not be thought that the tactics used here in a purely fighter versus fighter war, would necessarily be suitable to cope with other situations, for instance, escorted bomber raids on this country. During the six months we spent in

Korea considerable changes in flying tactics took place and will continue to take place.'[16]

The seconded CFE pilots commented on the aircraft they flew, their tactics and training, and the equipment they used, including the USAF's flying equipment. Merifield also noted that

> we did not like the American crash helmet. It is heavy, and unless a very good fit, it slips down over one's eyes if any 'G' is applied and at all times acts rather like horses' blinkers. In a break, when looking behind with many 'G's on, it is quite difficult to keep one's head up. Two of the team had their RAF leather helmets revised for the American R/T set and wore them for most of their tour. The improvements in comfort and visibility was most marked. Admittedly, in a crash, the head has less protection, but good all-round visibility is a *sine qua non* of the fighter pilot; we thought the advantage of comfort and good visibility easily outweighed the safety angle.[17]

Squadron Leader James Ryan led the next group of RAF pilots in early 1953, who commented, 'the American head gear is heavy and seriously limits all-round visibility. However, a lightweight "hard-hat" would carry considerable advantages for high-speed operations in bumpy conditions. Two members of the party experienced bumps caused by their aircraft being shaken around by the weather and flak, which could have produced serious results had it not been for the protection offered by the hard helmet.'[18] Although the benefits of the USAF flying helmet were understood, it did have its limitations. Although the comment is tactical in nature, the subject-matter and its limitations would become very relevant for Stephenson during his final flight.

Beyond the lectures, the convention was also an opportunity for some senior RAF officers to catch up with their flying currencies. For example, Assistant Chief of the Air Staff (Operations) Air Vice-Marshal Lawrence Sinclair flew eight sorties in the Gloster Meteor T7 during the early mornings and evenings while attending the conference during the normal working day.[19] It was not unusual for senior RAF officers to fly in modern fast jets. For example, just before the CFE visit to the United States, the Deputy Chief of the Air Staff, Air Marshal Tom Pike, visited West Raynham and flew in the

Hawker Hunter. However, not all senior officers' flights were as successful. Pike would also visit the United States later that month, and his itinerary would partly overlap with Stephenson's group. Both Pike and the CFE group would also meet up with the first commandant of the CFE, Air Vice-Marshal Richard Atcherley. 'Batchy' had only relinquished his post as Air Officer Commanding 12 Group a few weeks before the visit and taking up his new appointment as the head of the RAF staff of the British Joint Services Mission in Washington, DC. Before taking up his new position, Atcherley was keen to ensure he was in flying currency and credible in the eyes of his fellow fighter pilots, both at home and in the United States. Consequently, Atcherley visited West Raynham on 22 October 1953, and he endeavoured to fly in the Hawker Hunter and Supermarine Swift before departing for the United States. Weather precluded his Hawker Hunter flight, but he did manage to fly in the Supermarine Swift. However, his flying experiences in the United States would be more problematic.

Atcherley's Sabre Crash

As part of his new role in the United States, Atcherley was keen to continue to fly in fighter aircraft and, in particular, the cherished North American F-100 Super Sabre.[20] After much persuasion and cajoling of Pentagon officialdom and a thorough medical, he was cleared to fly by General Thomas White, the Vice Chief of the USAF. However, Atcherley had to prove himself first. Initially, he flew several sorties in a North American Sabre operated by the Canadian air force before flying the CF-100. Although the nomenclature is similar, the Avro Canada CF-100 Canuck was a straight-winged, twin-engined, two-seat interceptor and slower as well as less nimble than its Super Sabre counterpart. After his compressed introduction to fast-jet flying in North America, Atcherley flew to Los Angeles to visit the North American factory where the Super Sabre was built. Next, he headed to Edwards Air Force Base to fly in North American's latest supersonic fighter on 24 May 1954. However, before he could fly in the Super Sabre, the USAF wanted to ensure that Atcherley knew the nuances and challenges of landing on the dry lakebed runway. The plan was for Atcherley to fly three missions in one day and in three different aircraft types. First, a two-seat Lockheed T-33 Shooting Star jet trainer. Next, the latest F-86H variant of the Sabre before graduating to the F-100 Super Sabre. Atcherley's instructor for the day was none other than Major Chuck Yeager, the test pilot famed for being the first person to break the sound barrier a few years earlier in the Bell X-1. In the briefing, Atcherley was informed that he must remember that the F-100 Super Sabre 'was the first "unmodified" version and was a definite handful'.[21]

The first flight in the T-33 Shooting Star was flown with Yeager and without incident. However, the second mission on the F-86H Sabre most definitely ended in an incident! After a standard cockpit checkout by Major Austin Julian, Atcherley took off in the F-86H Sabre, serial number 52-1981A, at 1046, chased by Julian in the T-33 Shooting Star. The weather was perfect for the flight, with light winds of six miles per hour from the south-west, 20-mile visibility and high, thin scattered clouds at 30,000ft. Although Atcherley had flown the Sabre before, one significant difference on the F-86H was its brakes. The upgraded Sabre had a larger braking area and higher brake boost than earlier versions. Moreover, RAF pilots were accustomed to hand-operated differential brakes, whereas the USAF system used footbrakes. Consequently, Atcherley found that the Sabre's brakes were 'extremely sensitive and fierce'.

Twenty minutes into the sortie, Atcherley had familiarized himself with the aircraft and returned to the airfield for several touch and go's on the dry lake. Once content, Atcherley switched to the main runway, which benefitted from a four-mile over-run into the dry lake area. As a result of the unusually long runway and stopping area, there was no need for early or aggressive use of the brakes during the landing run. After an uneventful touch and go, Atcherley set himself up for a landing on the same runway. Despite landing with the flaps selected up and a slight tailwind, which would elongate the landing run, Atcherley elected to land on Runway 06.

Atcherley touched down at the correct point, some 1,000ft into the runway. However, something was wrong. Atcherley's personal staff officer, Wing Commander Stacey, recalls what happened next. 'I was somewhat surprised to see a cloud of black smoke, some flame and subsequently two tyres parting company with the wheels and soaring up into the air behind the aircraft . . . the Air Marshal swinging off the runway and vanishing into an enormous pall of dust.'[22]

Atcherley either landed with his feet on the brake pedals or, on landing, applied too much pressure onto the brakes. Either way, excessive braking was employed on touchdown, with the brakes immediately locking up and remaining so for the entirety of the landing run. The now out-of-control Sabre made a gradual turn to the left and departed the runway 3,000ft later, leaving behind broad black marks on the runway from the remnants of the tyres, traversing across a taxiway and 100ft of dirt before finally coming to rest 80 degrees left of the runway heading. Atcherley was fortunate; he walked away from the aircraft with only his pride damaged. However, the aircraft certainly bore the scars of Atcherley's little jaunt across the Edwards airfield.

All three tyres were blown. The main gear, nose gear, wheels and brakes were all damaged. On the inboard trailing edge of the wing, both flaps were dented. Both external fuel tanks were damaged on their underside. The stress of the incident caused a rippling of the fuselage skin aft of the main gear struts. The evidence was damning; Atcherley knew it, and so did the USAF.

The official USAF accident report shows that USAF senior leaders were acutely aware of the diplomatic sensitivities of a senior RAF officer crashing in a USAF aircraft. The accident report was 'streamlined so as to avoid unnecessary publicity'. Nevertheless, there was no cover-up. The USAF categorized the incident as a major accident; the aircraft was substantially damaged and caused by pilot error. The cost of the accident was a rather specific $5,297.49! Although the aircraft damage was considerable, it was not beyond economic repair, and the wounded Sabre would eventually return to flight status.[23] However, the reputational damage to the RAF and Atcherley was potentially greater. Despite the accident, Atcherley was still keen to fulfil his desire and fly the F-100 Super Sabre that very same day.

After much deliberation by the Edwards Air Force Base medical team and leadership, Atcherley was, amazingly, cleared to fly the F-100 Super Sabre that same afternoon. However, the weather took a turn for the worse, and only an afternoon dust storm at Edwards Air Force Base precluded the sortie from taking place. The mission was rescheduled for the following morning. Atcherley flew the F-100 sortie successfully, without incident, and with Yeager providing calm reassurance from the T-33 Shooting Star chase aircraft. The precedent was now set. RAF officers could now fly in the USAF's latest fighter – the F-100 Super Sabre. However, given what would happen when the next RAF officer flew the aircraft, perhaps Atcherley and the USAF may have reconsidered his desire and focus to fly the flawed Super Sabre.

Chapter 12

Letters From America

As part of the CFE's remit, the unit's charter tasked them to conduct 'liaison with Allied Air Forces to achieve maximum coordination of current thought and method'.[1] During his tenure as Commandant, Stephenson conducted at least three overseas trips, one to South Africa and two to the United States.

Over the period 2–27 February 1954, Stephenson visited South Africa with an entourage of CFE personnel. The visit would follow South African support to fighter operations over Korea. Again, the CFE monthly diary barely mentions the visit with only brief comment regarding the Air Fighting Development Unit's support to the visit.

Stephenson's letters from South Africa talk about his future in the RAF. He hints that promotion to Air Vice-Marshal was on the cards at the end of his current tour. Although his short-term prospects within the Service were looking rosy, his own longer-term commitment to the RAF was by no means assured. 'I don't know if I shall go on in the RAF for another ten years. If one is lucky, the prospect isn't too bad. It depends so much on our jobs.' While he was undoubtedly a product and advocate of the Cranwell system, he was becoming increasingly aware of his broader responsibilities and not limited to those of the RAF.

Stephenson's trip to South Africa was neither his first nor his most important overseas tour at the CFE. That honour would reside with the annual tour of the United States. Stephenson's fateful 1954 trip to the United States was not his first trip to the country as the CFE Commandant. He visited the United States the previous year from late October to early November 1953. Before Stephenson visited the United States, CFE hosted a reciprocal arrangement for the Air Proving Ground Command team the month prior. The CFE operations record book for the Air Fighting Development Squadron notes that their USAF counterparts 'paid several visits to the squadron during the second week of the month. The Venom aircraft was demonstrated to the team, and several members of the team flew the aircraft.'[2]

Although the CFE operations record book does not include a visit itinerary for the United States trip, a few of Stephenson's personal letters from the visit still exist. The 1953 visit included stops at Washington DC, Wright Patterson Air Force Base in Ohio, the home of the Air Development Center, Los Angeles to meet the various aircraft manufacturers, Edwards Air Force Base, the USAF's test and evaluation hub and the Air Defense Command headquarters at Colorado Springs in Denver. The last location on the schedule was Eglin Air Force Base in Florida, home of the Air Proving Ground Command.

In Stephenson's letters, he notes that the transatlantic journey was laborious.

We had lunch at Prestwick, tea in Iceland and then flew in the dark to Labrador, where we landed at Goose Bay, then on to Boston and finally, around 5.15, as dawn was breaking, in New York. We stopped [for] about an hour at each place, and it was a long night. We missed our stay in New York and got straight into another aeroplane, landed in Philadelphia, and got here shortly after 0900 on Thursday.'

As soon as the party arrived in Washington DC, their schedule was packed; work events during the day and a plethora of social activities in the evening, ranging from American football matches to dinner and the odd drink or two. One of the RAF team's favourite conversation-starters was to let it 'accidentally' slip to their American hosts that Stephenson's former role was as an *aide de camp* to the Queen. This situation led to the inevitable deluge of questions about the new Queen and the Royal Family. In one of his letters, Stephenson, perhaps feigning frustration, tells Maureen that 'out here, it is not amusing, at parties the chaps shoot a line about me and then some women comes up and say "oh, do tell me about the Queen"'. Nevertheless, the CFE team were bonding well together as a unit and as ambassadors for their Service and country. However, it came at a cost. Even though they were sometimes a little fragile in the mornings, the RAF team maintained the relentless tempo throughout the tour. Stephenson enjoyed it. He marvelled at Los Angeles, describing it as:

A coastal plain about 5–8 miles in width before the mountains rise up. It was once dry scrubland, but with water, it is fertile. The city stretches for miles and miles, streets are set at right angles, and the blocks are pretty large, except for the scattered shopping areas where the buildings are high. All the dwellings are bungalows with their unfenced garden and garage – not crowded and all fairly clean and tidy. At night, everything is a blaze of light, many street lights and every sort of neon sign. On Beverley Hills, there are bigger, more extravagant, more varied houses, but most are very huge. All sorts of architecture in there. I forgot to say that nearly all the bungalows are painted wooden construction. Then there are American cars galore. You can [not] believe it till you see it. Everyone must have one, and there are thousands of apparently brand-new, second-hand ones.

Not everything impressed Stephenson. 'The Grand Canyon didn't really look from the air any more imposing than Wadi Mujib.'[3] Surprisingly, Stephenson was somewhat underwhelmed with the National Park in Arizona, albeit he had seen it only from the air and had not had the experience of standing on its rim and taking in the amazing vista. Nevertheless, the 1953 United States tour left a lasting and positive impression on Stephenson. He made a series of connections that would stand him in good stead for the rest of his command tour. He also enjoyed the United States as a location and, in a classically understated way, thought he should consider a future posting there. His letter noted, 'I find the atmosphere entirely bearable and wouldn't mind living here on a job'. It would be another year before Stephenson returned to the United States.

The 1954 visit by the RAF team to Eglin Air Force Base was to continue to foster the strong working relationship between the two transatlantic fighter communities. Specifically, the visit was to look at the 'latest developments in the air defence of the US'.[4] The six-man CFE group was led by Stephenson and supported by Fred Rosier, Group Captain Operations at CFE. The additional members of the British party were Wing Commanders David Mawhood, Ricky Wright and Edward Crew, as well as Squadron Leader Dennis Walton.

Stephenson's party were a stellar bunch, consisting of decorated fighter pilots that covered the RAF's activities throughout the Second World War, including the Battle of France, the Battle of Britain, the Desert Air Force, the Italian campaign, the campaign for Western Europe and the Far East. One of the group was a night fighter ace with 15 kills and a further 31.5 kills against the dreaded V-1 missiles. Another had spent three years as a Japanese POW. The group had a remarkable set of personal histories, were at the forefront of RAF thinking at the dawn of the jet age, and most would go on to achieve senior positions within the Service. However, Stephenson nearly did not make it on the trip. A bout of pneumonia had been running through the household. Maureen had recovered from the illness, while Anna was admitted to Ely Hospital and missed the first six weeks of the first term of school. Stephenson avoided the illness. If Stephenson had caught pneumonia, he would not have been able to travel to the United States, a point that Maureen and her daughters did not miss.

The group's itinerary was similar to the previous year, with the group visiting the same places, organisations, and experts. However, not all of the cohort visited all of the locations. This revised schedule may have been an attempt to ease the furious tempo of the previous year's trip. Nevertheless, as noted in his letters, the pace was still relentless, and Stephenson's fatigue towards the end of the trip was evident. Moreover, and with echoes of the previous US tour and much to Stephenson's disappointment, the trip did not get off to a great start. Once again, technical issues thwarted Stephenson's attempts to spend time on the ground in New York. The group planned to depart London on Tuesday 19 October 1954, and fly on a British Overseas Airways Corporation Lockheed Constellation to New York's Idlewild airport via Prestwick in Scotland, Keflavik in Iceland, and Goose Bay in Canada.[5] Not only was the route circuitous compared to contemporary transatlantic travel, but it was not without its technical difficulties, as Stephenson notes in the first of his letters home to his wife. Frustratingly, he wrote his first letter home from his club in London, The Lansdowne Club, just off Berkeley Square in Mayfair, rather than New York!

Tuesday 11 pm. My Darling, It now doesn't go til tomorrow, so bang goes our chance of seeing New York. I gather that both engine trouble and bad weather are factors in our delay . . . The others have been dragged out by BOAC to a hotel several miles from Croydon! I really couldn't face it.

Five days later, Stephenson sent the following letter from Washington DC on Sunday, 24 October 1954. However, the letter was written a few days before, on Thursday 21st and on Royal Canadian Air Force headed paper from Goose Bay. The letter highlights the enduring challenges of a military officer travelling overseas! At the top of the first page and scribbled above the headed paper is a quick update – 'Sunday, we leave for Boston this lunchtime'. The letter continues:

My Darling, We are making the best of a bad job. It was very aggravating to get stuck for a night at Prestwick, and now we are stuck here. Yesterday to Iceland was lovely – a sunny, happy flight. There we met the Colonel I had written to and got VIP treatment. (How important it is to write good Battle of Britain letters!) He was our conducting officer last year at Colorado Springs. I could see the snow on the mountains to the north, and he says that it isn't too bad a place to be in. It was 35 degrees Fahrenheit so quite nippy. I passed the southern tip of Greenland in lovely weather. It looked very bleak and grim – like my idea of North Norway fiords, snow, deep water. We saw some icebergs – great big white masses floating along. We were at 18,000 feet at the time. I've got in here at 11:30 pm, and then, after a wait, we decided to come on up to the Mess. Their time was 7:30 pm. I've had supper, and so drank some good beer . . . Well, eventually, last night we heard that the engine could not be repaired and so it was arranged to put us up in the Mess. A long day but we had a good night's sleep. One feels very well here.

Well, we don't know when we shall be moving on. It is so difficult when one cannot say if one's messages for spare parts or a spare aeroplane have arrived in New York . . . The boys are in very good form. [Group Captain] Fred [Rosier], of course, claims to know everyone and everything in the States. I really am only amused, and the others too, I think.[6] I have no doubts that the party will be a very happy one. Sunday. I've, at last, got to Washington at 11:30 am and was rushed by [Air Vice-Marshal] Dick [Atcherley] straight into work.[7] He met us and was all smiles. He gave a party that night which was a great success, and I met lots of people, including [Group Captain Charles] Tomalin and [his wife] Maxie. . . . [Air Chief Marshal] Baker [Controller Aircraft]

and [Air Marshal] Tom Pike [Deputy Chief of Air Staff] were also there
and enjoying themselves very much . . . I think so much of you, darling,
I do hope you are happy through and through, and that strength is
coming back into you. I love you so very much always.

It took Stephenson's group six days to get from London to Washington, DC.
Nevertheless, the group were now in the United States and making up for lost
time. Stephenson's deputy, Fred Rosier, provides further details of the next
elements of the visit.

> After the initial briefing at the Pentagon, which I see from my notes
> I described as 'poor as it was superficial and most of the material was
> well known to us beforehand,' the team split into two parties, Air
> Commodore Stephenson, [Wing Commander David] Mawhood and
> I leaving for New England to go to MIT [Massachusetts Institute of
> Technology], the Cambridge Research Centre, Rome Air Development
> Centre and the GE [General Electric] factory plant at Syracuse, whilst
> Wright, Crew and Walton went to Wright Patterson Air Development
> Center and Edwards Air Force Base.[8]

Stephenson's following letter was hurriedly written at Boston Airport during a
brief lull in their hectic programme on Wednesday, 27 October 1954. The short
Air Mail 'Bluey' highlights the busy schedule, the growing team dynamic, the
value of the trip and the excellent US hospitality.

> My Darling Maureen, We are exhausted mentally. We really have
> worked hard for the last two and a half days. We all (Fred and David)
> admit that we are quite saturated and cannot, for the moment, absorb
> another drop of information. We have had explained a gigantic and very
> courageous and clever project.[9] Even at lunch, we ate sandwiches and
> talked or were talked to hard. That is the prime thought in my mind
> now. We have to wait here for an hour, having made a mistake in the
> time. Then we have about an hour's flight to Rome [the location of the
> Air Development Center at Griffiss Air Force Base in New York State],
> where we stay for two nights. I hope we get to bed early! We get to Los

Angeles at breakfast on Sunday next, and I hope there will be some letters there for us . . . I am very well. I can take these rather hectic tours, I think. This one is much more concentrated than last time . . . My love, my darling, Geoffrey.

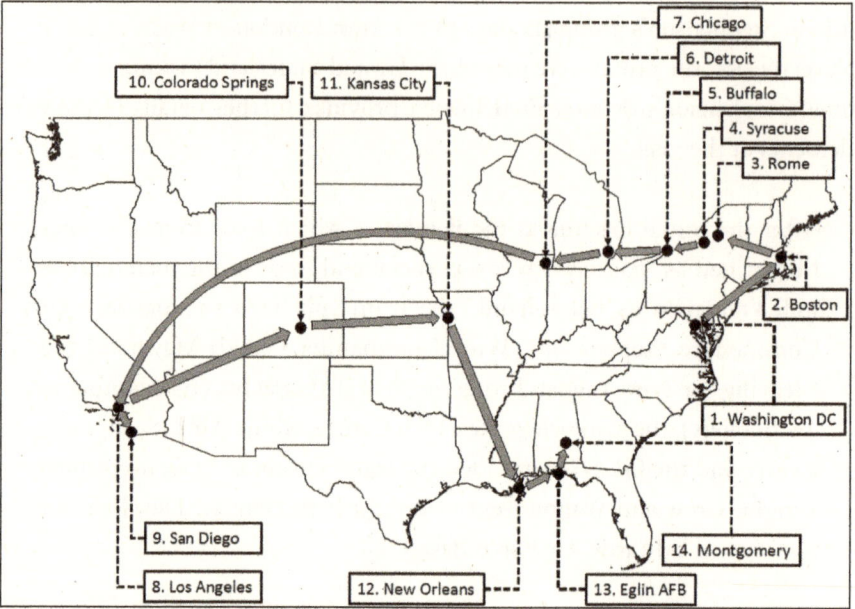

Figure 12.1 – The 1954 Central Fighter Establishment Tour of the United States.

Stephenson sent his subsequent letter from Chicago on Saturday, 30 October 1954. The Air Mail 'Bluey' was dated Friday, 29 October 1954, written during his journey westwards towards Los Angeles. The note also highlights the frenzied and intense nature of the visit. The tempo was starting to take its toll on Stephenson and his colleagues.

It is 11:30 pm at 8,000 feet with 40 people on board en route from Buffalo to Detroit after a very busy day. We land at Chicago after midnight and then have a long haul through a long night west to L.A., where we arrive at their breakfast time. What a week we have had – really, very hard at it. Amassing masses of information about new things and ideas. It is very exhausting, but we have managed to rise bright and chirpy each morning for more. I shall get an easy two days now to catch up on sleep and energy. I think I am putting on weight! I am eating too much and loving it! Everyone is outstandingly kind and friendly and most forthcoming . . . It will be interesting to hear what the rest of the team have been up to during the week. [Group Captain] Fred [Rosier] and [Wing Commander] David [Mawhood] are both in excellent form, tho' . . . I must doze now. I love you dearly, my darling, Geoffrey.

After a week apart, the two RAF parties regrouped in Los Angeles. Over three days, the RAF team aimed to visit four major military aircraft manufacturers' factories of Lockheed, Convair and Hughes and the producers of the F-100 Super Sabre, North American. Stephenson wrote his fourth letter of the tour to Maureen on Sunday, 31 October 1954, on Club Del Mar headed notepaper, located on Santa Monica Beach overlooking the Pacific Ocean. Stephenson was enjoying California, the opportunity to bond with his team and his seniors; the pace remained relentless, but Stephenson was apparently coping better than others. After visiting Los Angeles, Stephenson and his group flew east to visit Air Defense Command at Colorado Springs. His final letter was sent from there on Friday, 5 November 1954. However, Stephenson penned it on United Airlines headed notepaper two days prior on Wednesday, 3 November, during the flight between Los Angeles and Denver. The opportunity to recover some sleep and energy may not have been as successful as Stephenson had hoped. Ominously, Stephenson was also reflecting on the recent death of a friend and colleague. Air Vice-Marshal Johnny Hawtrey and his *aide de camp* were both killed in a car accident in Italy while returning from his tour as Air Officer Commanding Iraq.

My Darling, I last wrote to you on Sunday. The stay in L.A. was very comfortable indeed, and we had two cars for the party, which was an enormous benefit. I really had a very comfortable and pleasant room with bathroom attached; and the price was reasonable. Each day we visited a different firm going down to San Diego by air yesterday. We were wonderfully looked after both during the day and in the evenings. We ran into [Air Chief Marshal] Sir John Baker one evening quite unexpectedly and brought him back for a drink. He was particularly friendly. It is a clear blue day and perfectly lovely. The Rockies are all

covered in snow. We are short of sleep, but that's how it is on these trips
. . . I am at the Broadmoor (a fabulous place in American eyes, so you
know it must be about 10 star.) In a very great hurry written at breakfast,
I wonder about Johnny Hawtrey and am very sad. I must unhappily end
this now and send you all my very fondest and deepest love. I am very
well, Geoffrey.

Upon completing their visit to Air Defense Command at Colorado Springs,
the group moved to Eglin Air Force Base in Florida via Kansas City, New
Orleans, and Pensacola.[10] Stephenson was no stranger to Eglin Air Force Base
as he visited it during his 1953 tour.

Bizarrely, the CFE operations record book does not capture the events of
8 November 1954. Indeed, there is very little recorded in the unit's official
history regarding the six-man tour of the United States. The only comment
in the document is a passing comment in the November 1954 input from
the All-Weather Wing, which informs that Wing Commander Crew and
Squadron Leader Walton visited Fighter Command to 'lecture on the all-
weather aspects of the recent CFE team visit to the USA'.[11] Incredibly, there
is no mention of their Commandant's visit to the United States, his flight in
the F-100 Super Sabre nor, for that matter, his death. Indeed, at the time of
Stephenson's death, the CFE's operations record book focuses on the visit
of their former commandant, Air Vice-Marshal 'Paddy' Crisham, and now
Air Officer Commanding 12 Group, to West Raynham and his flight in the
new Hawker Hunter fighter on 9 November 1954. Nevertheless, why was
Stephenson visiting Eglin Air Force Base, what led up to the accident and
what actually happened on that fateful day?

Chapter 13

The Last Flight – 8 November 1954

'Lo I am with Thee, even unto the end.'

Mathew 28:20 and
Epitaph on Stephenson's Gravestone
Oakwood Cemetery Annex
Montgomery, Alabama

To keep abreast of the latest tactical thinking from its key strategic partner, CFE maintained regular dialogue and visits to its allied counterpart. The visits were not only about strategic leadership engagement at the Pentagon, insights into the latest developments in aviation research and visits to the aircraft manufacturers, there was also a more practical element of the visit. Consequently, it also included familiarization sorties in the latest jets from each air force's inventory. The RAF's key relationship during the post-Second World War era and in the early days of the Cold War was with the USAF. Therefore, a strong bilateral relationship between CFE and its USAF equivalent, Air Proving Ground Command based at Eglin Air Force Base in the Florida panhandle, was a focus for both Stephenson and his organization. The scale of the two operations was starkly different. The Air Proving Ground Command set-up was on a significantly larger scale, one that Stephenson and CFE could only dream of.

Eglin Air Force Base is located south of and adjacent to the town of Valparaiso in north-western Florida, some 30 miles east of Pensacola and situated on the shores of the Gulf of Mexico. Airfield construction of what was then called the Valparaiso Bombing and Gunnery Base began in March 1933, with the airfield becoming active just over two years later, on 14 June 1935.[1] As its name suggested, the initial role of the Valparaiso base was as a bombing and gunnery range. Consequently, to provide air-to-ground ranges, 383,744 acres of Choctawhatchee National Forest were added to the airfield's portfolio on 27 June 1940.[2] Throughout the 1940s, the base's expansion continued with the creation of ten auxiliary airfields in the local area.[3] By 31 December 1944, the base complex comprised 30 miles of runway and 882 buildings. The name Eglin Air Force Base was not adopted until 24 June 1948, in honour of Lieutenant Colonel Frederick Irving Eglin. Eglin was the first-rated US military aviator in 1917 and was responsible for training many US aviators during the First World War.[4] However, on 1 January 1937, Eglin was killed while flying his Northrop A-17 pursuit aircraft from Langley Field, Virginia, to Maxwell Field in Alabama.[5]

A 1954 article describes the role and the vast scale of the Air Proving Ground Command enterprise. 'The Air Proving Ground Reservation stretches over approximately 465,000 acres. The land area is 60 miles East-West by 25 miles North-South. In addition, water ranges are available along 100 miles of the coastline, extending into the Gulf of Mexico to approximately 150 miles. Test operations are conducted on 39 active ranges and 11 airfields.'[6] Air Proving Ground Command

represents one of the basic conceptions for the development of air power. Experience in all branches of military service has demonstrated repeatedly that only when there exists an independent, specially equipped agency to represent the using organization will there be adequate, realistic testing of military material. As a result, the Air Proving Ground Command was established to determine the operational suitability of aircraft, material, and other equipment used or proposed for use by the United States Air Force.[7]

By UK and RAF standards, the space, resources and talent at both Eglin Air Force Base and the Air Proving Ground Command were impressive and an instant draw for senior RAF leaders such as Stephenson and CFE.

During his 1953 visit to Eglin Air Force Base, Stephenson flew in the North American F-86 Sabre and the two-seat jet trainer, the Lockheed T-33 Shooting Star.[8] The former was famed for its recent stellar performance over its Soviet MiG-15 nemesis in the skies of 'MiG Alley' during the Korean War. The F-86 Sabre was not a new aircraft type for Stephenson as he had already flown the

Canadian-built Sabre variant. The RAF employed the Sabre as a short-term stopgap between the RAF's first generation of fighters and the delivery of the next group of RAF fighters, including the Hawker Hunter. Consequently, the RAF received its first Sabres in December 1952, with the first Sabre squadron becoming operational in May 1953. Ultimately, the F-86 Sabre would equip 12 RAF squadrons; ten in West Germany and two in the UK.[9]

The latter aircraft was the first USAF jet trainer. As a former CFS commandant overseeing RAF flying instructor training, Stephenson would have been intrigued by the Lockheed T-33 Shooting Star. The new USAF trainer was broadly comparable to its RAF opposite number, the Jet Provost, which flew for the first time in June 1954. There were no reported issues associated with Stephenson's previous flights in USAF aircraft.

Considering Atcherley's recent crash in the F-86H Sabre at Edwards Air Force Base, it was not a foregone conclusion that the USAF would approve the RAF's request for the CFE team to fly in their aircraft. There were several bureaucratic challenges to overcome before Stephenson, and his party would find themselves at the helm of the latest USAF fighter aircraft. An undated confidential note from the USAF Headquarters to the Air Proving Ground Command stipulated that 'no foreign nationals . . . will be cleared to fly test or late model tactical aircraft without written approval of this headquarters'.[10] Another note suggested that the approval rested with either the Chief of Staff or Vice Chief of Staff.[11]

In seeking an exemption from the USAF's policy, a response from the Air Proving Ground Command on 22 October 1954 noted that CFE had made reciprocal arrangements to allow USAF personnel to fly in the latest RAF front-line aircraft types.[12] The note also suggested that the unit could support North American F-100 Super Sabre, F-86H Sabre flights and possibly the Republic F-84F Thunderstreak flights.[13] Rather intriguingly, the note also alludes to the CFE's desire to fly the captured Soviet-built MiG-15 fighter, now located at Wright-Patterson Air Force Base, during the same trip.[14] The MiG-15 and its pilot had defected from North Korea to Seoul in September 1953. After evaluation in Japan by USAF test pilots, including Chuck Yeager, the MiG-15 was airlifted to its current location in Ohio in December 1953 for further flight testing.[15] The thought of RAF pilots flying the latest variant of the MiG-15 would have been an exciting prospect due to its exploits during the recently terminated Korean War.

On 29 October 1954, the Air Proving Ground Command headquarters informed the USAF headquarters that CFE

> representatives have voiced a desire to fly the [Northrop] F-89D [Scorpion] and F-86H during their visit to Eglin on 8 November 1954. A limited number of flights can be supported without undue interference with [Operational Suitability Test] programs. In the interest of maintaining excellent relations existing between this command and CFE authority is requested to permit one F-89D flight and two F-86H flights. Total flying time one plus 30 for the F-89D, 2 plus 30 for the F-86H.[16]

USAF headquarters quickly approved the request as it was a low-risk proposition.

On 5 November 1954, a telephone conversation between USAF headquarters and Air Proving Ground Command staff expanded the options of aircraft types that the RAF visitors could fly.[17] The records do not contain the rationale for including the F-84F and the F-100 in the CFE programme. Therefore, it is unclear if this was a request from the UK to include the most recent arrival at Eglin Air Force Base or if it was an internal USAF option to showcase their latest fighter aircraft. Following the telephone conversation, the USAF headquarters confirmed, via letter, the types of aircraft that the CFE pilots were permitted to fly in. The 5 November note confirmed that the RAF visitors could fly late model aircraft F-89D, F-86H and include the F-100 at the discretion of the Air Proving Ground Commander.[18] The USAF was incrementally developing their current fleet of front-line fighters, including the F-84F Thunderstreak, the F-86H Sabre and the F-89D Scorpion. As a result, the RAF had equivalent, if not similar, types in operational service. Moreover, the risk involved in flying these types was relatively minimal. For example, the F-89D Scorpion was a two-seat aircraft where a USAF pilot could mentor the visiting pilot from the other cockpit. Likewise, the F-86 Sabre was an aircraft that the RAF pilots were familiar with as it was in RAF service, and exchange pilots had flown it operationally with the USAF during the recent Korean War, albeit the F-86H was a more advanced variant and Atcherley's recent escapade in the Sabre did not help matters. Consequently, while interesting to see and fly in, these aircraft were not a paradigm shift from what CFE were flying daily back in the UK. However, the same was not true for the last aircraft on the list of aircraft the RAF flyers were allowed to fly. It was no longer a test aircraft but had just begun its operational test and evaluation. In parallel, it had just entered front-line service but had yet to be declared operational. Moreover, its introduction heralded the leap from the basic first generation of jet fighters to the dawn of more advanced second-generation high-performance, supersonic fighter aircraft. Therefore, the USAF's newest fighter aircraft truly caught the RAF visitors' attention and imagination – the North American F-100A Super Sabre.

The North American Aviation F-100A Super Sabre

As the company's first variant of the F-86 Sabre was entering front-line service in 1949, North American Aviation was already considering not only improvements to the aircraft but also its successor.[19] By January 1951, the company initiated a self-funded 'Sabre 45' study named after the more daring 45-degree sweep on the wing, rather than the sedate 35 degrees of its F-86 predecessor.[20] The new aircraft's design called for a single-seat, low-wing, high-performance air superiority fighter; in essence, the F-100 Super Sabre was to be a direct replacement for the F-86 Sabre. However, the F-100's unique selling point was its ability to achieve supersonic speeds in straight and level flight. This characteristic is a baseline requirement for any new fighter aircraft today. However, in the early 1950s, this was a global first, and the requirement occurred only a few years after Chuck Yeager's first supersonic flight on board the Bell X-1 in October 1947. The introduction of the F-100 Super Sabre, or 'Hun' as it was affectionately known, heralded the arrival of the century series of fighters that would provide the backbone of the USAF throughout the 1960s. The Super Sabre also marked the dawn of the second generation of fighter aircraft, which were distinguishable by a step change in aircraft performance, multi-role utility, as well as more advanced weapons and sensors.

Nevertheless, an advanced airframe design alone was insufficient to meet the demands of supersonic flight; the designers had to incorporate a more advanced jet engine. Pratt and Whitney developed the J57-P-7 turbojet engine for the early F-100 Super Sabre, which, when matched with the emerging concept of an afterburner, provided over 14,000lbs of thrust.[21] Consequently, North American believed that the proposed airframe and engine combination delivered on its promise of supersonic flight. Two further century-series fighters, the McDonnell F-101 Voodoo and the Convair F-102 Delta Dagger, as well as several naval fighter aircraft also used the same engine.[22] However, its utility was not only limited to fighter aircraft as eight J57s would be fitted to each Boeing B-52 Stratofortress while a single engine would power the Lockheed U-2 spy plane.[23] In its civilian TF3 form, the engine equipped the Boeing 707 (including the military variants, the KC-135 Stratotanker and C-135 Stratolifter) as well as the Douglas DC-8 airliners.[24] The Pratt and Whitney J57 was an era-defining engine.

On 14 May 1951, amid the Korean War, the company submitted a proposal for the new fighter concept to the USAF. In response, the USAF awarded a contract for two prototypes on 1 November 1951 and designated the new aircraft as the F-100A a month later, on 7 December 1951.[25] The following month, the USAF signed an initial contract with North American Aviation to produce 23 F-100A aircraft; it later extended the contract to 273 aircraft in August 1952.[26] The first of the two prototypes rolled off the production line on schedule on 24 April 1953.[27] After transferring the aircraft to Edwards Air Force Base, the North American Aviation Chief Test Pilot, George Welch, once again took the controls of another North American fighter on its maiden flight on 25 May 1953.[28] During the 57-minute inaugural flight, Welch demonstrated the F-100A's potential by achieving supersonic flight at 35,000ft.[29] Buoyed by their initial success, North American Aviation were keen to accelerate their test programme. The USAF pilots assigned to the F-100 test programme were, wisely, a little more circumspect in their approach. USAF test pilots confirmed that the aircraft outperformed any other production aircraft in the USAF's inventory and had potential as a weapons platform. However, there were concerns regarding the aircraft's stability at all flight conditions and altitudes.[30] The plane demonstrated an uncontrollable yaw and pitching motion near its stalling speed.[31] Despite these reservations, senior USAF officials endorsed the manufacturer's desire to continue to accelerate the F-100 development programme.[32]

Despite the emerging issues, North American Aviation was manufacturing the production F-100As in parallel to the test programme. The first F-100A came off the production line on 25 September 1953, with the first aircraft being accepted by the USAF the following month, on 26 October 1953.[33] As the USAF's Tactical Air Command began to accept the first F-100A into service on 18 September 1954, there were concerns as front-line pilots were also experiencing stability and control problems.[34] Less than a month later, on 12 October 1954, the F-100 programme suffered a significant setback. The test programme scheduled George Welch to undertake a demanding test sortie in one of the early F-100As from Edwards Air Force Base in the Mojave Desert. The profile called for a maximum speed dive from 45,000ft followed by a maximum G pull-up at 24,000ft.[35] In the dive, Welch achieved Mach 1.55 and a 7G pull-up. However, the aircraft disintegrated during the manoeuvre before crashing onto the dry lake at Edwards Air Force Base. Welch survived the crash, but he was mortally injured. The test pilot and Second World War ace, nominated for the Medal of Honor for his actions in the air against the Japanese attackers over Pearl Harbor on 7 December 1941, was pronounced dead on arrival at the nearby Palmdale hospital.[36] Less than a month later, Stephenson and his team would visit Eglin Air Force Base.

Stephenson and his party arrived at Eglin Air Force Base at 1900 on Sunday, 7 November.[37] The group retired to the Batchelor Officers' Quarters for the night 3 hours later at 2200.[38] They were well rested and was woken at 0630 by their escorting officer, Major Edward Johnston.[39] The plan for the day was for two British pilots to fly the Super Sabre; Stephenson was to fly first, chased by another Super Sabre flown by an experienced USAF pilot.[40] Group Captain Fred Rosier would replace Stephenson for the second sortie and follow the same profile.[41] The schedule called for a 1400 take-off for the first event.[42] Consequently, the British pilots had much to cover ahead of their afternoon F-100 familiarization sorties.

Flight Preparation

After meeting their hosts at 0800 and the usual pleasantries, the first briefing started at 0815. Lieutenant Colonel Henry 'Baby' Brown, the F-100 Super Sabre project officer at the Air Proving Ground Command, conducted the first brief.[43] Brown was a veteran fighter ace with considerable combat experience and time as a POW in Germany, albeit a much shorter period than Stephenson.

Brown's 45-minute briefing to the entire RAF party covered the handling characteristics of the F-100 Super Sabre and the Operational Suitability Testing on the aircraft to date. The briefing was generic and did not focus on the two RAF pilots who were selected to fly the F-100 Super Sabre that afternoon. Stephenson's recent visit to the North American plant in California proved to be a useful foundation ahead of Brown's briefing. During his visit to the Palmdale plant, Stephenson had several discussions with the engineers and test pilots. As a result, he was deemed well-informed on the Super Sabre and had shown significant interest in the aircraft.[44]

Following the briefing, Brown was only then informed that two of the RAF pilots were to be given a flight in the Super Sabres that afternoon. Brown sought permission to be excused from the remaining briefings and immediately departed 'to coordinate matters pertaining to the flights. At approximately 1015, [Brown] arrived at the Flight Line and found that there was only one F-100 in commission, and another expected in by noon.' Brown curtailed the morning flight of the sole serviceable Super Sabre to 30 minutes to ensure that the aircraft was available for the RAF flights later that day. At some time after 1100 and following Lieutenant Colonel Sharp's departure in the sole serviceable Super Sabre, Brown instructed 'that unless we had two F-100s in commission, I was going to get the flights cancelled. I wanted one of the F-100s to act as a chase aircraft. I told Captain Moore that he was to act as the chase pilot.'[45]

The pilot chosen to act as Stephenson's chase pilot was Captain Lonnie Moore. Although the most junior of the group in terms of rank, he was an experienced pilot in his own right. As mentioned, Moore had been at Eglin for over three years, including a stint in Korea, where he achieved ace status. Following his Korean War experience, Moore returned to his former unit at Eglin Air Force Base and served as the chief project officer for the

Operational Suitability Tests of the F-100A Super Sabre. From August 1954, the 3200th Test Wing operated six F-100A Super Sabres from Eglin Air Force Base.[46] Four of the aircraft were allocated to Moore's unit, the Air Force Operational Test Center, to conduct Operational Suitability Testing; the Air Force Armament Center used the remaining two Super Sabres to conduct the various weapon tests.[47]

As Brown frantically rearranged the flying programme, the engineers busily tried to generate two serviceable Super Sabres to meet the apparent short-notice demands to fly two RAF pilots. It was not until lunchtime that Brown discovered which two RAF pilots would fly in the Super Sabres and in what order. At approximately 1245, and after lunch at the Officers' Club, the group moved to the Flight Line Operations building, where Brown began the initial checkout procedures for Stephenson and Rosier.[48] Over the next 90 minutes, Brown 'went over the landing techniques with both officers. They seemed to have more questions on the landing pattern than any other phase of the flight. The Air Commodore was very meticulous in his questioning. On a knee pad, he wrote all the information pertaining to altitudes, direction of landing, air speeds, where to break on the initial, where to lower dive brakes and at what airspeed to lower gear.'[49]

Following the detailed discussion on landing techniques, the briefing turned its attention to the take-off characteristics of the Super Sabre. Brown explained the take-off trim button and the high break-out forces required on the horizontal stabilizer.[50] Brown then explained a porpoising effect that these high break-out forces could introduce to the aircraft. If the porpoising effect was evident, Brown briefed that the control column should be held in its current position and not to fight the controls; if that action did not remedy the problem, then the control column was to be released.[51] Brown also cautioned the RAF pilots to expect a yawing sensation as the wheels retracted into the airframe on take-off.[52]

The remainder of the briefing covered the climb-out, the supersonic portion of the mission, as well as a review of a map showing the local area, particularly the location of Eglin Air Force Base and Crestview and where his track was to be during his supersonic flight. 'The briefing was considered to be very thorough, covering all information he had to know prior to flight.'[53] Moore was perhaps less fulsome in his praise when he suggested that he 'considered this as an adequate briefing'.[54]

Brown asked Stephenson if he wished to read the 'Dash 1 handbook', the pilot's operations handbook, for the aircraft that stipulated the procedures for the specific aircraft type.[55] Surprisingly, he did not even answer the question. Upon completing the briefing, Stephenson visited the flying equipment section for a helmet and oxygen mask fitting. He was happy with his equipment. The helmet fitted well, and he tested the oxygen mask to prove it was in good working order.[56] Stephenson was familiar with the US oxygen mask as the RAF used an 'exact duplicate of the American type'.[57] Of note, the helmet did not have a visor fitted, nor were anti-G trousers offered or fitted.

Start-Up, Taxi, and Take Off

As Stephenson walked from the Flight Line Operations building to his allocated aircraft on the apron, the weather could not have been better. On 8 November 1954, northern Florida was blessed with clear skies, 15 miles visibility, a surface wind speed of 14 knots, 47 per cent humidity and a temperature of just over 20 degrees centigrade.[58] It was a lovely day to go flying.

Brown and Colonel Edward Szaniawski, the Deputy Commander Air Force Operational Center at the Air Proving Ground Command and another Second World War fighter ace and former POW, escorted Stephenson to his steed for the day – F-100A-10NA, serial number 53-1534A.[59] As was the USAF's custom at the time, the Super Sabre wore no camouflage scheme, and the bright silver aluminium skin was bare bar the mandatory USAF roundel located between the air intake and cockpit and serial numbers on the fuselage and tailfin. This next-generation fighter's sleek, clean lines must have looked both mesmerising and daunting to Stephenson as he strode towards the aircraft as it basked in the late autumn sunshine. His allocated aircraft was less than three months old, having rolled out of the North American Aviation Plant adjacent to Los Angeles International Airport on 11 August 1954.[60] Consequently, the aircraft had only flown for 38 hours and 55 minutes before this, its last mission.[61] Recently, the aircraft suffered a recurring technical issue associated with smoke and fumes in the cockpit.[62] However, the Eglin engineering team rectified the problem by replacing the heating vents.[63] The aircraft subsequently flew 12 uneventful sorties, including two flights during the morning of 8 November.[64]

Lieutenant Colonel Moreland got airborne at 0840 for a 1 hour and 15-minute flight.[65] Next, Lieutenant Colonel Daniel Sharp took the controls of the F-100 Super Sabre, which lasted 34 minutes and landed at 1145.[66] On neither sortie was there a recurrence of the smoke and fumes issues. Indeed, the aircraft was declared fully serviceable by both pilots after their respective sorties. Neither mission highlighted any indicators of what was to come as the engineers prepared the Super Sabre for Stephenson's mission.

During the pre-flight walk-round inspection, which Brown led, it was obvious from Stephenson's comments 'that he had a certain amount of previous knowledge of the aircraft'.[67] Moore joined the group at this point. Brown continued the walk-round while Stephenson and Moore discussed the taxi-out procedure, line-up, take-off, and air work to be performed. 'The Air Commodore was very interested in flying formation, and this took a lot of the discussion time. It was agreed that Captain Moore would make the radio calls after the Air Commodore checked in to make his initial radio check. This was agreed since the Air Commodore said that he has trouble making his transmission understood over the radio. Captain Moore was also to taxi out first to lead the Air Commodore to the take-off position.'[68]

Post the walk-round, Stephenson climbed into the cockpit with Brown on one side of the cockpit and Colonel Szaniawski on the other. Brown strapped Stephenson into the seat and explained how to tighten the shoulder straps and seat belt.[69] Next, Brown briefed him on how to use the ejection seat system. Once comfortable with his seating position and operation, Brown worked 'left to right' explaining the various panels and functions in the cockpit, starting with the Emergency Dive Brake Lever on the left to the Emergency Hydraulic Pump Lever on the right-hand side and everything in between![70] Brown showed how to set up the radio and its operation.[71] Finally, Stephenson was allowed to bring 'the Hun' to life. He dutifully followed the American's instructions. The aircraft started without issue. Brown confirmed that Stephenson was familiar with the location of the drag chute lever and could easily reach it.[72] Stephenson's 'oxygen mask was checked in the cockpit, and the oxygen system checked prior to closing the canopy'.[73]

After confirming that Stephenson had no more questions, the canopy was closed, and Brown confirmed that 'he himself double-checked the canopy, and it was definitely closed and locked'.[74] However, there was an issue. It should come as no surprise, given the complexity of the aircraft, Stephenson's lack of familiarity and his hasty introduction to the Super Sabre. Stephenson was confused regarding using the aircraft's communication system. As a result, he opened the canopy to seek advice from Brown, who had by now stepped away from the side of the cockpit to allow Stephenson to finish the start-up procedure.[75] Before Brown could approach the aircraft and assist him with the radio problem, the issue was resolved by Stephenson himself, and he re-closed the canopy.[76]

Airborne . . .

Contrary to the brief, Stephenson taxied first and 'used too much throttle on his initial roll but corrected very nicely prior to gaining the taxi strip. His use of brake and nose wheel steering was very good.'[77] The reason for the deviation from the brief was a simple one. Only one power unit was available between the two aircraft. Consequently, the new plan called for Stephenson to start first.

Additionally, once lined up on Eglin's Runway 19, there was another deviation from the brief. Instead of lighting the afterburner while stationary, Stephenson released his brakes first and started his take-off run before he selected the afterburner.[78] While not a serious safety issue in its own right, it suggests that Stephenson may not have had sufficient time or instruction to fully absorb the Super Sabre's operating procedures. Worse was to follow. Immediately after lifting off Eglin's southerly runway, Stephenson's aircraft began to violently pitch up and down, or 'porpoise'.

Of those who witnessed the take-off, Moore was probably in the best position. Sat on the end of the runway and then following Stephenson during his take-off gave him a unique perspective. Moore commented, 'this was the worst porpoise that I had ever seen. It was so bad that I thought he would crash back into the runway.'[79] 'Shortly after take-off, he pulled the aircraft up sharply, and the porpoising decreased considerably. It started immediately again. He porpoised on take-off for seven to eight miles. He would almost get under control, and then it would start again. After seven or eight miles, he got the porpoising stopped, and from then on, he had the aircraft under control.'[80]

Captain Eugene M. Faber was also on the ramp as the F-100s started up and was available to render assistance during the start-up procedure if required. Once the aircraft had taxied to the runway, Faber moved forward to the taxiway to get a better view of the take-off. Faber describes what he saw, 'the take-off roll and lift-off appeared to be normal up to the point when the gear was retracted, at which time the nose appeared to come down and the aircraft started a violent porpoising which continued through three or four cycles and then appeared to dampen out'.[81]

Standing on the same spot on the ramp where the aircraft taxied from, Brown described the take-off as 'Up to the point of his breaking ground on take-off, his take-off was very good. Upon lifting the aircraft from the runway, the Air Commodore greatly overcorrected on the horizontal stabilizer. It was the poorest take-off that I had seen while working with the F-100.'[82]

It took some time for Stephenson to remedy the situation. By the time he regained control, the aircraft had accelerated to 450 knots, crossed Choctawhatchee Bay and was now over the beautiful white sands of Fort Walton Beach, heading towards the massive expanse of the Gulf of Mexico, some 7 miles south of Eglin Air Force Base.[83] Stephenson had survived the take-off portion of the sortie, but only just.

After recovering from the 'porpoising' issue immediately after take-off, Stephenson turned left 180 degrees over the Gulf of Mexico onto a northerly heading, crossed the coastline and headed back overland as he climbed the Super Sabre up to 43,000ft in the clear skies of Florida.[84] Moore followed Stephenson but sat between 2,000 and 3,000ft behind the lead Super Sabre.[85] Upon levelling off at their assigned altitude, both Super Sabres crossed the US Highway 90 that ran east/west across northern Florida and marked the northernmost point of their circuit.[86] Both aircraft turned left 180 degrees, passing overhead the town of Crestview and pointed towards Eglin Air Force Base, some 20 miles away.[87] Once steady on a heading of south, both pilots selected afterburner to begin their supersonic acceleration.[88] The Super Sabre ably demonstrated its power by smoothly accelerating through the sound barrier before stabilizing at Mach 1.3 while maintaining level flight – this was the Super Sabre's party trick and unique selling point. This phase of the flight passed without any difficulty; there was a typical 'running conversation' between the two pilots on their dedicated radio channel, Channel 13, and nothing to indicate any issues.[89] Stephenson called on the radio to extend the dive brakes and reduce power. Simultaneously, Stephenson brought his aircraft out of the fuel-thirsty afterburner, selected the speed brake out, and began a descent down to 15,000ft.[90] Moore followed the leader's actions and maintained his position 2,000ft behind Stephenson. Next, as he approached the overhead of Eglin Air Force Base, Stephenson turned the aircraft left through 180 degrees to, once again, cross the Floridian coast and head inland on a heading of north.[91]

As he approached his planned height of 15,000ft, Stephenson shallowed the aircraft's rate of descent and increased the throttle setting up to 90 per cent power. Next, Stephenson called on the radio to direct Moore to bring his 'Speed Brakes Up' while retracting his own speed brake.[92] Once level at 15 000 feet and his speed now established at a more fuel-efficient 300 knots, Stephenson was ready for the next serial – close formation practice with Moore taking over as the formation leader. As a veteran flying instructor with a significant amount of close formation practice and aerobatic experience, Stephenson would have been in his element with this portion of the mission. As planned, Stephenson 'requested the chase pilot to come up even with him so he could fly formation. The chase pilot's rate of closure was slow, and when he came up even, he advised the pilot [Stephenson] that he would pass on the left. This transmission was "rogered"' – this simple acknowledgement would be Stephenson's last radio call, and the next move would be his last and proved fatal.[93]

After the last radio call, 'it appeared to the chase pilot that the pilot [Stephenson] started to cross under his aircraft to fly [on] his left wing'.[94] With the sun in their seven o'clock position and without the benefit of a visor, Stephenson may have elected to cross below and behind Moore's aircraft to take up a position on Moore's left-wing or echelon left in order to have the sun behind him to avoid the glare. Moore watched Stephenson cross behind him in his 5 o'clock position and estimated him to be 25–30ft below and 10–15ft behind his aircraft.[95] At this point, Stephenson's aircraft began to porpoise again. Moore believed the oscillations were not as severe as those witnessed during take-off and had no cause for concern.[96] Moore now lost sight of Stephenson as he crossed below the leader's tail and into the lead Super Sabre's blind spot.[97] Moore was expecting to see Stephenson emerge under control in his 7 o'clock position, but he did not appear.[98] After checking to confirm Stephenson had not returned to his original position on the right, Moore suspected that he had dropped back to stabilize and control the 'porpoising' Super Sabre.[99] Consequently, Moore remained unconcerned and elected to maintain his heading and height while continuing to travel north.[100] During this period, there was no radio communication between the two pilots. However, with the formation approaching the overhead of Eglin Auxiliary Airfield Number Two, Stephenson was in trouble.

Immediately after crossing behind and below Moore's lead Sabre, Stephenson entered a near vertical uncontrolled roll or spin down to approximately 5,000ft, where the aircraft appeared to make a momentary recovery to a relatively level flight path.[101]

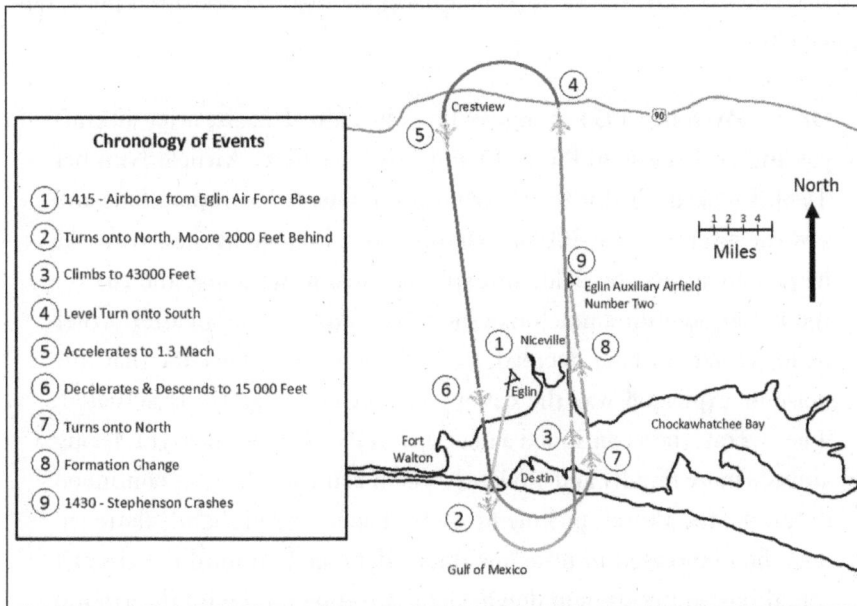

Figure 13.1 – Flight Path of Stephenson's F-100A Super Sabre Sortie.

The testimonies of 15 individuals who witnessed the final moments of the crash were captured and reproduced in the subsequent crash report. However, not all witnesses are equal; some saw very little, while others had neither the knowledge nor experience to describe what they saw in detail. Some narratives contradicted others in what they thought they observed as Stephenson's aircraft crossed over the airfield from the south-west and headed north-east.

However, several of those on the ground at Eglin Auxiliary Airfield Number Two who witnessed Stephenson's predicament were credible witnesses. This group were pilots from the 612th Fighter Bomber Squadron, a visiting F-86 Sabre squadron from Alexandria Air Force Base in Louisiana. One of the F-86 pilots from the 612th Fighter Bomber Squadron who witnessed the Super Sabre's last moments was First Lieutenant M. H. Lamb. In his testimony, Lamb said he saw: 'Two aircraft together in the air at a high level. He states that one aircraft broke away from the other to the left. He did not notice anything unusual until he saw one turn to the left.'[102]

The second witness from the 612th Fighter Bomber Squadron was First Lieutenant Harvey L. Brown, a flight commander and F-86 pilot. His statement reads:

On 8 November 1954 at approximately 1430, I heard a jet aircraft passing fairly close to Pierce Field [Eglin Auxiliary Airfield Number Two]. I looked up at it from my position outside base operations and saw the aircraft, an F-100 in a slightly nose-low, slight right turn. As he passed across the field, an explosion was heard above the roar of the F-100, sounding much like the initial explosion of an afterburner being actuated I later decided, from the sequence of events, that this noise or explosion was the canopy ejector cartridge being actuated. The aircraft then continued a nose-low roll or spin to the right, losing altitude more rapidly and obviously out of control. The nose continued dropping, the aircraft picking up more speed, the roll slightly flattened out, then increased in nose low pitch, tightened up until the aircraft was almost going straight down, slightly rolling until it hit the ground almost vertically. The aircraft appeared to me to be inverted when it struck the ground. Approximately 2 seconds after impact, I sighted an object that looked to me just like a canopy, falling rear end first and hitting fairly close to the wreckage of the aircraft. The speed of the aircraft at the time it struck the ground, I would judge to be about 250–270 knots. At the time I first sighted the aircraft, I would judge its altitude to be 3,000 to 3,500 feet. My impressions and recollections of the events lead me to believe that the canopy was jettisoned at some point previous to the entry into the right-hand, vertical roll . . . The explosion I heard was not followed by an increase in engine noise. The explosion was preceded by normal engine noise, and after the explosion, normal engine noise was again heard with no evident increase in power delivery.[103]

Another witness from the 612th Fighter Bomber Squadron was Captain Donald M. McCance, the Operations Officer and an F-86 pilot. At the time of the incident, McCance was sitting in the pilot ready room in the Operations Building in the middle of Eglin Auxiliary Airfield Number Two. McCance described the situation as follows:

I first observed this aircraft at approximately 5000 feet descending in what seemed to be a rather slow spin or vertical roll. When I first noticed the aircraft, I thought that the pilot would be able to recover from the manoeuvre all right. I believe the aircraft was either spinning or rolling to the right. I did not observe either afterburner or speedbrakes extended. The degree of nose-down attitude of the aircraft was approximately 60 degrees. This angle of descent seemed to remain fairly constant throughout my observation. The aircraft did not seem to be to flatten out at any time while in this manoeuvre. The speed of descent remained constant. The aircraft did not seem to be in a vicious manoeuvre. I saw no smoke coming off the aircraft or out of the tail. I did observe the canopy falling through the air. The canopy's position was between me and the flight of the aircraft. When I saw the canopy, it was at a higher altitude than the aircraft. I feel that I could have recovered from the manoeuvre the aircraft was in if it was in a roll when I first saw it. I am not sure I could have gotten the aircraft out of the manoeuvre it was in if this manoeuvre had been a spin because of the low altitude of the aircraft. It seemed as if there was no effort by the pilot to make a recovery. The thing that stays in my mind mostly about the manoeuvre the aircraft was in was how slowly the aircraft seemed to be descending right up until the time it crashed.[104]

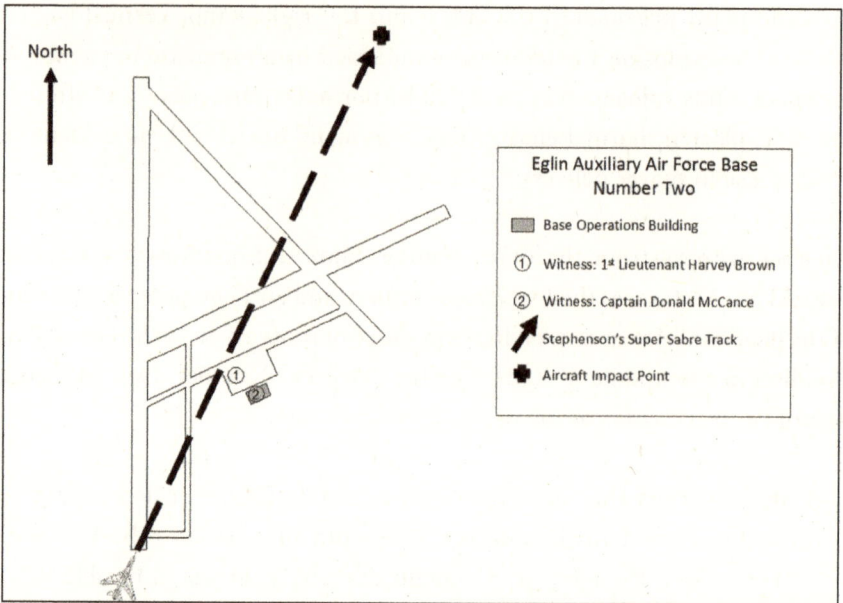

Figure 13.2 – Plan View of Stephenson's F-100A Super Sabre Crash.

At approximately 1430, Stephenson's Super Sabre crashed in an uninhabited wooded area approximately 1.5 miles north/north-east of Eglin Auxiliary Airfield Number Two.[105] At the point of impact, the aircraft attitude was inverted, with the left wing slightly lower than the right and the nose down approximately 45 degrees.[106] As determined by damage to trees adjacent to the impact point, the flight path indicated that the aft section of the aircraft was moving slightly to the right at impact.[107] Witnesses saw the canopy detaching from the aircraft during the latter stages of its descent. Investigators found it alongside another piece of equipment between the airfield and approximately 5,000ft short of the crash site.[108] A few witnesses reported seeing the aircraft make contact with the ground and an explosion.[109] Some observers spoke of seeing fire, but most reported seeing a black mushroom of smoke appearing above the trees.[110]

The air traffic control tower at Eglin Auxiliary Airfield Number Two also watched the tragic event unfold. Consequently, at 1428 they alerted the base fire department, who quickly dispatched four fire vehicles and 18 personnel under the command of Technical Sergeant William Donaldson to the crash site two miles north-east of the airfield.[111]

Meanwhile, above the carnage below, Moore was still unaware of the situation. After extending his flight path to the north, he began a slow left turn to expedite a join with his perceived errant wingman.[112] Halfway through the turn and heading west, Moore saw a plume of black smoke rise from the ground in his 8 o'clock position and to the north of Eglin Auxiliary Airfield Number Two.[113] The significance of the plume of smoke did not register with the chase pilot.[114] He tried to make radio contact with Stephenson but to no avail. Moore then switched radio frequencies to 'Tango Control', who informed the Super Sabre pilot of a crash north of Eglin Auxiliary Airfield Number Two and asked Moore to investigate.[115] From losing sight of Stephenson to being informed of the crash, a mere two and a half minutes had elapsed.[116]

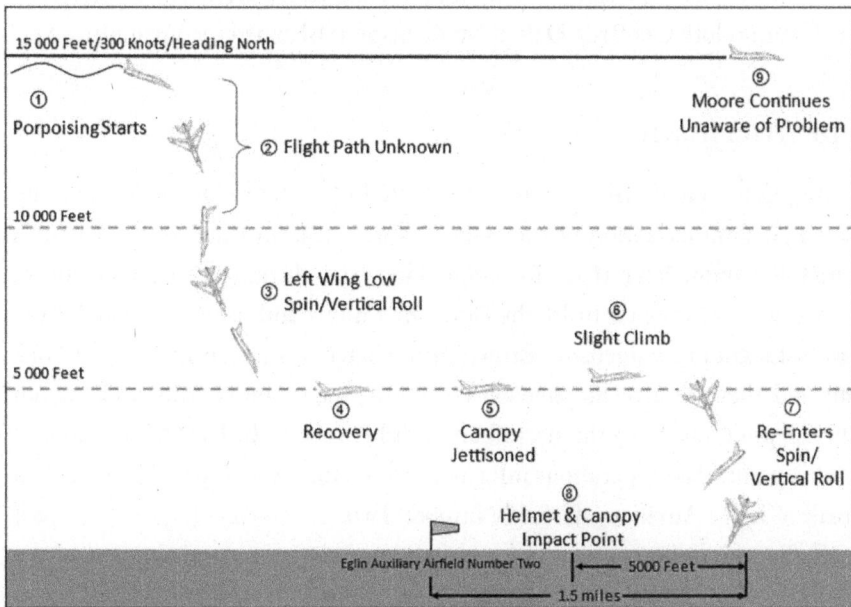

Figure 13.3 – Side View of Stephenson's F-100A Super Sabre Crash.

At 1436, Donaldson and his firefighters arrived at the crash site, a wooded area on level terrain to the north of the airfield and some 178 feet above sea level.[117] Using water turrets and hand lines to expel 2,300 gallons of water and an additional 200 gallons of foam, the firefighters were able to bring the fire under control within 11 minutes of their arrival on scene.[118] Donaldson and his team curtailed the spread of the fire to the surrounding woods by ploughing a fire lane around the entire area.[119] With the immediate danger now under control, the firefighters were left with an area of utter devastation. The impact point left a crater 20ft wide, 30ft long and 5ft deep.[120] The crater was at the southern end of the debris field, which headed north and covered an area 500ft long and 120ft wide.[121] The engine, aft section of the fuselage and empennage were found inverted and resting on the forward edge of the crater.[122] The remainder of the aircraft was scattered. Thrown furthest from the debris field were the lower portions of the fuselage.[123] Aside from the aft fuselage, engine, empennage and in-board wing panels, the entire aircraft had disintegrated on impact.[124] The nature of the failures and distribution of the wreckage indicated that the fire following the impact was a flash fire rather than an internal explosion.[125] The impact completely destroyed the aircraft. Air Commodore Geoffrey Dalton Stephenson CBE was killed instantly.

The Aftermath

Back at Eglin, Henry Brown was on the flight line with Fred Rosier conducting a cockpit familiarization of the Super Sabre ahead of the Group Captain's scheduled flight later that afternoon. However, during the cockpit check, Brown was summoned to Flight Line Operations and informed that Moore had lost sight of Stephenson. Brown immediately contacted Base Operations and told them to give Stephenson's aircraft priority on landing and that an English pilot was flying the aircraft and would probably be hard to understand. At this point, Base Operations informed Brown that an F-100 had just crashed north of Eglin Auxiliary Airfield Number Two.

Sadly, the military process for informing next of kin and the rest of the Service is a well-honed and oft-practised procedure. Consequently, Maureen was quickly told that her husband had been killed. Her younger daughters, Victoria and Veryan, were quickly whisked away to her parents' home while Maureen attempted to come to terms with the terrible news. Anna was informed and supported by the staff and her friends at her boarding school. Even if Maureen wanted her husband to be repatriated back to the United Kingdom, that request was not within her gift. In keeping with military protocols of the time, a service member killed overseas was buried at the nearest Commonwealth War Graves Commission site. In Stephenson's case, he would be buried at the Oakwood

Cemetery Annex in Montgomery, Alabama, 130 miles north of Eglin Air Force Base. As the funeral arrangements were finalised, another event showed that Stephenson's crash was not a one-off event.

On 9 November 1954, the day after Stephenson's death, another F-100A Super Sabre crashed in Nevada. During a gunnery test sortie, the experienced pilot lost control of the aircraft and was forced to eject. This time, Major Frank Emory, a Second World War veteran, survived the ordeal. This crash was the sixth major incident involving the Super Sabre since April 1954. Additionally, anecdotal evidence from USAF test pilots and front-line operators indicated that the F-100 Super Sabre was challenging to fly. Now, there was hard evidence to substantiate those claims. Although only two of the incidents were fatal, they were becoming more frequent, higher profile and increasingly severe. The F-100A Super Sabre programme was now under intense scrutiny.

Back at Eglin Air Force Base, the senior RAF officer in the United States arrived from Washington DC on 9 November 1954. Air Vice-Marshal Richard Atcherley, the head of the RAF staff at the British Joint Services Mission to the United States, was attending the funeral as part of his routine formal duties as the senior RAF airman in the United States. However, not only was it part of Atcherley's role to support major and high-profile Service events, particularly a fellow senior officer and aviator's funeral, but he was also attending the funeral of a friend and someone he had mentored and guided throughout their career. Most recently, he had met Stephenson at the start of their current US tour. He was not there merely to bury a colleague, he was there to say goodbye to a friend. In the end, and a far cry from his days on the run in Europe in 1940, Geoffrey Stephenson was not alone.

At 0900 the following morning, a memorial service was held at the Eglin Air Force Base chapel with Reverend Johnson Pace of St. Simons on the Sound Church, Fort Walton Beach, conducting the service. In addition to Atcherley and the RAF officers who were part of Stephenson's CFE visit, the congregation included Major General Patrick Timberlake and Brigadier General Daniel Campbell, the commander and deputy commander of the Air Proving Ground Command respectively, as well as several of their key staff officers.

At 1200, Stephenson's coffin was accompanied by 30 RAF and USAF officers and flown from Eglin to Maxwell Air Force Base in Montgomery,

Alabama. Although Maxwell Air Force Base has an active airfield and was responsible for training US, British and French pilots during the Second World War, its primary role was to host the USAF's various professional military education establishments. The courses at Maxwell range from initial officer training to the USAF's senior professional military education course – the year-long Air War College designed to develop Lieutenant Colonels and Colonels into senior strategic leaders. To foster stronger ties between joint and coalition partners, the USAF invites their naval, marine and army counterparts, as well as international partners, to participate in its professional military education programmes. Consequently, there has been an enduring RAF presence at Maxwell Air Force Base since the Second World War. Indeed, the first RAF student at Air War College in 1946 was Al Deere, who had also crash-landed a Spitfire on the beach during the Dunkirk evacuation in May 1940.

In November 1954, the senior RAF officer at Maxwell Air Force Base was Group Captain Maurice Robinson, a former Hurricane squadron commander during the Battle of Britain. Robinson and Stephenson would have known each other from their officer training days at Cranwell. Robinson was on the junior course to Stephenson and Bader. He officiated at Stephenson's internment ceremony at the Commonwealth War Graves Commission site at the Oakwood Cemetery Annex in downtown Montgomery. Ultimately, Stephenson was amongst friends and not simply buried in the corner of some foreign field.

Most of the 78 RAF graves at Oakwood Cemetery are those of young trainee pilots, taken in their prime and with insufficient time in their short lives to tell their story or leave a legacy. Although their lives are marked in the immaculately kept graves, there is very little to recant about their lives. Stephenson would be the 79th RAF airman buried at Oakwood cemetery, but he would not be the last. That dubious honour occurred in 1958, four years after Stephenson's death, when 30-year-old Squadron Leader Christopher Walker was killed flying the still-sensitive Lockheed U-2 spyplane while on a high-altitude training mission over Texas.

At the same time as Stephenson's burial, news of Stephenson's death was also reported in the British press. Several newspaper articles reflected on his remarkable career, with most articles covering his time as a prisoner of war, commanding CFS and his *aide de camp* role. One newspaper even gave an insight into Stephenson's crash. 'According to an American pilot of another plane, Air Commodore Stephenson went into a deep spiral from 15000 feet and crashed in a pine forest near the base. The cause of the accident is not known but is being investigated.' Most of the articles accurately reported the incident and Stephenson's background. However, one British tabloid newspaper got its facts badly wrong. Its obituary for Stephenson suggested that he was married to his former fiancée, the Honourable Anne Farrer. While the newspaper reporting was careless, other events leave endearing and tragic memories. Stephenson's daughter, Victoria, vividly recalls listening to a radio playing in an adjacent room that broadcast news of her father's death.

With Stephenson now laid to rest and the conclusion of the funeral arrangements in the United States, the remaining five dejected members of the CFE team returned home from New York onboard a Boeing Stratocruiser on Friday, 12 November 1954.[126] That same afternoon, a memorial service was held in the UK to allow Stephenson's family, friends and colleagues to pay their last respects. The service was held at the station church at RAF West Raynham and presided over by the chaplain-in-chief, Canon A.S. Giles, as well as the Station Chaplain, the Reverend T.A. Jenkins. The lesson was read by the station commander, Wing Commander A.S. Judson. The church was packed with additional mourners in the station theatre where the service was relayed. In addition to her daughter, Anna, Maureen was supported by her parents and Geoffrey's brothers, Urban and John. The list of senior RAF attendees was extensive. The highest-ranking attendee was Air Chief Marshal John Baker, who had met Stephenson during the early stages of his visit to the United States a fortnight earlier. Another attendee was Stephenson's superior, Air Marshal Sir Dermot Boyle, Air Officer Commander-in-Chief of Fighter Command, and his subordinates from 11 and 12 Group, Air Vice-Marshals H.L. Patch and Stephenson's immediate boss, 'Paddy' Crisham. Also in attendance were notable RAF retirees. Stephenson's old friend, Douglas Bader, was there as well as Group Captain John 'Cats Eyes' Cunningham, the former night fighter pilot who was now working for the aircraft manufacturing company, De Havilland. While the funeral and memorial service formalities were being completed, the USAF was focusing on understanding what had happened during Stephenson's last flight.

Accident Investigation Board

On the same day that the CFE team returned home, under the authority of the commander at Eglin Air Force Base, the Specialized Air Force-Industry F-100A Aircraft Accident Investigation Board convened formally for the first time. The president of the Accident Investigation Board was Colonel Edward 'Jonesy' Szaniawski. The Air Proving Ground Command Deputy Commander met Stephenson on the day of the accident. He had escorted him to his aircraft and sat on one side of the cockpit as Brown and Stephenson worked through the Super Sabre's start-up procedures. As the President of the Accident Investigation Board, the Second World War veteran fighter pilot and former *Stalag Luft* III POW was responsible to the Eglin Air Force Base commander for the delivery of three tasks. First, assemble the facts surrounding the accident. Second, analyse and evaluate the findings. Last, determine the causes. Within 16 days, Szaniawski's report would be with the Inspector General.

The first task of the Accident Investigation Board was to stipulate the who, what, where and when of the tragic events of 8 November. This task was completed relatively quickly and is the basis of the narrative in the previous chapter. Next, the Accident Investigation Board turned their attention to their second task – the analysis and evaluation of the findings. Two critical questions needed to be answered. First, why did the aircraft crash? Secondly, why did Stephenson not eject from the aircraft when it was apparent that it was doomed?

The Accident Investigation Board determined that the primary cause was the loss of control of the aircraft, with two contributory factors. First, the 'apparent instability of F-100 model aircraft'.[127] Additionally, 'pilot's inexperience with this type of control system'.[128] The early F-100A Super Sabres were challenging to fly. During his evidence, Brown suggested that 'this aircraft is not stable'.[129] Furthermore, 'at no time can you fly hands-off [the controls] with this aircraft. If you try to refer to technical material or anything you lose altitude or gain, get off your heading.'[130] Brown wrapped up his testimony by saying, 'If there is any time you can fly hands-off, I have not found it.' An experienced pilot and instructor like Stephenson should have been able to deal with the Hun's marginal stability flight characteristics.

However, the situation was exacerbated by a technical fault that would seal Stephenson's fate.

A faulty electrical connection between the trim button on the control column and the horizontal stabilizer materialized during the flight. Brown checked the functionality of the trim switch during the start-up procedure. During the post-crash investigation, it was discovered that due to improper assembly during manufacture, the electrical wire sheared from its plug, disconnecting the trim button from the horizontal stabilizer. The net result was that an aircraft already prone to stability issues needed even larger control inputs to control it. It was inevitable that the aircraft would be overcontrolled and induce the porpoising effect before losing control. Moreover, during the mission briefing, Brown informed Stephenson that, since the F-100A Super Sabre had yet to complete its spin trials. Therefore, Stephenson was told, 'in the event he got into a spin, to bail out'.[131] While the technical issue and the inherent instability were the cause of the accident, it does not explain why an experienced pilot like Stephenson did not complete the ejection sequence from an obviously stricken aircraft and contrary to his briefing from Brown.

Stephenson initiated the ejection procedure when it became evident that recovery from the spin was impossible. Unlike in modern fighter aircraft, where ejection is undertaken by a single action, the F-100 Super Sabre ejection requires two steps. First, the pilot jettisons the canopy and then pulls the ejection seat handle. The investigation determined that Stephenson had completed the first action but inexplicitly not the second. It seems inconceivable that once Stephenson decided to abandon the aircraft and jettison the canopy, he would not complete the second action and stay with his crippled fighter. So, what happened in the cockpit immediately after the canopy was jettisoned?

Stephenson's canopy and helmet were found adjacent to each other 5,000ft south-west of the crash site. Both items were determined to have left the aircraft at a similar time. On inspection, his helmet was 'very badly scarred'.[132] It was also noted that 'there are a brace of marks on the helmet and on the canopy which fairly well match up'.[133] The evidence was clear; the witness marks and paint on the canopy matched Stephenson's helmet. Through investigation, it was clear that the jettisoned canopy struck Stephenson's visor-less helmet during its departure from the aircraft. However, after some initial debate, it was deemed by aero-medical specialists that the canopy smashed Stephenson's helmet with a glancing but non-fatal blow. Exacerbating Stephenson's problems was that in the maelstrom of an open 350mph open cockpit, the chin strap of his helmet failed due to a manufacturing defect. Incredulously, the investigation board deemed that being struck by the canopy and having his helmet torn from his head were insufficient to cause injury to the pilot. Stephenson had made the critical decision to eject and had completed the first action but did not pull the ejection seat handle. The investigation board could not determine why Stephenson was unable to complete the second step of the ejection sequence.

Despite this apparent oversight, the Szaniawski-led investigation made five recommendations that would profoundly impact the F-100A Super Sabre project. First, 'all F-100 aircraft be grounded until all trim actuators manufactured by Hoover Electric Company have been inspected for proper assembly of all electric wiring'.[134] Second, 'a programme be initiated immediately to alleviate the present stability and flight control deficiencies of the F-100 type aircraft'.[135] Third, 'that the use of the take-off trim button as an alternate trim source be incorporated in the emergency section of the pilot's flight operations instructions'.[136] Fourth, 'spin tests be conducted immediately on the F-100 type aircraft'.[137] Finally, 'F-100 type aircraft not to be assigned to tactical organizations and put into general use until the control and stability problems are alleviated'.[138] The crash report also gave the cost of the accident as $1.8 million. Beyond the financial costs, there were the reputational damage implications for the USAF to address, both from a Super Sabre credibility perspective and the fact that an experienced senior RAF officer had been killed in the aircraft. F-100 Super Sabre production continued but at a reduced rate. However, the fleet was grounded and would remain so for three months. Flying operations recommenced on 21 February 1955, with aircraft deliveries resuming two months later. The modified F-100As now had a larger fin and a longer wingspan to mitigate, rather than eradicate, the Super Sabres' inherent design flaws.

The USAF declassified Stephenson's crash report on 30 August 1961, just shy of seven years after the incident. However, the primary source material is merely a collection of crash reports. The file does not include any details regarding the consequences of the flight. Moreover, the files contain no details of the RAF and USAF interactions on the subject. What is clear is that Stephenson's family appear not to have been informed of the background of the accident or the subsequent findings. Perhaps the RAF and USAF believed they were protecting the family who were attempting to recover from a devastating event. Re-opening those wounds in 1961 may have been deemed unpalatable. Nevertheless, the events of 8 November 1954 left Maureen Stephenson a widow for the second time at only 34 years of age and with the daunting prospect of bringing up her young family all on her own. Ultimately, the Stephenson family were left in the dark about the death of their father. The RAF may have lost a very senior officer who was demonstrating the potential for greater things in his career, but this wanes in significance with the colossal void suffered by the young Stephenson family. Perhaps, another way to look at Stephenson's death was that it saved countless others, by forcing the USAF to ground the Super Sabre and scrutinize then modify their new, but flawed, aircraft. Although the lessons identified did not completely eliminate the inherent stability issues of the Super Sabre, the changes and corporate knowledge unquestionably saved countless future F-100 Super Sabre fighter pilots. As a result, the Stephenson family can be assured that while their patriarch's death was a tragic affair, he certainly did not die in vain.

Chapter 14

Stephenson's Legacy

A t the time of Stephenson's death, Bader's biography *Reach for the Sky* had just been published to critical acclaim. Authored by fellow Spitfire pilot and prisoner of war Paul Brickhill, the book was hugely successful. The initial print run of 300,000 copies quickly sold out, and the book became the best-selling hardback in post-war Britain. Given their lifelong friendship, it is no surprise that Stephenson appears regularly throughout the biography. Stephenson was aware of the book's upcoming release and supported Bader by providing publicity material to help promote the book. The biography's success ensured that the film rights were quickly snapped up. In July 1956, the film version was released with Kenneth More playing Bader and Harry Day acting as a technical advisor to the film.[1]

There was one notable difference between the book and the film. While Stephenson was prominent in the former, he was not incorporated into the latter. Bader 'was adamant that everyone who had played a part in his life story should be faithfully represented', but the decision was not Bader's to make.[2] The film's producers wielded the axe to many of the supporting names. Regarding Stephenson, the decision rested not with the producers but with Maureen, Geoffrey's widow. Still hurting from losing her husband, Maureen vetoed Geoffrey's name from the film script. As a result, the producers were forced to create an alternative character to narrate the film and play the role of Bader's friend at Cranwell and the commanding officer of 19 Squadron. Played by the Canadian actor Lyndon Brook, the character 'Johnny Sanderson' is not a composite of multiple characters as claimed by some; 'Johnny Sanderson' is Geoffrey Stephenson.[3] Despite the minor adaptation, *Reach for the Sky* topped the British box office in 1956 and won the BAFTA Award for Best British film that year.

While the film undoubtedly reinforced Bader's reputation and credibility as a resilient and heroic fighter leader, and showed a softer side to his hard-nosed character, it was a subtle sign-off for his friend, Stephenson. Stephenson's story could have stopped there, just another tragic statistic from a generation of remarkable individuals conducting incredible feats who gave their all for their Monarch and country. Over the next three decades, the Stephenson family got on with their lives. Maureen subsequently re-married and moved to London to bring up her three daughters. Over the next few decades, the people who knew Stephenson best began to pass away. Even before *Reach for the Sky* hit the cinemas, the pilot who had flown alongside Stephenson on his last flight was also killed in a flying accident at Eglin Air Force Base in Florida. On 10 January 1956, 14 months after Stephenson's crash, the now Major Lonnie Moore was taking his first flight in another of the century-series fighters, the McDonnell F-101A Voodoo. As the fighter lifted off the Florida runway, the aircraft pitched up and crashed in the centre of the airfield. Moore was killed instantly; he left behind a wife and five children.

After attending Stephenson's funeral, Richard Atcherley stayed in the United States as the senior RAF officer in country for another year. He left Washington DC in 1955, on promotion to Air Marshal, to return to the United Kingdom to take up his last post as Air Officer-in-Command Flying Training Command. After introducing the Jet Provost basic trainer into service and recommending the diminutive Folland Gnat as the RAF's next-generation advanced trainer, Atcherley would eventually retire from the RAF in 1959. He remained connected with the aviation business by moving to the Folland Aircraft Company as a Sales Director. Atcherley finally retired in 1965. In April 1970, as he was preparing to set off to Florida to watch the Apollo 13 launch, Atcherley fell ill and died at the relatively young age of 66. Stephenson's other flight commander from their time at RAF Kenley, Harry Day was the subject of a 1961 edition of the TV programme *This Is Your Life*. Away from the limelight of TV programmes, technical advisor to blockbuster films and his wartime memoir, Day's domestic life was a more turbulent affair. His first marriage ended upon his return from his time as a POW. A second marriage also ended in divorce. Nevertheless, for the rest of his life, he lived with his partner, initially in Monaco, before moving to Malta. In March 1977, at the age of 78, the former Royal Marine, retired Group Captain and veteran of both World Wars died in a hospital on the island; he was buried nearby at Ta Braxia cemetery.

Bader was now the sole survivor of the group of four aviators at Kenley in the early 1930s. The success of *Reach for the Sky* ensured that he remained a household name for the rest of his life and beyond. After a second career lasting 23 years, Bader retired in 1969 from his role as a Managing Director for Shell Aviation. However, he had plenty of projects to keep him busy. First and foremost was his role as a technical advisor for the 1969 film *Battle of Britain*, much of which was shot at Duxford. He was one of many veterans from the Battle that supported the movie, including his old adversary and now friend, Adolf Galland. Although Bader was a divisive and forthright character, he also used his name for the greater good. His work supporting the disabled community was initially recognized by the appointment of a CBE in January 1956 before ultimately being knighted two decades later in 1976. As with Day, Bader was the subject of a *This Is Your Life* episode in March 1982. Sadly, a few months later, in September 1982 and at 72, Sir Douglas Bader CBE, DSO and Bar, DFC and Bar, DL, FRAeS, died from a heart attack.

1986 saw a pivotal moment. At the incredible age of 106, the Stephenson family lost their matriarch. Stephenson's mother, Jessie, died. With the passing of the generation who knew Stephenson best, there was a real chance he would fade from the collective memory. However, over three decades after Stephenson's death, just as his generation of friends and family were dwindling in number, an event occurred that would eventually bring his name back to prominence. In early 1986, strong currents in the English Channel uncovered an old friend.

The Resurrection of N3200

At Sangatte, the battered remains of a Spitfire emerged from the storm-damaged French beach. Although it was clear that the wreckage was from a Spitfire, its identity remained a mystery and would remain so until the early 2000s. The aircraft remains that rose from the sand showed the inevitable signs of over 40 years of corrosion. The aircraft was predominantly intact, but it was a blackened and wrecked airframe. In spring 1986, all that was left was a badly corroded and damaged aluminium airframe as well as the Rolls-Royce Merlin engine block. Nevertheless, a French team excavated the Spitfire's remains from the beach. The key question now was what to do with the shattered aircraft.

This was not the first Spitfire to be exhumed from a French beach following its Operation Dynamo exploits. That accolade went to the first of the nine Spitfires that crash-landed on the French beaches during the Dunkirk evacuation. On 24 May 1940, Spitfire Mark Ia P9374 was flown by 92 Squadron's Flying Officer Peter Cazenove when it was brought down by defensive gunfire from a Dornier Do.17 bomber.[4] As with Stephenson, Cazenove's Spitfire suffered a damaged radiator, forcing him to crash land on the beach at Calais, a few miles east of N3200's crash site. Like N3200, the French sands slowly consumed Cazenove's Spitfire and would not emerge again for another 40 years. In September 1980, P9374 appeared from the beach and was unceremoniously dragged from her slumber before moving to the *Musée d'l'Air* at Le Bourget, Paris.[5]

After it was recovered from the beach, N3200 was also moved to a museum. The unidentified Spitfire was put on display a few miles inland at *Forteresse de Mimoyecques*, a museum on the underground bunker site where the Germans intended to house their V-3 weapon. The unadulterated remains of N3200 remained on display at the museum for the next decade.

N3200 Returns Home

As the new century dawned, a *Financial Times* article sponsored by one of the restoration companies at Duxford stimulated a debate that would ultimately see N3200 returned to her former glory and her old base. The newspaper article spoke of the benefits of owning a warbird and its investment opportunities. The article triggered a discussion between two friends from their schoolboy days – American Tom Kaplan and his British business partner, Simon Marsh. In addition to being a successful businessman, Kaplan is a philanthropist passionate about wildlife conservation, collecting art and aviation. The latter two interest areas were piqued by the *Financial Times* article. With the financial means, passion, and business acumen to sniff out a prudent investment, Kaplan and Marsh were the perfect clients. However, Kaplan and Marsh needed a warbird to make their project viable. Together, they sought to answer the question what is the most graceful and artistic design available in warbird mode? Quickly, they settled on an answer. It had to be a thoroughbred design – the original Spitfire, the Mark I.

By December 2000, Kaplan and Marsh had purchased three wrecked Mark I Spitfires – including P9373 and P9374. By this stage, the third airframe was identified as Stephenson's N3200. Hindering the early identification process was the fact that early Spitfires did not carry data plates on their bulkheads. When a more detailed inspection took place, it was discovered that the serial number on the Merlin III engine plate matched the details contained within the RAF Records Card for N3200. Earlier suspicions that the unidentified wrecked Spitfire was indeed N3200 proved correct. It was then realised that N3200 was a 19 Squadron aircraft from Duxford and flown by Stephenson on its first and last operational mission in May 1940. From the restoration team's viewpoint, it was rapidly becoming apparent that the N3200 project would be different and very special. The aircraft had a stellar provenance and a remarkable story to tell, not only of the aircraft but its pilot and its home base – the same base where it flew from in 1940 would resurrect it to fly again over seven decades later. N3200 *was* Duxford. This was a Duxford aircraft with a Duxford aviator at the controls; N3200 was coming home. While N3200 may have been identified, the surviving members of the Stephenson family were still unaware that their father's aircraft had been found.

Marsh and Kaplan's intent was simple, to return the aircraft to flying status in an authentic condition replicating the build standard, modification status and paint scheme of the aircraft on the day it was lost. Marsh and Kaplan wanted 'to pay homage to those who Winston Churchill called "The Few", the pilots who were all that stood between Hitler's darkness and what was left of civilisation'.[6] The intent may have been simple, but the restoration would be long, expensive, and require meticulous attention to detail. Getting the right team in place to undertake the complex project was key.

Building the team to conduct the project was a long and arduous process. As a result, many companies were involved, but it was thought that no single company could oversee the exacting build standards stipulated by the demanding clients. In the meantime, the wrecked airframes were repatriated to the United Kingdom and stored in various locations. The next piece of the jigsaw fell into place at an art exhibition in London, when the event organiser and mutual friend played matchmaker. The art dealer knew the two individuals shared a passion for aviation and art. Consequently, knowing that one of them was looking for a warbird restoration company while the other was the owner of such a company. Karel Bos, a Dutchmen who had made his money in Belgium manufacturing exhaust systems and catalytic converters, also owned Historic Flying Limited, a Duxford-based company specializing in Spitfire restorations. Bos shared the Historic Flying Limited hangar with John Romain's Aircraft Restoration Company. While Bos' company focused on restoration, Romain's business catered for the longer-term maintenance needs of warbirds. Although Kaplan had chatted with various owners of restoration companies, he had not approached Bos as he was under the impression that Historic Flying Limited only restored Spitfires for themselves. Over dinner at the art exhibition, Bos corrected Kaplan's oversight and was impressed with the project's ambition. Consequently, Bos promised Kaplan that he would release his company to restore the wrecked Spitfires to the exacting standards laid out by his new client.

By 2006, the restoration team had finally been assembled; Bos had now retired, and the project now fell under the leadership of John Romain, who had taken over from Bos as the head of Historic Flying Limited and the Aircraft Restoration Company. Kaplan and Marsh, now working under the guise of Mark One Partners, commissioned Historic Flying Limited to undertake the intensive work required to return the Spitfires to their former glory. Beyond John Romain's Aircraft Restoration Company were two other major sub-contractors. First, RetroTrack and Air, based in Gloucestershire, rebuilt the Merlin III engines. Second, the Isle of Wight-based company Airframe Assemblies constructed the fuselage and tail unit. The same year, P9374 was the first airframe to arrive at Duxford. As it was the first to arrive, it was also the first to undergo restoration. N3200 finally returned to its former wartime home the following year. However, it would be another seven years before N3200 would slip the surly bonds. The near-term priority was P9374, and over the next four years, the focus was to get P9374 built and back into the air. With P9374 taking to the air in the summer of 2011, the focus turned to N3200. It was now the turn of Stephenson's aircraft to be restored, to research her provenance and tell the remarkable story of man, machine, and their home unit.

The Stephenson Connection

In early 2012, while awaiting the arrival of the N3200 fuselage from the Isle of Wight, there was a breakthrough in finding out more about Stephenson. Colin

Swann, the Senior Projects Engineer at the Aircraft Restoration Company, had led the charge to understand more about N3200's pilot. During one internet search, he stumbled across a *New York Times* obituary that referred to Stephenson leaving behind a wife and two daughters. However, he had no more luck identifying any living relatives. Simultaneously, enquiries on the other side of the Atlantic were also going on but looking at the problem from the opposite perspective. In parallel to Colin's search, a family friend of Stephenson's daughter was trying to learn more about her father's career. In January 2012, the two paths collided.

Peter Orgain was a long-time friend of Victoria's husband, David, and had known Victoria since the early 1970s when she moved to North America. Peter knew that Victoria's father had been an RAF pilot and had died in a flying accident. Stephenson's story intrigued Peter, and his naturally inquisitive nature took over. Consequently, Peter began to research elements of Stephenson's remarkable career. Peter's engagement included making a minor correction to a website containing information about Stephenson's career and mentioning that the information had come via Stephenson's daughter. The comment was noticed by Colin, who could not believe his luck. Colin immediately reached out to Peter and explained his situation. Peter informed Victoria and put her in touch with Colin and the team at Duxford. Fifty-eight years after their father's death and 72 years after crashing his Spitfire on the French beach, Stephenson's daughters became aware that their father's Spitfire was back in the UK and being rebuilt. Little did they realise that their father's name and story would become so well known amongst the warbird community. Moreover, that target audience would soon become even more extensive.

The catalyst for bringing Stephenson's name to a much broader audience was another fearless lad from Lincolnshire – Guy Martin. The intrepid motorbike racer had become a household name in the United Kingdom for his no-nonsense, down-to-earth, and practical documentaries. North One, the TV production company responsible for Guy's documentaries, were tasked by Channel 4 management to think bigger with a focus on engineering and history that would not only play to Guy's expertise but also appeal to the general public. In 2012, and just after Stephenson's daughters had been traced, the North One team became aware that N3200 was in the early stages of its rebuild – it was a perfect fit. Not only would Guy follow the engineering aspects of the build, but he would be able to showcase his engineering prowess on carefully supervised elements of the build! The producers also wanted to tell the human dimension of the story. Consequently, they set off to discover more about N3200's pilot. The subsequent tale blended the rebuild, Geoffrey's story and his daughters witnessing the grand reveal of the completed N3200.

N3200 Restoration

To understand the restoration process, you first need to understand the Spitfire Mark I and the various components that make it unique. Of note, the Spitfire Mark I was in a constant state of modification. The propeller is a case in point. When the Spitfire arrived on 19 Squadron in 1938, it was equipped with a twin-bladed propeller. However, when Stephenson arrived at Duxford, the aircraft was now sporting a metal three-bladed, twin-pitched propeller. That propeller was far from the finished article; it would be later refined to a wooden propeller connected to a constant speed unit; later models added additional blades. The later modifications allowed more carefree handling for the pilot while the wooden blades, unlike their metal counterparts, tended to shatter when aircraft tipped onto their nose during errant landings. In contrast, the energy of the metal propellers transferred into the engine, applying significant stresses and usually rendering it unusable.

The early Rolls-Royce Merlin III engine produced about 950 horsepower, which would double as the engine developed throughout the war. However, the early Merlin also had a shorter life when compared to the more reliable later variants.[7] Given the short life expectancy of fighters of that era, the Merlin's reliability issue was not too much of a concern. As a result, it becomes challenging when trying to restore a contemporary warbird. Consequently, many Spitfire restoration projects opt for the more reliable and practical Merlin 35 engine as its preferred powerplant. To keep N3200 in its original specification, it had to be fitted with the more fragile Merlin III engine.

The tyres of the Mark I Spitfires were also exclusive to the type. The original tyres were smooth and manufactured by Dunlop. This type of tyre was quickly replaced by grooved tyres, and soon Dunlop discontinued the manufacture of the smooth tyre design. However, during the restoration project, Dunlop were persuaded to manufacture a bespoke run of 50 new smooth tyres to the original Mark I Spitfire specification. The issue is not helped by the Spitfire's undercarriage suffering from a toe-in design that naturally increases the tyres' wear and tear. Nevertheless, the problem is mitigated by the aircraft tending to operate from grass airstrips rather than the more abrasive concrete and tarmac airfields.

The cockpit also had a few features unique to Stephenson's era of Spitfires. Externally, the Mark I canopy had a bulbous top but flat sides rather than the bulged canopies of the later models. Practically, the flat-sided canopy did not give the pilot much room to swivel his head, and pilots tended to complain about constantly banging their heads against the side of the canopy. As a result, the canopy is generally open during take-offs and landings. Additionally, the early Spitfires struggled to jettison the canopy. Therefore, to abandon the aircraft in flight, the pilot had to slide the canopy back, but at high speeds, the airflow and suction tended to keep the canopy in place. The punch-out piece incorporated into the side of the canopy allowed the pilot to break the suction, slide the canopy aft and bale out of a stricken aircraft.

While building the aircraft to the original specification 'as it was on the beach' was a requirement, it was a challenge but feasible. However, there was no point in making the aircraft if it was inherently unsafe to fly. Consequently, the restoration team considered flight safety from the outset. The build team were also fortunate to have a unique resource on hand to answer many of their safety-related questions – Alex Henshaw, a wartime Spitfire test pilot. Although Alex passed away before N3200 took to the air again, he was available to respond to John Romain's questions during the early scoping work of the project. One area of concern for John Romain was the fabric-covered ailerons and rudder as

it was a different animal to the other Spitfires I was used to flying which had metal flying controls. Most were modified in the later production Mark Is and later variants. The new metal flying surfaces were much more effective. However, at the time of its crash, N3200 had fabric-covered flying surfaces, but we needed to know if it was safe to fly in that configuration. We were fortunate that we could seek advice from Alex Henshaw during one of our regular discussions with him. Alex's sage guidance was, 'you will not have any trouble with those until you are doing about 320 miles per hour, and then they get stiff. At 400 miles per hour, it's like flying concrete. Below that speed, they are just fine and for a normal aerobatic display, they are lovely. So, leave them.'

The Spitfire was under constant modification, and understanding the standard of N3200 at the time of its demise and the rationale for those changes was one of the biggest challenges during the restoration. Nevertheless, the demand and ambition were unrelenting, the end-state was a fully-functioning Mark I Spitfire as flown by Stephenson on 26 May 1940. However, the front-line Spitfires were constantly being adapted with new modifications, instruments and paint schemes. Consequently, in 1940 it was not unusual to have several variants of Spitfire in a single squadron. Getting N3200 right was a complex affair. The Aircraft Restoration Company team was fully aware that the project would come under serious scrutiny from the warbird community and their clients, who were investing considerable time, effort and funds to create an authentic Mark I Spitfire. Indeed, the clients initially hired an independent external auditor to ensure authenticity was maintained throughout the project. When it became evident that the restoration was being conducted diligently, the auditor's role became redundant.

Given that it was the most visible element of the project, the area that was likely to come under the closest scrutiny was the cockpit. As a result, getting the instrument panel right was critical, whether that be the type of instruments used, layout and even down to the detail of the size and colour of the screws, piping, fasteners, cabling and wiring looms. All were researched and meticulously replicated to ensure they accurately reflected N3200 in late May 1940. There are a couple of modifications to ensure the restoration meets modern aviation standards, but their impact is reduced as much as possible. For example, a modern radio is discretely incorporated into what was the map case down by the pilot's left knee. Also, the pilot's harness had to be upgraded to meet modern safety standards, but the straps were colour-matched to make them look like their 1940s equivalent. The authenticity requirement is embedded throughout the aircraft, not just in visible areas. One example of the meticulous attention to detail is the nuts and bolts inside the aircraft and, ordinarily, out of view. Today, the nuts and bolts can be procured to the correct imperial measurements, but their cadmium plating is gold in colour, whereas in 1939, they were silver. Consequently, the nuts and bolts had to be stripped and re-plated to match the original silver colour – such is the attention to detail.

Although much of N3200 was largely intact when it was discovered, few parts could be salvaged. Consequently, the restoration combined restored parts and new sections built to the original specifications. The restoration of N3200 began in earnest in April 2012 with the arrival at Duxford of the fuselage and tail unit from the specialist manufacturer, Airframe Assemblies, based in the Isle of Wight. Much of the build is covered in the North One-produced documentary, 'Guy Martin's Spitfire', which shows Guy assisting the Aircraft Restoration Company team throughout the build, from constructing union joins, creating the metal wing ribs, installing the Merlin III engine to refining and fitting the wings. Initially, the build was straightforward, having benefitted from the lessons generated from the restoration of P9374. That good luck would soon become a distant memory as tragic news and engineering challenges hindered the latter stages of the project.

Halfway through the restoration of N3200, the project suffered a devastating blow. In July 2013, tragedy struck when one of the founding partners of the Mark One Partners, Simon Marsh, was killed in a flying accident in Italy. The likeable and enthusiastic Simon had been the driving force behind the project. Not only would he receive the monthly progress reports on the restoration projects, but he was also a regular visitor to Duxford during the restoration of P9374 and N3200. Simon's death profoundly impacted the project. Although he saw P9374 return to the air, he would not see N3200 repeat that feat. Moreover, while N3200 would complete its restoration, the third Spitfire Mark I scheduled for restoration, P9373, was put on hold. The impetus for the project was waning, but N3200 would be finished. It was a difficult time for the team, both emotionally and from an engineering perspective.

Despite N3200 being the second Spitfire to be restored and benefitting from many of the teething issues associated with P9374, the project was far from seamless. According to Martin 'Mo' Overall, the Hangar Manager at Aircraft Restoration Company, of the two Mark I Spitfires, restoring N3200 was problematic, particularly towards the end of the build in early 2014. 'Nothing went well; there were issues with the engine run and control surfaces.' So much so that Mo suggested to his boss, John Romain, 'It's fighting us'. Thankfully, the issues were relatively minor but required effort and time. Just over a month after the first engine run, N3200 was ready for its first flight since 26 May 1940. John Romain piloted N3200 on its 'maiden' flight on 26 March 2014. The Aircraft Restoration Company staff watched as Romain put N3200 through the first of its flights on its planned test schedule. Those on the ground were initially concerned that this was the longest first flight he had ever done. However, once N3200 eventually landed, they need not have worried. John Romain's immediate reaction was, 'That's the best one you have built!'

Once the flight test schedule was completed, Victoria and Veryan were invited to Duxford to see their father's long-lost Spitfire on the ground and in the air. The footage of Stephenson's daughter's standing outside the Duxford hangar awaiting the grand reveal of their father's aircraft for the first time made for memorable and emotional viewing. Both Victoria and Veryan awaited a tangible connection with their father, who they had last seen six decades earlier. The footage shows the ordinarily stoic daughters full of nervous excitement. Both daughters were beaming when they saw the time and effort the Aircraft Restoration Company team had put into restoring the aircraft and keeping their father's memory alive. Victoria noted that her father would have been overjoyed that it was up and flying again. While the event was a huge success, it also stirred some sad and profound reflections. The footage of a grinning Victoria sitting in the cockpit of N3200 was incredibly poignant to those who watched. From Veryan's perspective, she found it very moving to see her older sister, who bears a striking resemblance to her father, in N3200's cockpit. Consequently, there was a profound sense of something missing from this magical moment. One of the daughters reflected that the event had 'a tinge of sadness too', the remarkable reunion of family and fighter was missing one key component – Geoffrey Stephenson. The documentary was a huge success and would be called 'humbling' by the Channel 4 senior manager who initiated the project. For Neil Duncanson, the Chief Executive Officer at North One, it was one of his favourite projects over a career spanning 40 years.

The N3200 project was a career pinnacle for many involved in the restoration. It had set a new standard in warbird restoration. The rebuild of the two Spitfire Mark Is was the first time that aircraft had been restored to their original specification and from such a limited set of useable parts. The unique project provided an incredible insight and a snapshot into the time and life of a remarkable aircraft and individual. However, the special project was coming to an end.

The loss of Simon Marsh also meant bringing forward the plan to dispose of P9374 and N3200. After significant debate and negotiation, it was decided, due to its unique link to Duxford, to keep N3200 at its old base and auction P9374. Stephenson's Spitfire would be generously donated to the Imperial War Museum by Tom Kaplan. Although owned by the Imperial War Museum, N3200 would be maintained by the Aircraft Restoration Company. As the Imperial War Museum's sole flying exhibit, N3200 continues to tell the story of Stephenson and a remarkable group of individuals for generations to come. On 9 July 2015, Prince William, the grandson of Stephenson's principal when he was her *aide de camp*, received N3200 on behalf of the Imperial War Museum. During his visit, Prince William watched N3200 conduct an air display before sitting in its cockpit. That evening, Christies auctioned P9374 for £3.1 million – a record for a Spitfire. Proceeds went to charities, including the RAF Benevolent Fund, as 'a way to honour that breed who gave so much for Britain when its existence was imperilled'.[8] Overall, the disposal of both Spitfire Mark Is aided a broad range of individuals and organisations, but none more so than Stephenson himself. N3200 and Stephenson are inextricably linked; each time N3200 flies at an airshow, the commentary usually refers to its pilot and his wartime exploits. However, what is it like to fly in Stephenson's wartime steed?

Flying N3200

Pilots who are fortunate enough to fly N3200 all use the same one word to describe how she flies – 'lovely'.

When filming the Guy Martin documentary, 'Mo' Overall was not only busy overseeing the restoration of both Spitfire Mark Is, but he was also following a similar path to his boss, John Romain. Mo is not only an accomplished engineer but was also well on his way to becoming a warbird pilot. A few months after N3200 made its first flight, Mo joined an illustrious group – a qualified Spitfire pilot. He initially flew in a Mark IX before being let loose on N3200, the aircraft he helped restore. So, what makes N3200 such a 'lovely' aircraft to fly?

Perhaps 'lovely' is an interesting phrase to describe a war machine. Its role today may be very different to the one it faced in 1940. Stephenson was an operator focused on defeating a foe in the air to protect Allied forces on the ground. He may have been an experienced pilot and enjoyed flying the Spitfire, but it was built for a purpose. Stephenson may have used terms like 'lethal', 'fast' and 'agile', words contemporary fighter pilots may use to describe their current steeds. Perhaps in the future, the carefree handling aspects of a Typhoon or F-16 Fighting Falcon may be described as 'lovely', but those aspects are a means to an end. The cultured handling lets the pilot focus on the job at hand – attacking and killing the enemy. N3200 is no different; behind that beautiful, gentle façade is a potent fighter aircraft. However, getting N3200 into the air takes some focus.

N3200's pilots are given a pure Spitfire experience, just as R.J. Mitchell had intended it to be. Given its build to the original specification, N3200's pilots have the rare opportunity to experience what flying a Spitfire at the start of its military career was like. Later Spitfire marks would deviate from that original design and understanding. N3200's pilots get to see the original Spitfire in all its glory, including its vices, idiosyncrasies, and quirks – of which there are a few.

The aircraft is simple and quick to start. However, once the Merlin engine is up and running, time is of the essence as the engine can quickly overheat on the ground. Once on the runway, the take-off run requires constant care and attention from the pilot. Hands constantly move around the cockpit to ensure the aircraft remains in the correct configuration as the aircraft trundles down the runway. Due to the limitations of the two-pitch propeller, the take-off run is laborious rather than a sprightly affair. As the aircraft takes off in fine pitch, the aircraft is slowly winding up throughout the take-off run. The potential for more speed and energy is evident, but the aircraft initially feels sluggish and underwhelming. If you leave it in coarse pitch, just as Bader did, the speed simply does not build up quick enough and getting airborne before the airfield boundary becomes problematic. It would be akin to trying to cycle from a standing start in a big gear. Given this ponderous start to getting a Spitfire Mark I airborne, it is difficult to believe that the Spitfire will turn into a quick, sleek fighter aircraft. However, as it lifts off the ground, the aim is to release its potential by reducing the drag and bringing the undercarriage up as quickly as possible. Rather than the simple flick of a switch to bring the gear up, the early Mark Is had a manual pump! To bring the undercarriage up, the large, black metal handle on the right-hand side of the cockpit must be pumped nearly two dozen times. Consequently, just after the aircraft has left *terra firma*, the pilot needs to switch hands to fly with their left hand while pumping the undercarriage up with their right hand. For inexperienced pilots, there is a tendency for the aircraft to porpoise as the pilot's left hand tends to move the control column in sympathy with the pumps from the right hand! With the undercarriage lever becoming stiff – an indicator that the gear is up – it is time to change the propeller pitch. If left in fine pitch with +4lbs of boost, the take-off setting, the RPM would rise beyond prudent tolerances if the aircraft stayed in straight and level flight. However, if transitioning into a steep climb, the propellor can be left in fine pitch for a little longer. When the aircraft levels off, typically above 500ft, coarse pitch is set, and the RPM winds back. Next, the pilot must switch attention to the engine and boost settings. If left in the take-off configuration of +4lbs of boost, the engine will be over-boosted, which could result in damage to the engine and an unwelcome, expensive and lengthy engineering investigation post-flight. Getting a Mark I Spitfire airborne is very much a pilot-controlled adventure; they must constantly monitor the RPM, boost, temperatures, and pressures and physically operate the undercarriage during the take-off. N3200's pilots like the mechanical interaction combined with its simplicity. It works every time, but the pilot must think and read the aircraft for it to function correctly. To get the best out of the aircraft, the pilot must sense the aircraft and be one or two steps ahead to ensure it performs optimally.

While N3200 may be sluggish on the ground, its character quickly changes once airborne. When free of the ground, N3200 is in its prime and transitions from an ugly duckling into a graceful swan. The handling is beautiful, light and responsive. Bar empty ammunition tanks, and unlike many of the warbirds on the display circuit, N3200's configuration accurately represents an operational aircraft. With a complete set of eight Browning .303 machine guns and armour plating, N3200 flies and displays at operational weights. When airborne, N3200 has poise, but it does have its vices. Most notably, the early Merlin engines operated with a float-controlled carburettor. Consequently, under negative G, the engine is starved of fuel, causing the engine to splutter or, if sustained, force the engine to stop. During combat and low-level aerobatics, a sudden reduction in noise, thrust, and energy would undoubtedly grab a pilot's attention. As a result, pilots had to carefully plan their combat manoeuvres and aerobatics displays to cater for the limitation. Nevertheless, according to those that have flown N3200, it is a joy to display.

Whether on display on the ground at Duxford or on one of its aerobatic displays, N3200 turns heads. To be fair, any Spitfire will have a similar effect. A Spitfire aerobatic display is an attack on the physical senses via the evocative sound of a Merlin engine roaring overhead, as well as the sight of the graceful lines of its elliptical wings. It is the aircraft type that all warbirds aspire to be; N3200 is an icon.

N3200 today

When asked what N3200 means to him, John Romain responded,

> I love it because it is a pure Spitfire Mark I. N3200 is currently the only 'stock' Spitfire Mark I in existence, and I love it because of that fact. P9374, the other Spitfire Mark I we restored, now resides in the United States and has been upgraded to the later and more robust Merlin 35 engine. Consequently, N3200 is unique and is, in essence, a flying time capsule.

Amongst the warbird aficionado community, N3200 is the subject of debate. Given the limited number of original parts in the finished product, a few question whether N3200 is a restoration or a reconstruction? Many equate N3200 to 'Trigger's Broom'.[9] Unlike 'Trigger's Broom,' N3200 retains some originality, albeit a minimal number of parts. However, the large aluminium fuselage, wings and tail section were rebuilt to exacting original specifications. Moreover, is there such a thing as a pre-existing original Spitfire? During their service life, Mark I Spitfires were constantly modified. Additionally, the aircraft would have received constant rectification as part of its routine operating schedule and following any battle damage suffered during operational missions. The constant wear and tear on the airframe would have seen components constantly repaired and replaced. Consequently, any surviving Mark I Spitfire would look very different and contain few original parts compared to when it rolled off the factory floor. Although the restoration versus replica debate continues, perhaps the argument is missing the point of what N3200 actually represents.

All agree that N3200 is a remarkable engineering feat. Moreover, it is a tangible, living, breathing artefact that gives current and future generations an insight into a remarkable time and place. Perhaps N3200's charm is linked to its provenance and the associated narrative. It tells a story directly related to a defining moment in British history and to the story of a specific pilot and a remarkable generation. N3200 brings to life the emotional and human story of a special individual who flew the aircraft on its sole operational sortie. However, N3200 is more than just Stephenson's story; it is associated with our past. It reflects a bygone era when honour, duty and sacrifice were tangible deeds rather than empty platitudes. N3200 encapsulates all the nostalgia and tragedy of a former age. Also, it is a physical representation of a generation, like Stephenson, who are no longer with us, whether lost in battle or through a long life well lived but packed with hard-won experiences. The restoration versus replica debate pales into insignificance when you look at what N3200 means to those who understand that remarkable generation's sacrifices. To prove the point, one only has to look at the emotion and reactions of Stephenson's daughters, Victoria and Veryan, when they were introduced to N3200 for the first time. Both ladies were instantly transported back to the early 1950s, their childhood and loving memories of their father. Few pieces of hardware create that level of reaction and emotion – the Spitfire can and N3200 does.

While the contemporary narrative may focus on Stephenson's link to N3200, Stephenson's legacy is more varied, chaotic, and interesting than just the events of one Sunday morning over French beaches in May 1940.

Stephenson's Relevance Today

This biography sets out to tell the story of a remarkable individual buried thousands of miles from home, in a southern US state, one he had never visited or knew. He is laid to rest in Montgomery, Alabama, amongst 79 other airmen, people he did not know but with whom he shared common bonds and values – nationality, service to their Monarch and country, and a love for aviation. Stephenson's short life was crammed full of incredible experiences. Resilience, risk awareness and mentorship would be critical traits that he would develop in his formative years and recur throughout the periods of turmoil and change in his life.

While Stephenson certainly benefitted from a relatively privileged upbringing, it was far from a cosseted life. Growing up in the aftermath of the Great War left its scars and challenges on the Stephenson family. While he was raised in a wealthy farming family and was privately educated, life was far from simple and entry into Cranwell was not assured. Conflict, both on the Continent and in Ireland, and troublesome family finances were obstacles the Stephenson family had to contend with to get their eldest son a place at the coveted new RAF College at Cranwell. To get there, Stephenson showed that he was a resilient young man, able to cope independently in an increasingly foreign (and arguably hostile) country. Stephenson's resilience would stand him in good stead, not only for the remainder of his schooling but also when forced to live in isolation overseas in hostile situations in later life. Stephenson's robust and resilient nature imbued from an early age allowed him to handle the stresses and strains of five years as a prisoner of war and when separated from his wife and children in Egypt in the early 1950s. Others in a similar predicament fared less well.

In the late 1920s, Stephenson had joined an elite, select group to become an officer, a pilot and a future senior leader in the post-Great War air force. The junior Service was seen as a chivalrous, if not glamorous, life which offered an alternative to the miserable carnage of static, attritional trench warfare. It was a Service created in wartime; while its focus on strategic bombing maintained its independence in the parlous 1920s and early 1930s, it was air policing in the Middle East that showed the tangible value of air power. While Stephenson may have joined a peacetime air force, it was not without its risks. Rather than fighting a dastardly foe, the airmen of the 1920s were fighting a lack of funding, the unforgiving aviation environment and immature technology. Consequently, 25 per cent of his Cranwell cohort would be killed within 18 months of graduation, all bar one in flying accidents. Stephenson was an excellent pilot and lucky; he was wise enough to recognize his limits which kept him alive. Others in his cohort of young, head-strong aviators ran out of luck, ability, or both.

Stephenson's return from the Middle East in the mid-1930s coincided with the first signs of a resurgent Germany. With the clouds of war once again beginning to loom over Europe, the changing strategic context saw a paradigm shift for the peacetime RAF. Within a few short years, the RAF expanded and diversified. Fighter Command benefitted by introducing new fighters and radar, critical components for the world's first integrated air defence system. Equipment was simply not enough. The RAF also required a larger workforce to fuel its expansion. While Cranwell graduates remained first amongst equals, the trawl for officers and pilots came from a much wider sway of the British population, including candidates from broader social and class backgrounds. While the pool may have become larger, Stephenson could seek mentorship and advancement by virtue of his Cranwell credentials and experience.

Stephenson was always well connected to senior RAF officers who could mentor him, gain access to other senior officers to establish his credibility and ensure he was given the right career-enhancing job at the right time. Unusually, he worked as an aide to several senior RAF officers throughout his career. As a young Flying Officer in Iraq in the early 1930s, Stephenson worked for Air Vice-Marshal Charles Burnett. Later in that same decade, the then Squadron Leader Stephenson would be reunited with Burnett in the Inspector General role. Stephenson also worked with the former Chief of the Air Staff, Marshal of the RAF Sir Edward Ellington, in the same appointment. Working closely with two influential senior RAF leaders guaranteed Stephenson a prime appointment as a Spitfire squadron commander in Fighter Command; it was the place to be and an opportunity to fly the RAF's latest and most modern fighter. Indeed, after returning home after five years in captivity, it was to his old principal, Ellington, that Stephenson turned to for advice as he started to resurrect his plateauing career profile. In the post-war era, Stephenson again worked in the outer office of a senior RAF leader. As a Group Captain, Stephenson worked alongside Air Marshal 'Mary' Coningham, the famed New Zealander from the Western Desert campaign, as his Senior Personal Staff Officer at Flying Training Command. The net result was that Stephenson would always be the prime candidate for the upcoming CFS commandant position. Using mentors, he adroitly ensured his constant and timely progression through the rank structure and key command appointments.

Stephenson was undoubtedly a career RAF officer whose true potential and reach are difficult to quantify, as his career was abruptly cut short in a Florida forest in 1954. However, he was also an exceptionally gifted pilot and instructor.

Military flying was and remains a high-risk proposition. Stephenson and his colleagues knew the risks yet faced them daily despite seeing many friends and colleagues fall by the wayside. As a young, single aviator, it was easier to accept the risks and losses with youthful bravado, but skill and experience alone are sometimes not enough to save a life. The enemy and luck also vote on a fighter pilot's destiny. Stephenson duelled with the opposition only once; luck and skill saved him that day. However, luck is a finite resource, and Stephenson's luck would run out on 8 November 1954. It was a remarkable run. His flying career spanned 26 years and started in silver-painted, fabric-covered wooden biplanes that flew at less than 200mph and would finish in a sleek, bare-aluminium supersonic jet fighter. Sat near the middle of Stephenson's flying career is N3200. When asked what Geoffrey Stephenson meant to him, one of N3200's contemporary pilots, 'Mo' Overall reflected that:

Sometimes you sit there in the cockpit of N3200 flying over the beautiful Cambridgeshire countryside on a lovely day and simply enjoy the moment. However, it is something else to actually point this war machine across the English Channel and go across there knowing full well that someone is trying to shoot you down before you do the same to them. I am in awe of them all. I often wonder, if it was me, how quickly the thrill of the fight would have worn off as I saw my friends and colleagues being killed in action or failing to return from a mission. The thought of being let loose with a state-of-the-art Spitfire must have been exciting. However, the responsibility and the initial excitement of the impending battle must have been immense.

Yet, that is precisely what Stephenson and his colleagues did. All faced trauma and their fears in one form or another at some point. Stephenson paid a dear price on his first battle – the impact of his incarceration stayed with him for many years after his release. Others survived the initial onslaught, only to go up and repeat the event again and again. Some survived the constant struggle; others, like Stephenson and Bader, were captured, while some, like Brian Lane, made the ultimate sacrifice. Others never reached the front line; many of Stephenson's Cranwell friends were killed in pre-war peacetime training. Today, Stephenson rests in Oakwood Cemetery in downtown Montgomery,

Alabama alongside 79 other RAF airmen, all more junior and younger than Stephenson. Most are half his age and were killed during their Second World War pilot training, too young to have a legacy, no family of their own to tell their story and no experience of war to speak of their brave exploits fighting for their country. Therefore, Stephenson's story is important as he speaks on their behalf. However, Stephenson's tale is both remarkable and essential as it not only tells his life but also reflects on the incredible people, places and aircraft that he met along the way, many of whom were unable to tell their own story.

Lest we forget.

Appendix A

RAF Burials at The Commonwealth War Graves Commission Cemetery, Oakwood Annex, Montgomery, Alabama

Rank	Name	Age	Date of Death
LAC	Frank Victor Marhoff	29	13 November 1941
LAC	Richard Norman Moss	20	
LAC	Peter Greene	20	10 December 1941
LAC	Stanley Holden	30	
LAC	William Joseph Marchant	18	13 December 1941
LAC	John Keith Briers	21	26 December 1941
LAC	Douglas Fairer Leman	20	27 December 1941
LAC	Kenneth Barlass	21	7 January 1942
LAC	Kenneth Neil Thomson	27	8 January 1942
LAC	John Feldon Rimer	19	13 January 1942
LAC	George Benson Whigham	21	14 January 1942
LAC	Alfred Bolton Kinnear	20	20 January 1942
LAC	David William Turner	19	3 February 1942
LAC	Paul Derek Underwood	20	
LAC	George William Rowley	19	5 February 1942
LAC	Ronald George Robbins	21	7 February 1942
Cpl	Reginald Arthur Price	22	9 February 1942
LAC	Charles William Wadkinson	19	
LAC	John Ferrior Latta	25	18 March 1942
LAC	Richard Edward Davies	23	28 March 1942
LAC	Thomas Henry Hedger	20	
LAC	Reginald Arthur John Shotbolt	20	7 April 1942

LAC	George Leslie Simpson	21	9 April 1942
LAC	Thomas Walpole Atkin	23	10 April 1942
LAC	Frederick Nash	24	
LAC	Wilfred John Hawes	30	11 April 1942
LAC	Philip Walter Winter	20	
LAC	Ronald Arthur Parry	20	20 April 1942
LAC	Geoffrey Holmes	20	6 May 1942
Plt Off	George Henry Anthony Butler	19	7 May 1942
LAC	Oswald Hendrie McDonald	20	
LAC	Ernest George Gulliver	20	9 May 1942
LAC	Victor William Lear	19	21 May 1942
LAC	Arthur Vernon Lowe	22	
LAC	James Edward Maddick	21	
LAC	Patrick Geoffrey Marshall Overton	22	
LAC	Michael Ernest Peachell	22	
LAC	David Stanley Peattie	19	
LAC	Ronald Edward Randall	26	
LAC	Frank Rogers	23	
LAC	Arthur William Wakeley	20	28 May 1942
LAC	James Arthur Barnes	21	3 June 1942
LAC	Walter Samuel Bowden	20	17 June 1942
LAC	Charles Dean Junior Eaton	32	29 June 1942
LAC	Maurice Hislop	20	14 July 1942
LAC	Rowland William Holmes	–	
LAC	Bernard Walter Howcroft	22	
LAC	William Gibson Lamont	20	
LAC	Philip William Longbottom	28	
LAC	Ronald Bertram Pinsent	21	
LAC	Sidney Arthur Platt	19	
LAC	Kenward Frederick Stevens	21	
LAC	Eric William Frederick Charrosin	21	18 July 1942

LAC	Leonard Alfred Carter	21	22 July 1942
LAC	Herbert Riding	20	9 August 1942
LAC	Albert Edgar Ayling	19	10 August 1942
LAC	Cyril Evan Gray	26	
LAC	Douglas Warren Flatau	19	17 August 1942
LAC	Ernest Robert John Spooner	20	1 September 1942
LAC	Thomas Gilbert Hornsey	20	
LAC	Douglas Albert Gell	19	14 September 1942
LAC	Victor Holman	23	19 September 1942
LAC	Charles Norman Frederick Downs	20	24 September 1942
LAC	Kenneth McGregor Moore	26	4 October 1942
LAC	David James Calder	19	6 October 1942
Plt Off	Lorenzo Diaz Copeland	22	3 November 1942
Plt Off	Ronald William McIntosh Mackenzie	22	19 November 1942
LAC	Gordon Grieve Warner	24	25 November 1942
Fg Off	Douglas Arthur Crowther	20	6 December 1942
LAC	Leslie Herbert Carter	19	29 December 1942
Plt Off	Michael Tom Dickinson	21	31 December 1942
Fg Off	Philip Jones	25	
Plt Off	Anthony Guy Mole	26	13 January 1942
LAC	Felix Quinn	20	7 February 1942
Fg Off	Joshua Johnston	29	4 March 1943
Plt Off	George Lammie	20	27 May 1943
Fg Off	Frank Charles Creed	22	2 July 1943
Flt Lt	George William Nickerson MM	44	31 July 1943
Air Cdre	Geoffrey Dalton Stephenson	44	8 November 1954
Sqn Ldr	Christopher H Walker	29	6 July 1958

Notes

Chapter 1: The Early Days

1. TNA, WO 374/65220, William Stephenson.
2. TNA, WO 374/65220, William Stephenson.
3. TNA, WO 374/65220, William Stephenson.
4. TNA, WO 374/65220, William Stephenson.
5. TNA, WO 374/65220, William Stephenson.
6. TNA, WO 374/65220, William Stephenson.
7. TNA, WO 374/65220, William Stephenson.
8. TNA, WO 95/1113/2, 9 (Queen's Royal) Lancers.
9. Athies is located a few miles west of Arras.
10. TNA, WO 95/1113/2, 9 (Queen's Royal) Lancers.
11. TNA, WO 374/65220, William Stephenson.
12. *Yorkshire Post*, Monday 15 April 1918.
13. *Lincolnshire Echo*, Wednesday 16 July 1919.
14. Castle Park School. 'Further Information'. https://www.castleparkschool.ie/our-school/further-information/ (accessed 1 November 2022.)
15. Castle Park Old Boys' Society 1925, 5 and 1926, 8.
16. *The Lynn Advertiser, Wisbech Constitutional Gazette and Norfolk and Cambridgeshire Herald*, 25 June 1926.
17. *The London Gazette*, Friday 21 October 1927.
18. Haslam, *The History of Royal Air Force Cranwell*, 23.
19. Haslam, *The History of Royal Air Force Cranwell*, 23.
20. Haslam, *The History of Royal Air Force Cranwell*, 23.
21. Haslam, *The History of Royal Air Force Cranwell*, 23.
22. Haslam, *The History of Royal Air Force Cranwell*, 23.
23. Haslam, *The History of Royal Air Force Cranwell*, 23.

Chapter 2: Pre-War in the RAF

1. Haslam, *The History of Royal Air Force Cranwell*, 21.
2. Haslam, *The History of Royal Air Force Cranwell*, 20.
3. *The Journal of the Royal Air Force College*, Vol. XII No. 1 Spring 1932, 126.
4. *The Journal of the Royal Air Force College*, Vol. X No. 2 Autumn 1930, 178.

5. *The Journal of the Royal Air Force College*, Vol. X No. 2 Autumn 1930, 180.
6. *The Journal of the Royal Air Force College*, Vol. X No. 1 Spring 1930, 58.
7. *The Journal of the Royal Air Force College*, Vol. IX No. 2 Autumn 1929, 154.
8. *The Journal of the Royal Air Force College*, Vol. X No. 1 Spring 1930, 186.
9. Lucas, *Flying Colours – The Epic Story of Douglas Bader*, 36.
10. TNA, AIR 27/287/1, Squadron Number: 23 Summary of Events: Y.
11. TNA, AIR 27/287/1, Squadron Number: 23 Summary of Events: Y.
12. TNA, AIR 27/287/1, Squadron Number: 23 Summary of Events: Y.
13. TNA, AIR 27/287/1, Squadron Number: 23 Summary of Events: Y.
14. TNA, AIR 27/287/1, Squadron Number: 23 Summary of Events: Y.
15. Lucas, *Flying Colours – The Epic Story of Douglas Bader*, 47.
16. Lucas, *Flying Colours – The Epic Story of Douglas Bader*, 47.
17. TNA, AIR 27/287/1, Squadron Number: 23 Summary of Events: Y.
18. Brickhill, *Reach for the Sky*, 42.
19. Sarkar, *Fighter Ace*, 33.
20. TNA, AIR 27/287/1, Squadron Number: 23 Summary of Events: Y.
21. TNA, AIR 27/287/1, Squadron Number: 23 Summary of Events: Y.
22. Lucas, *Flying Colours – The Epic Story of Douglas Bader*, 51.
23. TNA, AIR 43/7, Royal Air Force courts martial charge book.
24. TNA, AIR 27/287/1, Squadron Number: 23 Summary of Events: Y.
25. TNA, AIR 27/287/1, Squadron Number: 23 Summary of Events: Y.
26. Brickhill, *Reach for the Sky*, 43.
27. Brickhill, *Reach for the Sky*, 45.
28. J.A. Chance was killed in a flying accident at Catterick in November 1930 while flying an Atlas with 26 Squadron. On 7 August 1931, D.G. Vaughan-Fowler was killed in a 41 Squadron Siskin when it overturned on landing at Hawkinge and caught fire. A.G. Cleland was killed in the Sudan in December 1932 when flying a 47 Squadron Fairey during a cooperation exercise with the Eastern Arab Corps. J.S. Newcombe had been attending the Bobsleigh World Championships in Switzerland in February 1931 when he died of peritonitis. Newcombe served as a brakeman in the British team, alongside the Sword of Honour winner, Paddy Coote.
29. TNA, AIR 10/1482. Report on Flying Accidents during July–Dec. 1931.
30. Warwick, *In Every Place*, 163.
31. Warwick, *In Every Place*, 170.
32. Castle Park Old Boys' Society 1932, 25.
33. TNA, AIR 29/604, Central Flying School. Formed at Upavon (UK) in May 1912. Disbanded in April 1942. Contains Defence Scheme of Vulnerable Points, newspaper cuttings and a water colour of the School's armorial bearings. Includes 8 photographs depicting: Central Flying School, RAF Upavon: aerial views: visit by HM King George VI: rows of aircraft (unidentified). Dated 1938. With appendices.
34. TNA, AIR 29/604, Central Flying School. Formed at Upavon (UK) in May 1912. Disbanded in April 1942. Contains Defence Scheme of Vulnerable Points,

newspaper cuttings and a water colour of the School's armorial bearings. Includes 8 photographs depicting: Central Flying School, RAF Upavon: aerial views: visit by HM King George VI: rows of aircraft (unidentified). Dated 1938. With appendices.

35. TNA, AIR 29/604, Central Flying School. Formed at Upavon (UK) in May 1912. Disbanded in April 1942. Contains Defence Scheme of Vulnerable Points, newspaper cuttings and a water colour of the School's armorial bearings. Includes 8 photographs depicting: Central Flying School, RAF Upavon: aerial views: visit by HM King George VI: rows of aircraft (unidentified). Dated 1938. With appendices.

36. All three pilots would go on to have stellar careers. Mermagen and Stephenson would be reunited in early 1940 as Spitfire squadron commanders at Duxford before he too would rise to the rank of Air Commodore. In 1937 Colin Scragg was the most junior of the three but was commissioned the following year. During the war's latter stages, he commanded 166 Squadron flying Lancaster bombers. However, his operational tour ended early in January 1945 when Scragg was the sole survivor after a German night fighter shot down his Lancaster. Although he spent the last few months as a prisoner of war, Scragg would rise through the ranks in the post-war era, eventually reaching the rank of Air Vice-Marshal, one level beyond his 1937 wingmen.

37. TNA, AIR 29/604, Central Flying School. Formed at Upavon (UK) in May 1912. Disbanded in April 1942. Contains Defence Scheme of Vulnerable Points, newspaper cuttings and a water colour of the School's armorial bearings. Includes 8 photographs depicting: Central Flying School, RAF Upavon: aerial views: visit by HM King George VI: rows of aircraft (unidentified). Dated 1938. With appendices.

38. Key Aero. 'Upside Down and Inside Out.' https://www.key.aero/article/upside-down-inside-out (accessed 23 January 2023.)

39. TNA, AIR 29/604, Central Flying School. Formed at Upavon (UK) in May 1912. Disbanded in April 1942. Contains Defence Scheme of Vulnerable Points, newspaper cuttings and a water colour of the School's armorial bearings. Includes 8 photographs depicting: Central Flying School, RAF Upavon: aerial views: visit by HM King George VI: rows of aircraft (unidentified). Dated 1938. With appendices.

40. Pudney, *A Pride of Unicorns*, 155.

Chapter 3: Spitfire Command

1. TNA, AIR 27/252/1, Squadron Number: 19 Records of Events: Y.
2. TNA, AIR 27/252/1, Squadron Number: 19 Records of Events: Y.
3. Sarkar, *Spitfire!*, 42.
4. Imperial War Museum. 'Unwin, George Cecil (Oral History.)' https://www.iwm.org.uk/collections/item/object/80011292 (accessed 21 January 2022.)

5. Smith, *Wings Day*, 17.
6. TNA, AIR 81/27. Wing Commander H M A Day: POW. Sergeant E B Hillier and Aircraftman 2nd Class F G Moller: report of deaths; Blenheim L1138 shot down near Ibar Oberstein, 13 October 1939.
7. Imperial War Museum. "Unwin, George Cecil (Oral History.)" https://www.iwm.org.uk/collections/item/object/80011292 (accessed 21 January 2022.)
8. TNA, AIR 27/252/6, Squadron Number: 19 Records of Events: Y.
9. TNA, AIR 27/252/10, Squadron Number: 19 Records of Events: Y.
10. Imperial War Museum. 'Unwin, George Cecil (Oral History.)' https://www.iwm.org.uk/collections/item/object/80011292 (accessed 21 January 2022.)
11. TNA, AIR 27/252/16, Squadron Number: 19 Records of Events: Y.
12. Sarkar, *Spitfire!*, 93.
13. Deere, *Nine Lives*, 36.
14. TNA, AIR 27/252/3, Squadron Number: 19 Records of Events: Y.
15. TNA, AIR 27/252/9, Squadron Number: 19 Records of Events: Y.
16. Deere, *Nine Lives*, 35.
17. Imperial War Museum. 'Unwin, George Cecil (Oral History.)' https://www.iwm.org.uk/collections/item/object/80011292 (accessed 21 January 2022.)
18. TNA, AIR 27/252/9, Squadron Number: 19 Records of Events: Y.
19. TNA, AIR 27/252/11, Squadron Number: 19 Records of Events: Y.
20. TNA, AIR 27/252/8, Squadron Number: 19 Records of Events: Y.
21. Imperial War Museum. "Unwin, George Cecil (Oral History.)" https://www.iwm.org.uk/collections/item/object/80011292 (accessed 21 January 2022.)
22. TNA, AIR 27/252/9, Squadron Number: 19 Records of Events: Y.
23. TNA, AIR 27/252/9, Squadron Number: 19 Records of Events: Y.
24. Flying Logbook of Douglas Bader, copy held at AFHRA.
25. Brickhill, *Reach for the Sky*, 155.
26. Sarkar, *Spitfire!*, 88.
27. Brickhill, *Reach for the Sky*, 159.
28. Sarkar, *Fighter Ace*, 93.
29. TNA, AIR 27/252/13, Squadron Number: 19 Records of Events: Y.
30. Saunders, *Spitfire Mark I P9374*, 114.
31. Saunders, *Spitfire Mark I P9374*, 118.
32. Saunders, *Spitfire Mark I P9374*, 117.
33. N3200 may have been Stephenson's personal aircraft but it was also used by other pilots. For example, on 24 May 1940, Flight Lieutenant Brian Lane flew N3200 on a training sortie.
34. Sarkar, *Spitfire!*, 95.
35. Levine, *Dunkirk*, 278.
36. Levine, *Dunkirk*, 278.
37. TNA, AIR 27/252/13, Squadron Number: 19 Records of Events: Y.
38. Lane, *Spitfire!*, 25.
39. Lane, *Spitfire!*, 26.

Chapter 4: Dogfight over Dunkirk

1. Lane, *Spitfire!*, 27.
2. Lane, *Spitfire!*, 27.
3. Sarkar, *Spitfire!*, 105.
4. TNA, AIR 50/10/23. Air Ministry: Combat Reports, Second World War. Fighter Command. No. 19 Squadron. Name: Lyne. Rank: Pilot Officer. Squadron: 19 Other Dates of Combat: 26 May 1940.
5. TNA, AIR 50/10/19. Air Ministry: Combat Reports, Second World War. Fighter Command. No. 19 Squadron. Name: Lane. Rank: Flight Lieutenant, Squadron Leader. Squadron: 19 Other Dates of Combat: 26 May 1940; 01 June 1940, 24 August 1940, 07 September 1940, 11 September 1940, 15 September 1940.
6. TNA, AIR 50/10/4. Air Ministry: Combat Reports, Second World War. Fighter Command. No. 19 Squadron. Name: Brinsden. Rank: Flying Officer. Squadron: 19 Other Dates of Combat: 26 May 1940, 09 September 1940.
7. TNA, AIR 50/10/34. Air Ministry: Combat Reports, Second World War. Fighter Command. No. 19 Squadron. Name: Sinclair. Rank: Flying Officer. Squadron: 19 Other Dates of Combat: 26 May 1940, 01 June 1940.
8. Sarkar, *Spitfire!*, 105.
9. TNA, AIR 50/10/23. Air Ministry: Combat Reports, Second World War. Fighter Command. No. 19 Squadron. Name: Lyne. Rank: Pilot Officer. Squadron: 19 Other Dates of Combat: 26 May 1940.
10. TNA, AIR 50/10/19. Air Ministry: Combat Reports, Second World War. Fighter Command. No. 19 Squadron. Name: Lane. Rank: Flight Lieutenant, Squadron Leader. Squadron: 19 Other Dates of Combat: 26 May 1940; 01 June 1940, 24 August 1940, 07 September 1940, 11 September 1940, 15 September 1940.
11. TNA, AIR 50/10/4. Air Ministry: Combat Reports, Second World War. Fighter Command. No. 19 Squadron. Name: Brinsden. Rank: Flying Officer. Squadron: 19 Other Dates of Combat: 26 May 1940, 09 September 1940.
12. TNA, AIR 50/10/146. Air Ministry: Combat Reports, Second World War. Fighter Command. No. 19 Squadron. Name: Clouston. Rank: Flight Lieutenant. Squadron: 19 Other Dates of Combat: 21 October 1939, 11 May 1940, 26 May 1940, 27 May 1940, 18 September 1940.
13. TNA, AIR 50/10/35. Air Ministry: Combat Reports, Second World War. Fighter Command. No. 19 Squadron. Name: Steere. Rank: Flight Sergeant. Squadron: 19 Other Dates of Combat: 11 May 1940, 26 May 1940, 27 May 1940, 28 May 1940, 01 June 1940.
14. TNA, AIR 50/10/139. Air Ministry: Combat Reports, Second World War. Fighter Command. No. 19 Squadron. Name: Ball. Rank: Flying Officer. Squadron: 19 Other Dates of Combat: 19 June 1940; 26 May 1940, 27 May 1940.
15. TNA, AIR 50/10/34. Air Ministry: Combat Reports, Second World War. Fighter Command. No. 19 Squadron. Name: Sinclair. Rank: Flying Officer. Squadron: 19 Other Dates of Combat: 26 May 1940, 01 June 1940.

16. Sarkar, *Spitfire!*, 106.
17. TNA, AIR 50/10/23. Air Ministry: Combat Reports, Second World War. Fighter Command. No. 19 Squadron. Name: Lyne. Rank: Pilot Officer. Squadron: 19 Other Dates of Combat: 26 May 1940.
18. TNA, AIR 50/10/19. Air Ministry: Combat Reports, Second World War. Fighter Command. No. 19 Squadron. Name: Lane. Rank: Flight Lieutenant, Squadron Leader. Squadron: 19 Other Dates of Combat: 26 May 1940; 01 June 1940, 24 August 1940, 07 September 1940, 11 September 1940, 15 September 1940.
19. TNA, AIR 50/10/19. Air Ministry: Combat Reports, Second World War. Fighter Command. No. 19 Squadron. Name: Lane. Rank: Flight Lieutenant, Squadron Leader. Squadron: 19 Other Dates of Combat: 26 May 1940; 01 June 1940, 24 August 1940, 07 September 1940, 11 September 1940, 15 September 1940.
20. TNA, AIR 50/10/28. Air Ministry: Combat Reports, Second World War. Fighter Command. No. 19 Squadron. Name: Potter. Rank: Flight Sergeant. Squadron: 19 Other Dates of Combat: 26 May 1940.
21. TNA, AIR 50/10/35. Air Ministry: Combat Reports, Second World War. Fighter Command. No. 19 Squadron. Name: Steere. Rank: Flight Sergeant. Squadron: 19 Other Dates of Combat: 11 May 1940, 26 May 1940, 27 May 1940, 28 May 1940, 01 June 1940.
22. TNA, AIR 50/10/27. Air Ministry: Combat Reports, Second World War. Fighter Command. No. 19 Squadron. Name: Petre Rank: Flying Officer. Squadron: 19 Other Dates of Combat: 11 May 1940; 26 May 1940, 27 May 1940, 18 June 1940.
23. TNA, AIR 50/10/139. Air Ministry: Combat Reports, Second World War. Fighter Command. No. 19 Squadron. Name: Ball. Rank: Flying Officer. Squadron: 19 Other Dates of Combat: 19 June 1940; 26 May 1940, 27 May 1940.
24. TNA, AIR 50/10/34. Air Ministry: Combat Reports, Second World War. Fighter Command. No. 19 Squadron. Name: Sinclair. Rank: Flying Officer. Squadron: 19 Other Dates of Combat: 26 May 1940, 01 June 1940.
25. TNA, AIR 50/10/28. Air Ministry: Combat Reports, Second World War. Fighter Command. No. 19 Squadron. Name: Potter. Rank: Flight Sergeant. Squadron: 19 Other Dates of Combat: 26 May 1940.
26. TNA, AIR 50/10/28. Air Ministry: Combat Reports, Second World War. Fighter Command. No. 19 Squadron. Name: Potter. Rank: Flight Sergeant. Squadron: 19 Other Dates of Combat: 26 May 1940.
27. TNA, AIR 50/10/34. Air Ministry: Combat Reports, Second World War. Fighter Command. No. 19 Squadron. Name: Sinclair. Rank: Flying Officer. Squadron: 19 Other Dates of Combat: 26 May 1940, 01 June 1940.
28. TNA, AIR 50/10/23. Air Ministry: Combat Reports, Second World War. Fighter Command. No. 19 Squadron. Name: Lyne. Rank: Pilot Officer. Squadron: 19 Other Dates of Combat: 26 May 1940.

29. Brickhill, *Reach for the Sky*, 174.
30. Cornwell, *The Battle of France: Then and Now*, 373.
31. Rudorffer would become a rising star within the *Luftwaffe* fighter pilot community. In keeping with *Luftwaffe* policy of keeping fighter pilots on the front line throughout the war, Rudorffer would see active service throughout the Second World War. Indeed, Rudorffer served during the Battle of Britain, in North Africa, and on the Eastern Front before returning to fly the Messerschmitt Me 262 jet fighter during the closing stages of the war on the Western Front. He rose through the ranks achieving the rank of Major by the war's end. Moreover, Rudorffer's tally of kills would increase to a remarkable 222 as the seventh-highest-scoring fighter pilot of all time. Rudorffer may have been young and relatively inexperienced in May 1940, but he was a competent individual at the start of a remarkable career as a fighter pilot.
32. TNA, AIR 27/252/16, Squadron Number: 19 Records of Events: Y.
33. Imperial War Museum. 'Unwin, George Cecil (Oral History.)' https://www.iwm.org.uk/collections/item/object/80011292 (accessed 21 January 2022.)
34. Deere, *Nine Lives*, 65

Chapter 5: I Walk Alone

1 Anne is Anne Farrer, his girlfriend at the time.
2. H.W. either refers to Henry Wilson Woollett, the commanding officer of 23 Squadron in the early 1930s during Stephenson's first front-line tour, or Herbert Waldemar 'Tubby' Mermagen, Bader's former aerobatics leader at CFS pre-war and his fellow Spitfire squadron commander at Duxford.
3. Lieutenant Malcolm Rogerson Rollo was the eldest son of the late the Honorable Gilbert de Ste Croix Rollo and Margaret Freda Evelyn Rollo. At the time of his interaction with Stephenson on 26 May 1940, Rollo served with the 173 Railway Tunnelling Company, Royal Engineers. He was wounded later the same day and captured before being taken as a POW. Sadly, he died aged 35 in a Berlin hospital 18 months later from blood poisoning on 5 December 1941. In 1948, Rollo was reburied in the Berlin 1939–1945 War Cemetery at Heerstrasse.
4. Literally translates as 'save who can' but has come to mean 'everyone for themselves'.
5. B.E.F. = British Expeditionary Force.
6. R.D.F. = Radio Direction Finding (radar).
7. The Me 109 unit that hosted Stephenson on 2 June 1940 at Evere was II./JG 27 which was located at the airfield over the period 22 May to 5 June 1940.
8. Oberleutnant Werner Seyfert was the *Staffelkapitän* (squadron commander) of 6/JG 27 from 10 May 1940. He would remain in command of the unit throughout the Battle of France and the Battle of Britain. With 10 air-to-air kills to his name, he would go on to command a training unit, JG 103, from December 1942 to January 1943.

Chapter 6: *Dulag Luft*

1. Smith, *Wings Day*, 36. The numbers in the advanced party are disputed in the official Camp History of *Dulag Luft* which suggests that the British cadre comprised five officers and two airmen while seven French officers and two other ranks made up the initial group of the Permanent Party. TNA, WO 208/3269. *Dulag Luft* (Oberusel): RAF personnel.
2. TNA, WO 208/3269. *Dulag Luft* (Oberusel): RAF personnel.
3. TNA, WO 208/3269. *Dulag Luft* (Oberusel): RAF personnel.
4. TNA, WO 208/3269. *Dulag Luft* (Oberusel): RAF personnel.
5. Smith, *Wings Day*, 46.
6. TNA, WO 208/3269. *Dulag Luft* (Oberusel): RAF personnel.
7. TNA, WO 208/3269. *Dulag Luft* (Oberusel): RAF personnel.
8. TNA, WO 208/3269. *Dulag Luft* (Oberusel): RAF personnel.
9. Smith, *Wings Day*, 47.
10. Smith, *Wings Day*, 47.
11. Smith, *Wings Day*, 81.
12. TNA, WO 208/3269. *Dulag Luft* (Oberusel): RAF personnel.
13. TNA, WO 208/3269. *Dulag Luft* (Oberusel): RAF personnel.
14. TNA, WO 208/3269. *Dulag Luft* (Oberusel): RAF personnel.
15. Smith, *Wings Day*, 45.
16. TNA, WO 208/3269. *Dulag Luft* (Oberusel): RAF personnel.
17. TNA, WO 208/3269. *Dulag Luft* (Oberusel): RAF personnel.
18. TNA, WO 208/3269. *Dulag Luft* (Oberusel): RAF personnel.
19. Smith, *Wings Day*, 37.
20. Smith, *Wings Day*, 41.
21. Smith, *Wings Day*, 41
22. Smith, *Wings Day*, 63.
23. Smith, *Wings Day*, 53.
24. TNA, WO 208/3269. *Dulag Luft* (Oberusel): RAF personnel.
25. TNA, WO 208/3269. *Dulag Luft* (Oberusel): RAF personnel.
26. TNA, WO 208/3269. *Dulag Luft* (Oberusel): RAF personnel.
27. TNA, WO 208/3269. *Dulag Luft* (Oberusel): RAF personnel.
28. Stephenson's reading list included works by C.S. Forester, P.G. Wodehouse, H.G. Wells, J.B. Priestley, Evelyn Waugh, Daphne de Maurier, Tolstoy, D.H. Lawrence, Jane Austin, Shakespeare, and Rudyard Kipling.
29. TNA, WO 208/3269. *Dulag Luft* (Oberusel): RAF personnel.
30. TNA, WO 208/3269. *Dulag Luft* (Oberusel): RAF personnel.
31. TNA, WO 208/3269. *Dulag Luft* (Oberusel): RAF personnel.
32. MacDonnell, *Dogfight to Diplomacy*, 86.
33. MacDonnell, *Dogfight to Diplomacy*, 86.
34. Eric Foster, *Life Hangs by a Silken Thread*, 71.
35. TNA, AIR 81/611. Squadron Leader G D Stephenson: POW; Spitfire N3200 force landed in the Dunkirk–Calais area, France, 28 May 1940.

36. TNA, AIR 81/611. Squadron Leader G D Stephenson: POW; Spitfire N3200 force landed in the Dunkirk-Calais area, France, 28 May 1940.
37. TNA, AIR 81/611. Squadron Leader G D Stephenson: POW; Spitfire N3200 force landed in the Dunkirk-Calais area, France, 28 May 1940.
38. Smith, *Wings Day*, 48.
39. Smith, *Wings Day*, 64.
40. MacDonnell, *Dogfight to Diplomacy*, 87.
41. Pearson, *The Great Escaper*, 270.
42. Smith, *Wings Day*, 38.
43. TNA, WO 208/3269. *Dulag Luft* (Oberusel): RAF personnel.
44. Smith, *Wings Day*, 63.
45. Smith, *Wings Day*, 65.
46. TNA, WO 208/5448. Sage – Sykes.
47. TNA, WO 208/3269. *Dulag Luft* (Oberusel): RAF personnel.
48. TNA, WO 208/3282, *Stalag Luft* I Barth.
49. Pearson, *The Great Escaper*, 180.

Chapter 7: *Stalag Luft* I

1. TNA, WO 208/3282, *Stalag Luft* I Barth.
2. TNA, WO 208/3282, *Stalag Luft* I Barth.
3. TNA, WO 208/3282, *Stalag Luft* I Barth.
4. TNA, WO 208/3282, *Stalag Luft* I Barth.
5. TNA, WO 208/3282, *Stalag Luft* I Barth.
6. Tunstall, *The Last Escaper*, 120.
7. TNA, WO 208/3282, *Stalag Luft* I Barth.
8. TNA, WO 208/3282, *Stalag Luft* I Barth.
9. TNA, WO 224/62, *Stalag Luft* I.
10. TNA, WO 208/3282, *Stalag Luft* I Barth.
11. TNA, WO 208/3282, *Stalag Luft* I Barth.
12. TNA, WO 208/3282, *Stalag Luft* I Barth.
13. TNA, WO 224/62, *Stalag Luft* I.
14. TNA, WO 224/62, *Stalag Luft* I.
15. TNA, WO 208/3282, *Stalag Luft* I Barth.
16. TNA, WO 208/3282, *Stalag Luft* I Barth.
17. Smith, *Wings Day*, 66.
18. Smith, *Wings Day*, 66.
19. Smith, *Wings Day*, 66.
20. Smith, *Wings Day*, 81.
21. Smith, *Wings Day*, 81.
22. Tunstall, *The Last Escaper*, 126.
23. Pearson, *The Great Escaper*, 173.

24. TNA, WO 208/3282, *Stalag Luft* I Barth.
25. MacDonnell, *Dogfight to Diplomacy*, 93.
26. MacDonnell, *Dogfight to Diplomacy*, 86.
27. MacDonnell, *Dogfight to Diplomacy*, 86.
28. TNA, WO 224/62, *Stalag Luft* I.
29. TNA, WO 224/62, *Stalag Luft* I.
30. Flight Lieutenant Harry Burton escaped from solitary confinement on 27 May 1941. Over the next four days, he walked to the German port of Sassnitz, where he caught a ferry to neutral Sweden and eventually flew back to the UK. Burton was the first British prisoner of the Second World War to achieve a 'home run'. For his escape endeavours, he was awarded the Distinguished Service Order.
31. TNA, WO 208/3282, *Stalag Luft* I Barth.
32. TNA, WO 208/3282, *Stalag Luft* I Barth.
33. TNA, WO 208/3282, *Stalag Luft* I Barth.
34. TNA, WO 224/62, *Stalag Luft* I.
35. TNA, WO 224/62, *Stalag Luft* I.
36. TNA, WO 224/62, *Stalag Luft* I.
37. MacDonnell, *Dogfight to Diplomacy*, 88.
38. MacDonnell, *Dogfight to Diplomacy*, 88.
39. MacDonnell, *Dogfight to Diplomacy*, 88.
40. TNA, WO 208/3282, *Stalag Luft* I Barth.
41. TNA, WO 224/62, *Stalag Luft* I.
42. MacDonnell, *Dogfight to Diplomacy*, 95.
43. Reid, *Colditz – The Full Story*, 37.
44. Reid, *Colditz – The Full Story*, 41.
45. Of note, one newspaper article informs that Stephenson was a POW held at *Stalag Luft* II. Stephenson's POW file at The National Archives and his Red Cross Record in Geneva both reference *Stalag Luft* II as his place of residence in late 1940. The confusion is clarified by the Red Cross file for *Stalag Luft* I, which informs that *Stalag Luft* I was previously known as *Stalag Luft* II.
46. TNA, HS 9/1021/1. James Francis George MENESSON, aka James Francis MENZIES, aka Jean François MARTINET, aka BIRCH – born 27.04.1916, executed 29.03.1945 at Flossenburg concentration camp.
47. TNA, HS 9/1021/1. James Francis George MENESSON, aka James Francis MENZIES, aka Jean François MARTINET, aka BIRCH – born 27.04.1916, executed 29.03.1945 at Flossenburg concentration camp.
48. TNA, HS 9/1021/1. James Francis George MENESSON, aka James Francis MENZIES, aka Jean François MARTINET, aka BIRCH – born 27.04.1916, executed 29.03.1945 at Flossenburg concentration camp.
49. Flying Logbook of Douglas Bader, copy held at AFHRA.
50. Flying Logbook of Douglas Bader, copy held at AFHRA. In reality, Bader's total has been subsequently pared back to 22.5. Sarkar, *Fighter Ace*, 314.
51. Sarkar, *Fighter Ace*, 284.

52. Galland, *First and the Last*, 85.
53. Sarkar, *Fighter Ace*, 294.

Chapter 8 – Colditz: The Allied Years

1. TNA, WO 40/1910. Camp history: Oflag IVC (Colditz): Army, Navy and Air Force personnel Nov 1940 – Apr 1945.
2. TNA, WO 224/69. Oflag IVC Saalhaus Coldlitz, Dresden.
3. TNA, WO 40/1910. Camp history: Oflag IVC (Colditz): Army, Navy and Air Force personnel Nov 1940 – Apr 1945.
4. Reid, *The Colditz Story*, x.
5. TNA, WO 224/69. Oflag IVC Saalhaus Coldlitz, Dresden.
6. Reid, *The Colditz Story*, 32.
7. Reid, *The Colditz Story*, x.
8. TNA, WO 40/190. Camp history: Oflag IVC (Colditz): Army, Navy and Air Force personnel Nov 1940 – Apr 1945.
9. TNA, WO 40/190. Camp history: Oflag IVC (Colditz): Army, Navy and Air Force personnel Nov 1940 – Apr 1945.
10. TNA, WO 40/190. Camp history: Oflag IVC (Colditz): Army, Navy and Air Force personnel Nov 1940 – Apr 1945.
11. TNA, WO 40/190. Camp history: Oflag IVC (Colditz): Army, Navy and Air Force personnel Nov 1940 – Apr 1945.
12. TNA, WO 224/69. Oflag IVC Saalhaus Coldlitz, Dresden.
13. TNA, WO 224/69. Oflag IVC Saalhaus Coldlitz, Dresden.
14. TNA, WO 224/69. Oflag IVC Saalhaus Coldlitz, Dresden.
15. TNA, WO 40/190. Camp history: Oflag IVC (Colditz): Army, Navy and Air Force personnel Nov 1940 – Apr 1945.
16. TNA, WO 224/69. Oflag IVC Saalhaus Coldlitz, Dresden.
17. TNA, WO 224/69. Oflag IVC Saalhaus Coldlitz, Dresden.
18. TNA, WO 40/190. Camp history: Oflag IVC (Colditz): Army, Navy and Air Force personnel Nov 1940 – Apr 1945.
19. TNA, WO 224/69. Oflag IVC Saalhaus Coldlitz, Dresden.
20. Reid, *Colditz – The Full Story*, 35.
21. Reid, *Colditz – The Full Story*, 35.
22. TNA, WO 40/190. Camp history: Oflag IVC (Colditz): Army, Navy and Air Force personnel Nov 1940 – Apr 1945.
23. TNA, WO 224/69. Oflag IVC Saalhaus Coldlitz, Dresden.
24. TNA, WO 224/69. Oflag IVC Saalhaus Coldlitz, Dresden.
25. TNA, WO 224/69. Oflag IVC Saalhaus Coldlitz, Dresden.
26. TNA, WO 224/69. Oflag IVC Saalhaus Coldlitz, Dresden.
27. TNA, WO 224/69. Oflag IVC Saalhaus Coldlitz, Dresden.
28. TNA, WO 224/69. Oflag IVC Saalhaus Coldlitz, Dresden.
29. TNA, WO 224/69. Oflag IVC Saalhaus Coldlitz, Dresden.

30. TNA, WO 224/69. Oflag IVC Saalhaus Coldlitz, Dresden.
31. TNA, WO 224/69. Oflag IVC Saalhaus Coldlitz, Dresden.
32. TNA, WO 224/69. Oflag IVC Saalhaus Coldlitz, Dresden.
33. In December 1941, the 400g of meat included 205g of meat, 70g of dried fish and 125g of sausage. TNA, WO 224/69. Oflag IVC Saalhaus Coldlitz, Dresden.
34. TNA, WO 40/190. Camp history: Oflag IVC (Colditz): Army, Navy and Air Force personnel Nov 1940 – Apr 1945.
35. TNA, WO 224/69. Oflag IVC Saalhaus Coldlitz, Dresden.
36. TNA, WO 224/69. Oflag IVC Saalhaus Coldlitz, Dresden.
37. TNA, WO 224/69. Oflag IVC Saalhaus Coldlitz, Dresden.
38. TNA, WO 40/190. Colditz Camp History of Oflag IVC (Colditz)
39. TNA, WO 224/69. Oflag IVC Saalhaus Coldlitz, Dresden.
40. Reid, *The Colditz Story*, 57.
41. TNA, WO 224/69. Oflag IVC Saalhaus Coldlitz, Dresden.
42. TNA, WO 224/69. Oflag IVC Saalhaus Coldlitz, Dresden.
43. TNA, WO 224/69. Oflag IVC Saalhaus Coldlitz, Dresden.
44. TNA, WO 224/69. Oflag IVC Saalhaus Coldlitz, Dresden.
45. TNA, WO 224/69. Oflag IVC Saalhaus Coldlitz, Dresden.
46. Reid, *The Colditz Story*, 63.
47. TNA, WO 224/69. Oflag IVC Saalhaus Coldlitz, Dresden.
48. TNA, WO 224/69. Oflag IVC Saalhaus Coldlitz, Dresden.
49. TNA, WO 224/69. Oflag IVC Saalhaus Coldlitz, Dresden.
50. TNA, WO 224/69. Oflag IVC Saalhaus Coldlitz, Dresden.
51. TNA, WO 224/69. Oflag IVC Saalhaus Coldlitz, Dresden.
52. Reid, *Colditz – The Full Story*, 125.
53. Reid, *Colditz – The Full Story*, 125.
54. Reid, *Colditz – The Full Story*, 349. Others suggest that Bader arrived a few days later on 18 August 1942. Sarkar, *Fighter Ace*, 308.
55. Sarkar, *Fighter Ace*, 305.
56. Brickhill, *Reach for the Sky*, 338.
57. Reid, *The Colditz Story*, 157.
58. TNA, WO 40/1910. Camp history: Oflag IVC (Colditz): Army, Navy and Air Force personnel Nov 1940 – Apr 1945.
59. TNA, WO 40/1910. Camp history: Oflag IVC (Colditz): Army, Navy and Air Force personnel Nov 1940 – Apr 1945.
60. Reid, *Colditz – The Full Story*, 120.
61. TNA, WO 40/1910. Camp history: Oflag IVC (Colditz): Army, Navy and Air Force personnel Nov 1940 – Apr 1945.
62. TNA, WO 40/1910. Camp history: Oflag IVC (Colditz): Army, Navy and Air Force personnel Nov 1940 – Apr 1945.
63. TNA, WO 40/1910. Camp history: Oflag IVC (Colditz): Army, Navy and Air Force personnel Nov 1940 – Apr 1945.
64. TNA, WO 40/1910. Camp history: Oflag IVC (Colditz): Army, Navy and Air Force personnel Nov 1940 – Apr 1945.

65. TNA, WO 224/69. Oflag IVC Saalhaus Coldlitz, Dresden.
66. TNA, WO 40/1910. Camp history: Oflag IVC (Coldlitz): Army, Navy and Air Force personnel Nov 1940 – Apr 1945.
67. TNA, WO 40/1910. Camp history: Oflag IVC (Coldlitz): Army, Navy and Air Force personnel Nov 1940 – Apr 1945.
68. TNA, WO 224/69. Oflag IVC Saalhaus Coldlitz, Dresden.
69. TNA, WO 40/190. Camp history: Oflag IVC (Coldlitz): Army, Navy and Air Force personnel Nov 1940 – Apr 1945.
70. The VC winner was Lieutenant Colonel Charles Merritt who earned Britain's highest gallantry award for his part in the controversial 1942 Dieppe raid.
71. TNA, WO 224/69. Oflag IVC Saalhaus Coldlitz, Dresden.
72. TNA, WO 224/69. Oflag IVC Saalhaus Coldlitz, Dresden.
73. Reid, *Colditz – The Full Story*, 238.
74. TNA, WO 224/69. Oflag IVC Saalhaus Coldlitz, Dresden.
75. TNA, WO 224/69. Oflag IVC Saalhaus Coldlitz, Dresden.
76. Sadly, on 25 September 1944 and during the last escape attempt from Colditz, Mike Sinclair was shot and this time the injury was fatal.
77. TNA, WO 224/69. Oflag IVC Saalhaus Coldlitz, Dresden.
78. TNA, HS 9/1021/1. James Francis George MENESSON, aka James Francis MENZIES, aka Jean François MARTINET, aka BIRCH – born 27.04.1916, executed 29.03.1945 at Flossenburg concentration camp.
79. TNA, HS 9/1021/1. James Francis George MENESSON, aka James Francis MENZIES, aka Jean François MARTINET, aka BIRCH – born 27.04.1916, executed 29.03.1945 at Flossenburg concentration camp.
80. TNA, HS 9/1021/1. James Francis George MENESSON, aka James Francis MENZIES, aka Jean François MARTINET, aka BIRCH – born 27.04.1916, executed 29.03.1945 at Flossenburg concentration camp.
81. TNA, HS 9/1021/1. James Francis George MENESSON, aka James Francis MENZIES, aka Jean François MARTINET, aka BIRCH – born 27.04.1916, executed 29.03.1945 at Flossenburg concentration camp.

Chapter 9: Colditz: The British Years

1. TNA, WO 224/69. Oflag IVC Saalhaus Coldlitz, Dresden.
2. TNA, WO 224/69. Oflag IVC Saalhaus Coldlitz, Dresden.
3. TNA, WO 224/69. Oflag IVC Saalhaus Coldlitz, Dresden.
4. Reid, *The Colditz Story*, 293.
5. TNA, WO 224/69. Oflag IVC Saalhaus Coldlitz, Dresden.
6. TNA, AIR 40/1910. Camp history: Oflag IVC (Colditz): Army, Navy and Air Force personnel Nov 1940 – Apr 1945.
7. Reid, *The Colditz Story*, 211.
8. TNA, AIR 40/1910. Camp history: Oflag IVC (Colditz): Army, Navy and Air Force personnel Nov 1940 – Apr 1945.

9. TNA, AIR 40/1910. Camp history: Oflag IVC (Colditz): Army, Navy and Air Force personnel Nov 1940 – Apr 1945.

10. TNA, AIR 40/1910. Camp history: Oflag IVC (Colditz): Army, Navy and Air Force personnel Nov 1940 – Apr 1945.

11. Reid, *The Latter Days at Colditz*, 223.

12. Champ, *The Diggers of Colditz*, 176.

13. MacIntyre, *Prisoners of the Castle*, 225.

14. Reid, *The Latter Days at Colditz*, 133.

15. Reid, *The Colditz Story*, 57.

16. Reid, *The Colditz Story*, 122.

17. Reid, *The Latter Days at Colditz*, 123.

18. TNA, WO 224/69. Oflag IVC Saalhaus Coldlitz, Dresden.

19. TNA, WO 224/69. Oflag IVC Saalhaus Coldlitz, Dresden.

20. TNA, WO 224/69. Oflag IVC Saalhaus Coldlitz, Dresden.

21. TNA, WO 224/69. Oflag IVC Saalhaus Coldlitz, Dresden.

22. Reid, *Colditz – The Full Story*, 290.

23. TNA, WO 224/69. Oflag IVC Saalhaus Coldlitz, Dresden.

24. TNA, WO 224/69. Oflag IVC Saalhaus Coldlitz, Dresden.

25. TNA, WO 224/69. Oflag IVC Saalhaus Coldlitz, Dresden.

26. TNA, AIR 40/1910. Camp history: Oflag IVC (Colditz): Army, Navy and Air Force personnel Nov 1940 – Apr 1945.

27. TNA, WO 224/69. Oflag IVC Saalhaus Coldlitz, Dresden.

28. TNA, WO 224/69. Oflag IVC Saalhaus Coldlitz, Dresden.

29. TNA, WO 224/69. Oflag IVC Saalhaus Coldlitz, Dresden.

30. TNA, WO 224/69. Oflag IVC Saalhaus Coldlitz, Dresden.

31. TNA, AIR 40/1910. Camp history: Oflag IVC (Colditz): Army, Navy and Air Force personnel Nov 1940 – Apr 1945.

32. Tunstall, *The Last Escaper*, 292.

33. TNA, WO 224/69. Oflag IVC Saalhaus Coldlitz, Dresden.

34. Reid, *The Colditz Story*, 264.

35. There are various stories, the most plausible being that Millar was recaptured two weeks later and taken to the POW camp at *Stalag* VIIIB. He was removed from there and taken under heavy guard by the German Secret Police to the Mauthausen concentration camp in Austria. It is believed that he was then shot dead on 15 July 1944, with his body being cremated there and his ashes scattered among those of other murdered camp inmates.

36. Reid, *The Latter Days at Colditz*, 177.

37. Eggers, *Colditz – The German Side*, 140.

38. TNA, AIR 40/1910. Camp history: Oflag IVC (Colditz): Army, Navy and Air Force personnel Nov 1940 – Apr 1945.

39. Reid, *Colditz – The Full Story*, 259.

40. TNA, AIR 40/1910. Camp history: Oflag IVC (Colditz): Army, Navy and Air Force personnel Nov 1940 – Apr 1945.

41. Others contest who conceived the glider project. For example, Bader suggests that it was Flight Lieutenant Lorne Welch, a pre-war gliding expert, with Flight Lieutenants Walter Morison and Jack Best supporting and Bader acting as a consultant. Welch, Morison and Best would all be involved in the project, but the architect of the project was Bill Goldfinch. Lorne Welch conducted stress calculations for the glider while Walter Morison 'made a few minor components'. *New York Times*, 'Lorne Welch, R.A.F. Pilot And Escape Artist, Dies at 81." https://www.nytimes.com/1998/06/08/world/lorne-welch-raf-pilot-and-escape-artist-dies-at-81.html (accessed 24 August 2022) and YouTube. 'One Way into Colditz.' https://www.youtube.com/watch?v=Rsq-5v3BqMI (accessed 24 August 2022.)
42. TNA, AIR 40/1910. Camp history: Oflag IVC (Colditz): Army, Navy and Air Force personnel Nov 1940 – Apr 1945.
43. Again, this position is contested. Pat Reid suggests it was Rolt's idea to build the glider and he brought Goldfinch in on the idea. Reid, *The Latter Days at Colditz*, 206.
44. TNA, AIR 40/1910. Camp history: Oflag IVC (Colditz): Army, Navy and Air Force personnel Nov 1940 – Apr 1945 and Hoskins, *The Colditz Cock*, 30.
45. Reid, *The Latter Days at Colditz*, 253.
46. Hoskins, *The Colditz Cock*, 38.
47. Hoskins, *The Colditz Cock*, 29.
48. Reid, *Colditz – The Full Story*, 306.
49. Hoskins, *The Colditz Cock*, 43.
50. Hoskins, *The Colditz Cock*, 43.
51. Reid, *The Latter Days at Colditz*, 242.
52. Hoskins, *The Colditz Cock*, 30.
53. TNA, AIR 40/1910. Camp history: Oflag IVC (Colditz): Army, Navy and Air Force personnel Nov 1940 – Apr 1945.
54. TNA, AIR 40/1910. Camp history: Oflag IVC (Colditz): Army, Navy and Air Force personnel Nov 1940 – Apr 1945.
55. TNA, AIR 40/1910. Camp history: Oflag IVC (Colditz): Army, Navy and Air Force personnel Nov 1940 – Apr 1945.
56. TNA, AIR 40/1910. Camp history: Oflag IVC (Colditz): Army, Navy and Air Force personnel Nov 1940 – Apr 1945.
57. Reid, *The Latter Days at Colditz*, 10.
58. TNA, AIR 40/1910. Camp history: Oflag IVC (Colditz): Army, Navy and Air Force personnel Nov 1940 – Apr 1945.
59. Reid, *The Latter Days at Colditz*, 279.
60. Reid, *The Latter Days at Colditz*, 284.
61. Brickhill, *Reach for the Sky*, 353.
62. RAF Museum. 'The Long Trip Home'. https://www.rafmuseum.org.uk/research/archive-exhibitions/freedom-liberty/the-long-trip-home/ (accessed 20 August 2022.)

63. RAF Museum. 'The Long Trip Home'. https://www.rafmuseum.org.uk/research/archive-exhibitions/freedom-liberty/the-long-trip-home/ (accessed 20 August 2022.)
64. Reid, *The Latter Days at Colditz*, 288.
65. Reid, *The Latter Days at Colditz*, 288.
66. Reid, *The Latter Days at Colditz*, 289.
67. Imperial War Museum. 'Goldfinch, Leslie James Edward 'Bill (Oral history)'. https://www.iwm.org.uk/collections/item/object/80025510 (accessed 20 August 2022.)
68. Tunstall, *The Last Escaper*, 302.
69. Tunstall, *The Last Escaper*, 302.
70. TNA, AIR 29/1102. Personnel Despatch and Reception Units.
71. TNA, AIR 29/1102. Personnel Despatch and Reception Units.
72. TNA, AIR 29/1102. Personnel Despatch and Reception Units.
73. TNA, AIR49/386. Prisoners of War: formation of No. 106 Personnel Reception Centre, Cosford (ex P.O.W.); administrative instructions for the post-hostilities evacuation of Air Force prisoners-of-war; miscellaneous papers.
74. Pudney, *A Pride of Unicorns*, 180.
75. Pudney, *A Pride of Unicorns*, 188.
76. Rosier, *Be Bold*, 191.
77. TNA, HS 9/1021/1. James Francis George MENESSON, aka James Francis MENZIES, aka Jean François MARTINET, aka BIRCH – born 27.04.1916, executed 29.03.1945 at Flossenburg concentration camp.
78. TNA, HS 9/1021/1. James Francis George MENESSON, aka James Francis MENZIES, aka Jean François MARTINET, aka BIRCH – born 27.04.1916, executed 29.03.1945 at Flossenburg concentration camp.

Chapter 10: A Return to Blighty then Overseas and Back Again

1. TNA, AIR 81/611. Squadron Leader G D Stephenson: POW; Spitfire N3200 force landed in the Dunkirk-Calais area, France, 28 May 1940.
2. TNA, AIR 81/611. Squadron Leader G D Stephenson: POW; Spitfire N3200 force landed in the Dunkirk-Calais area, France, 28 May 1940.
3. TNA, AIR 81/611. Squadron Leader G D Stephenson: POW; Spitfire N3200 force landed in the Dunkirk-Calais area, France, 28 May 1940.
4. In his logbook, Bader misspells Leigh's surname as Leah.
5. Brickhill, *Reach for the Sky*, 148.
6. TNA, AIR 28/105. Bradwell Bay.
7. TNA, AIR 28/105. Bradwell Bay.
8. TNA, AIR 28/105. Bradwell Bay.
9. TNA, AIR 28/105. Bradwell Bay.

10. TNA, AIR 28/105. Bradwell Bay.
11. TNA, AIR 28/105. Bradwell Bay.
12. There is some confusion over Peter Dollar's rank. Reid suggests that Dollar was a Major (Reid, *Colditz – The Full Story*, 351), while Brickhill informs that he was a Lieutenant Colonel (Brickhill, *Reach for the Sky*, 346.)
13. Brickhill, *Reach for the Sky*, 349.
14. TNA, HS 9/1021/1. James Francis George MENESSON, aka James Francis MENZIES, aka Jean François MARTINET, aka BIRCH – born 27.04.1916, executed 29.03.1945 at Flossenburg concentration camp.
15. TNA, AIR 28/723. Spilsby.
16. TNA, AIR 28/723. Spilsby.
17. TNA, AIR 28/723. Spilsby.
18. Rosier, *Be Bold*, 156.
19. Bader would retire less than a month later, on 21 July 1946.
20. Castle Park Old Boys' Society 1946, 36.
21. Coningham was killed in a commercial flying accident on 30 January 1948 when the Avro Tudor airliner he was flying in as a passenger disappeared off Bermuda.
22. MacDonnell, *Dogfight to Diplomacy*, 152.
23. TNA, AIR 29/1787. Central Flying Training School (Advanced), Little Rissington.
24. TNA, AIR 29/1788. Central Flying Training School (Advanced), Little Rissington. Appendices only.
25. TNA, AIR 29/1788. Central Flying Training School (Advanced), Little Rissington. Appendices only.
26. TNA, AIR 29/1788. Central Flying Training School (Advanced), Little Rissington. Appendices only.
27. TNA, AIR 29/1788. Central Flying Training School (Advanced), Little Rissington. Appendices only.
28. TNA, AIR 29/1787. Central Flying Training School (Advanced), Little Rissington.
29. TNA, AIR 29/1787. Central Flying Training School (Advanced), Little Rissington.
30. TNA, AIR 29/1787. Central Flying Training School (Advanced), Little Rissington.
31. Castle Park Old Boys' Society 1949, 32.
32. Castle Park Old Boys' Society 1949, 32.
33. Bagshaw et al, *RAF Little Rissington*, 36.
34. TNA, AIR 29/1787. Central Flying Training School (Advanced), Little Rissington.
35. TNA, AIR 29/1787. Central Flying Training School (Advanced), Little Rissington.
36. TNA, AIR 29/1787. Central Flying Training School (Advanced), Little Rissington.
37. TNA, AIR 29/1787. Central Flying Training School (Advanced), Little Rissington.

38. TNA, AIR 29/1787. Central Flying Training School (Advanced), Little Rissington.
39. TNA, AIR 29/1787. Central Flying Training School (Advanced), Little Rissington.
40. TNA, AIR 29/1787. Central Flying Training School (Advanced), Little Rissington.
41. TNA, AIR20/6703. Royal Air Force: Fighter Command (Code 67/12): Air defence in the Middle East.
42. TNA, AIR20/6703. Royal Air Force: Fighter Command (Code 67/12): Air defence in the Middle East.
43. TNA, AIR20/6703. Royal Air Force: Fighter Command (Code 67/12): Air defence in the Middle East.
44. TNA, AIR20/6703. Royal Air Force: Fighter Command (Code 67/12): Air defence in the Middle East.
45. Lee, *Wings in the Sun*, 46.
46. TNA. AIR20/9065. Royal Air Force Personnel (Code 68): Leave and travel: passages for families and evacuation of families from Middle East in 1952; papers held by Air Member for Personnel.
47. TNA. AIR20/9065. Royal Air Force Personnel (Code 68): Leave and travel: passages for families and evacuation of families from Middle East in 1952; papers held by Air Member for Personnel.
48. P. Chinnery, *Combat Over Korea* (Pen and Sword: Barnsley, 2011), 171.
49. Hall of Valor Project. "Lonnie Raymond Moore." https://valor.militarytimes.com/hero/7006 accessed 15 September 2021.
50. R.F. Futrell, *The United States Air Force in Korea, 1950-1953* (Center for Air Force History: Washington DC, 1981), 655.

Chapter 11: Central Fighter Establishment

1. Royal Air Force, Record of Service for Air Commodore G.D. Stephenson CBE.
2. TNA AIR16/1214. Central Fighter Establishment: drafting of charter, functions and organisation.
3. Rosier, *Be Bold*, 191.
4. TNA AIR16/1214. Central Fighter Establishment: drafting of charter, functions and organisation
5. TNA AIR16/1214. Central Fighter Establishment: drafting of charter, functions and organisation
6. Rosier, *Be Bold*, 192.
7. TNA AIR29/2432. Central Fighter Establishment, West Raynham.
8. Air Force Historical Research Agency (AFHRA), Reel 47050. USAF Directorate of Flight Safety Research, Norton Air Force Base, California, Aircraft Accidents for 1954.

9. AFHRA, Reel 47050. Aircraft Accidents for 1954.

10. AFHRA, Reel 47050. Aircraft Accidents for 1954.

11. TNA AIR29/2432. Central Fighter Establishment, West Raynham.

12. TNA AIR29/2432. Central Fighter Establishment, West Raynham.

13. Unusually there was no Fighter Conference held in 1953. The RAF's and the Central Fighter Establishment's commitment to the Queen's Coronation Parades may have played a part in the decision to cancel.

14. Rosier, *Be Bold*, 195.

15. At the 1951 Tactical Convention, Stephenson is incorrectly annotated as Stevenson in the attendees' list. TNA AIR64/179. 5th Fighter Tactical Convention 12th-15th June: report.

16. TNA AIR64/170. Report on aircraft in Korea.

17. TNA AIR64/170. Report on aircraft in Korea.

18. TNA AIR64/170. Report on aircraft in Korea.

19. TNA AIR29/2432. Central Fighter Establishment, West Raynham.

20. Pudney, *Pride of Unicorns*, 225.

21. Pudney, *Pride of Unicorns*, 225.

22. Pudney, *Pride of Unicorns*, 227.

23. The aircraft was returned to flight status but was destroyed in a fatal crash which killed the Korean War fighter ace, Captain Joseph McConnell Jr., at Edwards Air Force Base on 25 August 1954, a few weeks before Stephenson's death.

Chapter 12: Letters from America

1. TNA AIR16/1214. Central Fighter Establishment: drafting of charter, functions and organisation.

2. TNA AIR29/2432. Central Fighter Establishment, West Raynham.

3. Wadi Mujib is a 40-mile canyon in Jordan that runs into the Dead Sea.

4. Rosier, *Be Bold*, 200.

5. Rosier, *Be Bold*, 199.

6. 'Fred' was Group Captain Fred Rosier, Group Captain Operations at the Central Fighter Establishment – he had recently returned to the United Kingdom following an exchange tour in the United States, initially at the US Armed Forces Staff College before heading to Continental Air Command at Mitchell Field, Long Island and tasked with helping to set-up Air Defense Command. Rosier, *Be Bold*, 179.

7. 'Dick' was Air Vice-Marshal Richard Atcherley, the head of the British Joint Services Mission in Washington, DC.

8. Rosier, *Be Bold*, 199.

9. As part of his visit to MIT, Stephenson most likely visited the Lincoln Laboratory. The complex major project that Stephenson references in his letter is most likely to be SAGE (Semi-Automatic Ground Environment,) the

United States' first air defence system, an early Cold War version and a much upgraded equivalent of the RAF's Dowding System to cater for the emerging Soviet nuclear bomber threat. For more details see https://www.ll.mit.edu/about/history/sage-semi-automatic-ground-environment-air-defense-system.
10. Rosier, *Be Bold*, 200.
11. TNA AIR29/2432. Central Fighter Establishment, West Raynham.

Chapter 13: The Last Flight

1. R. Mueller, *Air Force Bases, Volume One* (Washington DC: Office of Air Force History, 1982), 133.
2. Mueller, *Air Force Bases*, 136.
3. Mueller, *Air Force Bases*, 136.
4. Mueller, *Air Force Bases*, 133.
5. Mueller, *Air Force Bases*, 133.
6. Wiley Online Library. 'The Role of Air Proving Ground Command in the Development of Navigational Equipment.' https://onlinelibrary.wiley.com/doi/10.1002/j.2161-4296.1955.tb00163.x (accessed 15 September 2021.)
7. Wiley Online Library. 'The Role of Air Proving Ground Command in the Development of Navigational Equipment.' https://onlinelibrary.wiley.com/doi/10.1002/j.2161-4296.1955.tb00163.x (accessed 15 September 2021.)
8. AFHRA, Reel 47050. Aircraft Accidents for 1954.
9. Weapons and Warfare. 'RAF Sabres.' https://weaponsandwarfare.com/2020/05/11/raf-sabres/ (accessed 15 September 2021.)
10. AFHRA, Reel 47050. Aircraft Accidents for 1954.
11. AFHRA, Reel 47050. Aircraft Accidents for 1954.
12. AFHRA, Reel 47050. Aircraft Accidents for 1954.
13. AFHRA, Reel 47050. Aircraft Accidents for 1954.
14. AFHRA, Reel 47050. Aircraft Accidents for 1954.
15. AFHRA, Reel 47050. Aircraft Accidents for 1954.
16. AFHRA, Reel 47050. Aircraft Accidents for 1954.
17. AFHRA, Reel 47050. Aircraft Accidents for 1954.
18. AFHRA, Reel 47050. Aircraft Accidents for 1954.
19. T. Gardner, *F-100 Super Sabre at War* (Minnesota: Zenith Press, 2007), 9.
20. Gardner, *Super Sabre at War*, 10.
21. Gardner, *Super Sabre at War*, 22.
22. Gardner, *Super Sabre at War*, 21.
23. Gardner, *Super Sabre at War*, 21.
24. Gardner, *Super Sabre at War*, 21.
25. Gardner, *Super Sabre at War*, 11.
26. Gardner, *Super Sabre at War*, 116.
27. Gardner, *Super Sabre at War*, 116.
28. Gardner, *Super Sabre at War*, 35.

29. Gardner, *Super Sabre at War*, 36.
30. Gardner, *Super Sabre at War*, 37.
31. Gardner, *Super Sabre at War*, 37.
32. Gardner, *Super Sabre at War*, 37.
33. Gardner, *Super Sabre at War*, 116.
34. Gardner, *Super Sabre at War*, 37.
35. Gardner, *Super Sabre at War*, 37.
36. Gardner, *Super Sabre at War*, 38.
37. AFHRA, Reel 47050. Aircraft Accidents for 1954.
38. AFHRA, Reel 47050. Aircraft Accidents for 1954.
39. AFHRA, Reel 47050. Aircraft Accidents for 1954.
40. AFHRA, Reel 47050. Aircraft Accidents for 1954.
41. AFHRA, Reel 47050. Aircraft Accidents for 1954.
42. AFHRA, Reel 47050. Aircraft Accidents for 1954.
43. AFHRA, Reel 47050. Aircraft Accidents for 1954.
44. AFHRA, Reel 47050. Aircraft Accidents for 1954.
45. AFHRA, Reel 47050. Aircraft Accidents for 1954.
46. '6 F-100s at Eglin for Test.' *Playground News*, 26 August 1956.
47. '6 F-100s at Eglin for Test.' *Playground News*, 26 August 1956.
48. AFHRA, Reel 47050. Aircraft Accidents for 1954.
49. AFHRA, Reel 47050. Aircraft Accidents for 1954.
50. AFHRA, Reel 47050. Aircraft Accidents for 1954.
51. AFHRA, Reel 47050. Aircraft Accidents for 1954.
52. AFHRA, Reel 47050. Aircraft Accidents for 1954.
53. AFHRA, Reel 47050. Aircraft Accidents for 1954.
54. AFHRA, Reel 47050. Aircraft Accidents for 1954.
55. AFHRA, Reel 47050. Aircraft Accidents for 1954.
56. AFHRA, Reel 47050. Aircraft Accidents for 1954.
57. AFHRA, Reel 47050. Aircraft Accidents for 1954.
58. AFHRA, Reel 47050. Aircraft Accidents for 1954.
59. AFHRA, Reel 47050. Aircraft Accidents for 1954.
60. AFHRA, Reel 47050. Aircraft Accidents for 1954.
61. AFHRA, Reel 47050. Aircraft Accidents for 1954.
62. AFHRA, Reel 47050. Aircraft Accidents for 1954.
63. AFHRA, Reel 47050. Aircraft Accidents for 1954.
64. AFHRA, Reel 47050. Aircraft Accidents for 1954.
65. AFHRA, Reel 47050. Aircraft Accidents for 1954.
66. AFHRA, Reel 47050. Aircraft Accidents for 1954.
67. AFHRA, Reel 47050. Aircraft Accidents for 1954.
68. AFHRA, Reel 47050. Aircraft Accidents for 1954.
69. AFHRA, Reel 47050. Aircraft Accidents for 1954.
70. AFHRA, Reel 47050. Aircraft Accidents for 1954.
71. AFHRA, Reel 47050. Aircraft Accidents for 1954.

72. AFHRA, Reel 47050. Aircraft Accidents for 1954.
73. AFHRA, Reel 47050. Aircraft Accidents for 1954.
75. AFHRA, Reel 47050. Aircraft Accidents for 1954.
75. AFHRA, Reel 47050. Aircraft Accidents for 1954.
76. AFHRA, Reel 47050. Aircraft Accidents for 1954.
77. AFHRA, Reel 47050. Aircraft Accidents for 1954.
78. AFHRA, Reel 47050. Aircraft Accidents for 1954.
79. AFHRA, Reel 47050. Aircraft Accidents for 1954.
80. AFHRA, Reel 47050. Aircraft Accidents for 1954.
81. AFHRA, Reel 47050. Aircraft Accidents for 1954.
82. AFHRA, Reel 47050. Aircraft Accidents for 1954.
83. AFHRA, Reel 47050. Aircraft Accidents for 1954.
84. AFHRA, Reel 47050. Aircraft Accidents for 1954.
85. AFHRA, Reel 47050. Aircraft Accidents for 1954.
86. AFHRA, Reel 47050. Aircraft Accidents for 1954.
87. AFHRA, Reel 47050. Aircraft Accidents for 1954.
88. AFHRA, Reel 47050. Aircraft Accidents for 1954.
89. AFHRA, Reel 47050. Aircraft Accidents for 1954.
90. AFHRA, Reel 47050. Aircraft Accidents for 1954.
91. AFHRA, Reel 47050. Aircraft Accidents for 1954.
92. AFHRA, Reel 47050. Aircraft Accidents for 1954.
93. AFHRA, Reel 47050. Aircraft Accidents for 1954.
94. AFHRA, Reel 47050. Aircraft Accidents for 1954.
95. AFHRA, Reel 47050. Aircraft Accidents for 1954.
96. AFHRA, Reel 47050. Aircraft Accidents for 1954.
97. AFHRA, Reel 47050. Aircraft Accidents for 1954.
98. AFHRA, Reel 47050. Aircraft Accidents for 1954.
99. AFHRA, Reel 47050. Aircraft Accidents for 1954.
100. AFHRA, Reel 47050. Aircraft Accidents for 1954.
101. AFHRA, Reel 47050. Aircraft Accidents for 1954.
102. AFHRA, Reel 47050. Aircraft Accidents for 1954.
103. AFHRA, Reel 47050. Aircraft Accidents for 1954.
104. AFHRA, Reel 47050. Aircraft Accidents for 1954.
105. AFHRA, Reel 47050. Aircraft Accidents for 1954.
106. AFHRA, Reel 47050. Aircraft Accidents for 1954.
107. AFHRA, Reel 47050. Aircraft Accidents for 1954.
108. AFHRA, Reel 47050. Aircraft Accidents for 1954.
109. AFHRA, Reel 47050. Aircraft Accidents for 1954.
110. AFHRA, Reel 47050. Aircraft Accidents for 1954.
111. AFHRA, Reel 47050. Aircraft Accidents for 1954.
112. AFHRA, Reel 47050. Aircraft Accidents for 1954.
113. AFHRA, Reel 47050. Aircraft Accidents for 1954.
114. AFHRA, Reel 47050. Aircraft Accidents for 1954.

115. AFHRA, Reel 47050. Aircraft Accidents for 1954.
116. AFHRA, Reel 47050. Aircraft Accidents for 1954.
117. AFHRA, Reel 47050. Aircraft Accidents for 1954.
118. AFHRA, Reel 47050. Aircraft Accidents for 1954.
119. AFHRA, Reel 47050. Aircraft Accidents for 1954.
120. AFHRA, Reel 47050. Aircraft Accidents for 1954.
121. AFHRA, Reel 47050. Aircraft Accidents for 1954.
122. AFHRA, Reel 47050. Aircraft Accidents for 1954.
123. AFHRA, Reel 47050. Aircraft Accidents for 1954.
124. AFHRA, Reel 47050. Aircraft Accidents for 1954.
125. AFHRA, Reel 47050. Aircraft Accidents for 1954.
126. Rosier, *Be Bold*, 200.
127. AFHRA, Reel 47050. Aircraft Accidents for 1954.
128. AFHRA, Reel 47050. Aircraft Accidents for 1954.
129. AFHRA, Reel 47050. Aircraft Accidents for 1954.
130. AFHRA, Reel 47050. Aircraft Accidents for 1954.
131. AFHRA, Reel 47050. Aircraft Accidents for 1954.
132. AFHRA, Reel 47050. Aircraft Accidents for 1954.
133. AFHRA, Reel 47050. Aircraft Accidents for 1954.
134. AFHRA, Reel 47050. Aircraft Accidents for 1954.
135. AFHRA, Reel 47050. Aircraft Accidents for 1954.
136. AFHRA, Reel 47050. Aircraft Accidents for 1954.
137. AFHRA, Reel 47050. Aircraft Accidents for 1954.
138. AFHRA, Reel 47050. Aircraft Accidents for 1954.

Chapter 14: Stephenson's Legacy

1. Day would reprise his technical advisor role on another film inspired by one of Brickhill's books – *The Great Escape*; both would have first-hand experience of *Stalag Luft* III, one as a 'stooge', the other as an escaper.
2. Sarkar, *Fighter Ace*, 323.
3. Ironically, Squadron Leader Sanderson, the commanding officer of 19 Squadron, actually existed. However, Clifford Sanderson led the Squadron in 1931, nine years before Stephenson.
4. Cornwell, *The Battle of France: Then and Now*, 356.
5. Christies. 'Last of its kind Supermarine Spitfire to be auctioned for charity.' https://www.christies.com/features/Last-of-its-kind-Spitfire-5969-3.aspx (accessed 27 January 2023.)
6. Christies. 'Last of its kind Supermarine Spitfire to be auctioned for charity.' https://www.christies.com/features/Last-of-its-kind-Spitfire-5969-3.aspx (accessed 27 January 2023.)

7. For example, the early engines did not like to operate at high boost settings for a prolonged period. In Brian Lane's account of the 26 May 1940 dogfight where Stephenson was shot down, Lane uses the full boost to extract himself from the melee over Dunkirk. Ordinarily, his aircraft would have required an extensive engineering investigation upon landing. Through necessity, Lane flew the same aircraft on the afternoon mission over Dunkirk without apparent ill effects.

8. *Daily Mail*, 'Spitfire faithfully restored after 40 years buried under a French beach sells for world record £3.1million fee at auction – with all the proceeds going to charity.' https://www.dailymail.co.uk/news/article-3155260/Spitfire-faithfully-restored-40-years-buried-French-beach-sells-world-record-3-1million-fee-auction-proceeds-going-charity.html (accessed 27 January 2023.)

9. A reference to the classic comedy show *Only Fools and Horses*, where the affable but simple character Trigger claims that he has used the same road sweeper's broom for 20 years, despite replacing the head and handle on numerous occasions.

Bibliography

Primary Sources

Air Force Historical Research Agency (AFHRA). Reel 47050. USAF Directorate of Flight Safety Research, Norton Air Force Base, California, Aircraft Accidents for 1954.
AFHRA. Aircraft Accident Report 54-5-24-6.

The National Archives (TNA.) AIR5/1255. Operations: Iraq, Chapters 34 to 39.
TNA. AIR5/1293. Iraq Command: monthly operation summaries, Volume VII.
TNA. AIR8/1634. Fortnightly Opsums: H.Q. Middle East Air Force.
TNA. AIR10/1482. Report on Flying Accidents during July-Dec. 1931.
TNA. AIR10/2242. Iraq Command Report December 1932 - December 1934.
TNA. AIR16/1214. Central Fighter Establishment: drafting of charter, functions and organisation.
TNA. AIR19/590. Middle East Air Force: general.
TNA. AIR20/6703. Royal Air Force: Fighter Command (Code 67/12): Air defence in the Middle East.
TNA. AIR20/9065. Royal Air Force Personnel (Code 68): Leave and travel: passages for families and evacuation of families from Middle East in 1952; papers held by Air Member for Personnel.
TNA. AIR23/8336. Formation of No. 1 Sector M.E.A.F.: organization.
TNA. AIR24/818. Operations record books.
TNA. AIR24/2344. Headquarters Middle East Air Force.
TNA. AIR24/2345. Headquarters Middle East Air Force.
TNA. AIR24/2346. Headquarters Middle East Air Force.
TNA. AIR27/252/1. Squadron Number: 19 Summary of Events: Y.
TNA. AIR27/252/2. Squadron Number: 19 Records of Events: Y.
TNA. AIR27/252/3. Squadron Number: 19 Records of Events: Y.
TNA. AIR27/252/4. Squadron Number: 19 Records of Events: Y.
TNA. AIR27/252/5. Squadron Number: 19 Records of Events: Y.
TNA. AIR27/252/6. Squadron Number: 19 Records of Events: Y.
TNA. AIR27/252/7. Squadron Number: 19 Records of Events: Y.
TNA. AIR27/252/8. Squadron Number: 19 Records of Events: Y.
TNA. AIR27/252/9. Squadron Number: 19 Records of Events: Y.

TNA. AIR27/252/10. Squadron Number: 19 Records of Events: Y.
TNA. AIR27/252/11. Squadron Number: 19 Records of Events: Y.
TNA. AIR27/252/12. Squadron Number: 19 Records of Events: Y.
TNA. AIR27/252/13. Squadron Number: 19 Records of Events: Y.
TNA. AIR27/252/14. Squadron Number: 19 Records of Events: Y.
TNA. AIR27/252/15. Squadron Number: 19 Records of Events: Y.
TNA. AIR27/252/16. Squadron Number: 19 Records of Events: Y.
TNA. AIR27/252/17. Squadron Number: 19 Records of Events: Y.
TNA. AIR27/252/18. Squadron Number: 19 Records of Events: Y.
TNA. AIR27/252/19. Squadron Number: 19 Records of Events: Y.
TNA. AIR27/287/1. Squadron Number: 23 Summary of Events: Y.
TNA. AIR27/2380. Squadron Number: Oxford University Air Squadron Summary of Events: Y.
TNA. AIR28/175. Cranwell.
TNA. AIR28/723. Spilsby.
TNA. AIR29/50. Air Ministry and Ministry of Defence: Operations Record Books, Miscellaneous Units. RAF Levies: Armoured Car Wing, Hinaidi, Iraq, formed 1 April 1927.
TNA. AIR29/604. Central Flying School. Formed at Upavon (UK) in May 1912. Disbanded in April 1942.
TNA. AIR29/1102. 106 Personnel Reception Centre, formed at Cosford March 1945 and disbanded August 1945 (PRC UK). With appendices.
TNA. AIR29/1787. Central Flying Training School (Advanced), Little Rissington.
TNA. AIR29/1788. Central Flying Training School (Advanced), Little Rissington. Appendices only.
TNA. AIR29/2432. Central Fighter Establishment, West Raynham.
TNA. AIR32/72. Flying Training Command: Statistical Summary 1948, including training progress utilization of aircraft, accidents, manpower and morale.
TNA. AIR32/120. Flying Training Command: programme of work.
TNA. AIR40/1910. Camp history: Oflag IVC (Colditz): Army, Navy and Air Force personnel Nov 1940 – Apr 1945.
TNA. AIR40/2645. Stalag Luft 3 (Sagan): camp history; air force personnel; Apr 1942 – Jan 1945.
TNA. AIR43/7. Royal Air Force courts martial charge book.
TNA. AIR43/8. Royal Air Force courts martial charge book.
TNA. AIR49/386. Prisoners of War: formation of No. 106 Personnel Reception Centre, Cosford (ex P.O.W.); administrative instructions for the post-hostilities evacuation of Air Force prisoners-of-war; miscellaneous papers.
TNA. AIR50/10/4. Air Ministry: Combat Reports, Second World War. Fighter Command. No. 19 Squadron. Name: Brinsden. Rank: Flying Officer. Squadron: 19 Other Dates of Combat: 26 May 1940, 09 September 1940.
TNA. AIR50/10/19. Air Ministry: Combat Reports, Second World War. Fighter Command. No. 19 Squadron. Name: Lane. Rank: Flight Lieutenant, Squadron

Leader. Squadron: 19 Other Dates of Combat: 26 May 1940; 01 June 1940, 24 August 1940, 07 September 1940, 11 September 1940, 15 September 1940.

TNA. AIR50/10/23. Air Ministry: Combat Reports, Second World War. Fighter Command. No. 19 Squadron. Name: Lyne. Rank: Pilot Officer. Squadron: 19 Other Dates of Combat: 26 May 1940.

TNA. AIR50/10/27. Air Ministry: Combat Reports, Second World War. Fighter Command. No. 19 Squadron. Name: Petre Rank: Flying Officer. Squadron: 19 Other Dates of Combat: 11 May 1940; 26 May 1940, 27 May 1940, 18 June 1940.

TNA. AIR50/10/28. Air Ministry: Combat Reports, Second World War. Fighter Command. No. 19 Squadron. Name: Potter. Rank: Flight Sergeant. Squadron: 19 Other Dates of Combat: 26 May 1940.

TNA. AIR50/10/30. Air Ministry: Combat Reports, Second World War. Fighter Command. No. 19 Squadron. Name: Potter. Rank: Flight Sergeant. Squadron: 19 Other Dates of Combat: 26 May 1940, 01 June 1940, 16 August 1940.

TNA. AIR50/10/34. Air Ministry: Combat Reports, Second World War. Fighter Command. No. 19 Squadron. Name: Sinclair. Rank: Flying Officer. Squadron: 19 Other Dates of Combat: 26 May 1940, 01 June 1940.

TNA. AIR50/10/35. Air Ministry: Combat Reports, Second World War. Fighter Command. No. 19 Squadron. Name: Steere. Rank: Flight Sergeant. Squadron: 19 Other Dates of Combat: 11 May 1940, 26 May 1940, 27 May 1940, 28 May 1940, 01 June 1940.

TNA. AIR50/10/139. Air Ministry: Combat Reports, Second World War. Fighter Command. No. 19 Squadron. Name: Ball. Rank: Flying Officer. Squadron: 19 Other Dates of Combat: 19 June 1940; 26 May 1940, 27 May 1940.

TNA. AIR50/10/146. Air Ministry: Combat Reports, Second World War. Fighter Command. No. 19 Squadron. Name: Clouston. Rank: Flight Lieutenant. Squadron: 19 Other Dates of Combat: 21 October 1939, 11 May 1940, 26 May 1940, 27 May 1940, 18 September 1940.

TNA. AIR64/169. Combat characteristics of the American F86 aircraft compared with the Russian MIG15 as demonstrated in NW Korea.

TNA. AIR64/170. Report on aircraft in Korea.

TNA. AIR64/179. 5th Fighter Tactical Convention 12th-15th June: report.

TNA. AIR64/180. 6th Fighter Tactical Convention 1st-4th July: report.

TNA. AIR64/181. 8th Fighter Tactical Convention 12th-14th July: report.

TNA. AIR64/235. CFE liaison visit to Middle East Air Forces Nov: 1952.

TNA. AIR64/268. Tactical trial of the Hunter Mk 1 as an interceptor fighter.

TNA. AIR64/392. Quarterly progress report.

TNA. AIR64/393. Quarterly progress report.

TNA. AIR64/464. Central Fighter Establishment: flight evaluation of United States Air Force (USAF) fighter aircraft.

TNA. AIR81/27. Wing Commander H M A Day: POW. Sergeant E B Hillier and Aircraftman 2nd Class F G Moller: report of deaths; Blenheim L1138 shot down near Ibar Oberstein, 13 October 1939.

TNA. AIR81/611. Squadron Leader G D Stephenson: POW; Spitfire N3200 force landed in the Dunkirk-Calais area, France, 28 May 1940.

TNA. AIR81/8187. Wing Commander D R S Bader: POW; mid air collision with enemy aircraft over France, aerial combat, Spitfire W3185, 616 Squadron, 9 August 1941.

TNA. HS 9/1021/1. James Francis George MENESSON, aka James Francis MENZIES, aka Jean François MARTINET, aka BIRCH – born 27.04.1916, executed 29.03.1945 at Flossenburg concentration camp.

TNA. WO 95/1113/2. (Queen's Royal) Lancers.

TNA. WO95/1166/12. Lancer Brigade: 9 (Queen's Royal) Lancers.

TNA. WO95/2691/1. 1/4 Battalion Lincolnshire Regiment. Diaries for 1915 March-1915 December added, May 1997 Disbanded Jan 1918; nucleus amalgamated with 2/4 Battalion.

TNA. WO95/2154/1. 1 Battalion Lincolnshire Regiment.

TNA. WO 167/958. 173 Railway Tunnelling Company Royal Engineers.

TNA. WO 208/3269. Dulag Luft (Oberusel): RAF personnel.

TNA. WO 208/3282. Stalag Luft I Barth.

TNA. WO 208/3288. Oflag IVC Colditz.

TNA. WO 208/5448. Sage – Sykes.

TNA. WO 224/62. Stalag Luft I.

TNA. WO 224/69. Oflag IVC Saalhaus Coldlitz, Dresden.

TNA. WO372/19/38741. Medal card of Stephenson, Eric Lionel.

TNA. WO372/19/40403. Medal card of Stephenson, Urban Arnold.

TNA. WO 374/65220. Captain William Dalton Stephenson. Lincolnshire Yeomanry.

Secondary Sources

Books

Bader, D., *Fight for the Sky*. New York: Doubleday and Company, 1973.

Bagshaw, R. et al., *RAF Little Rissington*. Barnsley: Pen and Sword Aviation, 2006.

Brickill, P., *Reach for the Sky*. Annapolis: Bluejacket Books, 2001.

Champ, J. and Burgess, C., *The Diggers of Colditz*. Kenthurst: Kangaroo Press, 1997.

Chinnery, P., *Combat over Korea*. Barnsley: Pen and Sword Aviation, 2011.

Cornwell, P.D., *The Battle of France Then and Now*. Old Harlow: Battle of Britain International Limited, 2007.

Corum, R., *Boyd – The Fighter Pilot Who Changed the Art of War*. Boston: Little, Brown and Company, 2002.

Crane, C.C., *American Air Power Strategy in Korea 1950-1953*. Lawrence: University of Kansas, 2000.

Deere, A.C., *Nine Lives*. Manchester: Goodall, 2009.

Futrell, R.F. *The United States Air Force in Korea, 1950-1953*. Washington DC: Center for Air Force History, 1981.

Galland, A. *The First and the Last*. New York: Buccaneer Books, 1954.

Gardner, T.E., *F-100 Super Sabre at War*. St. Paul: Zenith Press, 2007.

Gillies, M., *The Barbed Wire University*. London: Aurum Press, 2012.

Glancey, J., *Spitfire – The Biography*. London: Atlantic Books, 2007.

_____, *Wings Over Water*. London: Atlantic Books, 2020.

Haslam, E.B., *The History of Royal Air Force Cranwell*. London: Her Majesty's Stationery Office, 1982.

Hoskins, T., *Flight from Colditz*. Barnsley: Frontline Books, 2016.

Kane, R.B., *So Far From Home*. Montgomery: NewSouth Books, 2016.

Kennedy, E., *The Blenheim Bomber Story*. United Kingdom: Lundarien Press, 2015.

Knaack, M.S., *Encyclopaedia of US Air Force Aircraft and Missile Systems, Volume 1*. Washington DC: Office of Air Force History, 1978.

Lane, B., *Spitfire! The Experiences of a Battle of Britain Fighter Pilot*. Stroud: Amberley Publishing, 2011.

Lee, D., *Wings in the Sun*. London: Her Majesty's Stationery Office, 1989.

Levine, J., *Dunkirk*. New York: William Morrow, 2017.

Lucas, L., *Flying Colours – The Epic Story of Douglas Bader*. London; Hutchinson, 1981.

MacDonnell, A.R.D., *From Dogfight to Diplomacy*. Barnsley: Pen and Sword Aviation, 2009.

MacIntyre, B., *Prisoners of the Castle*. New York: Crown, 2022.

Mueller, R., *Air Force Bases, Volume One*. Washington DC: Office of Air Force History, 1982.

Napier, M., *Korean Air War*. Oxford: Osprey, 2021.

Newton Dunn, B., *Big Wing*. Shrewsbury: Airlife, 1992.

Nichol, J., *Spitfire*. London: Simon and Schuster, 2018.

Orange, V., *Coningham*. Washington DC: Center for Air Force History, 1992.

Pearson, S., *The Great Escaper*. New York: Skyhorse Publishing, 2021.

Pudney, J., *A Pride of Unicorns*. London: Oldbourne Book Company, 1960.

Reid, P.R., *Colditz – The Full Story*. London: Pan, 2002.

_____, *The Colditz Story*. London: Hodder and Stoughton, 2014.

_____, *The Latter Days at Colditz*. London: Hodder and Stoughton, 2014.

Rogers, J., *Tunnelling into Colditz*. London: Hale, 1986.

Rosier, F., *Be Bold*. London: Grub Street, 2011.

Sarkar, D., *Fighter Ace*. Stroud: Amberley, 2014.

_____, *Spitfire!*. Barnsley: Air World, 2019.

Saunders, A., *Spitfire Mark I P9374*. London: Grub Street, 2012.

Sebag-Montefiore, H., *Dunkirk*. London: Penguin, 2015.

Smith, R.C., *Al Deere*. London: Grub Street, 2003.

Smith, S., *Wings Day*. London: Pan Books Limited, 1977.

Townsend, P., *Duel of Eagles*. London: Phoenix Press, 2000.

Tunstall, P., *The Last Escaper*. New York: Overlook Duckworth, 2015.

Verkaik, R., *The Traitor of Colditz*. London: Welbeck, 2022.

Warwick, N.W.M., *In Every Place*. Rushden: Force and Corporate Publishing, 2014.

Wooton, C., *From Radley to Colditz and Sagan*. Radley: Radley History Club, 2009.

Online Material

Air Historical Branch. 'The RAF, Small Wars and Insurgencies in the Middle East, 1919-1939.' https://www.raf.mod.uk/our-organisation/units/air-historical-branch/regional-studies-post-coldwar-narratives/raf-small-wars-and-insurgencies-vol-1-middle-east-1919-1939/ (accessed 22 January 2023.)

American Air Museum. 'Henry William Brown.' https://www.americanairmuseum.com/person/93557 (accessed 15 September 2021.)

Castle Park School. 'Further Information.' https://www.castleparkschool.ie/our-school/further-information/ (accessed 1 November 2022.)

Christies. 'Last of its kind Supermarine Spitfire to be auctioned for charity.' https://www.christies.com/features/Last-of-its-kind-Spitfire-5969-3.aspx (accessed 27 January 2023.)

Daily Mail, "Spitfire faithfully restored after 40 years buried under a French beach sells for world record £3.1million fee at auction - with all the proceeds going to charity." https://www.dailymail.co.uk/news/article-3155260/Spitfire-faithfully-restored-40-years-buried-French-beach-sells-world-record-3-1million-fee-auction-proceeds-going-charity.html (accessed 27 January 2023.)

Hall of Valor Project. 'Lonnie Raymond Moore.' https://valor.militarytimes.com/hero/7006 (accessed 15 September 2021.)

Imperial War Museum. 'Carr, John Baker (Oral history).' https://www.iwm.org.uk/collections/item/object/80000988 (accessed 21 January 2022).

Imperial War Museum. 'Goldfinch, Leslie James Edward 'Bill (Oral history).' https://www.iwm.org.uk/collections/item/object/80025510 (accessed 21 January 2022).

Imperial War Museum. 'Unwin, George Cecil (Oral history).' https://www.iwm.org.uk/collections/item/object/80011292 (accessed 21 January 2022.)

Imperial War Museum. 'Wilson, John Carson (Oral history).' https://www.iwm.org.uk/collections/item/object/80014876 (accessed 21 January 2022.)

Key Aero. 'When the Queen First Reviewed Her Air Force.' https://www.key.aero/article/when-queen-first-reviewed-her-air-force (accessed 14 November 2022.)

Key Aero. 'Upside Down and Inside Out.' https://www.key.aero/article/upside-down-inside-out (accessed 23 January 2023.)

New York Times. 'Lorne Welch, R.A.F. Pilot And Escape Artist, Dies at 81.' https://www.nytimes.com/1998/06/08/world/lorne-welch-raf-pilot-and-escape-artist-dies-at-81.html (accessed 24 August 2022.)

Oxford Dictionary of National Biography. 'Burnett, Sir Charles Stuart.' https://doi.org/10.1093/ref:odnb/32188. (accessed 23 January 2023.)

RAF Historical Society. 'The RAF Armoured Car Companies in Iraq (Mostly) 1921-1947. https://www.rafmuseum.org.uk/documents/Research/RAF-Historical-Society-Journals/Journal_48_Seminar_the_ME_Mespot_Iraq_NW_Frontier_4_FTS.pdf (accessed 25 January 2023.)

RAF Museum. 'The Long Trip Home.' https://www.rafmuseum.org.uk/research/archive-exhibitions/freedom-liberty/the-long-trip-home/ (accessed 20 August 2022.)

Royal Air Force College Cranwell. 'The Journal of the Royal Air Force College, Vol. IX No.2 Autumn 1929.' http://www.cranwell-college.life/Journals/019/mobile/index.html (accessed 21 January 2023.)

Royal Air Force College Cranwell. 'The Journal of the Royal Air Force College, Vol. X No.1 Spring 1930.' http://www.cranwell-college.life/Journals/101/mobile/index.html (accessed 23 January 2023.)

Royal Air Force College Cranwell. 'The Journal of the Royal Air Force College, Vol. X No.2 Autumn 1930.' http://www.cranwell-college.life/Journals/102/mobile/index.html (accessed 23 January 2023.)

Royal Air Force College Cranwell. 'The Journal of the Royal Air Force College, Vol. XII No. 1 Spring 1932.' http://www.cranwell-college.life/Journals/121/mobile/index.html (accessed 23 January 2023.)

The Canadian Military Engineers Association. 'Lt William Anderson Millar.' https://cmea-agmc.ca/award/gallantry/lt-william-anderson-millar-mid-7th-fd-coy (accessed 3 August 2022.)

Weapons and Warfare. 'RAF Sabres.' https://weaponsandwarfare.com/2020/05/11/raf-sabres/ (accessed 15 September 2021.)

Wiley Online Library. 'The Role of Air Proving Ground Command in the Development of Navigational Equipment.' https://onlinelibrary.wiley.com/doi/10.1002/j.2161-4296.1955.tb00163.x (accessed 15 September 2021.)

YouTube. 'One Way into Colditz.' https://www.youtube.com/watch?v=Rsq-5v3BqMI (accessed 24 August 2022.)

YouTube. 'Colditz: The Best of British.' https://www.youtube.com/watch?v=G1P2Pb2aeP4 (accessed 22 January 2023.)

YouTube. 'Colditz: The Legend.' https://www.youtube.com/watch?v=VJC7ivpH6qc (accessed 22 January 2023.)

YouTube. 'Escape from Colditz.' https://www.youtube.com/watch?v=LmaIuH94Vwg (accessed 22 January 2023.)

YouTube. 'Escape From Nazi Alcatraz | Escape Plan: Colditz Cock Documentary | Military Documentary F.' https://www.youtube.com/watch?v=tlkgSiOWIH0 (accessed 22 January 2023.)

YouTube. 'Guy Martin's Spitfire: The Full Documentary | Guy Martin Proper.' https://www.youtube.com/watch?v=mxnGJsVPIFA (accessed 22 January 2023.)

Podcasts

The Fighter Pilot Podcast. '103 - F-100 Super Sabre.' https://www.fighterpilotpodcast.com/episodes/103-f-100-super-sabre/ (accessed 22 January 2023.)

We Have Ways of Making You Talk. '141. Dunkirk - Day 1.' https://wehavewayspod.com/episodes/ (accessed 22 January 2023.)

We Have Ways of Making You Talk. '142. Dunkirk – Day 2.' https://wehavewayspod.com/episodes/ (accessed 22 January 2023.)

We Have Ways of Making You Talk. '143. Dunkirk – Day 3.' https://wehavewayspod.com/episodes/ (accessed 22 January 2023.)

Index

0–9

5 Group, 188
7th Panzer (Ghost) Division, 38
8 Maintenance Unit, 37
9th Lancers (Special Reserve), 5
9th (Queen's Royal) Lancers, 5
12 (Bombing) Squadron, 19
11 Group, 129, 179
   Battle of Britain, 109
   Battle of France, 39, 40
12 Group, 30, 31, 33, 35, 39, 108, 109,
   129, 188, 196, 201, 209, 220
19 Squadron, xi, 27–33, 35–41, 43,
   45–6, 48–9, 53–6, 101, 108, 129,
   144, 155–6, 178, 184, 188, 196, 248,
   252, 255
23 Squadron, 16–20, 25, 28, 32, 144, 179
23 (Training) Group, 24
25 Squadron, 156, 186
40 Squadron, 113
53-1534A, 230
54 Squadron, 57
57 Squadron, 27
65 Squadron, 58
74 Squadron, 55, 57
85 Squadron, 186
92 Squadron, 57, 251
106 Personnel Reception Centre, 177–8
111 Squadron, 27
124 Squadron, 186
126 Squadron, 186
205 Group, 195–8, 207
207 Squadron, 188
211 Group, 180
219 Squadron, 179

222 Squadron, 35, 108, 188
226 Squadron, 105
242 Squadron, 108, 129
307 Squadron, 186
335th Fighter Interceptor
   Squadron, 199
397th Bomb Group, 181
596th Bomb Squadron, 181
612th Fighter Bomber Squadron, 236–7
707, Boeing, 226

A

A-17, Northrop, 222
Abbeville, 38
Abinger Hall, 101
Abwehr, 113, 149
Accident Investigation Board, 244
Adastral House, 2
Aden, 196
Air Defense Command, 213, 219–20
Air Development Center, 213, 217
Air Fighting Development Squadron,
   202, 212
Air Fighting Development Unit, 202,
   204, 212
Air Force Operational Test Center, 229
Air Member for Personnel, 32
Air Ministry, 32, 34, 37, 73, 78, 99,
   193–6, 201, 203
Air Proving Ground Command, 207,
   212–13, 221–4, 228, 230, 241, 244
Air War College, xv, 242
Aircraft Restoration Company, xii–xiii,
   xiv, xvii, 253–4, 257–60
Aire, 70–1

Airframe Assemblies, 253–8
Airspeed, AS.10 Oxford, 185
Alabama, xv–xix, 156–7, 221–2, 241–2,
    264, 268
Alexandria Air Force Base, 236
All-Weather Wing, 202
Allen, Ron, 193
Allied Expeditionary Air Force, 180
Althorpe, 3, 8
Amman, 196
Anderson, William Faithfull, 163
Andover, 17, 19
Aqaba, 196
Appel, 113, 150, 167,
Arcadian, RMS, 7
Arkwright, Gentleman Cadet, 15
Armstrong Whitworth Siskin, 14
Army Education Corps, 9
Army Group A, 38
Army Group B, 38
Army Group C, 38
Arras, 5, 7
Arrestbau, 181
AS.10, Airspeed Oxford, 185
Assistant Chief of the Air Staff
    (Operations), 208
Atcherley, David, 195, 197
Atcherley, Richard, 25, 179, 180, 195,
    198, 201, 203
    23 Squadron, 17
    CFE, 180
    death, 249
    Sabre crash, 209–11, 223, 225
    USA, 216, 241
Athies, 6
Audley End, xiii
Aussenstelle, 125
Austin Reed, 41, 64
Avro, 14
    504N, 14
    Lancaster, 188, 191
    Tutor, 23, 32
Avro Canada CF-100 Canuck, 209

B

B-26, Martin Marauder, 181, 199
B-52, Boeing Stratofortress, 226
Bader, Douglas, 1–2, 54–5, 109, 129–30,
    188, 243, 248, 261, 267
    19 Squadron, 32–5
    23 Squadron, 16–20, 23, 179
    222 Squadron, 35, 108
    242 Squadron, 108, 129
    Best Man, 189
    Big Wing controversy, 109
    Bradwell Bay, 185–7
    CFE, 180, 184–5, 202
    Cranwell, 3, 11, 14–16, 242
    death, 250
    PoW, 129, 144–6, 150, 174–5
Baker, Pilot Officer, 31
Baker, Sir John, 195, 216, 219, 243
Ball, Flying Officer Eric, 108
    death, 188
    Dunkirk, 42, 48–9, 52
    PoW, 129
Ballyfair, 8
Barbarossa, Operation, 130
Barth, 107, 111, 114, 118–19, 121–2, 125, 143
    see also Stalag Luft I

Basra, 21
Battle, Fairey, 32, 105
Battle of Britain, 35, 42, 44, 58, 87,
    108–09, 129, 156, 179, 184–6, 191,
    196, 215–16, 242
    film, xi, 250
Beaumont, Lieutenant J.W., 162
Beethoven, 140
Beirut, 196
Bell X-1, 210
Berkeley Square, 215
Berkhamstead, 5
Berlin, 44, 111
Best, Flight Lieutenant Jack, 167–8,
    170–2, 175
    see also Colditz *and* Colditz Cock

Bethune, 6, 130
Beveridge Plan, 163
Binbrook, 7, 200
Birch, 181
  see also Henri, Martinet, Mennesson,
    Menzies
Bird-Wilson, Wing Commander 'Birdy',
    202
Birmingham, 177
Bishop's Stortford College, 4
Blenheim, Bristol, xii–xii, 28–30, 44,
    113, 118, 179
Blitzkrieg, 38–9, 44
Bodleian Library, 96
Boeing:
  707, 226
  B-52 Stratofortress, 226
  C-135 Stratolifter, 226
  KC-135 Stratotanker, 226
  Stratocruiser, 243
Boer War, 3–4, 7
Booth, Anne Jean Maureen, 129, 157,
    181–2, 187–8, 197, 205, 213, 215,
    217, 219, 240, 247–9
  Coronation, 198
  First Aid Nursing Yeomanry, 128
  memorial service, 243
  wedding, 189
  see also Mennesson, Jean François
    Georges, Menzies, Anna
Booth, Lady Agnes, 129
Booth, Sir Paul, 128
Bor-Komorvski, General, 174
Boscombe Down, RAF, 202
Bos, Karel, xiii, 252–3
Boston, 213, 216–17
Boulogne, 39, 59–60
Bovingdon, 176
Boyle, Dermot, 194–5, 199, 201, 243
Bracknell, RAF Staff College, 188–9
Bradwell Bay, RAF, 186–8
Brickhill, Paul, 248
Brie, 6

Brinsden, Flying Officer Frank,
  Dunkirk, 45, 47, 53
  PoW, 156
Bristol:
  Blenheim, xii–xii, 28–30, 44, 113,
    118, 179
  Buckmaster, 191
  Bulldog, 17–19, 32
British Expeditionary Force, 39, 179
British Joint Services Mission, 209, 241
British Overseas Airways Corporation,
    215
Brize Norton, RAF, 190
Brook, Lyndon, 248
Brooke-Popham Cup, 18
Brown, First Lieutenant Harvey L., 236
Brown, Lieutenant Colonel Henry
    'Baby', 228, 230–3, 240, 244–5
Bruce, Flight Lieutenant Dominic, 153
Brussels, 60–1, 73, 76–8, 80, 84, 177
Buckley, Lieutenant Commander
    Jimmy, 106
Buffalo, 218
Bulldog, Bristol, 17–19, 32
Buckmaster, Bristol, 191
Burnett, Charles, 21–2, 25, 266
Burnham-on-Crouch, 129, 157, 185,
    187, 189, 197
Burton, Harry, 127
Bushell, Squadron Leader Roger, 57,
    106, 173

C
C-135, Boeing Stratolifter, 226
Caen, 160
Calais, 7, 38, 41, 45–6, 48, 50–2, 57–60,
    63, 76, 80, 130, 155, 177, 180, 251
Cambridge Research Center, 217
Campbell, Brigadier General Daniel, 241
Canadian Engineers, 6
Canal Zone, 195–7
Canuck, Avro Canada CF-100, 209
Carsen, Lee, 175

Castle Park Preparatory School, xvii, 9
Catterick, RAF, 9, 179
Cazenove, Flying Officer Peter, 57, 251
Central Fighter Establishment, 184–5,
    198, 200–04, 206
  birth, 180
  Coronation Review, 199
  Tactical Convention, 206–09
  US visit, 212–4, 220–5, 241, 243–4
  see also Bader, Atcherley, RAF West
    Raynham
Central Flying School, 32–3, 35, 46,
    184, 202
  Association, xvii
  Commandant, 190–5, 223, 243, 266
  Qualified Flying Instructor, 22–4
  see also RAF Wittering, RAF
    Upavon, RAF Little Rissington
CF-100, Avro Canada Canuck, 209
Chamberlain, Prime Minister Neville, 24
Channel 4, xviii, 254, 259
Charleroi, 73
Chicago, 218
Chief of the Air Staff, 24–5, 39, 266
Chilbolton, 202
Chipmunk, De Havilland, xiii, 194
Chisholm, Captain C.J., 6
Choctawhatchee, 221, 233
Churchill, Prime Minister Winston,
    39, 252
Clacton, 204
Clade, Oberfeldwebel, 55
Clouston, Wilf, 179, 196
  Dunkirk, 30, 42, 47, 53
  PoW, 155–6
Club Del Mar, 218
Cochrane, Ralph, 190
Colditz, Oflag IVC, xvii, xix, 2, 55, 57,
    126–7, 131, 133–40, 142–5, 147–8,
    150, 152–6, 159–61, 163–9, 174–6,
    181, 184, 187,
  The Colditz Story, 132
  Colditz Cock, 170–3

Colnbrook, 183
Cologne, 84–5
Colorado Springs, 213, 216, 219–20
Coltishall, RAF, 108–09
Commonwealth War Graves
    Commission, xv–xvi, 157, 240, 242
Coningham, Arthur 'Mary', 14–15,
    189–90
Constellation, Lockheed, 215
Convair, 219
  F-102 Delta Dagger, 226
Coote, Paddy, 13, 16
Cosford, RAF, 177–8
Courtenay, Lieutenant J.M., 162
Coward, Noel, 162
Cox, Paul, xvii
Cozens, Squadron Leader Henry, 27, 29
Cramlington, 18
Cranwell, RAF College, 14, 20, 22–3,
    32–5, 56, 104, 125, 184, 189, 194,
    212, 242, 248, 265–7
Cranwellian Historical Society, xvii
Cree, Wing Commander J.R., 188
Crestview, 229, 233
Crew, Wing Commander Edward, 214,
    217, 220
Crisham, Air Marshal 'Paddy', 201, 203,
    220, 243
Croix de Guerre avec Palme, 187
Crouch Haven, 187
Crown Deep, 168–9, 171
Croydon, 215
Crozier, Hazel, xvii
Cunningham, Group Captain John
    'Cats Eyes', 243
Curragh, 7
Cyprus, 196–7

D
Dakota, Douglas DC-3, 176, 193
Dalkey, 9
Darlan, General, 146
Davies, Pilot Officer GGA, 58

Day, Harry, 23, 28, 114, 179, 248, 250
    death, 249
    Dulag Luft, 90–8, 103–07
    Hendon, 17, 23
    Red Cross Parcels, 117–22
    Stalag Luft 1, 122, 125
    Stalag Luft 3, 57, 144
    The 'Great Escape', 173
Day Fighter Leaders School, 202, 204
DC-3, Douglas Dakota, 176, 193
DC-8, Douglas, 226
Deal, 55
De Havilland, 243
    Chipmunk, xiii, 194
    DH9A, 14
    Mosquito, 156, 160, 179, 186, 191
    Tiger Moth, 190–1
    Vampire, 191, 195
    Venom, 199, 203–04, 213
Deere, Al, 57–8, 242
Delta Dagger, Convair F-102, 226
Denver, 213, 219
De Panne, 58
Deputy Chief of the Air Staff, 208, 217
Der Darss, 111
Desert Air Force, 180, 215
Desores, 65
Detroit, 218
Deutschfiendlich, 127
Deversoir, 195
DH9A, De Havilland, 14
Distinguished Conduct Medal, 3–4, 6, 9
Distinguished Flying Cross, 108, 129,
    144, 188, 190, 195, 250
Distinguished Service Order, 16, 109,
    121, 130, 144, 195, 250
Dobell, Pilot Officer A.E., 18
Do 17, Dornier, 251
Doingt, 5
Dollar, Peter, 187
Dolly Ball, 163
Donaldson, Technical Sergeant
    William, 238–9

Doran, Squadron Leader, 117
Dornier, Do 17, 251
Dostoevsky, 151
Douai, 73, 78
Douglas:
    DC-3 Dakota, 176, 193
    DC-8, 226
Dowding System, 42
Dresden, 133
Dublin, xvii, 9, 21, 192
Dulag Luft, 57, 89–90, 93–6, 99–100,
    102–07, 109, 112–13, 116–22, 133,
    144, 151
Duncanson, Neil, xviii, 259
Dunkirk, 1, 39–42, 44–6, 48, 55–8, 70,
    87, 106–08, 129, 155, 173, 176, 178,
    188, 242, 251
Dunlop, 255
Duxford, 31, 33, 144, 183, 250, 253–4
    19 Squadron, 27, 29, 36, 39–40, 255
    222 Squadron, 35, 108
    Aircraft Restoration Company, 251
    John Romain, xi–xiv
    N3200, xvii, 1, 36–7, 41, 252, 258–60,
        263
Dynamo, Operation, 39, 42, 55, 87, 108,
    113, 251

E
East Dudgeon, 29
Edlington, 4
Edwards Air Force Base, 209, 211, 213,
    217, 223, 226–7
Egham, 178, 183
Eglin, Lieutenant Colonel Frederick
    Irving, 222
Eglin Air Force Base, 199, 213–14,
    220–2, 224, 227–30, 233–4, 240–1,
    244, 249
Eglin Auxiliary Airfield Number 2,
    235–9
El Alamein, 180
El Firdan, 196

Ellington, Marshal of the RAF Edward, 25, 266
Elwell, Lieutenant Charles, 153
Ely, 215
Embassy, 126, 141
  United States, 61, 73, 78
Emory, Major Frank, 241
Evere, 79, 80
Exodus, Operation, 175

F
F-16, Fighting Falcon, 261
F-84F, Republic Thunderstreak, 223–4
F-86, North American Sabre, 203, 207, 222–5, 236–7
  Atcherley Crash, 210, 223
  F-86F, 199
  see also Korean War
F-89D, Northrop Scorpion, 224
F-100, North American Super Sabre, 1, 199, 219–20, 223–7, 241
  Accident Investigation Board, 244–7
  Atcherley's flight, 209–11
  handling issues, 226–7, 241, 244
  last flight, 232–6, 238–40
  origins, 225–6
  pre-flight, 228–32
  see also Air Proving Ground Command, Brown, Eglin Air Force Base, Moore, Welch
F-101, McDonnell Voodoo, 226, 249
F-102, Convair Delta Dagger, 226
Faber, Captain Eugene M., 232–3
Fairey:
  Battle, 32, 105
  Firefly, 194
Fakenham, 200
Farnborough, 194
Farrer, The Right Honourable Anne, 101, 127, 187, 243
Farrer, Thomas Cecil, 101
Fayid, 195
Ferfay, 71–2

Festubert, 6
Fighter Command, xi, 30, 34, 44, 56, 87, 109, 129, 180, 186, 188, 196, 199–201, 220, 243, 266
Fighting Area Attacks, 30
Fighting Falcon, F-16, 261
Financial Times, 251
Firefly, Fairey, 194
First Aid Nursing Yeomanry, 128
Florida, 1, 199, 207, 213, 219–21, 230, 233, 249, 266
Flossenberg, 181
Flying Training Command, 189, 249, 266
Focke-Wulf Fw 190, 155, 179, 184
Folland, 249
  Gnat, 202, 249
  Midge, 202
Forteresse de Mimoyecques, 251
Fort Mardyck, 58
Fort Walton, 233, 241
Fowler, Flight Lieutenant Bill, 143
Frankfurt, 58, 82, 85, 90, 93, 144
Freiberger Mulde, 133
Fresnes, 181
Fruges, 66, 68
Furtstenhaus, 135, 172

G
Galland, Adolf, 130, 250
Gamecock, Gloster, 17, 18
Gardiner, Jim, xvii
Gaskell-Blackburn, Wing Commander Vivian, 21
Gauntlet, Gloster, 27
General Electric, 217
Geneva Convention, 95, 106, 142, 163
German, Lieutenant Colonel Guy, 136, 140
Gestapo, 158
Giles, Canon A.S., 243
Gloster:
  Gamecock, 17, 18

Gauntlet, 27
Javelin, 199, 203
Meteor, 185, 188, 191, 197, 202–04, 208
Gloucester Aviation Services, 191–2
Gnat, Folland, 202, 249
Goldsmith, Flight Lieutenant Bill, 176
Goose Bay, 213, 215–16
Göring, Hermann, 94
Grand Canyon, 214
Griffiss Air Force Base, 217
Groves, Mr M.P., 78–80
Groves, R.M.:
    Memorial Prize, 15, 17
Gubbins, Major General, 158
Gulf of Mexico, 221–2, 233
Gunter, 157

H
Hamburg, 144
Hamilton, Patrick, 162
Hanbury, Air Commandant Felicity, 192
Handley Page Hastings, 197
Hannover, 28, 125, 144
Harvard, North American T-6, 157
Hastings, Handley Page, 197
Hawker, 27
    Hunter, 199, 202–4, 209, 220, 223
Hurricane, xii, 27–8, 32–3, 39, 87, 108,
        129, 156, 184, 191, 242
    Sea Fury, xii
    Sea Hawk, 204
Hawtrey, Air Vice-Marshal Johnny, 219–20
Hayden Baillie, Ormond, xii
Hendon, RAF, 93
Hendon Air Pageant, 17, 23–4, 56
Henri, 181
    see also Birch, Martinet, Mennesson,
        Menzies
Henshaw, Alex, 256
Hill, Air Marshal Roderic, 200
Hillier, Acting Sergeant Eric, 28
Hinaidi, RAF, 21
Historic Flying Limited, xiii, 253

Hitler, Adolf, 84, 94, 126
Horncastle, 4, 188
Hornchurch, RAF, 40–1, 45, 53, 55
Howe, Dick, 172
Hudson, Lockheed, 158
Hughes, 219
Hullavington, RAF, 184, 190
Hunter, Hawker, 199, 202–04, 209, 220,
        223
Hurricane, Hawker, xii, 27–8, 32–3, 39,
        87, 108, 129, 156, 184, 191, 242

I
Idlewild, 215
Illustrious, HMS, 193
Imperial War Museum, xiv, 163, 260
Imperial Yeomanry, 3
Inns of Court Officer Training Corps, 5
Institut Français, 128
Instrument Training Squadron, 202
Interception Analysis Unit, 202
Ireland, Pilot Officer, 18
Irwin, Sergeant Charles, 45, 55
Ismailia, RAF, 195–6

J
J57, Pratt and Whitney, 226
Jagdeschwader 2, 42, 44
Jam-Alc, 163
Jarman, Group Captain J.T., 195
Javelin, Gloster, 199, 203
Jenkins, Reverend T.A., 243
Jenkinson, Lieutenant, 6
Jerusalem, 196
Jet Provost, Percival, 223, 249
Johnston, Major Edward, 227
Josef, Franz, 154–5
Judson, Wing Commander A.S., 243
Julian, Major Austin, 210
Junkers:
    Ju 52, 84
    Ju 87 Stuka, 42, 44–52, 54
    Ju 88, 29

K

Kansas City, 220
Kaplan, Tom, xiv, 251–3, 260
KC-135, Boeing Stratotanker, 226
Keflavik, 215
Kellerhaus, 135–6, 161, 168
Kenley, RAF, 16–19, 28, 32, 90, 179, 194, 201, 249–50
Kew, xvii
Khormaksar, RAF, 196
King George VI, 24, 192, 194, 197
Kommandantur, 92, 134,
Korean War, 193, 199, 203, 207–08, 212, 222–6, 228
Kosse, *Leutnant*, 130
Kriegdgefangener, 87
Kut, 7

L

Labrador, 213
La Fere, 5
Lamb, First Lieutenant M.H., 236
Lancaster, Avro, 188, 191
Lansdowne Club, 215
Lane, Brian, 29, 108, 129, 156, 267
   death, 155
   Dunkirk, 42, 45, 47, 51, 55
Langley Field, 222
Laon, 205
Latimer-Needham, Cecil Hugh, 171
Le Bourget, 251
Le Havre, 7
Leicestershire Regiment, 136
Leigh, Group Captain Rupert, 184
Leigh-Mallory, Trafford, 31, 33, 39, 108, 129
Leipzig, 133
Le Mensil, 6
Lens, 73
Le Touquet, 205
Lichenburgh, 4
Lille, 60, 70
Lincolnshire Regiment, 6–7, 16

Little Rissington, RAF, 35–6, 190–2, 194–5, 205
Lockett, Squadron Leader Charles 'Lucy', 105, 111, 169, 171
Lockheed, 219
   T-33 Shooting Star, xii, 209–11, 222–3
   Constellation, 215
   Hudson, 158
   U-2, xvi, 226, 242
Longmore, Air Vice-Marshal A.M., 16
Los Angeles, 209, 213, 218–9, 230
Louth, 7
Lubeck, *Oflag* XC, 144, 152–3
Lucas, Laddie, 18–19
Luftgau XI, 125, 127
Lundin, Luke, xviii
Lundin, Veryan, xviii, 192, 240, 259, 264
Luton, 176
Lyne, Pilot Officer Michael, 45–6, 50–1, 53, 55, 108, 129
Lyneham, RAF, 197
Lypmne, 205

M

MacDonald, Group Captain W.L.M., 190
MacDonnell, Squadron Leader Donald, 121, 124–6
Maginot Line, 38
Magister, Miles, 31
Malta, 196–7, 249
Mangan, Philip, xvii
Marauder, Martin B-26, 181, 199
Marham, 10
Marhoff, Leading Aircraftman Frank, 157
Mark One Partners, 253, 258
Marsh, Simon, 251–2, 253, 258, 260
Martin B-26 Marauder, 181, 199
Martin, Guy, xviii, 254, 260
Martinet, Jean François, 181
Martinet, Miles, 186
Massachusetts Institute of Technology, 217

Mawhood, Wing Commander David, 213, 217, 219
Maxwell Air Force Base, xv–xvi, xviii, 156, 222, 241–2
Mayfair, 215
McCallum, David, 132
McCance, Captain Donald M., 237
McCue, Paul, xvii
McDonnell, F-101 Voodoo, 226, 249
Mennesson, Jean François Georges, 127–8, 157–8, 187, 205
  see also Birch, Henri, Martinet, Menzies
Mentioned in Dispatches, 7
Menzies, Anna, xviii
Menzies, James Francis George, 128–9, 181–2, 187
  see also Birch, Henri, Martinet, Mennesson
Merifield, Squadron Leader J.R.H., 207–08
Mermagen, Herbert 'Tubby', 23, 35
Mesopotamia, 7
Messerschmitt:
  Me 109, 28, 42, 44–7, 49–55, 81, 113, 130
  Me 110, 156
Meteor, Gloster, 185, 188, 191, 197, 202–04, 208
Metz, 28
Meyer, Oberfeldwebel Walter, 130
MI9, 98, 148, 161, 176–7
Michael, Operation, 5, 17
Middle East Air Force, 195, 207
Midge, Folland, 202
MiG-15, 199, 207, 222–4
Miles:
  Magister, 31
  Martinet, 186
Military Cross, 7
Millar, Lieutenant Bill, 168
Milne, Keith, 170
Mitchell, R.J., xi, 261

Moller, Aircraftsman Second Class Frederick, 28
Monaco, 249
Mont Saint Eloi, 7
Montgomery, Alabama, xv, xviii–xix, 156–7, 221, 241–2, 264, 267
Moore, Captain Lonnie, 188, 191, 228–9, 231–5, 239–40, 249
Moreland, Lieutenant Colonel, 231
Moreton-on-the-Marsh, RAF, 190
Mosquito, De Havilland, 156, 160, 179, 186, 191
Moss, Leading Aircraftman Richard, 157
Mosul, 21
Murphy, Private First Class Alan, 174
Musée d'l'Air, 251
Mustang, North American P-51, xiii, 186

N
N3200, xiii–xiv, xvii–xviii, 1, 267
  arrival, 35–8
  discovery, 251
  documentary, 254
  Dunkirk, 41, 46, 55, 57, 110
  flying, 260–3
  re-build, 252–60
  Trigger's Broom, 263–4
Narborough, 10
National Archives, The, xvii, 2, 90, 122, 128, 133, 148, 158, 170–1
Naunberg, 175
Naval Air Fighting Development Unit, 204
Neave, Lieutenant Airey, 143
New Orleans, 220
Newall, Cyril, 39
Newport Pagnall, 4
New York, 213, 215–17, 243
New York Times, 254
Nivelle, 77
No1 Armoured Car Company, 19
No1 Sector, 196

North American, 209, 219, 225–8, 230
    F-86 Sabre, *see* F-86
    F-100 Super Sabre, *see* F-100
    P-51 Mustang, xiii, 186
    T-6 Texan/Harvard, 157
North One, xviii, 249, 254, 258
    see also Martin, Guy
Northolt, RAF, 27
Northrop:
    A-17, 222
    F-89D Scorpion, 224
North Weald, RAF, 185
Nottingham:
    Dairy College, 4
    University, 4
Number 2 Armament Practice Station,
    185
Nuremburg, 181

O
Oakwood Cemetery Annex, xv–xvi, 157,
    221, 240, 242, 267
Oberkommando der Wehrmacht, 152
Oberursel, 85, 89, 91, 93–5, 97, 99,
    106–08, 111–12, 114, 119, 121
    see also Dulag Luft
Odiham, RAF, 198
Oflag IVC, Colditz, *see* Colditz
Oflag VIB, Warburg, 144
Oflag VIIB, 153
Oflag IX-A, Spangenberg, 91
Oflag XC, Lubeck, 145, 152
Operational Suitability Test, 224, 228–9
Orgain, Peter, xviii, 254
Overall, Martin 'Mo', xvii, 258
Overlord, Operation, 180
Oxford, Airspeed AS.10, 226, 249
Oxford University Air Squadron, 23

P
P-51, North American Mustang, xiii, 186
P9373, 252, 258
P9374, xiii–xiv, 57, 251–3, 258, 260, 263
Pace, Reverend Johnson, 241

Paddon, Squadron Leader Brian
    'Auntie', 113–41, 118–20, 122, 143
Palestine, 7, 21
Palmdale, 227–8
Paris, 158, 181, 251
Parker, Flight Lieutenant Vincent
    'Bush', 146
Pas de Calais, 7, 38, 130, 180
Pearl Harbor, 131, 227
Pearson, Simon, 104–05, 119
Peenemunde, 156
Pensacola, 220–1
Percival:
    Jet Provost, 223, 249
    Proctor, 186–7
Petra, 196
Petre, Flying Officer George, 30, 48,
    52, 55
Philadelphia, 213
Phillips, Flying Officer G.W., 19
Phoney War, 28–9, 37
Pierce Field, *see* Eglin Auxiliary Airfield
    Number 2
Pike, Air Marshal Tom, 208–09, 217
Pinkham, Squadron Leader Philip
    'Tommy', 108
Pioneer Regiment, 6
Pollock, Margo, 249
Portal, Air Marshal Sir Charles, 32
Post Office Rifles Cemetery, 6
Potter, Sergeant James, 46, 51, 53–4, 108
Pratt and Whitney:
    J57, 226
    TF3, 226
Preston, 157
Prestwick, 213, 215–16
Proctor, Percival, 186–7
Prominenter, 174
Purdy, Sub-Lieutenant Walter, 169, 177

Q
Qualified Flying Instructor, 22–3, 31,
    171, 190
Queen's Coronation Review, 198–200

Queen Elizabeth II, 2, 24, 197, 199, 213
Queen of the Belgians' Medal, 7

R
RAF:
  Benevolent Fund, xiv, 191, 260
  Binbrook, 200
  Boscombe Down, 202
  Bracknell, 188–9
  Bradwell Bay, 186–8
  Brize Norton, 190
  Catterick, 9, 179
  College Cranwell, 14, 20, 22–3, 32–5,
    56, 104, 125, 184, 189, 194, 212,
    242, 248, 265–7
  Coltishall, 108–09
  Cosford, 177–8
  Hendon, 93
  Hinaidi, 21
  Hornchurch, 40–1, 45, 53, 55
  Hullavington, 184, 190
  Ismailia, 195–6
  Kenley, 16–19, 28, 32, 90, 179, 194,
    201, 249–50
  Khormaksar, 197
  Little Rissington, 35–6, 190–2,
    194–5, 205
  Lyneham, 197
  North Weald, 185
  Northolt, 27
  Odiham, 198
  South Cerney, 190
  Spilsby, 188
  Tangmere, 129, 184–6, 200
  Tempsford, 158
  Upavon, 23–4, 32, 190
  Wittering, 22–3, 200
Ramsgate, 46
Reach for the Sky, 248–50
Reading Aero Club, 19
Red Cross, 93, 95–6, 99, 113–14, 141,
  162, 181
  parcels, 75, 86, 96–7, 100, 102, 117,
    120–1, 124, 139–40, 154, 163–4
reports, 123, 124, 126, 133–7, 140,
  142, 153–5, 159, 165–6
visits, 96, 114–15, 122–3, 138–9,
  151–2, 164
Reid, Captain Pat, 132, 134, 137, 140,
  143, 148, 161, 168–9, 172, 174, 176
RetroTrack, 253
Republic F-84F Thunderstreak, 223–4
R.M. Groves Memorial Prize, 15, 17
Robinson, Group Captain Maurice, 242
Robinson, Wing Commander, 18
Rollo, Lieutenant, 60–1
Rolls-Royce:
  Armoured Car, 21
  Merlin, 27, 36, 250, 255
Rolt, Lieutenant Tony, 170
Romain, John, xiv, xvii, 253, 256,
  258–60, 263
Rome Air Development Center, 217
Rommel, General Erwin, 38
Rosier, Group Captain Frederick, 206,
  214, 216–17, 219, 227, 229, 240
Rostock, 125
Rouen, 176
Rudorffer, *Oberfeldwebel* Erich, 44, 55
Rumpel, Major Theo, 94–5, 106, 111

S
Saalhaus, 132, 135, 137, 161
Sabre, North American F-86, *see* F-86
Sagan, 144
  see also Stalag Luft III
Saint-Quentin, 5
Salvation Army, 176
San Diego, 219
Sanderson, Johnny, 248
Sandringham, 205
Sangatte, 55, 57, 59, 99, 109, 250
Santa Monica, 219
Sarkar, Dilip, xvii, 46, 50
Sclater, William, xviii
Scorpion, Northrop F-89D, 224
Scragg, Sergeant Colin, 23
Sea Fury, Hawker, xii

Sea Hawk, Hawker, 204
Secours National, 158
Senior British Officer, 89, 91–2, 97, 107, 113–14, 117–20, 122, 125–7, 136–7, 139, 143–4, 159, 169, 173–4, 177
Seyfert, Lieutenant, 81
Sharp, Lieutenant Colonel Daniel, 231
Shell Aviation, 250
Sherwood Rangers Yeomanry, 4
Shinfield Park, 189
Shooting Star, Lockheed T-33, xii, 209–11, 222–3
Shrewsbury School, 1, 9–10
Signy-le-Petit, 44
Simmeleit, *Hauptmann*, 115, 124
Sinclair, Flying Officer Gordon, 49, 53–5
Sinclair, Air Vice-Marshal Lawrence, 208
Sinclair, Lieutenant Mike, 154–5, 167–8, 170, 173
Siskin, Armstrong Whitworth, 14
Skegness, 188
Smart, Pilot Officer, 58
Smith, Donald, 128
Smith, Sydney, 90, 103, 114, 117
Somersetshire, HMT, 20
Somme, 5, 61, 70, 177
Sonderlager, 126
Soucelles, 158
South Africa, 3, 11, 156, 211–2
South Cerney, RAF, 190
Southampton, 7, 20, 36
Spangenberg, 91, 118, 153
    see also *Oflag* IX-A
Special Operations Executive, xvii, 128, 157, 181–2
Spencer, William, xvii
Spilsby, RAF, 188
Spitfire, Supermarine, *see* P9373, P9374, N3200
Stacey, Wing Commander, 210
Stainforth, Wing Commander George, 32

Stalag Luft I, Barth, 57, 92, 107, 109, 111–13, 115–22, 125, 133, 144, 151, 177
Stalag Luft III, Sagan, 57, 121, 141, 144, 156, 173, 244
Stalag XXA, 119
Stamford, 22
Stapleton-Bretherton, Lieutenant O.F., 6
Steere, Flight Sergeant Harry, 30, 48, 52–3, 178–9
Stephenson, Charles, 7
Stephenson, Clare, 4
Stephenson, Eric, 4, 7
Stephenson, Geoffrey Leonard Huson, 170
Stephenson, George, 6
Stephenson, George Urban Eric, 8, 101, 243
Stephenson, Harold, 7
Stephenson, Jessica Eileen, 4, 101
Stephenson, Jessie (née Scorer), 4, 250
Stephenson, John Dalton, 4, 243
Stephenson, Lilian, 7
Stephenson, Philip, xviii
Stephenson, Reginald, 7
Stephenson, Susannah, 4
Stephenson, Urban Arnold, 4, 6
Stephenson, William Dalton, 2–11, 38, 99, 102, 127
Stevenson, Pilot Officer P.C.F., 58
Steward, Ian, xvii
St. Malo, 160
St. Omer, 144
St. Pol, 60
St Simons on the Sound Church, 241
Stoolball, 142, 163
Stratocruiser, Boeing, 243
Stratofortress, Boeing B-52, 226
Stratolifter, Boeing C-135, 226
Stratotanker, Boeing KC-135, 226
Strawderman, David, xviii, 254
Strawderman, Victoria, xviii, 190, 205, 240, 243, 254, 259, 264

Strugnell, Wing Commander William, 21
Sturzkampfgeschwader, 42
Stubley & Stephenson, 10
Suez, 195–7
Supermarine:
   Spitfire, *see* N3200, P9373, P9374
   Swift, 199, 202–03, 209
Super Sabre, North American F-100,
   see F-100
Surfleets Preparatory School, 7
Sutton Bridge, 17–18, 31
Swann, Colin, xvii, 254
Swift, Supermarine, 199, 202–03, 209
Syracuse, 217
Szaniawski, Colonel Edward 'Jonesy',
   230–1, 244, 246

T
T-6, North American Texan/Harvard,
   157
T-33, Lockheed Shooting Star, xii,
   209–11, 222–3
Ta Braxia, 249
Tangmere, RAF, 129, 184–6, 200
Taranto, 193
Taylor, Lieutenant Commander
   Reginald, 204
Tchaikovsky, 140
Tehran, 21
Tempsford, RAF, 158
Texan/Harvard, North American T-6,
   157
TF3, Pratt and Whitney, 226
The Brothers Karamazov, 151
This Is Your Life, 249–50
   see also Bader, Day
Thunderstreak, Republic F-84F, 223–4
Tiger Moth, De Havilland, 190–1
Timberlake, Major General Patrick, 241
Tod, Lieutenant Colonel, 174–5
Tomalin, Group Captain Charles, 216
Tournai, 76
Training Command, 24, 189, 249, 266

Trenchard, Pilot Officer Horace, 31
Trenchard, Marshal of the RAF Sir
   Hugh, 11, 13
Tripoli, 180
Tunis, 153, 180
Tunstall Peter, Flight Lieutenant,
   119, 166
Tutor, Avro, 23, 32
Typhoon, Eurofighter, 261

U
U-2, Lockheed, xvi, 226, 242
Unwin, Flight Sergeant George
   'Grumpy', 29, 31, 56
Upavon, RAF, 23–4, 32, 190

V
Valparaiso Bombing and Gunnery
   Range, 221
Vampire, De Havilland, 191, 195
Venom, De Havilland, 199, 203–04, 213
Vice Chief of the USAF, 209, 223
von Bock, General, 38
von Leeb, General, 38
von Richthofen, Manfred, 42
von Rundstedt, General, 38
Voodoo, McDonnell F-101, 226, 249
Vorlager, 112

W
Wadi Mujib, 214
Wagner, Robert, 132
Wakefield, Sir Charles, 11, 16
Walker, Squadron Leader Christopher,
   xvi, 242
Walker, Captain David, 170
Walton, Squadron Leader Dennis, 214,
   217, 220
Wapiti, Westland, 21
Warburg, *Oflag* VIB, 144
Wardle, Lieutenant, 170
Warner, Graeme, xiii
War Office, The, 3, 176

Washington DC, 209, 213, 216–17, 241, 249
Watson, Pilot Officer Peter, 31, 51, 54–5, 57
Welch, George, 226–7
Wells, H.G., 141
Westminster Abbey, 198
White, General Thomas, 209
Wiggenhall St Mary the Virgin, 10
William, Prince, 260
Williams, Hank, xv
Williams, Reverend, 189
Wilson, Flight Lieutenant J.C., 148
Wittering, RAF, 22–3, 200
Wolff, General Ludwig, 125–6
Wood, Lieutenant, 118
Woodley, 19
Woollett, Squadron Leader Henry, 16–18

Woolston, 36
Wright, Wing Commander Ricky, 214, 217
Wright Patterson Air Force Base, 213, 217, 223

X
X-1, Bell, 210

Y
Yeager, Major Chuck, 210–11, 223, 225
YMCA, 96
Young, Lieutenant Colonel George, 148
Ypres, 6

Z
Zwickavee Mulde, 133